STRANGE CULTS AND UTOPIAS OF 19th-CENTURY AMERICA

(Formerly titled: History of American Socialisms)

John Humphrey Noyes

With a New Introduction by
Mark Holloway

DOVER PUBLICATIONS, INC.
NEW YORK

Published in Canada by General Publishing Company, Ltd., 30 Lesmill Road, Don Mills, Toronto, Ontario.

Published in the United Kingdom by Constable and Company, Ltd., 10 Orange Street, London W. C. 2.

This Dover edition is an unaltered and unabridged republication of the work first published by J. B. Lippincott & Co., Philadelphia, in 1870, under the title: *History of American Socialisms*. The Introduction by Mark Holloway was written for the first Dover edition, published in 1966 under the original title.

International Standard Book Number: 0-486-21581-4
Library of Congress Catalog Card Number: 66-11430

Manufactured in the United States of America
Dover Publications, Inc.
180 Varick Street
New York, N. Y. 10014

INTRODUCTION TO THE
DOVER EDITION

The History of American Socialisms is an account of
the numerous utopian communities which were formed
by various sects and societies in America from the
middle of the eighteenth century onwards. The most
widely known of these communities were the Shaker
societies ; the communities started or inspired by Robert
Owen, centered on New Harmony ; Brook Farm ; and
Oneida Community, founded by the author of this book.
The book itself is often regarded as the first history of its
kind ; but in fact there were three earlier accounts, one
written at second hand, and two first-hand accounts that
were never published in book form.* The two earliest
were largely superseded by the present work, and much
of the third, which had only existed in manuscript, was

---

* Mary Hennell, *Outline of the Various Social Systems &
Communities Which Have Been Founded on the Principle of Co-
operation*, London (1844). John Finch, " Notes on Travel in the
United States," in *The New Moral World*, xii, 232—xiii, 10–11
(January to July, 1844). A. J. Macdonald, Manuscripts and
Collections in Yale University Library (c. 1842–1854).

incorporated into it.   John Humphrey Noyes, whose
name appears on the title page, did not write more than
a sixth of the book himself, but it is his contribution
which is responsible for the book's reputation and for its
intrinsic and unique interest.   As Noyes was the first in
the field with a substantial volume on the subject, so he
was also the first historian of the movement with interesting theories of his own, and the first with intimate
experience of his subject matter.

Noyes was described by Bernard Shaw as " one of
those chance attempts at the Superman which occur
from time to time in spite of the interference of Man's
blundering institutions."*   He was certainly a bold and
commanding figure, and a sketch of his character is a
necessary prelude to any consideration of his work.

At the time when Noyes was alive any marked deviation from the established churches of Christianity was
likely to provoke a vigorous reaction.   Consequently,
initiators and leaders of sects had to be men of excep-
tionally strong character, especially if they were
evangelically minded, for then they had to be capable
of keeping the allegiance of their original members and
of winning converts even in the midst of antagonism or
actual physical persecution.

A fanatic might get this far, might indeed get further,
as Ann Lee got to America from Lancashire and Joseph
Smith got to Nauvoo ; but other qualities were required
in order to maintain the initial impetus.   As well as the
absolute conviction that they and they alone had chosen
the right path, and the ability to persuade others that
this was so, leaders of this kind needed exceptional

* " The Revolutionist's Handbook," Section iii (see *Prefaces;
Man & Superman*).

organizing ability and foresight, balanced judgment, and a quality that can best be described as " intuitive astuteness." Joseph Meacham, who organized the Shakers into communities, and Brigham Young, who commanded the Mormon hegira, must have been endowed with these qualities; and no doubt other examples of " second-generation " wisdom of this kind could be cited. It was a characteristic that was less common among initiators, and this is one reason why Noyes is such an exceptional and fascinating character.

Noyes was truly original. In him the simple vision, the strength of character and the evangelical fire of the fanatical initiator were blended with the balanced judgment and practical managerial capacity of the successful consolidator. This was an unusual combination of characteristics; and in view of Noyes's background, his absolute rejection of orthodoxy was also unusual. His father had sat in Congress for Vermont, and his mother was the aunt of Rutherford B. Hayes, nineteenth President of the United States. He attended Dartmouth College and read law and theology at Andover and Yale. He married the granddaughter of a lieutenant-governor of the State. He was the educated and moderately cultivated son of a socially well-placed family. Yet as far as morals are concerned, particularly sexual morals, he was one of the most extreme revolutionaries that Western Civilization has produced.

He was extreme, but logical and realistic; revolutionary, but not violent. He believed that the Second Advent of Christ had occurred in A.D. 70, and with it the First Day of Judgment. The Kingdom of Heaven was already established on earth, at any rate for all who believed in it.   It was independent of and superior to human government ; and in it exclusive possession in marriage and in goods was abolished in accordance with certain Biblical texts (see pp. 621–28). Therefore all men are virtually married to all women, and vice versa. But "virtually" is a word that is never permitted by men of Noyes's character to stand between belief and action. If he and his followers believed that all men are married to all women, then all should, if they wished, be married to all in reality. Such was the simple basis on which Complex Marriage, a regulated form of promiscuity, was introduced into Noyes's community.

Noyes also regarded the propagative function of sexual intercourse as distinct and separate from what he called the amative function, and insisted that the former must not be permitted to jeopardize the latter.   To this end, he advocated and himself practiced Male Continence, or *coitus reservatus*. That Complex Marriage and Male Continence were both put into practice with evident success for a period of twenty-five years or more in the nineteenth century by people who could not be regarded by the severest psychological critics as in any way mad, is a matter for wonder and congratulation. Also, during part of the time when these customs were continually and without any fuss or bother made use of by Oneida Community, a further experiment was made with an elementary form of eugenics which Noyes called " stirpiculture."

It is difficult to think of a situation in which greater moral courage might be required ; but it is of the essence of Noyes's character that, just as the concept of all of one sex being married to all of the other was so sensibly not allowed to be mere " free love " or random promiscuity, so also having had the courage to initiate and the ability to control his experiments, Noyes had the even rarer form of courage which enabled him to decide to abandon them when it was evident that opposition to them was likely to bring the community to an end. Thirty years is a generation, and for almost a generation a group of about two hundred and fifty men, women and children lived happy, useful and successful lives while taking part in sexual experiments which would cause a sensation even today. Oneida Community proved a thesis which no one, thus far, has been bold enough to continue or elaborate.

When the religious fire, moral courage, and good judgment of Noyes have all been given due credit, something remains unexplained—some ingredient of the personality which could exercise such thorough control over so many individuals while they were experimenting with one of the most explosive of psychophysical complexes. I think that this unnamed quality can without sentimentality be called " love of life." I believe that Noyes, unlike many sectarians, was a great yea-sayer, an enhancer of life, a confident and optimistic embracer of truth and freedom, broadminded, receptive to new ideas, generous and without meanness or pettiness. There were many indications of this in Oneida Community, and there is some evidence of the same kind in the *History*.

At Oneida it was thought that everybody " should be surrounded with circumstances favoring the best development of heart, mind and body." [See *Handbook of the Oneida Community*, Oneida , N.Y. (1875), p. 25.] They had a library of 5000 books, tolerantly including

Darwin, Huxley and Herbert Spencer, and subscribed to all the leading newspapers and periodicals. They had a large orchestra, and performed plays, dances and pantomimes. They played chess, draughts and cards. And they surrounded their handsome family home with trees, ornamental shrubs and wide lawns on which they played croquet and held picnics. There was little sign of the restrictive, taboo-haunted mentality of the narrow-minded sectarian.

With similar tolerance, Noyes writes in the *History* of the non-religious communities in exactly the same spirit as he writes of the sectarians. In his view, all have their due influence in the development of the communitarian movement and are good, bad or indifferent whether religious or not. He regards Oneida as a " continuation of Brook Farm " (which was not particularly religious), and sees the spirit of socialism working its way through Owenite and Fourierist experiences and through Oneida in a kind of evolutionary search for satisfactory expression.

His pragmatic liberalism scorns blind adherence to theory : " We insist that God's appointed way for man to seek the truth in all departments, and above all in Social Science, which is really the science of righteousness, is to combine and alternate thinking with experiment and practice, and constantly submit all theories, whether obtained by scientific investigation or by intuition and inspiration, to the consuming ordeal of practical verification " (p. 668).

Noyes was also a compassionate man, who incidentally owed his discovery of Male Continence to sympathy for his wife, who had given birth to five babies in six years, four of them stillborn. Here is a passage from

the *History* which expresses an imaginative understanding of the sorrows of some unsuccessful com-
muniteers :

Think of the great hope at the beginning ; the heroism
of the long struggle ; the bitterness of the end. This
human group was made up of husbands and wives,
parents and children, brothers and sisters, friends and
lovers, and had two hundred hearts, longing for
blessedness. Plodding on their weary march of life,
Association rises before them like the *mirage* of the
desert. They see in the vague distance, magnificent
palaces, green fields, golden harvests, sparkling
fountains, abundance of rest and romance ; in one
word, HOME—which also is HEAVEN. They rush like
the thirsty caravan to realize their vision. And now the
scene changes. Instead of reaching palaces, they find
themselves huddled together in loose sheds—thirty-five
families trying to live in dwellings built for one. They
left the world to escape from want and care and temptation ; and behold, these hungry wolves follow them in
fiercer packs than ever. The gloom of debt is over them
from the beginning. Again and again they are on the
brink of bankruptcy. It is a constant question and
doubt whether they will " SUCCEED," which means,
whether they will barely keep soul and body together,
and pacify their creditors. But they cheer one another
on. " They must succeed ; they *will* succeed ; they
are already succeeding ! " These words they say over
and over to themselves, and shout them to the public.
Still debt hangs over them. . . . All through the sultry
months which should have been their working time,
they lie idle in their loose sheds, or where they can find a
place, sweating and shivering in misery and despair.
Human parasites gather about them, like vultures
scenting prey from afar. Their own passions torment
them. They are cursed with suspicion and the evil eye.
They quarrel about religion. They quarrel about their
food. They dispute about carrying out their principles.

Eight or ten families desert. The rest worry on through the long years. Foes watch them with cruel exultation. Friends shout to them, " Hold on a little longer! " They hold on just as long as they can, insisting that they are successful, or are just going to be, till the last. Then comes the " break up ; " and who can tell the agonies of that great corporate death! . . . We ourselves are thoroughly acquainted with these heights and depths. These men and women seem to us like brothers and sisters. We could easily weep with them and for them, if it would do any good. But the better way is to learn what such sufferings teach, and hasten to find and show the true path, which these pilgrims missed ; that so their illusions may not be repeated forever.*

By about the year 1870 Noyes had brought Oneida to the pinnacle of success. Dissension, resulting in the abdication of Noyes, and eventually in the abandonment of Complex Marriage and then of Communism, lay ahead. But during the seventh decade of the century, Noyes, having already succeeded so brilliantly in the community stakes, had begun to look about him and take stock of the rest of the field. He remembered A. J. Macdonald, " the sombre pilgrim " who had been collecting information from communities, and was lucky enough to obtain his manuscripts. Noyes published extracts from these in *The Circular*, the official journal of Oneida. At first the extracts appeared apologetically under the heading " Our Muck Heap," but after two or three months Noyes seems to have realized that the material was worthwhile and impressive. He then changed the title of the weekly column to " American Socialisms " and gave notice that he

* pp. 351–53.

would produce a history of socialism in America. After a run of about nine months, the extracts finished in July, 1869 ; and in December (but dated for the following year) *The History of American Socialisms* appeared.

Macdonald had assembled his information in the decade preceding his death in 1854, so that even his latest notes were fourteen years old by the time they were printed in *The Circular*. It does not seem that Noyes checked or questioned them ; he merely added comments of his own, or further extracts from communitarian publications and from books and correspondence. Consequently, it is not always possible to rely on the accuracy of the information, which requires checking, when feasible, against scholarly accounts published later.

Noyes's handling of Macdonald's material is of considerable interest. In Chapter II he gives a complete list of all the communities described by Macdonald with the number of manuscript pages devoted to each. The greatest amount of space is given to the Shakers (93 pages), Icarians (82 pages), and New Harmony (60 pages). There is then a decrease to 38 pages for the North American Phalanx, and all the other societies are given less than 30 pages each, with 50 out of a total of 74 societies having less than ten pages each. Altogether, Owenite societies receive about 120 pages, and Fourierist societies about 250.

Noyes transforms some of these figures : he gives the Shakers only 18 pages, and leaves out the Icarians. However the bulk of the book is concerned with the Owenite and Fourierist phases of communitarianism in much the same ratio to each other as in Macdonald's manuscripts. Within the limitations implied by the adjective in the title, this redistribution of space is justifiable if we accept Noyes's virtual exclusion of the Shakers (except in their spiritualistic aspect) on the grounds of their being well enough known through their own publications. I find this to be a thin excuse : no society, by Noyes's own admission, had greater influence on its successors ; and at the time he wrote there was no reliable objective account of them. Nor were the Rappites—to name only one of the " societies of foreigners " which Noyes excludes—without far-reaching influence. It could be argued too that some of these " foreigners " were as " American " as any other immigrants of the same period.

It is always difficult to define limits in a study of communities. Nordhoff,* five years later, restricted himself to societies which were still in existence ; Hinds,† in 1908, wrote the most inclusive study, but at the expense of perspective and illumination. Rigid definitions exclude, and loose definitions include, too much. Ultimately, most limits are arbitrary : one has to draw the line somewhere, and it is not always an unbroken one. In the present work, it is clear that Noyes was fascinated by the organic unity of the communitarian movement as a whole (including the reciprocal influences of the different communities), and also by the closely connected and sometimes alternating phases of revivalism and communitarianism. These are the themes of his book, and the material selected from Macdonald is that which best

---

* *The Communistic Societies of the United States*, Harper & Brothers, New York (1875). (Dover, 1966.)

† *American Communities*, 2nd revision, Charles H. Kerr Co., Chicago (1908).

illustrates them.   Rappites, Amanites and Icarians would hardly have been relevant to them.

It is largely due to Noyes that these themes have been recognized and established, but excessive enthusiasm and lack of information from abroad caused him to stretch historical theory too far.   There is no evidence that the Shakers were the " original socialists " or that they were " known and watched in Germany " or that the Rappites, Zoarites and Amanites were encouraged by their example to emigrate and form communities. Nor is there any evidence that Owen, who had already made plans for colonies when he first heard of the Shakers, was imitating them ;   nor that St. Simon and Fourier were led by the Shaker example to become socialists (see pp. 669–70).   In any case, the communities of Bohemia Manor, The Woman in the Wilderness, Ephrata, and others, were all founded before Ann Lee was born or the Shakers were thought of.   But it is true and apt to describe the success of the Shakers as the " ' specie basis ' that has upheld all the paper theories and counteracted the failures, of the French and English schools " (p. 670).

Noyes's second theory, of the interacting influences of what he calls " socialistic excitements " and religious revivals, is one of the most perceptive and useful contributions to the history of the communitarian movement.   It is described in typically vigorous and enthusiastic language (pp. 24–29) which is not invalidated in the least by the rather fanciful declaration that Oneida Community may be said to be the continuation of Brook Farm :   " Look at the dates.   Brook Farm deceased in October 1847.   Oneida Community commenced in November 1847.   It is a simple case of transmigration, or in the latest language, persistence of force."*

As an illustration of the continuity of theme from Owenite to Fourierist communities, Noyes refers to the communitarian movement as " *the enlargement of home —the extension of family union beyond the little man-and-wife circle to large corporations* " (p. 23). This is a favorite concept with Noyes, one of the few statements he thought worthy of italics ; it is repeated on pp. 292 and 351, and although it too may be thought a little fanciful even if approximately true, it is interesting for what it reveals about Noyes himself. It is not the sort of concept that would have occurred to Owen or to Fourier, both of whom had blueprints for the re-organization of mankind. It is the pronouncement of a paterfamilias who felt that the kingdom of heaven could best be realized by enlarging the scope of married love.

This idea was central to Noyes's whole way of thinking and acting. Why should such a valuable, intense and true emotion be restricted, thus cutting off one couple from another and forcibly inhibiting what was essentially a unifying emotion? How much better that all should love all, through the love of God. But if this was to be achieved, then the sexual relation must be subjected to the communistic principle (p. 139) ; and in his reviews of the religious communities, as being the most successful, Noyes concludes that their success is due to a " more or less stringent " control over " the sexual relation " (p. 147). This usually took the form of celibacy (as with the Shakers), or at least of dis-

* *The Circular*, n.s. V, 348 (Jan. 18, 1869) ; quoted from A. E. Bestor, *Backwoods Utopias*, pp. 53–54.

couragement of sexual intercourse. At Oneida it took the form of regulated promiscuity; and although Noyes did not live at a time when the conclusion that now seems to us obvious would have been drawn—that living under a ban on a natural instinct cannot be as conducive to healthiness and liveliness of mind and body as living in a society which gives this instinct means and meaning of expression—Oneida seems to us to stand as proof that the conclusion is right.

The success of this particular community was due to the outgoing constructive optimism of Noyesian Perfectionism, with its ingenious permissiveness, combined with Noyes's business ability and common sense. (It should be noted in passing that prosperity at Oneida resulted in more hired labor than in any other community, and this undoubtedly had much to do with the ease and culture that were almost exclusive to Oneida.) A combination of luck (finding Sewell Newhouse, the trap-maker who laid the foundations of Oneida's manufacturing enterprises) and business ability set Noyes on the right path—that of industry rather than agriculture. It was therefore not difficult for him to criticize the land-mania which had seized so many communities: ". . . we incline to think," he wrote, " that this fondness for land, which has been the habit of Socialists, had much to do with their failures. . . . We should have advised the Phalanxes to limit their land-investments to a minimum, and put their strength as soon as possible into some form of manufacture "(p. 19); and " If our experience is worth any thing, and if we might offer our advice, we should say, Sell two-thirds of that domain and put the proceeds into a machine-shop " (p. 594). He thought Fourier was responsible for this land-mania : " He is always talking in grand style about vast domains—three miles square, we believe, was his standard—and his illustrations of attractive industry are generally delicious pictures of fruit-raising and romantic agriculture " (p. 266).

Fourier, the timid impoverished bachelor living in one room waiting for a millionaire to translate his fantastic dreams into reality, was a very different character from the vigorously active and pragmatic Noyes. " We do not believe," wrote Noyes, " that cogitation without experiment is the right way to a true social theory. With us induction is first ; deduction second ; and verification by facts or the logic of events, always and everywhere the supreme check on both. For the sake of this principle we have been studying and bringing to light the lessons of American Socialisms. If Fourier and Brisbane are on the right track, we are on the wrong. Let science judge between us " (p. 667).

" Science," in the form of " the logic of events," has judged. There have been no more Phalanxes since Noyes wrote their epitaphs. Oneida, on the other hand, though no longer a community, is still a thriving business largely owned and run by those who work in it, and to this extent still bearing the imprint of its founder and his successors. And whereas Fourier turned out to be a wonderful but impractical dreamer, Noyes, who so happily combined idealism and practicality, devised and conducted one of the most original and successful social experiments in American history.

MARK HOLLOWAY

Sussex, England
August, 1965

PREFACE

THE object of this book is to help the study of Socialism by the inductive method. It is, first and chiefly, a collection of facts ; and the attempts at interpretation and generalization which are interspersed, are secondary and not intentionally dogmatic.

It is certainly high time that Socialists should begin to take lessons from experience ; and for this purpose, that they should chasten their confidence in flattering theories, and turn their attention to actual events.

This country has been from the beginning, and especially for the last forty years, a laboratory in which Socialisms of all kinds have been experimenting. It may safely be assumed that Providence has presided over the operations, and has taken care to make them instructive. The disasters of Owenism and Fourierism have not been in vain ; the successes of the Shakers and Rappites have not been set before us for nothing. We may hope to learn something from every experiment.

The author, having had unusual advantages for observing the Socialistic movements, and especial good fortune in obtaining collections of observations made by others, has deemed it his duty to devote a year to the preparation of this history.

As no other systematic account of American Socialisms exists, the facts here collected, aside from any interpretation of them, may be valuable to the student of history, and entertaining to the general reader.

The present issue may be considered a proof-sheet, as carefully corrected as it can be by individual vigilance. It is hoped that it will call out from experts in Socialism and others, corrections and additions that will improve it for future editions.

Wallingford, Conn.
December, 1869

CONTENTS.

HISTORY OF
AMERICAN
SOCIALISMS

AMERICAN SOCIALISMS.

CHAPTER I.

INTRODUCTORY.

MANY years ago, when a branch of the Oneida Community lived at Willow Place in Brooklyn, near New York, a sombre pilgrim called there one day, asking for rest and conversation. His business proved to be the collecting of memoirs of socialistic experiments. We treated him hospitably, and gave him the information he sought about our Community. He repeated his visit several times in the course of some following years, and finally seemed to take a very friendly interest in our experiment. Thus we became acquainted with him, and also in a measure with the work he had undertaken, which was nothing less than a history of all the Associations and Communities that have lived and died in this country, within the last thirty or forty years.

This man's name was A. J. Macdonald. We remember that he was a person of small stature, with black hair and sharp eyes. He had a benevolent air, but seemed a little sad. We imagined that the sad

scenes he had encountered while looking after the
stories of so many short-lived Communities, had given
him a tinge of melancholy. He was indeed the " Old
Mortality" of Socialism, wandering from grave to
grave, patiently deciphering the epitaphs of defunct
" Phalanxes." We learned from him that he was a
Scotchman by birth, and a printer by trade ; that he
was an admirer and disciple of Owen, and came from
the " old country" some ten years before, partly to see
and follow the fortunes of his master's experiments in
Socialism: but finding Owenism in ruins and Fourierism going to ruin, he took upon himself the task of
making a book, that should give future generations
the benefit of the lessons taught by these attempts
and failures.

His own attempt was a failure. He gathered a huge
mass of materials, wrote his preface, and then died in
New York of the cholera. Our record of his last
visit is dated February, 1854.

Ten years later our attention was turned to the
project of writing a history of American Socialisms.
Such a book seemed to be a want of the times.
We remembered Macdonald, and wished that by some
chance we could obtain his collections. But we had
lost all traces of them, and the hope of recovering
them from the chaos of the great city where he died,
seemed chimerical. Nevertheless some of our associates, then in business on Broadway, commenced
inquiring at the printing offices, and soon found
acquaintances of Macdonald, who directed them to
the residence of his brother-in-law in the city. There,
to our joyful surprise, we found the collections we were
in search of, lying useless except as mementos, and a

gentleman in charge of them who was willing we should take them and use them as we pleased.

On examining our treasure, we found it to be a pile of manuscripts, of letter-paper size and three inches thick, with printed scraps from newspapers and pamphlets interspersed. All was in the loosest state of disorder; but we strung the leaves together, paged them, and made an index of their contents. The book thus extemporized has been our companion, as the reader will see, in the ensuing history. The number of its pages is seven hundred and forty-seven. The index has the names of sixty-nine Associative experiments, beginning with Brook Farm and ending with the Shakers. The memoirs are of various lengths, from a mere mention to a narrative of nearly a hundred pages. Among them are notices of leading Socialists, such as Owen, Fourier, Frances Wright, &c. The collection was in no fit condition for publication; but it marked out a path for us, and gave us a mass of material that has been very serviceable, and probably could not elsewhere be found.

The breadth and thoroughness of Macdonald's intention will be seen in the following circular which, in the prosecution of his enterprise, he sent to many leading Socialists.

PRINTED LETTER OF INQUIRY.

" *New York, March,* 1851.

" I have been for some time engaged in collecting the necessary materials for a book, to be entitled ' *The Communities of the United States,*' in which I propose giving a brief account of all the social and co-operative experiments that have been made in this country

—their origin, principles, and progress ; and, particularly, the causes of their success or failure.

" I have reason to believe, from long experience among social reformers, that such a work is needed, and will be both useful and interesting. It will serve as a guide to all future experiments, showing what has already been done ; like a light-house, pointing to the rocks on which so many have been wrecked, or to the haven in which the few have found rest. It will give facts and statistics to be depended upon, gathered from the most authentic sources, and forming a collection of interesting narratives. It will show the errors of enthusiasts, and the triumphs of the cool-thinking ; the disappointments of the sanguine, and the dear-bought experience of many social adventurers. It will give mankind an idea of the labor of body and mind that has been expended to realize a better state of society; to substitute a social and co-operative state for a competitive one ; a system of harmony, for one of discord.

" To insure the truthfulness of the work, I propose to gather most of my information from individuals who have actually been engaged in the experiments of which I treat. With this object in view, I take the liberty to address you, asking your aid in carrying out my plan. I request you to give me an account of the experiment in which you were engaged at ———. For instance, I require such information as the following questions would call forth, viz :

" 1. Who originated it, or how was it originated ?

" 2. What were its principles and objects ?

" 3. What were its means in land and money ?

" 4. Was all the property put into common stock ?

" 5. What was the number of persons in the Association?

" 6. What were their trades, occupations and amount of skill?

" 7. Their education, natural intelligence and morality?

" 8. What religious belief, and if any, how preached and practised?

" 9. How were members admitted? was there any standard by which to judge them, or any property qualification necessary?

" 10. Was there a written or printed constitution or laws? if so can you send me a copy?

" 11. Were pledges, fines, oaths, or any coercive means used?

" 12. When and where did the Association commence its experiment? Please describe the locality; what dwellings and other conveniences were upon it; how many persons it could accommodate; how many persons lived on the spot; how much land was cultivated; whether there were plenty of provisions; &c., &c.

" 13. How was the land obtained? Was it free or mortgaged? Who owned it?

" 14. Were the new circumstances of the associates superior or inferior to the circumstances they enjoyed previous to their associating?

" 15. Did they obtain aid from without?

" 16. What particular person or persons took the lead?

" 17. Who managed the receipts and expenditures, and were they honestly managed?

" 18. Did the associates agree or disagree, and in what?

" 19. How long did they keep together?

"20. When and why did they break up? State the causes, direct and indirect.

"21. If successful, what were the causes of success?

"Any other information relating to the experiment, that you may consider useful and interesting, will be acceptable. By such information you will confer a great favor, and materially assist me in what I consider a good undertaking.

"The work I contemplate will form a neat 12mo. volume, of from 200 to 280 pages, such as Lyell's 'Tour in the United States,' or Gorrie's 'Churches and Sects of the United States.' It will be published in New York and London at the lowest possible price, say, within one dollar; and it is my intention, if possible, to illustrate the work with views of Communities now in progress, or of localities rendered interesting by having once been the battle grounds of the new system against the old.

"Please make known the above, and favor me with the names and addresses of persons who would be willing to assist me with such information as I require.

"Trusting that I shall receive the same kind aid from you that I have already received from so many of my friends,

"I remain, very respectfully, yours,

"A. J. MACDONALD."

Among the manuscripts in Macdonald's collection are many that were evidently written in response to this circular. Many others were written by himself as journals or reports of his own visits to various Associations. We have reason to believe that he spent most of his time from his arrival in this country in

1842 till his death in 1854, in pilgrimages to every Community, and even to every grave of a Community, that he could hear of, far and near.

He had done his work when he died. His collection is nearly exhaustive in the extent of its survey. Very few Associations of any note are overlooked. And he evidently considered it ready for the press; for most of his memoirs are endorsed with the word *"Complete,"* and with some methodical directions to the printer. He had even provided the illustrations promised in his circular. Among his manuscripts are the following pictures:

A pencil sketch and also a small wood engraving of the buildings of the North American Phalanx;

A wood engraving of the first mansion house of the Oneida Community;

A pencil sketch of the village of Modern Times;

A view in water-colors of the domain and cabin of the Clermont Phalanx;

A pencil sketch of the Zoar settlement;

Four wood engravings of Shaker scenes; two of them representing dances; one, a kneeling scene: and one, a "Mountain meeting;" also a pencil sketch of Shaker dwellings at Watervliet;

A portrait of Robert Owen in wood;

A very pretty view of New Harmony in India ink;

A wood-cut of one of Owen's imaginary palaces;

Two portraits of Frances Wright in wood; one representing her as she was in her prime of beauty, and the other, as she was in old age;

A fine steel engraving of Fourier.

In the following preface, which was found among Macdonald's manuscripts, and which is dated a few

months before his death, we have a last and sure signal that he considered his collection finished :

PREFACE TO THE BOOK THAT WAS NEVER PUBLISHED.

" I performed the task of collecting the materials
which form this volume, because I thought I was
doing good. At one time, sanguine in anticipating
brilliant results from Communism, I imagined mankind
better than they are, and that they would speedily prac-
tise those principles which I considered so true. But
the experience of years is now upon me ; I have mingled
with 'the world,' seen *stern reality*, and now am anxious
to do as much as in me lies, to make known to the
many thousands who look for a 'better state' than this
on earth as well as in heaven, the amount (as it were
at a glance) of the labors which have been and are
now being performed in this country to realize that
' better state'. It may help to waken dreamers, to
guide lost wanderers, to convince skeptics, to re-assure
the hopeful ; it may serve the uses of Statesmen and
Philosophers, and interest the general reader ; but it is
most desirable that it should increase the charity of
all those who may please to examine it, when they see
that it was for Humanity, in nearly all instances, that
these things were done.

" Of necessity the work is imperfect, because of the
difficulty in obtaining information on such subjects ; but
the attempt, whatever may be its result, should not be
put off, since there is reason to believe that if not now
collected, many particulars of the various movements
would be forever lost.

" It remains for a future historian to continue the
labor which I have thus superficially commenced ; for

the day has not yet arrived when it can be said that Communism or Association has ceased to exist ; and it is possible yet, in the progress of things, that man will endeavor to cure his social diseases by some such means ; and a future history may contain the results of more important experiments than have ever yet been attempted.

" I here return my thanks to the fearless, confiding, and disinterested friends, who so freely shared with me what little they possessed, to assist in the completion of this work. I name them not, but rejoice in their assistance.   A. J. MACDONALD.

" *New York City*, 1854."

The tone of this preface indicates that Macdonald was discouraged. The effect of his book, if he had lived to publish it, would have been to aggravate the re-action against Socialism which followed the collapse of Fourierism. We hope to make a better use of his materials.

It should not be imagined that we are about to edit his work. A large part of his collections we shall omit, as irrelevant to our purpose. That part which we use will often be reconstructed and generally condensed. Much of our material will be obtained from other sources. The plan and theory of this history are our own, and widely different from any that Macdonald would have been willing to indorse. With these qualifications, we still acknowledge a large debt of gratitude to him and to the Providence that gave us his collections.

CHAPTER II.

BIRDS-EYE VIEW OF THE EXPERIMENTS.

A GENERAL survey of the Socialistic field will be useful, before entering on the memoirs of particular Associations ; and for this purpose we will now spread before
us the entire Index of Macdonald's collections, adding
to it a schedule of the number of pages which he gave
to the several Associations, and the dates of their
beginning and ending, so far as we have been able to
find them. Many of the transitory Associations, it
will be seen, "made no sign" when they died. The
continuous Communities, such as the Shakers, of course
have no terminal date.

INDEX OF MACDONALD'S COLLECTION.

Associations, &c.	No. of Pages.	Dates.
Alphadelphia Phalanx . .	7	1843—6.
Auxiliary Branch of the Association of All Classes of All Nations .	3	1836.
Blue Spring Community . .	1	1826—7.
Brazilian Experiment . .	1	1841.
Brook Farm . . .	20	1842—7.
Brooke's Experiment . .	5	1844.
Brotherhood of the Union .	1	1850—1.
Bureau Co. Phalanx . .	1	1843.

Cincinnati Brotherhood . .	5	1845—8.
Clarkson Industrial Association .	11	1844.
Clermont Phalanx . .	13	1844—7.
Colony of Bethel . .	11	1852.
Columbian Phalanx . .	1	1845.
Commonwealth Society . .	1	1819.
Communia Working Men's League	1	1850.
Convention at Boston of the Friends of Association . .	2	1843.
Convention in New York for organizing an Industrial Congress .	1	1845.
Co-operating Society of Alleghany Co.	1	1825.
Coxsackie Community . .	2	1826—7.
Davis' Harmonial Brotherhood .	2	1851.
Dunkers	4	1724.
Ebenezer Community . .	5	1843.
Emigration Society, 2d Section .	4	1843.
Forrestville Community . .	1	1825.
Fourier, Life of . . .	3	
Franklin Community . .	1	1826.
Garden Grove . . .	1	1848.
Goose Pond Community . .	1	1843.
Grand Prairie Community .	2	184–.
Grand Prairie Harmonial Institute	8	1853.
Guatemala Experiment . .	1	1843.
Haverstraw Community . .	3	1826.
Hopedale Community . .	13	1842.
Hunt's Experiment of Equality .	12	1843—7.
Icaria	82	1849.
Integral Phalanx . . .	5	1845.
Jefferson County Industrial Association	3	1843.
Kendal Community . .	4	1826.
Lagrange Phalanx . .	2	1843.
Leraysville Phalanx . .	5	1844.
Macluria . .	7	1826.
Marlboro Association . .	10	1841.

McKean County Association .	1	1843.
Modern Times . . .	3	1851.
Moorhouse Union . .	6	1843.
Moravians, or United Brethren .	9	1745.
Murray, Orson S. . .	3	
Nashoba	14	1825—8.
New Lanark . . .	10	1799.
New Harmony . . .	60	1825—7.
North American Phalanx .	38	1843–55.
Northampton Association .	7	1842.
Ohio Phalanx . . .	11	1844—5.
Oneida Community . .	27	1847.
One-mentian Community .	6	1843.
Ontario Phalanx . .	1	1844.
Owen, Robert . .	25	
Prairie Home Community .	23	1844.
Raritan Bay Union . .	5	1853.
Sangamon Phalanx . .	1	1845.
Shakers . . .	93	1776.
Skaneateles Community . .	18	1843—6.
Social Reform Unity . .	23	1842.
Sodus Bay Phalanx . .	3	1844.
Spiritual Community at Mountain Cove	3	1853.
Spring Farm Association .	3	1846—9.
St. Louis Reform Association .	1	1851.
Sylvania Association .	25	1843—5.
Trumbull Phalanx . .	13	1844—7.
United Germans . .	2	1827.
Venezuelan Experiment .	25	1844—6.
Warren, Josiah, Time Store &c.	11	1842.
Washtenaw Phalanx . .	1	1843.
Wisconsin Phalanx . .	21	1844–50.
Wright, Frances . .	9	
Wilkinson, Jemima, and her Community	5	1780.
Yellow Springs Community .	1	1825.
Zoar . .	8	1819.

On general survey of the matter contained in this index, we may begin to sort it in the following manner:

First we will lay aside the antique *religious* Associations, such as the Dunkers, Moravians, Zoarites, &c. We count at least seven of these, which do not properly belong to the modern socialistic movement, or even to American life. Having their origin in the old world, and most of them in the last century, and remaining without change, they exist only on the outskirts of general society.

Next we put out of account the *foreign* Associations, such as the Brazilian and Venezuelan experiments. With these may be classed those of the Icarians and some others, which, though within the United States, are, or were, really colonies of foreigners. We see six of this sort in the index.

Thirdly, we dismiss two or three Spiritualistic attempts that are named in the list; first, because they never attained to the dignity of Associations; and secondly, because they belonged to a later movement than that which Macdonald undertook to record. The social experiments of the Spiritualists should be treated by themselves, as the *sequelæ* of the Fourier excitement of Macdonald's time.

The Associations that are left after these exclusions, naturally fall into two groups, viz.; those of the OWEN MOVEMENT, and those of the FOURIER MOVEMENT.

Robert Owen came to this country and commenced his experiments in Communism in 1824. This was the beginning of a national excitement, which had a course somewhat like that of a religious revival or a political campaign. This movement seems to have culminated in 1826; and, grouped around or near that year, we find in Macdonald's list, the names of eleven Communities. These were not all strictly Owenite Communities, but probably all owed their birth to the general excitement that followed Owen's labors, and may therefore, properly be classified as belonging to the Owen movement.

Fourierism was introduced into this country by Albert Brisbane and Horace Greeley in 1842, and then commenced another great national movement similar to that of Owenism, but far more universal and enthusiastic. We consider the year 1843 the focal period of this social revival; and around that year or following it within the forties, we find the main group of Macdonald's Associations. Thirty-four of the list may clearly be referred to this epoch. Many, and perhaps most of them, never undertook to carry into practice Fourier's theories in full; and some of them would disclaim all affiliation with Fourierism; but they all originated in a common excitement, and that excitement took its rise from the publications of Brisbane and Greeley.

Confining ourselves, for the present, to these two groups of Associations, belonging respectively to the Owen movement of 1826 and the Fourier movement of 1843, we will now give a brief statistical account of each Association; i. e., all we can find in Macdonald's collection, on the following points: 1, Locality; 2, Number of members; 3, Amount of land; 4, Amount of debt; 5, Duration. We give the amount of land instead of any other measurement of capital, because all and more than all the capital of the Associations was generally invested in land, and because it is difficult to distinguish, in most cases, between the cash capital that was actually paid in, and that which was only subscribed or talked about.

As to the reliability of these statistics, we can only say that we have patiently picked them out, one by one, like scattered bones, from Macdonald's heap. Though they may be faulty in some details, we are confident that the general idea they give of the attempts and experiences of American Socialists, will not be far from the truth.

Experiments of the Owen Epoch.

Blue Spring Community ; Indiana ; no particulars, except that it lasted " but a short time."

Co-operative Society ; Pennsylvania ; no particulars.

Coxsackie Community ; New York ; capital " small ;" " very much in debt ;" duration between 1 and 2 years.

Forrestville Community ; Indiana ; " over 60 members ;" 325 acres of land ; duration more than a year.

Franklin Community ; New York ; no particulars.

Haverstraw Community ; New York ; about 80 members ; 120 acres ; debt $12,000 ; duration 5 months.

Kendal Community ; Ohio ; 200 members ; 200 acres ; duration about 2 years.

Macluria ; Indiana ; 1200 acres ; duration about 2 years.

New Harmony ; Indiana ; 900 members ; 30,000 acres, worth $150,000 ; duration nearly 3 years.

Nashoba ; Tennessee ; 15 members ; 2,000 acres ; duration about 3 years.

Yellow Spring Community ; Ohio ; 75 to 100 families ; duration 3 months.

Experiments of the Fourier Epoch.

Alphadelphia Phalanx ; Michigan ; 400 or 500 members ; 2814 acres ; duration 2 years and 9 months.

Brook Farm ; Massachusetts ; 115 members ; 200 acres ; duration 5 years.

Brooke's experiment; Ohio; few members; no further particulars.

Bureau Co. Phalanx; Illinois; small; no particulars.

Clarkson Industrial Association; New York; 420 members; 2000 acres; duration from 6 to 9 months.

Clermont Phalanx; Ohio; 120 members; 900 acres; debt $19,000; duration 2 years or more.

Columbian Phalanx; Ohio; no particulars.

Garden Grove; Iowa; no particulars.

Goose Pond Community; Pennsylvania; 60 members; duration a few months.

Grand Prairie Community; Ohio; no particulars.

Hopedale; Massachusetts; 200 members; 500 acres; duration not stated, but commonly reported to be 17 or 18 years.

Integral Phalanx; Illinois; 30 families; 508 acres; duration 17 months.

Jefferson Co. Industrial Association; New York; 400 members; 1200 acres of land; duration a few months.

Lagrange Phalanx; Indiana; 1000 acres; no further particulars.

Leraysville Phalanx; Pennsylvania; 40 members; 300 acres; duration 8 months.

Marlboro Association; Ohio; 24 members; had "a load of debt;" duration nearly 4 years.

McKean Co. Association; Pennsylvania; 30,000 acres; no further particulars.

Moorhouse Union; New York; 120 acres; duration "a few months."

North American Phalanx; New Jersey; 112 members; 673 acres; debt $17,000; duration 12 years.

Northampton Association; Massachusetts; 130 members; 500 acres of land; debt $40,000; duration 4 years.

Ohio Phalanx; 100 members; 2,200 acres; deeply in debt; duration 10 months.

One-mentian (meaning probably one-mind) Community; Pennsylvania; 800 acres; duration one year.

Ontario Phalanx; New York; brief duration.

Prairie Home Community; Ohio; 500 acres; debt broke it up; duration one year.

Raritan Bay Union; New Jersey; few members; 268 acres.

Sangamon Phalanx; Illinois; no particulars.

Skaneateles Community; New York; 150 members; 354 acres; debt $10,000; duration 2 1-2 years.

Social Reform Unity; Pennsylvania; 20 members; 2,000 acres; debt $2,400; duration about 10 months.

Sodus Bay Phalanx; New York; 300 members; 1,400 acres; duration a "short time."

Spring Farm Association; Wisconsin; 10 families; duration 3 years.

Sylvania Association; Pennsylvania; 145 members; 2394 acres; debt $7,900; duration nearly 2 years.

Trumbull Phalanx; Ohio; 1500 acres; duration 2 1-2 years.

Washtenaw Phalanx; Michigan; no particulars.

Wisconsin Phalanx; 32 families; 1,800 acres; duration 6 years.

Recapitulation and Comments.

1. *Localities.* The Owen group were distributed among the States as follows: in Indiana, 4; in New York, 3; in Ohio, 2; in Pennsylvania, 1; in Tennessee, 1.

The Fourier group were located as follows: in Ohio, 8; in New York, 6; in Pennsylvania, 6; in Massachusetts, 3; in Illinois, 3; in New Jersey, 2; in Michigan, 2; in Wisconsin, 2; in Indiana, 1; in Iowa, 1.

Indiana had the greatest number in the first group, and the least in the second.

New England was not represented in the Owen group; and only by three Associations in the Fourier group; and those three were all in Massachusetts.

The southern states were represented by only one Association—that of Nashoba, in the Owen group—and that was little more than an eleemosynary attempt of Frances Wright to civilize the negroes.

The two groups combined were distributed as follows: in Ohio, 10; in New York, 9; in Pennsylvania, 7; in Indiana, 5; in Massachusetts, 3; in Illinois, 3; in New Jersey, 2; in Michigan, 2; in Wisconsin, 2; in Tennessee, 1; in Iowa, 1.

2. *Number of members.* The figures in our epitome (reckoning five persons to a family when families are mentioned), give an aggregate of 4,801 members: but these belong to only twenty-five Associations. The numbers of the remaining twenty are not definitely reported. The average of those reported is about 192 to an Association. Extending this average to the rest, we have a total of 8,641.

The numbers belonging to single Associations vary from 15 to 900; but in a majority of cases they were between 100 and 200.

3. *The amount of land* reported is enormous. Averaging it as we did in the case of the number of members, we make a grand total of 136,586 acres, or about

3,000 acres to each Association! This is too much for any probable average. We will leave out as exceptional, the 60,000 acres reported as belonging to New Harmony and the McKean Co. Association. Then averaging as before, we have a grand total of 44,624 acres, or about 1,000 acres to each Association.

Judging by our own experience we incline to think that this fondness for land, which has been the habit of Socialists, had much to do with their failures. Farming is about the hardest and longest of all roads to fortune: and it is the kind of labor in which there is the most uncertainty as to modes 'and theories, and of course the largest chance for disputes and discords in such complex bodies as Associations. Moreover the lust for land leads off into the wilderness, " out west," or into by-places, far away from railroads and markets; whereas Socialism, if it is really ahead of civilization, ought to keep near the centers of business, and at the front of the general march of improvement. We should have advised the Phalanxes to limit their land-investments to a minimum, and put their strength as soon as possible into some form of manufacture. Almost any kind of a factory would be better than a farm for a Community nursery. We find hardly a vestige of this policy in Macdonald's collections. The saw-mill is the only form of mechanism that figures much in his reports. It is really ludicrous to see how uniformly an old saw-mill turns up in connection with each Association, and how zealously the brethren made much of it; but that is about all they attempted in the line of manufacturing. Land, land, land, was evidently regarded by them as the mother of all gain and comfort. Considering how much they must have run in debt for land, and how little profit they got from it, we may say of them almost literally, that they were "wrecked by running aground."

4. *Amount of debt.* Macdonald's reports on this point are few and indefinite. The sums owed are stated for only seven of the Associations. They vary from $1,000 to $40,000. Five other Associations are reported as "very much in debt," "deeply in debt," &c. The exact indebtedness of these and of the remaining thirty-three, is probably beyond the reach of history. But we have reason to think that nearly all of them bought, to begin with, a great deal more land than they paid for. This was the fashion of the socialistic schools and of the times.

5. *The duration* of fourteen Associations is not reported; twelve lasted less than 1 year; two 1 year; four between 1 and 2 years; three 2 years; four between 2 and 3 years; one between 3 and 4 years; one 4 years; one 5 years; one 6 years; one 12 years, and one (it is said) 17 years. All died young, and most of them before they were two years old.

CHAPTER III.

THEORY OF NATIONAL EXPERIENCE.

Now that our phenomena are fairly before us, a little speculation may be appropriate. One wants to know what position these experiments, which started so gaily and failed so soon, occupy in the history of this country and of the world ; what relation they have to Christianity ; what their meaning is in the great scheme of Providence. Students of Socialism and history must have some theory about their place and significance in the great whole of things. We have studied them somewhat in the circumspective way, and will devote a few pages to our theory about them. It will at least correct any impression that we intend to treat them disrespectfully.

And first we keep in mind a clear and wide distinction between the Associations and the movements from which they sprung. The word *movement* is very convenient, though very indefinite. We use it to designate the wide-spread excitements and discussions about Socialism which led to the experiments we have epitomized. In our last chapter we incidentally compared the socialistic movements of the Owen and

Fourier epochs to religious revivals. We might now complete the idea, by comparing the Associations that issued from those movements, to churches that were organized in consequence of the revivals. A vast spiritual and intellectual excitement is one thing; and the *institutions* that rise out of it are another. We must not judge the excitement by the institutions.

We get but a very imperfect idea of the Owen and Fourier movements from the short-lived experiments whose remains are before us in Macdonald's collections. In the first place Macdonald, faithful as he was, did not discover all the experiments that were made during those movements. We remember some that are not named in his manuscripts. And in the next place the numbers engaged in the practical attempts were very small, in comparison with the masses that entered into the enthusiasm of the general movements and abandoned themselves to the idea of an impending social revolution. The eight thousand and six hundred that we found by averaging Macdonald's list, might probably be doubled to represent the census of the obscure unknown attempts, and then multiplied by ten to cover the outside multitudes that were converted to Socialism in the course of the Owen and Fourier revivals.

Owen in 1824 stirred the very life of the nation with his appeals to Kings and Congresses, and his vast experiments at New Harmony. Think of his family of nine hundred members on a farm of thirty thousand acres! A magnificent beginning, that thrilled the world! The general movement was proportionate to this beginning; and though this great Community and all the little ones that followed it failed and disappeared in a few years, the movement did not cease. Owen and his followers—especially his son Robert Dale Owen and Frances Wright—continued to agitate the country with newspapers, public lectures, and " Fanny Wright societies," till their ideas actually got foot-hold and influence in the great Democratic party. The special enthusiasm for practical attempts at Association culminated in 1826, and afterwards subsided ; but the excitement about Owen's ideas, which was really the Owen movement, reached its height after 1830 ; and the embers of it are in the heart of the nation to this day.

On the other hand, Fourier (by proxy) started another national excitement in 1842. With young Brisbane for its cosmopolitan apostle, and a national newspaper, such as the *New York Tribune* was, for its organ, this movement, like Owen's, could not be otherwise than national in its dimensions. We shall have occasion hereafter to show how vast and deep it was, and how poorly it is represented by the Phalanxes that figure in Macdonald's memoirs. Meanwhile let the reader consider that several of the men who were leaders in this excitement, were also leaders then and afterwards in the old Whig party ; and he will have reason to conclude that Socialism, in its duplex form of Owenism and Fourierism, has touched and modified both of the party-sections and all departments of the national life.

We must not think of the two great socialistic revivals as altogether heterogeneous and separate. Their partizans maintained theoretical opposition to each other ; but after all the main idea of both was *the enlargement of home—the extension of family union beyond the little man-and-wife circle to large corporations*. In this idea the two movements were one ; and this was the charm-

ing idea that caught the attention and stirred the enthusiasm of the American people. Owenism prepared the
way for Fourierism. The same men, or at least the
same sort of men that took part in the Owen movement, were afterward carried away by the Fourier
enthusiasm. The two movements may, therefore, be
regarded as one ; and in that view, the period of the
great American socialistic revival extends from 1824,
through the final and overwhelming excitement of 1843,
to the collapse of Fourierism after 1846.

As a man who has passed through a series of
passional excitements, is never the same being afterward, so we insist that these socialistic paroxysms have
changed the heart of the nation ; and that a yearning
toward social reconstruction has become a part of the
continuous, permanent, inner experience of the American people. The Communities and Phalanxes died
almost as soon as they were born, and are now almost
forgotten. But the spirit of Socialism remains in the
life of the nation. It was discouraged and cast down
by the failures of 1828 and 1846, and thus it learned
salutary caution and self-control. But it lives still, as a
hope watching for the morning, in thousands and perhaps millions who never took part in any of the experiments, and who are neither Owenites nor Fourierites,
but simply Socialists without theory—believers in the
possibility of a scientific and heavenly reconstruction of
society.

Thus our theory harmonizes Owenism with Fourierism, and regards them both as working toward the same
end in American history. Now we will go a step further
and attempt the reconciling of still greater repugnances.

Since the war of 1812—15, the line of socialistic excitements lies parallel with the line of religious Revivals. Each had its two great leaders, and its two epochs of enthusiasm. Nettleton and Finney were to Revivals, what Owen and Fourier were to Socialism. Nettleton prepared the way for Finney, though he was opposed to him, as Owen prepared the way for Fourier. The enthusiasm in both movements had the same progression. Nettleton's agitation, like Owen's, was moderate and somewhat local. Finney, like Fourier, swept the nation as with a tempest. The Revival periods were a little in advance of those of Socialism. Nettleton commenced his labors in 1817, while Owen entered the field in 1824. Finney was at the height of his power in 1831—3, while Fourier was carrying all before him in 1842—3. Thus the movements were to a certain extent alternate. Opposed as they were to each other theologically—one being a movement of Bible men, and the other of infidels and liberals—they could not be expected to hold public attention simultaneously. But looking at the whole period from the end of the war in 1815 to the end of Fourierism after 1846, and allowing Revivals a little precedence over Socialism, we find the two lines of excitement parallel, and their phenomena wonderfully similar.

As we have shown that the socialistic movement was national, so, if it were necessary, we might here show that the Revival movement was national. There was a time between 1831 and 1834 when the American people came as near to a surrender of all to the Kingdom of Heaven, as they came in 1843 to a socialistic revolution. The Millennium seemed as near in 1831, as Fourier's Age of Harmony seemed in 1843. And the final effect of Revivals was a hope watching for the morning, which remains in the life of the nation, side by side, nay identical with, the great hope of Socialism.

And these movements—Revivalism and Socialism—opposed to each other as they may seem, and as they have been in the creeds of their partizans, are closely related in their essential nature and objects, and manifestly belong together in the scheme of Providence, as they do in the history of this nation. They are to each other as inner to outer—as soul to body—as life to its surroundings. The Revivalists had for their great idea the regeneration of the soul. The great idea of the Socialists was the regeneration of society, which is the soul's environment. These ideas belong together, and are the complements of each other. Neither can be successfuly embodied by men whose minds are not wide enough to accept them both.

In fact these two ideas, which in modern times are so wide apart, were present together in original Christianity. When the Spirit of truth pricked three thousand men to the heart and converted them on the day of Pentecost, its next effect was to resolve them into one family and introduce Communism of property. Thus the greatest of all Revivals was also the great inauguration of Socialism.

Undoubtedly the Socialists will think we make too much of the Revival movement ; and the Revivalists will think we make too much of the Socialistic movement ; and the politicians will think we make too much of both, in assigning them important places in American history. But we hold that a man's deepest experiences are those of religion and love ; and these are just the experiences in respect to which he is most apt to be ashamed, and most inclined to be silent. So the nation says but little, and tries to think that it thinks but little, about its Revivals and its Socialisms ; but they are nevertheless the deepest and most interesting passages of its history, and worth more study as determinatives of character and destiny, than all its politics and diplomacies, its money matters and its wars.

Doubtless the Revivalists and Socialists despise each other, and perhaps both will despise us for imagining that they can be reconciled. But we will say what we believe ; and that is, that they have both failed in their attempts to bring heaven on earth, *because* they despised each other, and would not put their two great ideas together. The Revivalists failed for want of regeneration of society, and the Socialists failed for want of regeneration of the heart.

On the one hand the Revivalists needed daily meetings and continuous criticism to save and perfect their converts ; and these things they could not have without a thorough reconstruction of domestic life. They tried the expedient of "protracted meetings," which was really a half-way attack on the fashion of the world ; but society was too strong for them, and their half-measures broke down, as all half-measures must. What they needed was to convert their churches into unitary families, and put them into unitary homes, where daily meetings and continuous criticism are possible ;—and behold, this is Socialism !

On the other hand the Socialists, as often as they came together in actual attempts to realize their ideals, found that they were too selfish for close organization. The moan of Macdonald was, that after seeing the stern reality of the experiments, he lost hope, and was obliged to confess that he had "imagined mankind better than they are." This was the final confession of the leaders in the Associative experiments generally, from Owen to the last of the Fourierites; and this confession means, that Socialism needed for its complement, regeneration of the heart;—and behold, this is Revivalism!

These discords and failures of the past surely have not been in vain. Perhaps Providence has carried forward its regenerative designs in two lines thus far, for the sake of the advantage of a "division of labor." While the Bible men have worked for the regeneration of the soul, the infidels and liberals have been busy on the problem of the reconstruction of society. Working apart and in enmity, perhaps they have accomplished more for final harmony than they could have done together. Even their failures when rightly interpreted, may turn to good account. They have both helped to plant in the heart of the nation an unfailing hope of the "good time coming." Their lines of labor, though we have called them parallel, must really be convergent; and we may hope that the next phase of national history will be that of Revivalism and Socialism harmonized, and working together for the Kingdom of Heaven.

To complete our historical theory, we must mention in conclusion, one point of contrast between the Socialisms and the Revivals.

The Socialisms were imported from Europe; while the Revivals were American productions.

Owen was an Englishman, and Fourier was a Frenchman; but Nettleton and Finney were both Americans—both natives of Connecticut.

In the comparison we confine ourselves to the period since the war of 1812, because the history of the general socialistic excitements in this country is limited to that period. But the Revivals have an anterior history, extending back into the earliest times of New England. The great American *system* of Revivals, of which the Nettleton and Finney excitements were the continuation, was born in the first half of the last century, in central Massachusetts. Jonathan Edwards, whose life extended from 1703 to 1758, was the father of it. So that not only since the war of 1812, but before the Revolution of 1776, we find Revivalism, *as a system*, strictly an American production.

We call the Owen and Fourier movements, *American* Socialisms, because they were national in their dimensions, and American life chiefly was the subject of them. But looking at what may be called the *male* element in the production of them, they were really European movements, propagated in this country. Nevertheless, if we take the view that Socialism and Revivalism are a unit in the design of Providence, one looking to the regeneration of externals and the other to the regeneration of internals, we may still call the entire movement American, as having Revivalism, which is American, for its inner life, though Socialism, the outer element, was imported from England and France.

CHAPTER IV.

NEW HARMONY.

AMERICAN Socialisms, as we have defined them and grouped their experiments, may be called *non-religious* Socialisms. Several religious Communities flourished in this country before Owen's attempts, and have continued to flourish here since the collapse of Fourierism. But they were originally colonies of foreigners, and never were directly connected with movements that could be called national. Owen was the first Socialist that stirred the enthusiasm of the whole American people; and he was the first, so far as we know, who tried the experiment of a non-religious Community. And the whole series of experiments belonging to the two great groups of the Owen and Fourier epochs, followed in his footsteps. The exclusion of theology was their distinction and their boast.

Our programme, limited as it is by its title to these national Socialisms, does not strictly include the religious Communities. Yet those Communities have played indirectly a very important part in the drama of American Socialisms, and will require considerable incidental attention as we proceed.

In attempting to make out from Macdonald's collection an outline of Owen's great experiment at New Harmony (which was the prototype of all the Owen and Fourier experiments), we find ourselves at the outset quite unexpectedly dealing with a striking example of the relation between the religious and non-religious Communities.

Owen did not build the village of New Harmony, nor create the improvements which prepared his 30,000 acres for his family of nine hundred. He bought them outright from a previous religious Community; and it is doubtful whether he would have ever gathered his nine hundred and made his experiment, if he had not found a place prepared for him by a sect of Christian Communists.

Macdonald was an admirer, we might almost say a worshiper, of Owen. He gloats over New Harmony as the very Mecca of his devotion. There he spent his first eighteen months in this country. The finest picture in his collection is an elaborate India-ink drawing of the village. But he scarcely mentions the Rappites who built it. No separate account of them, such as he gives of the Shakers and Moravians, can be found in his manuscripts. This is an unaccountable neglect; for their pre-occupation of New Harmony and their transactions with Owen, must have thrust them upon his notice; and their history is intrinsically as interesting, to say the least, as that of any of the religious Communities.

A glance at the history of the Rappites is in many ways indispensable, as an introduction to an account of Owen's New Harmony. We must therefore address ourselves to the task which Macdonald neglected.

THE HARMONISTS.

In the first years of the present century, old Würtemburg, a province always famous for its religious enthusiasms, was fermenting with excitement about the Millennium ; and many of its enthusiasts were expecting the speedy personal advent of Christ   Among these George Rapp became a prominent preacher, and led forth a considerable sect into doctrines and ways that brought upon him and them severe persecutions. In 1803 he came to America to find a refuge for his flock.   After due exploration he purchased 5000 acres of land in Butler Co., Pennsylvania, and commenced a settlement which he called Harmony.   In the summer of 1804 two ship-loads of his disciples with their families— six hundred in all—came over the ocean and joined him   In 1805 the Society was formally organized as a Christian Community, on the model of the Pentecostal church.   For a time their fare was poor and their work was hard.   An evil eye from their neighbors was upon them.   But they lived down calumny and suspicion by well-doing, and soon made the wilderness blossom around them like the rose.   In 1807 they adopted the principle of celibacy ; but in other respects they were far from being ascetics.   Music, painting, sculpture, and other liberal arts flourished among them.   Their museums and gardens were the wonder and delight of the region around them.   In 1814, desiring warmer land and a better location for business, they sold all in Pennsylvania and removed to Indiana.   On the banks of the Wabash they built a new village and again called it Harmony.   Here they prospered more than ever, and their number increased to nearly a thousand.   In 1824 they again became discontented with their location, on account of bad neighbors and malaria. Again they sold all, and returned to Pennsylvania ; but not to their old home. They built their third and final village in Beaver Co, near Pittsburgh, and called it Economy. There they are to this day. They own railroads and oil wells and are reported to be millionaires of the unknown grade. In all their migrations from the old world to the new, from Pennsylvania to Indiana, and from Indiana back to Pennsylvania ; in all their perils by persecutions, by false brethren, by pestilence, by poverty and wealth, their religion held them together, and their union gave them the strength that conquers prosperity. A notable example of what a hundred families can do when they have the wisdom of harmony, and fight the battle of life in a solid phalanx ! A nobler " six hundred" than the famous dragoons of Balaklava !

Such were the people who gave Robert Owen his first lessons in Communism, and sold him their home in Indiana. Ten of their best years they spent in building a village on the Wabash, not for themselves (as it turned out), but for a theater of the great infidel experiment. Rev. Aaron Williams, D. D., the historian to whom we are indebted for the facts of the above sketch, thus describes the negotiations and the transfer :

" The Harmonists, when they began to think of returning to Pennsylvania, employed a certain Richard Flower, an Englishman, and a prominent member of an English settlement in their vicinity, to negotiate for a sale of their real estate, offering him five thousand dollars to find a purchaser. Flower went to England for this purpose, and hearing of Robert Owen's Community at New Lanark, he sought him out and succeeded in selling to him the town of Harmony, with all its houses,

mills, factories and thirty thousand acres of land, for one
hundred and fifty thousand dollars. This was an immense sacrifice ; but they were determined to leave the
country, and they submitted to the loss. Having in the
meantime made a purchase of their present lands in
Pennsylvania, on the Ohio river, they built a steamboat
and removed in detachments to their new and final place
of settlement."

Thus Owen, the first experimenter in non-religious
Association, had substantially the ready-made material
conditions which Fourier and his followers considered
indispensable to success.

We proceed now to give a sketch of the Owen
experiment chiefly in Macdonald's words. When our
own language occurs it is generally a condensation
of his.

OWEN'S NEW HARMONY.

"Robert Owen came to the United States in December 1824, to complete the purchase of the settlement at
Harmony. Mr. Rapp had sent an agent to England to
dispose of the property, and Mr. Owen fell in with him
there. In the spring of 1825 Mr. Owen closed the bargain. The property consisted of about 30,000 acres of
land ; nearly 3,000 acres under cultivation by the society ;
19 detached farms ; 600 acres of improved land occupied by tenants ; some fine orchards ; eighteen acres
of full-bearing vines ; and the village, which was a
regularly laid out town, with streets running at right
angles to each other, and a public square, around which
were large brick edifices, built by the Rappites for
churches, schools, and other public purposes."

We can form some idea of the size of the village from

the fact which we learn from Mr. Williams, that the Rappites, while at Harmony, numbered one thousand souls. It does not appear from Macdonald's account that Owen and his Community made any important additions to the village.

"On the departure of the Rappites, persons favorable to Mr. Owen's views came flocking to New Harmony (as it was thenceforth called) from all parts of the country. Tidings of the new social experiment spread far and wide; and, although it has been denied, yet it is undoubtedly true, that Mr Owen in his public lectures invited the 'industrious and well disposed of all nations' to emigrate to New Harmony. The consequence was, that in the short space of six weeks from the commencement of the experiment, a population of eight hundred persons was drawn together, and in October 1825, the number had increased to nine hundred."

As to the character of this population, Macdonald insists that it was "as good as it could be under the circumstances," and he gives the names of "many intelligent and benevolent individuals who were at various times residents at New Harmony." But he admits that there were some "black sheep" in the flock. "It is certain," he says, "that there was a proportion of needy and idle persons, who crowded in to avail themselves of Mr. Owen's liberal offer; and that they did their share of work more in the line of *destruction* than *construction*"

Constitution No. 1.

On the 27th of April 1825, Mr. Owen instituted a sort of provisional government. In an address to the people in New Harmony Hall, he informed them, "that he had bought that property, and had come there to introduce the practice of the new views ; but he showed them the impossibility that persons educated as they were, should change at once from an irrational to a rational system of society, and the necessity for a 'half-way house,' in which to be prepared for the new system." Whereupon he tendered them a *Constitution*, of which we find no definite account, except that it was not fully Communistic, and was to hold the people in probationary training three years, under the title of the *Preliminary Society of New Harmony*. "After these proceedings Mr. Owen left New Harmony for Europe, and the Society was managed by the *Preliminary Committee.*(!)" We may imagine, each one for himself, what the nine hundred did while Mr. Owen was away. Macdonald compiled from the *New Harmony Gazette* a very rapid but evidently defective account of the state of things in this important interval. He says nothing about the work on the 30,000 acres, but speaks of various minor businesses as "doing well." The only manufactures that appear to have "exceeded consumption" were those of soap and glue. A respectable apothecary "dispensed medicines without charge," and "the store supplied the inhabitants with all necessaries"—probably at Mr. Owen's expense. Education was considered "public property," and one hundred and thirty children were schooled, boarded and clothed from the public funds— probably at Mr, Owen's expense. Amusements flour- ished. The Society had a band of music ; Tuesday evenings were appropriated to balls ; Friday evenings to concerts—both in the old Rappite church. There was no provision for religious worship. Five military companies, "consisting of infantry, artillery, riflemen, veterans and fusileers," did duty from time to time on the public square.

Constitution No. 2.

"Mr. Owen returned to New Harmony on the 12th of January, 1826, and soon after the members of the Preliminary Society held a convention, and adopted a constitution of a Community, entitled *The New Harmony Community of Equality*. Thus in less than a year, instead of three years as Mr. Owen had proposed, the 'half-way house' came to an end, and actual Communism commenced. A few of the members, who, on account of a difference of opinions, did not sign the new constitution, formed a second Community on the New Harmony estate about two miles from the town, in friendly connection with the first."

The new government instituted by Mr. Owen, was to be in the hands of an *Executive Council*, subject at all times to the direction of the Community; and six gentlemen were appointed to this function. But Macdonald says: "Difficulties ensued in organizing the new Community. It appears that the plan of government by executive council would not work, and that the members were unanimous in calling upon Mr. Owen to take the sole management, judging from his experience that he was the only man who could do so. This call Mr. Owen accepted, and we learn that soon after general satisfaction and individual contentment took the place of suspense and uncertainty."

This was in fact the inauguration of

Constitution No. 3.

"In March the *Gazette* says that under the indefatigable attention of Mr. Owen, order had been introduced into every department of business, and the farm presented a scene of active and steady industry. The Society was rapidly becoming a Community of Equality. The streets no longer exhibited groups of idle talkers, but each one was busily engaged in the occupation he had chosen. The public meetings, instead of being the arenas for contending orators, were changed into meetings of business, where consultations were held and measures adopted for the comfort of all the members of the Community.

"In April there was a disturbance in the village on account of negotiations that were going on for securing the estate as private property. Some persons attempted to divide the town into several societies. Mr Owen would not agree to this, and as he had the power, he made a selection, and by solemn examination constituted a *nucleus* of twenty-five men, which *nucleus* was to admit members, Mr. Owen reserving the power to *veto* every one admitted. There were to be three grades of members, viz., conditional members, probationary members, and persons on trial. (?) The Community was to be under the direction of Mr. Owen, until two-thirds of the members should think fit to govern themselves, provided the time was not less than twelve months."

This may be called,

Constitution No. 4.

In May a third Community had been formed; and the population was divided between No. 1, which was Mr. Owen's Community, No. 2, which was called Macluria, and No. 3, which was called *Feiba Peven*—a name designating in some mysterious way the latitude and longitude of New Harmony.

"May 27. The immigration continued so steadily, that it became necessary for the Community to inform the friends of the new views that the accommodations were inadequate, and call upon them by advertisement not to come until further notice."

Constitution No. 5.

"May 30. In consequence of a variety of troubles and disagreements, chiefly relating to the disposal of the property, a great meeting of the whole population was held, and it was decided to form four separate societies, each signing its own contract for such part of the property as it should purchase, and each managing its own affairs ; but to trade with each other by paper money."

Mr. Owen was now beginning to make sharp bargains with the independent Communities. Macdonald says, "He had lost money, and no doubt he tried to regain some of it, and used such means as he thought would prevent further loss."

On the 4th of July Mr. Owen delivered his celebrated *Declaration of Mental Independence*, from which we give the following specimen :

" I now declare to you and to the world, that Man, up to this hour, has been in all parts of the earth a slave to a Trinity of the most monstrous evils that could be combined to inflict mental and physical evil upon his whole race. I refer to Private or Individual Property, Absurd and Irrational systems of Religion, and Marriage founded on Individual Property, combined with some of these Irrational systems of Religion."

" August 20. After Mr. Owen had given his usual address, it was unanimously agreed by the meeting that

the entire population of New Harmony should meet
three times a week in the Hall, for the purpose of being
educated together. This practice was continued about
six weeks, when Mr. Owen became sick and it was
discontinued."

Constitution No. 6.

"August 25. The people held a meeting at which
they *abolished all officers* then existing, and appointed
three men as *dictators*."

Constitution No. 7.

"Sept. 17. A large meeting of all the Societies and
the whole population of the town took place at the Hall,
for the purpose of considering a plan for the '*ameliora-
tion of the Society*, to improve the condition of the people,
and make them more contented.' A message was received from Mr. Owen proposing to form a Community
with as many as would join him, and put in all their
property, save what might be thought necessary to reserve to help their friends; the government to consist of
Robert Owen and four others of his choice, to be
appointed by him every year; and not to be altered
for five years. This movement of course nullified all
previous organizations. Disagreements and jealousies
ensued, and, as was the case on a former change being
made, many persons left New Harmony.

"Nov. 1. The *Gazette* says: 'Eighteen months experience has proved to us, that the requisite qualifications
for a permanent member of the Community of Common
Property are, 1, Honesty of purpose; 2, Temperance;
3, Industry; 4, Carefulness; 5, Cleanliness; 6, Desire
for knowledge; 7, A conviction of the fact that the
character of man is formed for, and not by, himself.'

"Nov. 8. Many persons leaving. The *Gazette* shows how impossible it is for a Community of common property to exist, unless the members comprising it have acquired the genuine Community character.

"Nov. 11. Mr. Owen reviewed the last six months' progress of the Community in a favorable light.

"In December the use of ardent spirits was abolished.

"Jan. 1827. Although there was an appearance of increased order and happiness, yet matters were drawing to a close. Owen was selling property to individuals; the greater part of the town was now resolved into individual lots; a grocery was established opposite the tavern; painted sign-boards began to be stuck up on the buildings, pointing out places of manufacture and trade; a sort of wax-figure-and-puppet-show was opened at one end of the boarding-house; and every thing was getting into the old style."

It is useless to follow this wreck further. Everybody sees it must go down, and *why* it must go down. It is like a great ship, wallowing helpless in the trough of a tempestuous sea, with nine hundred *passengers*, and no captain or organized crew! We skip to Macdonald's picture of the end.

"June 18, 1827. The *Gazette* advertised that Mr. Owen would meet the inhabitants of New Harmony and the neighborhood on the following Sunday, to bid them farewell. I find no account of this meeting, nor indeed of any further movements of Mr. Owen in the *Gazette*. After his departure the majority of the population also removed and scattered about the country. Those who remained returned to individualism, and settled as farmers and mechanics in the ordinary way. One portion of the estate was owned by Mr. Owen, and the other by Mr. Maclure. They sold, rented, or gave away the houses and lands, and their heirs and assigns have continued to do so to the present day."

Fifteen years after the catastrophe Macdonald was at New Harmony, among the remains of the old Community population, and he says: "I was cautioned not to speak of Socialism, as the subject was unpopular. The advice was good; Socialism was unpopular, and with good reason. The people had been wearied and disappointed by it; had been filled full with theories, until they were nauseated, and had made such miserable attempts at practice, that they seemed ashamed of what they had been doing. An enthusiastic socialist would soon be cooled down at New Harmony."

The strength of the reaction against Communism caused by Owen's failure, may be seen to this day in the sect devoted to "Individual Sovereignty." Josiah Warren, the leader of that sect, was a member of Owen's Community, and a witness of its confusions and downfall; from which he swung off into the extreme of anti-Communism. The village of "Modern Times," where all forms of social organization were scouted as unscientific, was the electric negative of New Harmony.

Macdonald thus moralizes over his master's failure:

" Mr. Owen said he wanted honesty of purpose, and he got dishonesty. He wanted temperance, and instead, he was continually troubled with the intemperate. He wanted industry, and he found idleness. He wanted cleanliness, and found dirt. He wanted carefulness, and found waste. He wanted to find desire for knowledge, but he found apathy. He wanted the principles of the formation of character understood, and he found them misunderstood. He wanted these good qualities combined in one and all the individuals of the Community, but he could not find them; neither could he find those who were self-sacrificing and enduring enough, to prepare and educate their children to possess these qualities. Thus it was proved that his principles were either entirely erroneous, or much in advance of the age in which he promulgated them. He seems to have forgotten, that if one and all the thousand persons assembled there, had possessed the qualities which he wished them to possess, there would have been no necessity for his vain exertions to form a Community; because there would of necessity be brotherly love, charity, industry and plenty. We want no more than these; and if this is the material to form Communities of, and we can not find it, we can not form Communities; and if we can not find parents who are ready and willing to educate their children, to give them these qualities for a Community life, then what hope is there of Communism in the future?"

Almost the only redeeming feature in or near this whole scene of confusion—which might well be called New Discord instead of New Harmony—was the silent retreat of the Rappite thousand, which was so orderly that it almost escaped mention. Remembering their obscure achievements and their persistent success, we can still be sure that the *idea* of Owen and his thousand was not a delusion, but an inspiration, that only needed wiser hearts, to become a happy reality.

CHAPTER V.

INQUEST ON NEW HARMONY.

THE only laudable object any one can have in rehearsing and studying the histories of the socialistic failures, is that of learning from them practical lessons for guidance in present and future experiments. With this in view, the great experiment at New Harmony is well worth faithful consideration. It was, as we have said, the first and most notable of the entire series of non-religious Communities. It had for its antecedent the vast reputation that Owen had gained by his success at New Lanark. He came to this country with the prestige of a reformer who had the confidence and patronage of Lords, Dukes and Sovereigns in the old world. His lectures were received with attention by large assemblies in our principal cities. At Washington he was accomodated by the Speaker and President with the Hall of Representatives, in which he delivered several lectures before the President, the President elect, all the judges of the Supreme Court, and a great number of members of Congress. He afterwards presented to the Government an expensive and elaborate model, with interior and working drawings, elevations, &c., of one of the magnificent communal edifices which he had projected. He had a large private fortune, and drew into his schemes other capitalists, so that his experiment had the advantage of unlimited wealth. That wealth, as we have seen, placed at his command unlimited land and a ready-made village. These attractions brought him men in unlimited numbers.

How stupendous the revolution was that he contemplated as the result of his great gathering, is best seen in the famous words which he uttered in the public hall at New Harmony on the 4th of July, 1826. We have already quoted from this speech a paragraph (underscored and double-scored by Macdonald) about the awful Trinity of man's oppressors—" Private property, Irrational Religion, and Marriage." In the same vein he went on to say :

" For nearly forty years have I been employed, heart and soul, day by day, almost without ceasing, in preparing the means and arranging the circumstances, to enable me to give the death-blow to the tyranny which, for unnumbered ages, has held the human mind spellbound in chains of such mysterious forms that no mortal has dared approach to set the suffering prisoner free ! Nor has the fullness of time for the accomplishment of this great event, been completed until within this hour ! Such has been the extraordinary course of events, that the Declaration of Political Independence in 1776, has produced its counterpart, the *Declaration of Mental Independence* in 1826; the latter just half a century from the former. * * *

" In furtherance of our great object we are preparing the means to bring up our children with industrious and useful habits, with national and of course rational ideas and views, with sincerity in all their proceedings ; and to give them kind and affectionate feelings for each other, and charity, in the most extensive sense of the term, for all their fellow creatures.

"By doing this, uniting our separate interests into one, by doing away with divided money transactions, by exchanging with each other our articles of produce on the basis of labor for equal labor, by looking forward to apply our surplus wealth to assist others to attain similar advantages, and by the abandonment of the use of spiritous liquors, we shall in a peculiar manner promote the object of every wise government and all really enlightened men.

"And here we now are, as near perhaps as we can be in the center of the United States, even, as it were, like the little grain of mustard seed! But with these *Great Truths* before us, with the practice of the social system, as soon as it shall be well understood among us, our principles will, I trust, spread from Community to Community, from State to State, from Continent to Continent, until this system and these *truths* shall overshadow the whole earth, shedding fragrance and abundance, intelligence and happiness, upon all the sons of men!"

Such were the antecedents and promises of the New Harmony experiment. The Professor appeared on the stage with a splendid reputation for previous thaumaturgy, with all the crucibles and chemicals around him that money could buy, with an audience before him that was gaping to see the last wonder of science : but on applying the flame that was to set all ablaze with happiness and glory, behold! the material prepared would not burn, but only sputtered and smoked ; and the" curtain had to come down upon a scene of confusion and disappointment !

What was the difficulty? Where was the mistake? These are the questions that ought to be studied till they are fully answered; for scores and hundreds of just such experiments have been tried since, with the same disastrous results; and scores and hundreds will be tried hereafter, till we go back and hold a faithful inquest, and find a sure verdict, on this original failure.

Let us hear, then, what has been, or can be said, by all sorts of judges, on the causes of Owen's failure, and learn what we can.

Macdonald has an important chapter on this subject, from which we extract the following:

"There is no doubt in my mind, that the absence of Robert Owen in the first year of the Community was one of the great causes of its failure; for he was naturally looked up to as the head, and his influence might have kept people together, at least so as to effect something similar to what had been effected at New Lanark. But with a people free as these were from a set religious creed, and consisting, as they did, of all nations and opinions, it is doubtful if even Mr. Owen, had he continued there all the time, could have kept them permanently together. No comparison can be made between that population and the Shakers, Rappites, or Zoarites, who are each of one religious faith, and, save the Shakers, of one nation.

"Mr. Samson, of Cincinnati, was at New Harmony from the beginning to the end of the Community; he went there on the boat that took the last of the Rappites away. He says the cause of failure was a rogue, named Taylor, who insinuated himself into Mr. Owen's favor, and afterward swindled and deceived him in a variety of ways, among other things establishing a distillery, contrary to Mr. Owen's wishes and principles, and injurious to the Community.

"Owen always held the property. He thought it would be ten or twelve years before the Community would fill up; but no sooner had the Rappites left, than the place was taken possession of by strangers from all parts, while Owen was absent in England and the place under the management of a committee. When Owen returned and found how things were going, he deemed it necessary to make a change, and notices were published in all parts, telling people not to come there, as there were no accommodations for them ; yet still they came, till at last Owen was compelled to have all the log-cabins that harbored them pulled down.

"Taylor and Fauntleroy were Owen's associates. When Owen found out Taylor's rascality he resolved to abandon the partnership with him, which Taylor would only agree to upon Owen's giving him a large tract of land, upon which he proposed to form a Community of his own. The agreement was that he should have the land and *all upon it*. So on the night previous to the execution of the bargain, he had a large quantity of cattle and farm implements put upon the land, and he thereby came into possession of them ! Instead of forming a Community, he built a distillery, and also set up a tan-yard in opposition to Mr. Owen !

In the *Free Enquirer* of June 10th, 1829, there is an article by Robert Dale Owen on New Lanark and New Harmony, in which, after comparing the two places and showing the difference between them, he makes the following remark relative to the experiment at New Harmony : "There was not disinterested industry, there was not mutual confidence, there was not practical experience, there was not unison of action, because there was not unanimity of counsel: and these were the points of difference and dissension—the rocks on which the social bark struck and was wrecked."

A letter in the *New Harmony Gazette*, of January 31, 1827, complains of the "slow progress of education in the Community—the heavy labor, and no recompense but *cold water* and *inferior provisions.*"

Paul Brown, who wrote a book entitled " Twelve months at New Harmony," among his many complaints says, " There was no such thing as real general *common stock* brought into being in this place." He attributes all the troubles, to the anxiety about "*exclusive property,*" principally on the part of Owen and his associates. Speaking of one of the secondary Societies, he says there were "class distinctions" in it; and Macluria or the School Society he condemns as being most aristocratical, "its few projectors being extremely wealthy."

In the *New Moral World* of October 12, 1839, there is an article on New Harmony, in which it is asserted that Mr. Owen was induced to purchase that place on the understanding that the Rappite population then residing there would remain, until he had gradually introduced other persons to acquire from them the systematic and orderly habits, as well as practical knowledge, which they had gained by many years of practice. But by the removal of Rapp and his followers, Mr. Owen was left with all the property on his hands, and he was thus compelled to get persons to come there to prevent things from going to ruin.

Mr. Josiah Warren, in his "Practical Details of Equitable Commerce," says: "Let us bear in mind that during the great experiments in New Harmony in

1825 and 1826, every thing went delightfully on, except pecuniary affairs! We should, no doubt, have succeeded but for property considerations. But then the experiments never would have been commenced but for property considerations. It was to annihilate social antagonism by a system of *common property*, that we undertook the experiments at all."

Mr. Sargant, the English biographer of Owen, intimates several times that *religion* was the first subject of discord at New Harmony. His own opinion of the cause of the catastrophe, he gives in the following words:

"What were the causes of these failures? People will give different answers, according to the general sentiments they entertain. For myself I should say, that such experiments must fail, because it is impossible to mould to Communism the characters of men and women, formed by the present doctrines and practices of the world to intense individualism. I should indeed go further by stating my convictions, that even with persons brought up from childhood to act in common and live in common, it would be impossible to carry out a Communistic system, unless in a place utterly removed from contact with the world, or with the help of some powerful religious conviction. Mere benevolence, mere sentiments of universal philanthropy, are far too weak to bind the self-seeking affections of men."

John Pratt, a Positivist, in a communication to *The Oneida Circular*, contributes the following philosophical observations:

"Owen was a Scotch metaphysician of the old school. As such, he was a most excellent fault-finder and *disorganizer*. He could perceive and depict the existing discord, but knew not better than his contemporaries Shelley and Godwin, where to find the New Harmony. Like most men of the last generation he looked upon society as a manufactured product, and not as an organism endued with imperishable vitality and growth. Like them he attributed all the evils it endured to priests and politicians, whose immediate annihilation would be followed by immediate, everlasting and universal happiness. It would be astonishing if an experiment initiated by such a class of thinkers should succeed under the most favorable auspices. One word as to mere externals. Owen was a skeptic by training, and a cautious man of business by nature and nationality. He was professedly an entire convert to his own principles ; yet set an example of distrust by holding on to his thirty thousand acres himself. This would do when dealing with starving Scotch peasantry, glad of the privilege of moderately remunerated labor, good food and clothing. Had he been a benevolent Southern planter he would have succeeded admirably with negro slaves, who would have been only too happy to accept any ' Principles.' He had to do with people who had individual hopes and aspirations. The internal affinities of Owen's Commune were too weak to resist the attractions of the outer world. Had he brought his New Lanark disciples to New Harmony, the result would not have been different. Removed from the mechanical pressure of despair and want, his weakly cohered elements would quickly have crumbled away."

Our chapter on New Harmony was submitted, soon after it was written, to an evening gathering of the Oneida Community, for the purpose of eliciting discussions that might throw light on the failure ; and we take the liberty here to report some of the observations made on that occasion. They have the advantage of coming from persons who have had long experience in Community life.

E. H. Hamilton said—" My admiration is excited, to see a man who was prospering in business as Mr Owen was, turn aside from the general drift of the world, toward social improvement. I have the impression that he was sincere. He risked his money on his theories to a certain extent. His attempt was a noble manifestation of humanity, so far as it goes. But he required other people to be what he was not himself. He complains of his followers, that they were not teachable. I do not think he was a teachable man. He got a glimpse of the truth, and of the possibilities of Communism ; but he adopted certain ideas as to the way in which these results are to be obtained, and it seems to me, in regard to those ideas, he was not docile. It must be manifest to all candid minds, that all the improvement and civilization of the present time, go along with the development of Christianity ; and I am led to wonder why a man with the discernment and honesty of Mr. Owen, was not more impressible to the truth in this direction. It seems to me he was as unreceptive to the truths of Christianity, as the people he got together at New Harmony were to his principles. His favorite dogma was that a man's character is formed for him, and not by himself. I suppose we might admit, in a certain sense, that a man's character is formed for him by the grace of God, or by evil spirits. But the notion that man is wholly the creature of external circumstances, irrespective of these influences, seems foolish and pig-headed."

H. J. Seymour,—"I should not object to Owen's doctrine of circumstances, if he would admit that the one great circumstance of a man's life is the possibility of finding out and doing the will of God, and getting into vital connection with him."

S. R. Leonard.—"The people Mr. Owen had to deal with in Scotland were of the servile class, employes in his cotton-factories, and were easily managed, compared with those he collected here in the United States. When he went to Indiana, and undertook to manage a family of a thousand democrats, he began to realize that he did not understand human nature, or the principles of Association."

T. R. Noyes.—"The novelty of Owen's ideas and his rejection of all religion, prevented him from drawing into his scheme the best class in this country. Probably for every honest man who went to New Harmony, there were several parasites ready to prey on him and his enterprise, because he offered them an easy life without religion. Even if he might have got on with simple-minded men and women like his Lanark operatives, it was out of the question with these greedy adventurers."

G. W. Hamilton.—"At the west I met some persons who claimed to be disciples of Owen. From what I saw of them, I should judge it would be very difficult to form a Community of such material. They were very strong in the doctrine that every man has a right to his own opinion; and declaimed loudly against the effect of religion upon people. They said the common ideas of God and duty operated a great deal worse upon the characters of men, than southern slavery. There is enough in such notions of independence, to break up any attempt at Communism."

F. W. Smith.—" I understand that Owen did not educate and appoint men as leaders and fathers, to take care of the society while he was crossing the ocean back and forth. He undertook to manage his own affairs, and at the same time to run this Community. Our experience has shown that it is necessary to have a father in a great family for daily and almost hourly advice. I should think it would be doubly necessary in such a Community as Owen collected, to have the wisest man always at his post."

C. A. Burt.—" There are only two ways of governing such an institution as a Community ; it must be done either by law or by grace. Owen got a company together and abolished law, but did not establish grace ; and so, necessarily failed."

L. Bolles.—" The popular idea is that Owen and his class of reformers had an ideal that was very beautiful and very perfect ; that they had too much faith for their time—too much faith in humanity; that they were several hundred years in advance of their age ; and that the world was not good enough to understand them and their beautiful ideas. That is the superficial view of these men. I think the truth is, they were not up to the times ; that mankind, in point of real faith, were ahead of them. Their view that the evil in human nature is owing to outward surroundings, is an impeach- ment of the providence of God. It is the worst kind of unbelief. But they have taught us one great lesson ; and that is, that good circumstances do *not* make good men. I believe the circumstances of mankind are as good as Providence can make them, consistently with their own state of development and the well-being of their souls. Instead of seeking to sweep away existing governments and forms of outward things, we should thank God that he has given men institutions as good as they can bear. We know that he will give them better, as fast as they improve beyond those they have."

J. B. Herrick —"Although the apparent effect of the failure of Owen's movement was to produce discouragement, still below all that discouragement there is, in the whole nation, generated in part by that movement, a hope watching for the morning. We have to thank Owen for so much, or rather to thank God, for using Owen to stimulate the public mind and bring it to that state in which it is able to receive and keep this hope for the future."

C. W. Underwood.—"Owen's experiment helped to demonstrate that there is no such thing as organization or unity without Christ and religion. But on the other hand we can see that Owen did much good. The churches were compelled to adopt many of his ideas. He certainly was the father of the infant-school system ; and it is my impression that he started the reform-schools, houses of refuge, etc. He gave impulse, at any rate, to the present reformatory movements."

It is noticeable, as a coïncidence with our obser-vations on the lust for land in a preceding chapter, that Owen succeeded admirably in a factory, and failed miserably on a farm. Whether his 30,000 acres had anything to do with his actual failure or not, they would probably have been the ruin of his Community, if it had not failed from other causes.

We have reason to believe from many hints, that *whisky* had considerable agency in the demoralization and destruction of New Harmony. The affair of

Taylor's distillery is one significant fact. Here is another from Macdonald:

"I was one day at the tan-yard, where Squire B. and some others were standing, talking around the stove. During the conversation Squire B. asked us if he had ever told us how he had served 'old Owen' in Community times. He then informed us that he came from Illinois to New Harmony, and that a man in Illinois was owing him, and asked him to take a barrel of whisky for the debt. He could not well get the money; so took the whisky. When it came to New Harmony he did not know where to put it, but finally hid it in his cellar. Not long after Mr. Owen found that the people still got whisky from some quarter, he could not tell where, though he did his best to find out. At last he suspected Squire B., and came right into his shop and accused him of it ; on which Squire B. had to own that it was he who retailed the whisky. 'It was taken for a debt,' said he, 'and what else was I to do to get rid of it?' Mr. Owen turned round, and in his simple manner said, 'Ah, I see you do not understand the principles.' This story was finished with a hearty laugh at 'old Owen.' I could not laugh, but felt that such men as Squire B. really did not understand the principles ; and no wonder there are failures, when such men as he thrust themselves in, and frustrate benevolent designs."

It was too early for a Community, when this country was a "nation of drunkards," as it was in 1825.

Owen's method of getting together the material of his Community, seems to us the most obvious *external* cause of his failure. It was like advertising for a wife ; and we never heard of any body's getting a good wife by advertising. A public invitation to "the industrious and well-disposed of all nations," to come on and take possession of 30,000 acres of land and a ready-made village, leaving each one to judge as to his own industry and disposition, would insure a prompt gathering—and also a speedy scattering.

This method, or something like it, has been tried in most of the non-religious experiments. The joint-stock principle, which many of them adopted, necessarily invites all who choose to buy stock. That principle may form organizations that are able to carry on the businesses of banks and railroads after a fashion; because such businesses require but little character, except zeal and ability for money-making. But a true Community, or even a semi-Community, like the Fourier Phalanxes, requires far higher qualifications in its members and managers.

The socialistic theorizers all assume that Association is a step in advance of civilization. If that is true, we must assume also that the most advanced class of civilization is that which must take the step; and a discrimination of some sort will be required, to get that class into the work, and shut off the barbarians who would hinder it.

Judging from all our experience and observation, we should say that the two most essential requisites for the formation of successful Communities, are *religious principle* and *previous acquaintance* of the members. Both of these were lacking in Owen's experiment. The advertising method of gathering necessarily ignores both.

Owen, in his old age, became a Spiritualist, and in the light of his new experience confessed what seems to us the principal cause of his failure. Sargant, his biographer, referring to chapter and verse in his writings says:

"He confessed that until he received the revelations of Spiritualism, he had been quite unaware of the necessity of good *spiritual conditions* for forming the character of men. The physical, the intellectual, the moral, and the practical conditions, he had understood, and had known how to provide for; but the spiritual he had overlooked. *Yet this, as he now saw, was the most important of all in the future development of mankind.*"

In the same new light, Owen recognized the principal cause of all real success. Sargant continues:

"Owen says, that in looking back on his past life, he can trace the finger of God directing his steps, preserving his life under imminent dangers, and impelling him onward on many occasions. It was under the immediate guidance of the Spirit of God, that during the inexperience of his youth, he accomplished much good for the world. The preservation of his life from the peculiar dangers of childhood, was owing to the monitions of this good Spirit. To this superior invisible aid he owed his appointment, at the age of seven years, to be usher in a school, before the monitorial system of teaching was thought of. To this he must ascribe his migration from an inaccessible Welsh county to London, and then to Stamford, and his ability to maintain himself without assistance from his friends. So he goes on recounting all the events of his life, great and small, and attributing them to the SPECIAL PROVIDENCE OF GOD."

CHAPTER VI.

THE fame of New Harmony has of course overshadowed and obscured all other experiments that resulted from Owen's labors in this country. It is perhaps scarcely known at this day that a Community almost as brilliant as Brook Farm, was started by his personal efforts at Cincinnati, even before he commenced operations at New Harmony. The following sketch, clipped by Macdonald from some old newspaper (the name and date of which are missing), is not only pleasant reading, but bears internal marks of painstaking and truthfulness. It is a model memoir of the life and death of a non-religious Community ; and would serve for many others, by changing a few names, as ministers do when they re-preach old funeral sermons. The moral at the close, inferring the impracticability of Communism, may probbly be accepted as sound, if restricted to non-religious experiments. The general career of Owen is sketched correctly and in rather a masterly manner: and the interesting fact is brought to light, that the beginning of the Owen movement in this country was signalized by a conjunction with Swedenborgianism. The significance of this fact will appear more fully, when we come to the history of the marriage between Fourierism and

Swedenborgianism, which afterwards took place at Brook Farm.

" The narrative here presented," says the unknown writer, " was prepared at the request of a minister who had looked in vain for any account of the Communities established by Robert Owen in this country. It is simply what it pretends to be, reminiscences by one who, while a youth, resided with his parents as a member of the Community at Yellow Springs. For some years together since his manhood, he has been associated with several of the leading men of that experiment, and has through them been informed in relation to both its outer and *inner* history. The article may contain some errors, as of dates and other matters unimportant to a just view of the Community ; but the social picture will be correct. With the hope that it may convey a useful lesson, it is submitted to the reader.

" Robert Owen, the projector of the Communities at Yellow Springs, Ohio, and New Harmony, Indiana, was the owner of extensive manufactories at New Lanark, Scotland. He was a man of considerable learning, much observation, and full of the love of his fellow men ; though a disbeliever in Christianity. His skeptical views concerning the Bible were fully announced in the celebrated debate at Cincinnati between himself and Dr. Alexander Campbell. But whatever may have been his faith, he proved his philanthropy by a long life of beneficent works. At his manufactories in Scotland he established a system based on community of labor, which was crowned with the happiest effects. But it should be remembered that Owen himself was the owner of the works, and controlled all things by a

single mind. The system, therefore, was only a beneficent scheme of government by a manufacturer, for the
good of himself and his operatives.

"Full of zeal for the improvement of society, Owen
conceived that he had discovered the cause of most of
its evils in the laws of *meum et tuum;* and that a state
of society where there is nothing *mine* or *thine*, would
be a paradise begun. He brooded upon the idea of a
Community of property, and connected it with schemes
for the improvement of society, until he was ready to
sacrifice his own property and devote his heart and his
life to his fellow men upon this basis. Too discreet to
inaugurate the new system among the poorer classes of
his own country, whom he found perverted by prejudice
and warped by the artificial forms of society there, he
resolved to proceed to the United States, and among the
comparatively unperverted people, liberal institutions
and cheap lands of the West, to establish Communities,
founded upon common property, social equality, and the
equal value of every man's labor.

"About the year 1824 Owen arrived in Cincinnati.
He brought with him a history of his labors at New
Lanark; with glowing and not unjust accounts of the
beneficent effects of his efforts there. He exhibited
plans for his proposed Communities here; with model
farms, gardens, vineyards, play-grounds, orchards, and
all the internal and external appliances of the social
paradise. At Cincinnati he soon found many congenial
spirits, among the first of whom was Daniel Roe, minister of the "New Jerusalem Church," a society of the
followers of Swedenborg. This society was composed
of a very superior class of people. They were intelligent, liberal, generous, cultivated men and women—

many of them wealthy and highly educated.   They were
apparently the best possible material to organize and
sustain a Community, such as Owen proposed.   Mr Roe
and many of his congregation became fascinated with
Owen and his Communism ; and together with others in
the city and elsewhere, soon organized a Community and
furnished the means for purchasing an appropriate site
for its location.   In the meantime Owen proceeded to
Harmony, and, with others, purchased that place, with
all its buildings, vineyards, and lands, from Rapp, who
emigrated to Pennsylvania and established his people at
Economy.   It will only be added of Owen, that after
having seen the New Harmonians fairly established, he
returned to Scotland.

" After careful consultation and selection, it was
decided by the Cincinnati Community to purchase a
domain at Yellow Springs, about seventy-five miles
north of the city, [now the site of Antioch College] as
the most eligible place for their purpose.   It was really
one of the most delightful regions in the whole West,
and well worthy the residence of a people who had
resolved to make many sacrifices for what they honestly
believed to be a great social and moral reformation.

" The Community, as finally organized consisted of
seventy-five or one hundred families ; and included professional men, teachers, merchants, mechanics, farmers,
and a few common laborers.   Its economy was nearly as
follows :

" The property was held in trust forever, in behalf of
the members of the Community, by the original purchasers, and their chosen successors, to be designated
from time to time by the voice of the Community.   All
additional property thereafter to be acquired, by labor,

purchase, or otherwise, was to be added to the common stock, for the benefit of each and all. Schools were to be established, to teach all things useful (except religion). Opinion upon all subjects was free; and the present good of the whole Community was the standard of morals. The Sabbath was a day of rest and recreation, to be improved by walks, rides, plays, and pleasing exercises; and by public lectures. Dancing was instituted as a most valuable means of physical and social culture; and the ten-pin alley and other sources of amusement were open to all.

"But although Christianity was wholly ignored in the system, there was no free-loveism or other looseness of morals allowed. In short, this Community began its career under the most favorable auspices; and if any men and women in the world could have succeeded, these should have done so. How they *did* succeed, and how they did not, will now be shown.

"For the first few weeks, all entered into the new system with a will. Service was the order of the day. Men who seldom or never before labored with their hands, devoted themselves to agriculture and the mechanic arts, with a zeal which was at least commendable, though not always according to knowledge. Ministers of the gospel guided the plough; called the swine to their corn, instead of sinners to repentance; and let patience have her perfect work over an unruly yoke of oxen. Merchants exchanged the yard-stick for the rake or pitch-fork. All appeared to labor cheerfully for the common weal. Among the women there was even more apparent self-sacrifice. Ladies who had seldom seen the inside of their own kitchens, went into that of the common eating-house (formerly a hotel), and made themselves useful among pots and kettles: and refined young ladies, who had all their lives been waited upon, took their turns in waiting upon others at the table. And several times a week all parties who chose mingled in the social dance, in the great dining-hall.

But notwithstanding the apparent heartiness and cordiality of this auspicious opening, it was in the social atmosphere of the Community that the first cloud arose. Self-love was a spirit which would not be exorcised. It whispered to the lowly maidens, whose former position in society had cultivated the spirit of meekness—"You are as good as the formerly rich and fortunate; insist upon your equality." It reminded the favorites of former society of their lost superiority ; and in spite of all rules, tinctured their words and actions with the love of self. Similar thoughts and feelings soon arose among the men ; and though not so soon exhibited, they were none the less deep and strong. It is unnecessary to descend to details : suffice it to say, that at the end of three months—*three months !*—the leading minds in the Community were compelled to acknowledge to each other that the social life of the Community could not be bounded by a single circle. They therefore acquiesced, but reluctantly, in its division into many little circles. Still they hoped. and many of them no doubt believed, that though social equality was a failure, community of property was not. But whether the law of *mine and thine* is natural or incidental in human character, it soon began to develop its sway. The industrious, the skillful and the strong, saw the products of their labor enjoyed by the indolent, the unskilled, and the improvident ; and self-love rose against benevolence. A band of musicians insisted that their brassy harmony was as necessary to the common happiness as bread and meat ; and declined to enter the harvest field or the work-shop. A lecturer upon natural science insisted upon talking only, while others worked. Mechanics, whose day's labor brought two dollars into the common stock, insisted that they should, in justice, work only half as long as the agriculturist, whose day's work brought but one.

"For a while, of course, these jealousies were only felt; but they soon began to be spoken also. It was useless to remind all parties that the common labor of all ministered to the prosperity of the Community. *Individual* happiness was the law of nature, and it could not be obliterated ; and before a single year had passed, this law had scattered the members of that society, which had come together so earnestly and under such favorable circumstances, back into the selfish world from which they came.

" The writer of this sketch has since heard the history of that eventful year reviewed with honesty and earnestness by the best men and most intelligent parties of that unfortunate social experiment. They admitted the favorable circumstances which surrounded its commencement ; the intelligence, devotion, and earnestness which were brought to the cause by its projectors ; and its final, total failure. And they rested ever after in the belief that man, though disposed to philanthropy, is essentially selfish ; and that a community of social equality and common property is impossible."

CHAPTER VII.

NASHOBA.

MACDONALD erects a magniloquent monument over the remains of Nashoba, the experiment of Frances Wright. This woman, little known to the present generation, was really the spiritual helpmate and better-half of the Owens, in the socialistic revival of 1826. Our impression is, not only that she was the leading woman in the communistic movement of that period, but that she had a very important agency in starting two other movements, that have had far greater success, and are at this moment strong in public favor ; viz., Anti-Slavery and Woman's Rights. If justice were done, we are confident her name would figure high with those of Lundy, Garrison, and John Brown on the one hand, and with those of Abby Kelly, Lucy Stone and Anna Dickinson on the other. She was indeed the pioneer of the "strong-minded women." We copy the most important parts of Macdonald's memoir of Nashoba :

"This experiment was made in Shelby Co., Tennessee, by the celebrated Frances Wright. The objects were, to form a Community in which the negro slave should be educated and upraised to a level with the whites, and thus prepared for freedom ; and to set an example, which, if carried out, would eventually abolish slavery in the Southern States ; also to make a home for good and great men and women of all countries, who might there sympathize with each other in their love and labor for humanity. She invited congenial minds from every quarter of the globe to unite with her in the search for truth and the pursuit of rational happiness. Herself a native of Scotland, she became imbued with these philanthropic views through a knowledge of the sufferings of a great portion of mankind in many countries, and of the condition of the negro in the United States in particular.

"She traveled extensively in the Southern States, and explained her views to many of the planters. It was during these travels that she visited the German settlement of Rappites at Harmony, on the Wabash river, and after examining the wonderful industry of that Community, she was struck with the appropriateness of their system of coöperation to the carrying out of her aspirations. She also visited some of the Shaker establishments then existing in the United States, but she thought unfavorably of them. She renewed her visits to the Rappites, and was present on the occasion of their removal from Harmony to Economy on the Ohio, where she continued her acquaintance with them, receiving valuable knowledge from their experience, and, as it were, witnessing a new village, with its fields, orchards, gardens, vineyards, flouring-mills and manufactories, rise out of the earth, beneath the hands of some eight hundred trained laborers."

Here is another indication of the important part the Rappites played in the early history of Owenism. As they cleared the 30,000 acres and built the village which was the theatre of Owen's great experiment, so it is evident from the above account and from other hints, that their Communistic ideas and manner of living were systematically studied by the Owen school, before and after the purchase of New Harmony. Indeed it is more than intimated in a passage from the *New Moral World* quoted in our 5th chapter, that Owen depended on their assistance in commencing his Community, and attributed his failure to their premature removal. On the whole we may conclude that Owen learned all he really knew about practical Communism, and more than he was able to imitate, from the Rappites. They learned Communism from the New Testament and the day of Pentecost.

" In the autumn of 1825 [when New Harmony was under full sail in the absence of Mr. Owen], Frances Wright purchased 2,000 acres of good and pleasant woodland, lying on both sides of the Wolf river in west Tennessee, about thirteen miles above Memphis. She then purchased several negro families, comprising fifteen able hands, and commenced her practical experiment."

Her plan in brief was, to take slaves in large numbers from time to time (either by purchase, or by inducing benevolent planters to donate their negroes to the institution), and to prepare them for liberty by education, giving them half of what they produced, and making them pay their way and purchase their emancipation, if necessary, by their labor. The working of the negroes and the general management of the Community was to be in the hands of the philanthropic and wealthy whites associated with the lady-founder. The theory was benevolent ; but practically the institution must have been a two-story commonwealth, somewhat like the old Grecian States which founded liberty on Helotism. Or we might define it as a Brook Farm *plus* a negro basis. The trouble at Brook Farm, according to Hawthorne, was, that the amateurs who took part in that 'pic-nic,' did not like to serve as 'chambermaids to the cows.' This difficulty was provided against at Nashoba.

"We are informed that Frances Wright found in her new occupation intense and ever-increasing interest. But ere long she was seized by severe and reïterated sickness, which compelled her to make a voyage to Europe for the recovery of her health. 'During her absence,' says her biographer, 'an intriguing individual had disorganized every thing on the estate, and effected the removal of persons of confidence. All her serious difficulties proceeded from her white assistants, and not from the blacks.'"

In December of the following year, she made over the Nashoba estate to a board of trustees, by a deed commencing thus:

"I, Frances Wright, do give the lands after specified, to General Lafayette, William Maclure, Robert Owen, Cadwallader Colden, Richardson Whitby, Robert Jennings, Robert Dale Owen, George Flower, Camilla Wright, and James Richardson, to be held by them and their associates and their successors in perpetual trust for the benefit of the negro race."

By another deed she gave the slaves of Nashoba to the before-mentioned trustees: and by still another she gave them all her personal property.

In her appeal to the public in connection with this transfer, she explains at length her views of reform, and her reasons for choosing the abovednamed trustees instead of the Emancipation or Colonization Societies ; and in respect to education says: 'No difference will be made in the schools between the white children and the children of color, whether in education or any other advantage.' After further explanation of her plans she goes on to say:

" ' It will be seen that this establishment is founded on the principle of community of property and labor: presenting every advantage to those desirous, not of accumulating money, but of enjoying life and rendering services to their fellow-creatures ; these fellow-creatures, that is, the blacks here admitted, requiting these services by services equal or greater, by filling occupations which their habits render easy, and which, to their guides and assistants, might be difficult or unpleasing.' [Here is the 'negro basis.']

" ' No life of idleness, however, is proposed to the whites. Those who cannot work must give an equivalent in property. Gardening or other cultivation of the soil, useful trades practiced in the society or taught in the school, the teaching of every branch of knowledge, tending the children, and nursing the sick, will present a choice of employment sufficiently extensive.' "

In the course of another year trouble had come and disorganization had begun.

" In March, 1828, the trustees published a communication in the *Nashoba Gazette*, explaining the difficulties they had to contend with, and the causes why the experience of two years had modified the original plan of Frances Wright. They show the impossibility of a co-operative Community succeeding without the members composing it are superior beings ; 'for,' say they, 'if there be introduced into such a society thoughts of evil and unkindness, feelings of intolerance and words of dissension, it can not prosper. That which produces in the world only common-place jealousies and every-day squabbles, is sufficient to destroy a Community.'

"The society had admitted some members to labor, and others as boarders from whom no labor was required; and in this they confess their error, and now propose to admit those only who possess the funds for their support.

"The trustees go on to say that 'they desire to express distinctly that they have deferred, for the present, the attempt to form a society of co-operative labor; and they claim for the association only the title of a Preliminary Social Community.'

"After describing the moral qualifications of members, who may be admitted without regard to color, they propose that each one shall yearly throw $100 into the common fund for board alone, to be paid quarterly in advance. Each one was also to build for himself or herself a small brick house, with a piazza, according to a regular plan, and upon a spot of ground selected for the purpose, near the center of the lands of Nashoba."

This communication is signed by Frances Wright, Richardson Whitby, Camilla Wright Whitby, and Robert Dale Owen, as resident trustees, and is dated Feb. 1, 1828.

"It is probable that success did not further attend the experiment, for Frances Wright abandoned it soon after, and in June following removed to New Harmony, where, in conjunction with William Owen, she assumed for a short time the management of the *New Harmony Gazette*, which then had its name altered to the *New Harmony and Nashoba Gazette or Free Enquirer.*

"Her biographer says that she abandoned, though not without a struggle, the peaceful shades of Nashoba, leaving the property in the charge of an individual, who

was to hold the negroes ready for removal to Hayti the
year following. In relinquishing her experiment in favor
of the race, she held herself equally pledged to the col-
ored families under her charge, to the southern state in
which she had been a resident citizen, and to the
American community at large, to remove her dependents
to a country free to their color. This she executed a
year after."

This Communistic experiment and failure was nearly
simultaneous with that of New Harmony, and was the
immediate antecedent of Frances Wright's famous
lecturing-tour. In December 1828 she was raising
whirlwinds of excitement by her eloquence in Baltimore,
Philadelphia and New York; and soon after the *New
Harmony Gazette*, under the title of *The Free Enquirer*,
was removed to the latter city, where it was ably edited
several years by Frances Wright and Robert Dale
Owen.

CHAPTER VIII.

SEVEN EPITAPHS.

WE have passed the most notable monuments of the Owen epoch, and come now to obscurer graves. Doubtless many of the little Communities that followed New Harmony, and in a small way repeated its fortunes, were buried without memorial. We have on Macdonald's list the names of only seven more, and their epitaphs are for the most part very brief. We may as well group them all in one chapter, and copy what Macdonald says about them, without comment.

EPITAPH NO. I.   CO-OPERATIVE SOCIETY, 1825.

" Located at Pittsburg, Pennsylvania. Founded on the principles of Robert Owen. Benjamin Bakewell, President ; John Snyder, Treasurer ; Magnus M. Murray, Secretary."

EPITAPH NO. II.   FRANKLIN COMMUNITY, 1826.

" Located somewhere in New York. Had a printed Constitution ; also a 'preparatory school.' No further particulars."

EPITAPH NO. III.   BLUE SPRINGS COMMUNITY. 1826—7.

" A gathering under the above title, existed for a short time near Bloomington, Ind. It was said [by

somebody] to be 'harmonious and prosperous' as late as
Jan. 1, 1827; but as I find no trace of it in my re-
searches, it is fair to conclude that it is numbered with
the dead, like others of its day."

EPITAPH NO. IV.   FORRESTVILLE COMMUNITY. (INDIANA.)

"This Society was formed on the 16th day of December, 1825, of four families consisting of thirty-one
persons.   March 26, 1826, the constitution was printed.
During the year their number increased to over sixty.
The business was transacted by three trustees, to be
elected annually, together with a secretary and treasurer.
The principles were purely republican. They had no
established religion, the constitution only requiring that
all candidates should be of good moral character, sober
and industrious.   They declared that 'a baptist, a methodist, a universalist, a quaker, a calvinist, a deist, or any
other *ist*, provided he or she is a genuine good moralist,
are equally privileged and equally esteemed.' They
occupied 325 acres of land, two saw-mills, one grist-mill,
a carding machine, and a tannery, and carried on wagon-
making, shoe-making, blacksmithing, coopering, agriculture, &c."

EPITAPH NO. V.   HAVERSTRAW COMMUNITY.

"This Society was formed in the year 1826 by a Mr.
Fay (an attorney), Jacob Peterson and George Houston
of New York, and Robert L Ginengs of Philadelphia.
It is probable that it originated in consequence of the
lectures which were at that time delivered by Robert
Owen in this country.

"The principles and objects of the Society, as far as I
can learn, were to better the condition of themselves

and their fellowmen, which they conceived could be done by living in Community, having all things in common, giving equal rights to each, and abolishing the terms 'mine and thine.'

"They increased their numbers to eighty persons, including women and children, and purchased an estate at Haverstraw, two miles back from the Hudson river, on the west side, about thirty miles above New York. There were 120 acres of wood land, two mansion houses, twelve or fourteen out-buildings, one saw-mill, and a rolling and splitting-mill: and the estate had a noble stream of water running through it. The property was owned by a Major Suffrens of Haverstraw, who demanded $18,000 for it. On this sum $6,000 were paid, and bond and mortgage were given for the remainder. To raise the $6,000 and to defray other expenses, Jacob Peterson advanced $7,000; another individual $300; and others subscribed sums as low as $10. Money, land, and every thing else were held as common stock for the equal benefit of all the members.

" Among the members, were persons of various trades and occupations, such as carpenters, cabinet-makers, tailors, shoe-makers and farmers. It was the general opinion that the society, as a whole, possessed a large amount of intelligence; and both men and women were of good moral character. I was acquainted with two or three persons who were engaged in this enterprise, and must say I never saw more just and honorable old men than they were when I knew them.

"It appears that they formed a church among themselves, which they denominated the *Church of Reason;* and on Sundays they attended meetings, where lectures were delivered to them on Morals, Philosophy, Agriculture and various scientific subjects. They had no religious ceremonies or articles of faith.

"They admitted members by ballot. The details of their rules and regulations were never printed. I have reason to believe that they had an abundance of laws and by-laws ; and that they disagreed upon these, as well as upon other matters.

"While the Community lasted, they were well supplied with the necessaries of life, and generally speaking their circumstances were by no means inferior to those they had left.

"The splitting and rolling mill was not used, but farming and mechanical operations were carried on ; and it is supposed (as in many other instances) that if the officers of the society had acted right, the experiment would have succeeded ; but by some means the affairs soon became disorderly, and though so much money had originally been raised, and assistance was received from without, yet the experiment came to an end after a struggle of only five months.

"An informant asserts that dishonesty of the managers and want of good measures were the causes of failure, and expresses himself thus :   'We wanted men and women of skillful industry, sober and honest, with a knowledge of themselves, and a disposition to command and be commanded, and not men and women whose sole occupation is parade and talk.'

"In this experiment, like many others, several individuals suffered pecuniary loss. Those who had but a home, left it for Community, and of course were thrown back in their progress. Those who had money and invested there, lost it. Jacob Peterson, of New York, who advanced $7,000, never got more than $300 of it

back, and even that was lost to him through the dishonesty of those with whom he did business."

EPITAPH NO. VI. COXSACKIE COMMUNITY.

" This experiment also was commenced in 1826, and
members from the Haverstraw experiment joined it on
the breaking up of their Society.

" The principal actors in this attempt, were Samuel
Underhill, John Norberry, Nathaniel Underhill, Wm. G.
Macy, Jethro Macy and Jacob Peterson. The objects
were the same as at Haverstraw, but in trying to carry
them out they met with no better success. It appears
that the capital was small, and the estate, which was
located seven miles back from Coxsackie on the Hudson
river, was very much in debt. From the little information I am enabled to gather concerning this attempt, I
judge that they made many laws, that their laws were
bad, and that they had many persons engaged in talking
and law-making, who did not work at any useful employment. The consequences were, that after struggling on
for a little more than a year, this experiment came to an
end. One of my informants thus expresses himself
about this failure : ' There were few good men to steer
things right. We wanted men and women who would
be willing to live in simple habitations, and on plain and
simple diet ; who would be contented with plain and
simple clothing, and who would band together for each
others' good. With such we might have succeeded ;
but such attempts can not succeed without such people.'

" In this little conflict there were many sacrifices ; but
those who survived and were still imbued with the principles, emigrated to Ohio, to fight again with the old
system of things."

EPITAPH NO. VII.   KENDAL COMMUNITY.

" This was an attempt to carry out the views of Mr. Owen. It was located near Canton, Stark County. Ohio. The purchase of the property was made in June 1826, by a body of freeholders, whose farms were mortgaged for the first payment, and who, on account of the difficulty of realizing cash for their estates, were under some embarrassment in their operations, though the property was a great bargain."

Of this enterprise in its early stage the *Western Courier* (Dec., 1826,) thus speaks :

" The Kendal Community is rapidly on the increase ; a number of dwellings have been erected in addition to those previously built ; yet the increase of families has been such that there is much inconvenience experienced for want of house-room. The members are now employed in erecting a building 170 by 33 feet, which is intended to be temporarily occupied as private dwellings, but ultimately as work-shops. This and other improvements for the convenience of the place, will soon be completed.

" Kendal is pleasantly and advantageously situated for health. We are informed that there is not a sick person on the premises. Mechanics of various professions have joined the Community, and are now occupied in prosecuting the various branches of industry. They have a woolen factory in which many hands are employed. Everything appears to be going on prosperously and harmoniously. There is observed a bustling emulation among the members. They labor hard, and are probably not exempt from the cares and perplexities incident to all worldly undertakings ; and what society or system can claim immunity from them? The question is, whether they may not be mitigated. Trouble we believe to be a divisible quantity; it may be softened by sympathy and intercourse, as pleasure may be increased by union and companionship. These advantages have already been experienced at the Kendal Community, and its members are even now in possession of that which the poet hath declared to be the sum total of human happiness, viz., Health, Peace and Competence."

"Several families from the Coxsackie Community," says Macdonald, "had joined Kendal when the above was written, and the remainder were to follow as soon as they were prepared. The Kendal Community then numbered about one hundred and fifty members including children. They were engaged in manufacturing woolen goods on a small scale, had a few hops, and did considerable business on the farm. They speak of their '*choice spirits;*' and anticipate assistance to carry out their plans, and prove the success of the social system beyond all contradiction, by the disposal of property and settlement of affairs at Coxsackie. In their enthusiasm they assert, 'that unaided, and with only their own resources and experience, and above all, with their little band of *invincible spirits*, who are tired of the old system and are determined to conquer or die, they *must* succeed.' I conclude they did not conquer but died, for I can learn nothing further concerning them."

A recent letter from Mr. John Harmon, of Ravenna, Ohio, who was a member of the Kendal Community, gives a more definite account of its failure, as follows:

" Our Community progressed harmoniously and prosperously, so long as the members had their health and a hope of paying for their domain. But a summer-fever attacked us, and seven heads of families died, among whom were several of our most valued and useful members. At the same time the rich proprietors of whom we purchased our land urged us to pay; and we could not sell a part of it and give a good title, because we were not incorporated. So we were compelled to give up and disperse, losing what we had paid, which was about $7,000. But we formed friendships that were enduring, and the failure never for a moment weakened my faith in the value of Communism."

We group the three last Communities together, because they were evidently closely related by members passing from one to another, as the earlier ones successively failed. This habit of migrating from one Community to another is an interesting characteristic of the veterans of Socialism, which we shall meet with frequently hereafter.

CHAPTER IX.

OWEN'S GENERAL CAREER.

CONFINING ourselves strictly to memoirs of Associations, we might leave Owen now and go on to the experiments of the Fourier school. But this would hardly be doing justice to the father of American Socialisms. We have exhibited his great failure; and we must stop long enough to acknowledge his great success, and say briefly what we think of his whole life and influence. Indeed such a review is necessary to a just estimate of the Owen movement in this country.

We accept what he himself said about his early achievements, that he was under the guidance of the Spirit of God, and was carried along by a wonderful series of special providences in his first labors for the good of the working classes. The originality, wisdom and success of his doings at New Lanark were manifestly supernatural. His factory village was indeed a light to the world, that gave the nations a great lesson in practical beneficence; and shines still amid the darkness of money-making selfishness and industrial misery. The single fact that he continued the wages of his operatives when the embargo stopped his business, actually paying out $35,000 in four months, to men who had nothing to do but to oil his machinery and keep it

clean, stamps him as a genius of an order higher than
Napoleon. By this bold maneuver of benevolence he
won the confidence of his men, so that he could manage
them afterwards as he pleased ; and then he went on to
reform and educate them, till they became a wonder to
the world and a crown of glory to himself. So far we
have no doubt that he walked with inspiration and
special providence.

On the other hand, it is also manifest, that his inspiration and success, so far at least as practical attempts
were concerned, deserted him afterwards, and that much
of the latter part of his life was spent in disastrous
attempts to establish Communism, without the necessary
spiritual conditions. His whole career may be likened
to that of the first Napoleon, whose "star" insured victory till he reached a certain crisis ; after which he lost
every battle, and sunk into final and overwhelming
defeat.

In both cases there was a turning-point which can be
marked. Napoleon's star deserted him when he put
away Josephine. Owen evidently lost his hold on practical success when he declared war against religion. In
his labors at New Lanark he was not an active infidel.
The Bible was in his schools. Religion was at least tolerated and respected. He there married the daughter of
Mr. Dale, a preacher of the Independents, who was his
best friend and counsellor through the early years of
his success. But when his work at New Lanark became famous, and he rose to companionship with
dukes and kings, he outgrew the modesty and practical
wisdom of his early life, and undertook the task of Universal Reform. Then it was that he fell into the mistake
of confounding the principles of the Bible with the char-

acter and pretensions of his ecclesiastical opposers, and so came into the false position of open hostility to religion. Christ was in a similar temptation when he found the Scribes and Pharisees arrayed against him, with the Old Testament for their vantage ground ; but he had wisdom enough to keep his foothold on that vantage ground, and drive them off. His programme was, " Think not that I am come to destroy the law and the prophets. I am not come to destroy, but to fulfill." Whereas Owen, at the turning-point of his career, abandoned the Bible with all its magazines of power to his enemies, and went off into a hopeless warfare with Christianity and with all God's past administrations. From that time fortune deserted him. The splendid success of New Lanark was followed by the terrible defeat at New Harmony. The declaration of war against all religion was between them. Such is our interpretation of his life ; and something like this must have been his own interpretation, when he confessed in the light of his later experience, that by overlooking spiritual conditions, he had missed the most important of all the elements of human improvement.

And yet we must not push our parallel too far. Owen, unlike Napoleon, never knew when he was beaten, and fought on thirty years after his Waterloo. It would be a great mistake to imagine that the failure of New Harmony and of the attempts that followed it, was the end of Owen's achievements and influence, even in this country. Providence does not so waste its preparations and inspirations. Let us see what was left, and what Owen did, after the disasters of 1826—7.

In the first place the failure of his Community at New Harmony was not the failure of the *village* which he bought of the Rappites. That was built of substantial brick and stone. The houses and a portion of the population which he gathered there, remained and have continued to be a flourishing and rather peculiar village till the present time. Several Communities that came over from England in after-years made New Harmony their rendezvous, either on their arrival or when they broke up. So Macdonald, with the enthuiasm of a true Socialist, on landing in this country in 1842 first sought out New Harmony. There he found Josiah Warren, the apostle of Individualism, returned from his wanderings and failures, to set up a "Time Store" in the old seat of Socialism. We remember also, that Dr. J. R. Buchanan, the anthropologist, was at New Harmony in 1842, when he astonished the world with his novel experiments in Mesmerism, which Robert Dale Owen reported in a famous letter to the *Evening Post*, and which gave impetus and respectability to the beginnings of modern Spiritualism. These facts and many others indicate that New Harmony continued to be a center and refuge of Socialists and innovators long after the failure of the Community. Notwithstanding the unpopularity of Communism which Macdonald says he found there, it is probably a semi-socialist village to this day, representing more or less the spirit of Robert Owen.

In the next place, with all his failures, Owen was successful in producing a fine family; and though he himself returned to England after the disaster at New Harmony, he bequeathed all his children to this country. Macdonald, writing in 1842, says: "Mr. Owen's family all reside in New Harmony. There are four sons and one daughter; viz., William Owen, who is a merchant and bank director; Robert Dale Owen, a lawyer and politician, who attends to the affairs of the Owen Estate ; David Dale Owen, a practical geologist ; Richard Owen, a practical farmer ; and Mrs. Fauntleroy. The four brothers, with the wives and families of three of them, live together in one large mansion."

Mr. Owen in his published journal says that "his eldest son Robert Dale Owen, after writing much that was excellent, was twice elected member of Congress, and carried the bill for establishing the Smithsonian Institute in Washington ; that his second son, David Dale Owen, was professor of chemistry, mineralogy and geology, and had been employed by successive American governments as their accredited geologist ; that his third son, Major Richard Owen, was a professor in a Kentucky Military College; and that his only daughter living in 1851, was the widow of a distinguished American officer."

Robert Dale Owen undoubtedly has been and is, the spiritual as well as natural successor of Robert Owen. Wiser and more moderate than his father, he has risen out of the wreck of New Harmony to high stations and great influence in this country. He was originally associated with Frances Wright in her experiment at Nashoba, her lecturing career, and her editorial labors in New York. At that time he partook of the antireligious zeal of his father. Opposition to revivals was the specialty of his paper, the *Free Enquirer*. In those days, also, he published his " Moral Physiology," a little book teaching in plain terms a method of controlling propagation—*not* " Male Continence." This bold issue, attributed by his enemies to licentious proclivities, was really part of the socialistic movement of the time ; and indicated the drift of Owenism toward sexual freedom and the abolition of marriage.

Robert Dale Owen originated and carried the law in Indiana giving to married women a right to property separate from their husbands ; and the famous facilities of divorce in that State are attributed to his influence.

He, like his father, turned toward Spiritualism, notwithstanding his non-religious antecedents. His report of Dr. Buchanan's experiments, and his books and magazine-articles demonstrating the reality of a world of spirits, have been the most respectable and influential auxiliaries to the modern system of necromancy. There is an air of respect for religion in many of his publications, and even a happy freedom of Bible quotation, which is not found in his father's writings. Perhaps the variation is due to the blood of his mother, who was the daughter of a Bible man and a preacher.

So much Mr. Owen left behind. Let us now follow him in his after career. He bade farewell to New Harmony and returned to England in June 1828. Acknowledging no real defeat or loss of confidence in his principles, he went right on in the labors of his mission, as Apostle of Communism for the world, holding himself ready for the most distant service at a moment's warning. His policy was slightly changed, looking more toward moving the nations, and less toward local experiments. In April 1828, he was again in this country, settling his affairs at New Harmony, and preaching his gospel among the people. During this visit the challenge to debate passed between him and Rev. Alexander Campbell, and an arrangement was made for a theological duel. He returned to England in the summer, and in November of the same year

(1828) sailed again for America on a scheme of obtaining from the Mexican government a vast territory in Texas on which to develop Communism. After finishing the negotiations in Mexico (which negotiations were never executed), he came to the United States, and in April 1829 met Alexander Campbell at Cincinnati in a debate which was then famous, though now forgotten. From Cincinnati he proceeded to Washington, where he established intimate relations with Martin Van Buren, then Secretary of State, and had an important interview with Andrew Jackson, the President, laboring with these dignitaries on behalf of national friendship and his new social system. In the summer of 1829 he returned to England, and for some years after was engaged in labors for the conversion of the English government, and in some local attempts to establish "Equitable Commerce," "Labor Exchange" and partial Communism, all of which failed. Here Mr. Sargant, his English biographer, gives up the pursuit of him, and slurs over the rest of his life as though it were passed in obscurity and dotage. Not so Macdonald. We learn from him that after Mr. Owen had exceeded the allotment of three-score years and ten, he twice crossed the ocean to this country. Let us follow the faithful record of the disciple. We condense from Macdonald:

In September 1844, Mr. Owen arrived in New York and immediately published in the *Herald* (Sept. 21) an address to the people of the United States proclaiming his mission "to effect in peace the greatest revolution ever yet made in human society." Fourierism was at that time in the ascendant. Mr. Owen called at the office of the *Phalanx*, the organ of Brisbane, and was received with distinction. In October he visited his family at New Harmony.   On his way he stopped at the Ohio Phalanx.   In December he went to Washington with Robert Dale Owen, who was then member of Congress.   The party in power was less friendly than that of 1829, and refused him the use of the National Halls.   He lectured, or advertised to lecture, in Concert Hall, Pennsylvania Avenue.   " In March 1845," says Macdonald, "I had the pleasure of hearing him lecture at the Minerva rooms in New York, after which he lectured in Lowell and other places."   In May he visited Brook Farm.   In June he published a manifesto, appointing a World's Convention, to be held in New York in October; and soon after sailed for England.   Stopping there scarcely long enough to turn round, he was in this country again in season to give a course of lectures preparatory to the October Convention.   After that Convention (which Macdonald confesses was a trifling affair) he continued his labors in various places.   On the 26th of October Macdonald met him on the street in Albany, and spent some time with him at his lodgings in much pleasant gossip about New Lanark.   In November he called at Hopedale.   Adin Ballou, in a published report of the visit, dashed off a sketch of him and his projects, which is so good a likeness that we copy it here:

"Robert Owen is a remarkable character.   In years nearly seventy-five: in knowledge and experience superabundant; in benevolence of heart transcendental; in honesty without disguise; in philanthropy unlimited; in religion a skeptic ; in theology a Pantheist : in metaphysics a necessarian circumstantialist ; in morals a universal excusionist; in general conduct a philosophic non-resistant ; in socialism a Communist; in hope a terrestrial elysianist; in practical business a methodist; in deportment an unequivocal gentleman.   *   *

" Mr. Owen has vast schemes to develop, and vast hopes of speedy success in establishing a great model of the new social state ; which will quite instantaneously, as he thinks, bring the human race into a terrestrial Paradise. He insists on obtaining a million of dollars to be expended in lands, buildings, machinery, conveniences and beautifications, for his model Community ; all to be finished and in perfect order, before he introduces to their new home the well-selected population who are to inhabit it. He flatters himself he shall be able, by some means, to induce capitalists, or perhaps Congress, to furnish the capital for this object. We were obliged to shake an incredulous head and tell him frankly how groundless, in our judgment, all such splendid anticipations must prove. He took it in good part, and declared his confidence unshaken, and his hopes undiscourageable by any man's unbelief."

The winter of 1845—6 Mr. Owen appears to have spent in the west, probably at New Harmony. In June 1846, he was again in Albany, and this time for an important purpose. The Convention appointed to frame a new Constitution for the State of New York was then in session. He obtained the use of the Assembly Chamber and an audience of the delegates ; and gave them two lectures on " Human Rights and Progress," and withal on their own duties. Macdonald was present, and speaks enthusiastically of his energy and dignity. After reminding the Convention of the importance of the work they were about, he went on to say that "all religious systems, Constitutions, Governments and Laws are and have been founded in *error*, and that error is the false supposition that *man forms his own character.* They were about to form another Constitution based upon that error, and ere long more Constitutions would have to be made and altered, and so on, until the truth that the *character of man is formed for him* shall be recognized, and the system of society based upon that principle become national and universal." " After the lecture," says Macdonald, " I lunched with Mr. Owen at the house of Mr. Ames. We had conversation on New Harmony, London, &c. Mr. Ames having expressed a desire for a photograph of Mr. Owen, I accompanied them to a gallery at the Exchange where I parted with him—perhaps forever! He returned soon after to England where he remains till the present time." [1854.]

Six times after he was fifty years old, and twice after he was seventy, he crossed the Atlantic and back in the service of Communism! Let us not say that all this wonderful activity was useless. Let us not call this man a driveller and a monomaniac. Let us rather acknowledge that he was receiving and distributing an inspiration unknown even to himself, that had a sure aim, and that is at this moment conquering the world. His hallucination was not in his expectations, but in his ideas of methods and times.

Owen had not much theory. His main idea was Communism, and that he got from the Rappites. His persistent assertion that man's character is formed for him by his circumstances, was his nearest approach to original doctrine ; and this he virtually abandoned when he came to appreciate spiritual conditions. The rest of his teaching is summed up in the old injunction, " Be good," which is the burden of all preaching.

But theory was not his function. Nor yet even practice. His business was to seed the world, and especially this country, with an unquenchable desire and hope for Communism ; and this he did effectually.

We call him the Father of American Socialisms, because he took possession of this country first. Fourierism was a secondary infusion. His English practicality was more in unison with the Yankee spirit, than the theorizing of the French school. He himself claimed the Fourierites as working on his job, grading the track by their half-way schemes of joint-stock and guaranteeism for his Rational Communism. And in this he was not far wrong. Communism or nothing, is likely to be the final demand of the American people.

The most conspicuous trait in all Owen's labors and journeyings is his indomitable perseverance. And this trait he transmitted to a large breed of American Socialists. Read again the letter of John Harmon at the close of our last chapter. He is now an old man, but his faith in Communism remains unshaken ; it is failure-proof. See how the veterans of Haverstraw, when their Community fell in pieces, moved to Coxsackie, and when the Coxsackie Community broke up, migrated to Ohio and joined the Kendal Community ; and perhaps when the Kendal Community failed, they joined another, and another ; and probably never gave up the hope of a Community-home. We have met with many such wanderers—men and women who were spoiled for the world by once tasting or at least imagining the sweets af Communism, and would not be turned back by any number of failures. Alcander Longley is a fine specimen of this class. He has tried every kind of Association, from Co-operation to Communism, including Fourierism and the nameless combinations of Spiritualism ; and is now hard at work in the farthest corner of Missouri on his sixth experiment, as enthusiastic as ever ! J. J. Franks is a still finer specimen. He began with Owenism. When that failed he enlisted with the Fourierites. During their campaign he bought five-thousand acres of land in the mountains of Virginia for a prospective Association, the Constitution of which he prepared and printed, though the Association itself never came into being. When Fourierism failed he devoted himself to Protective Unions. For twenty years past he has been a faithful disciple and patron of the Oneida Community. In such examples we trace the image and spirit of Robert Owen.

CHAPTER X.

CONNECTING LINKS.

In the transition from Owenism to Fourierism and later socialist movements, we find that Josiah Warren fulfills the function of a modulating chord. As we have already said, after seeing the wreck of Communism at New Harmony, he went clear over to the extreme doctrine of "Individual Sovereignty," and continued working on that theme through the period of Fourierism, till he founded the famous village of Modern Times on Long Island, and there became the master-spirit of a school, which has developed at least three famous movements, that are in some sense alive yet, long after the Communities and Phalanxes have gone to their graves.

Imprimis, Dr. Thomas L. Nichols was a fellow of the royal society of Individual Sovereigns, and an *habitué* of Modern Times, when he published his "Esoteric Anthropology" in 1853, and issued his printed catalogue of names for the reciprocal use of affinity-hunters all over the country; whereby he inaugurated the system of "Free Love" or Individual Sovereignty in sexual intercourse, that prevailed among the Spiritualists. He afterwards fell into a reaction opposite to Warren's, and swung clear back into Roman Catholicism. But "though dead, he yet speaketh."

Secondly, Stephen Pearl Andrews was publishing-partner of Josiah Warren in the propagandism of Individual Sovereignty; and built or undertook to build a notable edifice at Modern Times, when that village was in its glory. He subsequently distinguished himself by instituting, in connection with Nichols and others, a series of "Sociables" for the Individual Sovereigns in New York city, which were broken up by the conservatives. He is also understood to have originated a great spiritual or intellectual hierarchy, called the "Pantarchy," and a system of Universology, which is not yet published, but has long been on the eve of organizing science and revolutionizing the world. On the whole he may be regarded as the American rival of Comte, as A. J. Davis is of Swedenborg.

Lastly, Henry Edger, the actual hierarch of Positivism, one of the ten apostles *de propaganda fide* appointed by Comte, was called to his great work from Warren's school at Modern Times. He is still a resident of that village, and has attempted within a year or two to form a Positivist Community there, but without success.

The genealogy from Owen to these modern movements may be traced thus:

Owen begat New Harmony; New Harmony (by reaction) begat Individual Sovereignty; Individual Sovereignty begat Modern Times; Modern Times was the mother of Free Love, the Grand Pantarchy, and the American branch of French Positivism. Josiah Warren was the personal link next to Owen, and deserves special notice. Macdonald gives the following account of him:

JOSIAH WARREN.

"This gentleman was one of the members of Mr. Owen's Community at New Harmony in 1826, and from the experience gained there, he became convinced that there was an important error in Mr. Owen's principles, and that error was *combination*. It was then that he developed the doctrine of Individual Sovereignty, and devised the plan of Equitable Commerce, which he labored on incessantly for many years. He communicated his views on Labor Exchange to Mr. Owen, who endeavored to practice them in London upon a large scale, but failed, as Mr Warren asserts, through not carrying out the principle of *Individuality*. A similar attempt was made in Philadelphia, but also failed for the same cause.

" After the failure of the New Harmony Community, Mr. Warren went to Cincinnati, and there opened a Time Store, which continued in operation long enough, as he says, to demonstrate the truth of his principles. After this, in association with others, he commenced an experiment in Tuscarawas Co., Ohio; but in consequence of sickness it was abandoned. His next experiment was at Mount Vernon, Indiana, which was unsuccessful. After that he opened a Time Store in New Harmony, which he was carrying on when I became acquainted with him in 1842.

" The following must suffice as a description of

THE NEW HARMONY TIME STORE.

" A portion of a room was divided off by a lattice-work, in which were many racks and shelves containing a variety of small articles. In the center of this lattice an opening was left, through which the store-keeper could hand goods and take pay. On the wall at the back of the store-keeper and facing the customer, hung a clock, and underneath it a dial. In other parts of the room were various articles, such as molasses, corn, buckets, dry-goods, etc. There was a board hanging on the wall conspicuous enough for all persons to see, on which were placed the bills that had been paid to wholesale merchants for all the articles in the store; also the orders of individuals for various things.

" I entered the store one day, and walking up to the wicket, requested the store-keeper to serve me with some glue. I was immediately asked if I had a ' *Labor note*,' and on my saying no, I was told that I must get some one's note. My object in going there was to inquire if Mr. Warren would exchange labor with me ; but this abrupt reception scared me, and I hastily departed. However, upon my becoming further acquainted with Mr. Warren, we exchanged labor notes, and I traded a little at the Time Store in the following manner:

" I made or procured a written labor note, promising so many hours labor at so much per hour. Mr. Warren had similar labor notes. I went to the Time Store with my note and my cash, and informed the keeper that I wanted, for instance, a few yards of Kentucky jean. As soon as he commenced conversation or business with me, he set the dial which was under the clock, and marked the *time*. He then attended to me, giving me what I wanted, and in return taking from me as much cash as he paid for the article to the wholesale merchant, and as much time out of my labor note as he spent for me, according to the dial, in the sale of the article. I believe five per cent. was added to the cash cost, to pay rent and cover incidental expenses. The change for the labor notes was in small tickets representing time by the five, ten, or fifteen minutes ; so that if I presented a note representing an hour's labor, and he had been occupied only ten minutes in serving me, he would have to give me forty minutes in change. I have seen Mr. Warren with a large bundle of these notes, representing various kinds and quantities of labor, from mechanics and others in New Harmony and its vicinity. Each individual who gave a note, affixed his or her own price per hour for labor. Women charged as high, or nearly as high, as men ; and sometimes unskillful hands over-rated their services. I knew an instance where an individual issued too many of his notes, and they became depreciated in value. I was informed that these notes were refused at the Time Store. It was supposed that public opinion would regulate these things, and I have no doubt that in time it would. In this experiment Mr. Warren said he had demonstrated as much as he intended. But I heard him complain of the difficulties he had to contend with, and especially of the want of common honesty.

"The Time Store existed about two years and a half, and was then discontinued. In 1844 Mr. Warren went to Cincinnati and lectured upon his principles. On the breaking up of the Clermont Phalanx and the Cincinnati Brotherhood, Mr. Warren went to the spot where both failures had taken place, and there found four families who were disposed to try 'Equitable Commerce.' With these and a few other friends he started a village which he called Utopia, where he published the *Peaceful Revolutionist* for a time.

"His next and last movement was at Modern Times, on Long Island, a few miles from New York, whither he came in 1851."

From a copy of the *Peaceful Revolutionist*, published by Warren at Utopia in 1845, we take the first of the two following extracts. The second, relating to Modern Times, is from a newspaper article pasted into Macdonald's collection, without date, but probably printed in 1853. These will give a sufficient idea of the reaction from New Harmony, which, on several important lines of influence, connects Owen with the present time.

A PEEP INTO UTOPIA.

From an editorial by J. Warren.

"Throughout the whole of our operations at this village, everything has been conducted so nearly on the *Individual* basis, that not one meeting for legislation has taken place. No organization, no delegated power, no constitutions, no laws or bye-laws, rules or regulations, but such as each individual makes for himself and his own business; no officers, no priests nor prophets have been resorted to; nothing of this kind has been in demand. We have had a few meetings, but they were for friendly conversation, for music, dancing or some other social and pleasant pastime. Not even a single lecture upon the principles upon which we were acting, has been given on the premises! It was not necessary; for, as a lady remarked, 'the subject once stated and understood, there is nothing left to talk about; all is action after that.'

"I do not mean to be understood that all are of one mind. On the contrary, in a progressive state there is no demand for conformity. We build on *Individuality;* any difference between us confirms our position. Differences, therefore, like the admissible discords in music, are a valuable part of our harmony! It is only when the rights of persons or property are actually invaded that collisions arise. These rights being clearly defined and sanctioned by public opinion, and temptations to encroachments being withdrawn, we may then consider our great problem practically solved. With regard to mere difference of opinion in taste, convenience, economy, equality, or even right and wrong, good and bad, sanity and insanity—all must be left to the supreme decision of each *Individual*, whenever he can take on himself the *cost* of his decisions ; which he cannot do while his interests or movements are united or combined with others. It is in combination or close connection only, that compromise and conformity are required. Peace, harmony, ease, security, happiness, will be found only in *Individuality*."

A PEEP INTO MODERN TIMES.

Conversation between a Resident and a Reporter.

"We are not Fourierites. We do not believe in Association. Association will have to answer for very many of the evils with which mankind are now afflicted. We are not Communists ; we are not Mormons ; we are not Non-Resistants. If a man steals my property or injures me, I will take good care to make myself square with him. We are Protestants, we are Liberals. We believe in the SOVEREIGNTY OF THE INDIVIDUAL. We protest against all laws which interfere with INDIVIDUAL RIGHTS—hence we are Protestants. We believe in perfect liberty of will and action—hence we are Liberals. We have no compacts with each other, save the compact of individual happiness ; and we hold that every man and every woman has a perfect and inalienable right to do and perform, all and singular, just exactly as he or she may choose, now and hereafter. But, gentlemen, this liberty to act must only be exercised at the *entire cost* of the individuals so acting. They have no right to tax the community for the consequences of their deeds."

" Then you go back to nearly the first principles of government, and acknowledge the necessity of some controlling power other than individual will?"

" Not much—not much. In the present depraved state of society generally, we—few in numbers—are forced by circumstances into courses of action not precisely compatible with our principles or with the intent of our organization, thus: we are a new colony; we can not produce all which we consume, and many of our members are forced to go out into the world to earn what people call money, so that we may purchase our groceries, &c. We are mostly mechanics—eastern men. There is not yet a sufficient home demand for our labor to give constant employment to all. When we increase in numerical strength, our tinsmiths and shoemakers and hatters and artisans of that grade will not only find work at home, but will manufacture goods for sale. That will bring us money. We shall establish a Labor Exchange, so that if my neighbor, the blacksmith, wants my assistance, and I in turn desire his services, there will be a scale to fix the terms of the exchange."

" But this would disturb Individual Sovereignty."

" I don't see it. No one will be *forced* to barter his labor for another's. If parties don't like the terms, they can make their own. There are three acres of corn across the way—it is good corn—a good crop—it is mine. You see that man now at work in the field cutting and stacking it. His work as a farmer is not so valuable as mine as a mason. We exchange, and it is a mutual benefit. Corn is just as good a measure of value as coin. You should read the pamphlet we are getting out. It will come cheap. Andrews has published an excellent work on this subject of Individual Sovereignty."

" Have you any schools ?"

" Schools ? Ah! we only have a sort of primary affair for small children. It is supported by individual subscription. Each parent pays his proportion."

" How about women ?"

"Well, in regard to the ladies, we let them do about as they please, and they generally please to do about right. Yes, *they* like the idea of Individual Sovereignty. We give them plenty of amusement; we have social parties, music, dancing, and other sports. They are not all Bloomers : they wear such dresses as suit the individual taste, *provided they can get them !*"

"And the *breeches* sometimes, I suppose ?"

" Certainly they can *wear the breeches* if they choose."

" Do you hold to marriage?"

"Oh, marriage! Well, folks ask no questions in regard to *that* among us. We, or at least some of us, do not believe in life-partnerships, when the parties can not live happily. Every person here is supposed to know his or her own intrests best. We don't interfere ; there is no eaves-dropping, or prying behind the curtain. Those are good members of society, who are industrious and mind their own business. The individual is sovereign and independent, and all laws tending to restrict the liberty he or she should enjoy, are founded in error, and should not be regarded."

CHAPTER XI.

CHANNING'S BROOK FARM.

WE are now on the confines of the Fourier movement. The time-focus changes from 1826 to 1843. As the period of our history thus approaches the present time, our resources become more ample and authentic. Henceforward we shall not confine ourselves so closely to Macdonald's materials as we have done. The printed literature of Fourierism is more abundant than that of Owenism ; and while we shall still follow the catalogue of Associations which we gave from Macdonald in our third chapter, and shall appropriate all that is interesting in his memoirs, we shall also avail ourselves freely of various publications of the Fourierists themselves. A full set of their leading periodicals, (probably the only one in existence) was thrust upon us by the freak of a half-crazed literary gentleman, nearly at the very time when we had the good fortune to find Macdonald's collections. We shall hereafter refer most frequently to the files of *The Dial*, *The Present*, *The Phalanx*, *The Harbinger*, and *The Tribune*.

In order to understand the Fourier movement, we must look at the preparations for it. This we have already been doing, in studying Owenism. But there were other preparations. Owenism was the socialistic prelude. We must now attend to what may be called the religious preparations.

Owenism was limited and local, chiefly because it was thoroughly non-religious and even anti-religious. In order that Fourierism might sweep the nation, it was necessary that it should ally itself to some form of popular religion, and especially that it should penetrate the strongholds of religious New England.

To prepare for this combination, a differentiation in the New England church was going on simultaneously with the career of Owenism. After the war of 1815, the division of Congregationalism into Orthodoxy and Unitarianism, commenced. Excluding from our minds the doctrinal and ecclesiastical quarrels that attended this division, it is easy to see that Providence, which is always on both sides of every fight, aimed at division of labor in this movement. One party was set to defend religion ; the other liberty. One stood by the old faith, like the Jew ; the other went off into free-thinking and the fine arts, like the Greek. One worked on regeneration of the heart ; the other on culture of the external life. In short, one had for its function the carrying through of the Revival system ; the other the development of Socialism.

The royal men of these two "houses of Israel" were Dr. Beecher and Dr. Channing ; and both left royal families, direct or collateral. The Beechers are leading the Orthodox to this day ; and the Channings, the Unitarians. We all know what Dr. Beecher and his children have done for revivals. He was the pivotal man between Nettleton and Finney in the last generation, and his children are the standard-bearers of revival religion in the present. What the Channings have done for Socialism is not so well known, and this is what we must now bring to view.

First and chief of all the experiments of the Fourier epoch was BROOK FARM. And yet Brook Farm in its original conception, was not a Fourier formation at all, but an American seedling. It was the child of New England Unitarianism. Dr. Channing himself was the suggester of it. So says Ralph Waldo Emerson. As this is an interesting point of history, we have culled from a newspaper report of Mr. Emerson's lecture on Brook Farm, the following summary, from which it appears that Dr. Channing was the pivotal man between old-fashioned Unitarianism and Transcendentalism, and the father of *The Dial* and of Brook Farm:

EMERSON'S REMINISCENCES OF BROOK FARM.

" In the year 1840 Dr. Channing took counsel with Mr. George Ripley on the point if it were possible to bring cultivated, thoughtful people together, and make a society that deserved the name. He early talked with Dr. John Collins Warren on the same thing, who admitted the wisdom of the purpose, and undertook to make the experiment. Dr. Channing repaired to his house with these thoughts ; he found a well chosen assembly of gentlemen ; mutual greetings and introductions and chattings all around, and he was in the way of introducing the general purpose of the conversation, when a side-door opened, the whole company streamed in to an oyster supper with good wines, and so ended that attempt in Boston. Channing opened his mind then to Ripley, and invited a large party of ladies and gentlemen. I had the honor to be present. No important consequences of the attempt followed. Margaret Fuller,

Ripley, Bronson and Hedge, and many others, gradually came together, but only in the way of students. But I think there prevailed at that time a general belief in the city that this was some concert of doctrinaires to establish certain opinions, or to inaugurate some movement in literature, philosophy, or religion, but of which these conspirators were quite innocent. It was no concert, but only two or three men and women, who read alone with some vivacity. Perhaps all of them were surprised at the rumor that they were a school or sect, but more especially at the name of ' Transcendentalism.' Nobody knows who first applied the name. These persons became in the common chance of society acquainted with each other, and the result was a strong friendship, exclusive in proportion to its heat. * * *

" From that time, meetings were held with conversation—with very little form—from house to house. Yet the intelligent character and varied ability of the company gave it some notoriety, and perhaps awakened some curiosity as to its aims and results. But nothing more serious came of it for a long time. A modest quarterly journal called *The Dial*, under the editorship of Margaret Fuller, enjoyed its obscurity for four years, when it ended. Its papers were the contributions and work of friendship among a narrow circle of writers Perhaps its writers were also its chief readers. But it had some noble papers; perhaps the best of Margaret Fuller's. It had some numbers highly important, because they contained papers by Theodore Parker. * *

" I said the only result of the conversations which Dr. Channing had was to initiate the little quarterly called *The Dial;* but they had a further consequence in the creation of the society called the " Brook Farm " in

1841. Many of these persons who had compared their
notes around in the libraries of each other upon specu-
lative matters, became impatient of speculation, and
wished to put it into practice. Mr. George Ripley,
with some of his associates, established a society, of
which the principle was, that the members should be
stockholders, and that while some deposited money others
should be allowed to give their labor in different kinds
as an equivalent for money. It contained very many
interesting and agreeable persons. Mr. Curtis of New
York, and his brother of English Oxford, were members
of the family; from the first also was Theodore Parker;
Mr. Morton of Plymouth—engaged in the fisheries—
eccentric; he built a house upon the farm, and he and
his family continued in it till the end; Margaret Fuller,
with her joyous conversations and sympathies. Many
persons gave character and attractiveness to the place.
The farm consisted of 200 acres, and occupied some
spot near Reedville camp of later years. In and around
it, whether as members, boarders, or visitors, were
remarkable persons for character, intellect and accomplishments. * * * The Rev. Wm. H. Channing,
now of London, student of Socialism in France and
England, was a frequent sojourner here, and in perfect
sympathy with the experiment. * * *

"Brook Farm existed six or seven years, when the
society broke up and the farm was sold, and all parties
came out with a loss; some had spent on it the accumulations of years. At the moment all regarded it as a
failure; but I do not think that all so regard it now,
but probably as an important chapter in their experience, which has been of life-long value. What knowledge
has it not afforded them! What personal power which

the studies of character have given : what accumulated culture many members owe to it ; what mutual pleasure they took of each other ! A close union like that in a ship's cabin, of persons in various conditions ; clergymen, young collegians, merchants, mechanics, farmers' sons and daughters, with men of rare opportunities and culture."

Mr. Emerson's lecture is doubtless reliable on the main point for which we quote from it—the Unitarian and Channing-arian origin of Brook Farm—but certainly supfiercial in its view of the substantial character and final purpose of that Community. Brook Farm, though American and Unitarian in its origin, became afterward the chief representative and propagative organ of Fourierism, as we shall ultimately show. The very blossom of the experiment, by which it seeded the nation and perpetuated its species, was its periodical, *The Harbinger*, and this belonged entirely to the Fourieristic period of its career. Emerson dilates on *The Dial*, but does not allude to *The Harbinger*. In thus ignoring the public function by which Brook Farm was signally related to the great socialistic revival of 1843, and to the whole of American Socialism, Emerson misses what we conceive to be the main significance of the experiment, and indeed of Unitarianism itself.

And here we may say, in passing, that this brilliant Community has a right to complain that its story should have to be told by aliens. Emerson, who was not a member of it, nor in sympathy with the socialistic movement to which it abandoned itself, has volunteered a lecture of reminiscences ; and Hawthorne, who joined it only to jilt it, has given the world a poetico-sneering romance about it ; and that is all the first-hand information we have, except what can be gleaned from obsolete periodicals. George William Curtis, though he was a member, coolly exclaims in *Harper's Magazine:*

"Strangely enough, Hawthorne is likely to be the chief future authority upon 'the romantic episode' of Brook Farm. Those who had it at heart more than he, whose faith and energy were all devoted to its development, and many of whom have every ability to make a permanent record, have never done so, and it is already so much a thing of the past, that it will probably never be done."

In the name of history we ask, Why has not George William Curtis himself made the permanent record? Why has not George Ripley taken the story out of the mouths of the sneerers? Brook Farm might tell its own story through him, for he *was* Brook Farm. It was George Ripley who took into his heart the inspiration of Dr. Channing, and went to work like a hero to make a fact of it; while Emerson stood by smiling incredulity. It was Ripley who put on his frock and carted manure, and set Hawthorne shoveling, and did his best for years to keep work going, that the Community might pay as well as play. It was no "picnic" or "romantic episode" or chance meeting "in a ship's cabin" to him. His whole soul was bent on making a *home* of it. If a man's first-born, in whom his heart is bound up, dies at six years old, that does not turn the whole affair into a joke. There were others of the same spirit, but Ripley was the center of them.

Brook Farm came very near being a *religious* Community. It inherited the spirit of Dr. Channing and of Transcendentalism. The inspiration in the midst of which it was born, was intensely literary, but also religious. The Brook Farmers refer to it as the " revi-

val," the "*newness*," the "*renaissance*." There was
evidently an afflatus on the men, and they wrote and
acted as they were moved. *The Dial* was the original
organ of this afflatus, and contains many articles that are
edifying to Christians of good digestion. It was published quarterly, and the four volumes of it (sixteen
numbers) extended from July 1840 to April 1844.

The first notice we find of Brook Farm is in connection with an article in the second volume of *The Dial*
(Oct. 1841), entitled, "*A Glimpse of Christ's Idea of
Society*." The writer of this most devout essay was
Miss Elizabeth P. Peabody, then and since a distinguished literary lady. She was evidently in full
sympathy with the "newness" out of which Brook Farm
issued. Margaret Fuller, one of the constituents of
Brook Farm, was editress of *The Dial*, and thus
sanctioned the essay. Its reference to Brook Farm is
avowed in a note at the end, and in a subsequent article.
The following extracts give us

THE ORIGINAL IDEAL OF BROOK FARM.

[From *The Dial*, Oct. 1841.]

"While we acknowledge the natural growth, the good
design, and the noble effects of the apostolic church,
and wish we had it, in place of our own more formal
ones, we should not do so small justice to the divine
soul of Jesus of Nazareth, as to admit that it was a
main purpose of his to found it, or that when it was
founded it realized his idea of human society. Indeed
we probably do injustice to the apostles themselves, in
supposing that they considered their churches anything
more than initiatory. Their language implies that they
looked forward to a time when the uttermost parts of

the earth should be inherited by their beloved master ; and beyond this, when even the name, which is still above every name, should be lost in the glory of the Father, who is to be all in all.

"Some persons, indeed, refer all this sort of language to another world ; but this is gratuitously done. Both Jesus and the apostles speak of life as the same in both worlds. For themselves individually they could not but speak principally of another world ; but they imply no more than that death is an accident, which would not prevent, but hasten the enjoyment of that divine life, which they were laboring to make possible to all men, in time as well as in eternity.   *   *   *

"The Kingdom of Heaven, as it lay in the clear spirit of Jesus of Nazareth, is rising again upon vision. Nay, this Kingdom begins to be seen not only in religious ecstasy, in moral vision, but in the light of common sense, and the human understanding. Social science begins to verify the prophecy of poetry. The time has come when men ask themselves what Jesus meant when he said, 'Inasmuch as ye have not done it unto the least of these little ones, ye have not done it unto me.'

"No sooner is it surmised that the Kingdom of Heaven and the Christian Church are the same thing, and that this thing is not an association outside of society, but a reörganization of society itself, on those very principles of love to God and love to man, which Jesus Christ realized in his own daily life, than we perceive the day of judgment for society is come, and all the words of Christ are so many trumpets of doom. For before the judgment-seat of his sayings, how do our governments, our trades, our etiquettes, even our benevolent institutions and churches look ? What church in

Christendom, that numbers among its members a pauper or a negro, may stand the thunder of that one word, 'Inasmuch as ye have not done it to the least of these little ones, ye have not done it unto me?' And yet the church of Christ, the Kingdom of Heaven, has not come upon earth, according to our daily prayer, unless not only every church, but every trade, every form of social intercourse, every institution political or other, can abide this test.   *   *   *

"One would think from the tone of conservatives, that Jesus accepted the society around him, as an adequate framework for individual development into beauty and life, instead of calling his disciples 'out of the world.' We maintain, on the other hand, that Christ desired to reörganize society, and went to a depth of principle and a magnificence of plan for this end, which has never been appreciated, except here and there, by an individual, still less been carried out.   *   *   *

"There *are* men and women, who have dared to say to one another, Why not have our daily life organized on Christ's own idea? Why not begin to move the mountain of custom and convention? Perhaps Jesus's method of thought and life is the Savior—is Christianity! For each man to think and live on this method is perhaps the Second Coming of Christ. To do unto the little ones as we would do unto *him*, would be perhaps the reign of the Saints—the Kingdom of Heaven. We have hitherto heard of Christ by the hearing of the ear; now let us see him, let us be him, and see what will come of that. Let us communicate with each other and live.   *   *   *

"There have been some plans and experiments of Community attempted in this country, which, like those elsewhere, are interesting chiefly as indicating paths in which we should *not* go. Some have failed because their philosophy of human nature was inadequate, and their establishments did not regard man as he is, with all the elements of devil and angel within his actual constitution. Brisbane has made a plan worthy of study in some of its features, but erring in the same manner. He does not go down into a sufficient spiritual depth, to lay foundations which may support his superstructure. Our imagination before we reflect, no less than our reason after reflection, rebels against this attempt to circumvent moral freedom, and imprison it in his Phalanx.   *   *

" *The* church of Christ's Idea, world-embracing, can be founded on nothing short of faith in the universal man, as he comes out of the hands of the Creator, with no law over his liberty, but the Eternal Ideas that lie at the foundation of his Being. Are you a man ? This is the only question that is to be asked of a member of human society. And the enounced laws of that society should be an elastic medium of these Ideas ; providing for their everlasting unfolding into new forms of influence, so that the man of time should be the growth of eternity, consciously and manifestly.

" To form such a society as this is a great problem, whose perfect solution will take all the ages of time ; but let the Spirit of God move freely over the great deep of social existence, and a creative light will come at his word ; and after that long evening in which we are living, the morning of the first day shall dawn on a Christian society.   *   *   *

" N. B. A Postscript to this Essay, giving an account of a specific attempt to realize its principles, will appear in the next number."

Thus, according to this writer, Brook Farm, in its inception, was an effort to establish the kingdom of God on earth ; that kingdom in which " the will of God shall be done as it is done in heaven ; " a higher state than that of the apostolic church ; worthy even to be called the Second Coming of Christ, and the beginning of the day of judgment ! A high religious aim, surely ! and much like that proposed by the Shakers and other successful Communities, that have the reputation of being fanatical.

The reader will notice that Miss Peabody, on behalf of Brook Farm, disclaims Fourierism, which was then just beginning to be heard of through Brisbane's *Social Destiny of Man*, first published in 1840.

In the next number of *The Dial* Miss Peabody fulfills her promise of information about Brook Farm, in an article entitled, " *Plan of the West Roxbury Community*." Some extracts will give an idea of the first tottering steps of the infant enterprise :

THE ORIGINAL CONSTITUTION OF BROOK FARM.

[From *The Dial*, Jan. 1842.]

" In the last number of *The Dial*, were some remarks, under the perhaps ambitious title of, 'A Glimpse of Christ's Idea of Society;' in a note to which it was intimated, that in this number would be given an account of an attempt to realize in some degree this great Ideal, by a little company in the midst of us, as yet without name or visible existence. The attempt is made on a very small scale. A few individuals, who, unknown to each other, under different disciplines of life, reacting from different social evils, but aiming at the same object,—of being wholly true to their natures as men and women—have been made acquainted with one another, and have determined to become the Faculty of the Embryo University.

"In order to live a religious and moral life worthy the name, they feel it is necessary to come out in some degree from the world, and to form themselves into a community of property, so far as to exclude competition and the ordinary rules of trade; while they reserve sufficient private property, or the means of obtaining it, for all purposes of independence, and isolation at will. They have bought a farm, in order to make agriculture the basis of their life, it being the most direct and simple in relation to nature. A true life, although it aims beyond the highest star, is redolent of the healthy earth. The perfume of clover lingers about it. The lowing of cattle is the natural bass to the melody of human voices. [Here we have the old farming hobby of the socialists.]   *   *   *

"The plan of the Community, as an economy, is in brief this : for all who have property to take stock, and receive a fixed interest thereon : then to keep house or board in commons, as they shall severally desire, at the cost of provisions purchased at wholesale, or raised on the farm ; and for all to labor in community, and be paid at a certain rate an hour, choosing their own number of hours, and their own kind of work. With the results of this labor and their interest, they are to pay their board, and also purchase whatever else they require at cost, at the warehouses of the Community, which are to be filled by the Community as such. To perfect this economy, in the course of time they must have all trades and all modes of business carried on among them-

selves, from the lowest mechanical trade, which contributes to the health and comfort of life, to the finest
art, which adorns it with food or drapery for the mind.

"All labor, whether bodily or intellectual, is to be paid
at the same rate of wages; on the principle that as the
labor becomes merely bodily, it is a greater sacrifice to
the individual laborer to give his time to it; because
time is desirable for the cultivation of the intellectual,
in exact proportion to ignorance. Besides, intellectual
labor involves in itself higher pleasures, and is more
its own reward, than bodily labor.   *   *   *

"After becoming members of this Community, none
will be engaged merely in bodily labor. The hours of
labor for the Association will be limited by a general
law, and can be curtailed at the will of the individual
still more ; and means will be given to all for intellectual improvement and for social intercourse, calculated to
refine and expand. The hours redeemed from labor by
community, will not be re-applied to the acquisition of
wealth, but to the production of intellectual goods.
This Community aims to be rich, not in the metallic
representative of wealth, but in the wealth itself, which
money should represent; namely, LEISURE TO LIVE IN
ALL THE FACULTIES OF THE SOUL. As a Community,
it will traffic with the world at large, in the products of
agricultural labor; and it will sell education to as many
young persons as can be domesticated in the families,
and enter into the common life with their own children.
In the end it hopes to be enabled to provide, not only
all the necessaries, but all the elegances desirable for
bodily and for spiritual health : books, apparatus, collections for science, works of art, means of beautiful
amusement. These things are to be common to all ;

and thus that object, which alone gilds and refines the
passion for individual accumulation, will no longer exist
for desire, and whenever the sordid passion appears, it
will be seen in its naked selfishness. In its ultimate
success, the Community will realize all the ends which
selfishness seeks, but involved in spiritual blessings,
which only greatness of soul can aspire after.

"And the requisitions on the individuals, it is believed, will make this the order forever. The spiritual
good will always be the condition of the temporal.
Every one must labor for the Community in a reasonable degree, or not taste its benefits.   *   *   *
Whoever is willing to receive from his fellow men that
for which he gives no equivalent, will stay away from
its precincts forever. But whoever shall surrender himself to its principles, shall find that its yoke is easy and
its burden light. Everything can be said of it, in a
degree, which Christ said of his kingdom, and therefore
it is believed that in some measure it does embody his
idea. For its gate of entrance is strait and narrow. It
is literally a pearl hidden in a field. Those only who are
willing to lose their life for its sake shall find it. Its
voice is that which sent the young man sorrowing away:
'Go sell all thy goods and give to the poor, and then
come and follow me.' 'Seek first the kingdom of
Heaven and its righteousness, and all other things shall
be added to you.'   *   *   *

"There may be some persons at a distance, who will
ask, To what degree has this Community gone into
operation? We can not answer this with precision, but
we have a right to say that it has purchased the farm
which some of its members cultivated for a year with
success, by way of trying their love and skill for agricul-

tural labor; that in the only house they are as yet rich enough to own, is collected a large family, including several boarding scholars, and that all work and study together. They seem to be glad to know of all who desire to join them in the spirit, that at any moment, when they are able to enlarge their habitations, they may call together those that belong to them."

Thus far it is evident that Brook Farm was not a Fourier formation. Whether the beginnings of the excitement about Fourierism may not have secretly affected Dr. Channing and the Transcendentalists, we can not say. Brisbane's first publication and Dr. Channing's first suggestion of a Community (according to Emerson) took place in the same year—1840. But Brook Farm, as reported by Miss Peabody, up to January 1842 had nothing to do with Fourierism, but was an original Yankee attempt to embody Christianity as understood by Unitarians and Transcendentalists; having a constitution (written or unwritten) invented perhaps by Ripley, or suggested by the collective wisdom of the associates. Without any great scientific theory, it started as other Yankee experiments have done, with the purpose of feeling its way toward co-operation, by the light of experience and common sense; beginning cautiously, as was proper, with the general plan of joint-stock; but calling itself a Community, and evidently bewitched with the idea which is the essential charm of all Socialisms, that it is possible to combine many families into one great home. Moreover thus far there was no "advertising for a wife," no gathering by public proclamation. The two conditions of success which we named as primary in a previous chapter, viz., *religious principle* and *previous acquaintance*, were apparently secured. The nucleus was small in number, and well knit together by mutual acquaintance and spiritual sympathy. In all this, Brook Farm was the opposite of New Harmony.

If we take Rev. William H. Channing, nephew and successor of Dr. Channing, as the exponent of Brook Farm—which we may safely do, since Emerson says he was "a frequent sojourner there, and in perfect sympathy with the experiment "—we have evidence that the Community had not fallen into the ranks of Fourierism at a considerably later period. On the 15th of September 1843, Mr. Channing commenced publishing in New York a monthly Magazine called *The Present*, the main object of which was nearly the same as that of *The Dial*, viz., the discussion of religious Socialism, as understood at Brook Farm and among the Transcendentalists ; and in his third number (Nov. 15) he used language concerning Fourier, which *The Phalanx*, Brisbane's organ (then also just commencing), criticised as disrespectful and painfully offensive.

From this indication, slight as it is, we may safely conclude that the amalgamation of Brook Farm and Fourierism had not taken place up to November 1843, which was more than two years after Miss Peabody's announcement of the birth of the Community. So far Brook Farm was American and religious, and stood related to the Fourier revival only as a preparation. So far it was *Channing's* Brook Farm. Its story after it became *Fourier's* Brook Farm will be reserved for the end of our history of Fourierism.

CHAPTER XII.

HOPEDALE.

THIS Community was another anticipation of Fourierism, put forth by Massachusetts. It was similar in many respects to Brook Farm, and in its origin nearly contemporaneous. It was intensely religious in its ideal. As Brook Farm was the blossom of Unitarianism, so Hopedale was the blossom of Universalism. Rev. Adin Ballou, the founder, was a relative of the Rev. Hosea Ballou, and thus a scion of the royal family of the Universalists. Milford, the site of the Community, was the scene of Dr. Whittemore's first ministerial labors.

Hopedale held on its way through the Fourier revival, solitary and independent, and consequently never attained so much public distinction as Brook Farm and other Associations that affiliated themselves to Fourierism; but considered by itself as a Yankee attempt to solve the socialistic problem, it deserves more attention than any of them. Our judgment of it, after some study, may be summed up thus: As it came nearest to being a religious community, so it commenced earlier, lasted longer, and was really more scientific and sensible than any of the other experiments of the Fourier epoch.

Brook Farm was talked about in 1840, but we find no evidence of its organization till the fall of 1841. Whereas Mr. Ballou's Community dates its first compact from January 1841; though it did not commence operations at Hopedale till April 1842.

The North American Phalanx is reputed to have outlived all the other Associations of the Fourier epoch; but we find, on close examination of dates, that Hopedale not only was born before it, but lived after it. The North American commenced in 1843, and dissolved in 1855. Hopedale commenced in 1841, and lasted certainly till 1856 or 1857. Ballou published an elaborate exposition of it in the winter of 1854—5, and at that time Hopedale was at its highest point of success and promise. We can not find the exact date of its dissolution, but it is reported to have attained its seventeenth year, which would carry it to 1858. Indeed it is said there is a shell of an organization there now, which has continued from the Community, having a President, Secretary, &c., and holding occasional meetings; but its principal function at present is the care of the village cemetery

As to the theory and constitutional merits of the Hopedale Community, the reader shall judge for himself. Here is an exposition published in tract form by Mr. Ballou in 1851, outlining the scheme which was fully elaborated in his subsequent book :

" The Hopedale Community, originally called Fraternal Community, No. 1, was formed at Mendon, Massachusetts, January 28, 1841, by about thirty individuals from different parts of the State.   In the course of that year they purchased what was called the ' Jones Farm,' *alias*

'The Dale,' in Milford. This estate they named HOPEDALE—joining the word 'Hope' to its ancient designation, as significant of the great things they hoped for from a very humble and unpropitious beginning. About the first of April 1842, a part of the members took possession of their farm and commenced operations under as many disadvantages as can well be imagined. Their present domain (December 1, 1851), including all the lands purchased at different times, contains about 500 acres. Their village consists of about thirty new dwelling-houses, three mechanic shops, with water-power, carpentering and other machinery, a small chapel, used also for the purposes of education, and the old domicile, with the barns and out-buildings much improved. There are now at Hopedale some thirty-six families, besides single persons, youth and children, making in all a population of about 175 souls.

"It is often asked, What are the peculiarities, and what the advantages of the Hopedale Community? Its leading peculiarities are the following :

" 1. It is a church of Christ (so far as any human organization of professed Christians, within a particular locality, have the right to claim that title), based on a simple declaration of faith in the religion of Jesus Christ, as he taught and exemplified it, according to the scriptures of the New Testament, and of acknowledged subjection to all the moral obligations of that religion. No person can be a member, who does not cordially assent to this comprehensive declaration. Having given sufficient evidence of truthfulness in making such a profession, each individual is left to judge for him or herself, with entire freedom, what abstract doctrines are taught, and also what external religious rites are enjoined in the religion of Christ. No precise theological dogmas, ordinances or ceremonies are prescribed or prohibited. In such matters all the members are free, with mutual love and toleration, to follow their own highest convictions of truth and religious duty, answerable only to the great Head of the true Church Universal. But in practical Christianity this church is precise and strict. There its essentials are specific. It insists on supreme love to God and man—that love which 'worketh no ill' to friend or foe. It enjoins total abstinence from all God-contemning words and deeds; all unchastity; all intoxicating beverages; all oath-taking; all slave-holding and pro-slavery compromises; all war and preparations for war; all capital and other vindictive punishments; all insurrectionary, seditious, mobocratic and personal violence against any government, society, family or individual; all voluntary participation in any anti-Christian government, under promise of unqualified support—whether by doing military service, commencing actions at law, holding office, voting, petitioning for penal laws, aiding a legal posse by injurious force, or asking public interference for protection which can be given only by such force; all resistance of evil with evil; in fine, from all things known to be sinful against God or human nature. This is its acknowledged obligatory righteousness. It does not expect immediate and exact perfection of its members, but holds up this practical Christian standard, that all may do their utmost to reach it, and at least be made sensible of their short-comings. Such are the peculiarities of the Hopedale Community as a church.

"2. It is a Civil State, a miniature Christian Republic, existing within, peaceably subject to, and tolerated by the governments of Massachusetts and the United States, but otherwise a commonwealth complete within itself. Those governments tax and control its property, according to their own laws, returning less to it than they exact from it. It makes them no criminals to punish, no disorders to repress, no paupers to support, no burdens to bear. It asks of them no corporate powers, no military or penal protection. It has its own Constitution, laws, regulations and municipal police; its own Legislative, Judiciary and Executive authorities; its own educational system of operations; its own methods of aid and relief; its own moral and religious safeguards; its own fire insurance and savings institutions; its own internal arrangements for the holding of property, the management of industry, and the raising of revenue; in fact, all the elements and organic constituents of a Christian Republic, on a miniature scale. There is no Red Republicanism in it, because it eschews blood; yet it is the seedling of the true Democratic and Social Republic, wherein neither caste, color, sex nor age stands proscribed, but every human being shares justly in 'Liberty, Equality and Fraternity.' Such is The Hopedale Community as a Civil State.

" 3. It is a universal religious, moral, philanthropic, and social reform Association. It is a Missionary Society, for the promulgation of New Testament Christianity, the reformation of the nominal church, and the conversion of the world. It is a moral suasion Temperance Society on the teetotal basis. It is a moral power Anti-Slavery Society, radical and without compromise. It is a Peace Society on the only impregnable foundation of Christian non-resistance. It is a sound theoretical and practical Woman's Rights Association. It is a

Charitable Society for the relief of suffering humanity, to the extent of its humble ability. It is an Educational Society, preparing to act an important part in the training of the young. It is a socialistic Community, successfully actualizing, as well as promulgating, practical Christian Socialism—the only kind of Socialism likely to establish a true social state on earth. The members of this Community are not under the necessity of importing from abroad any of these valuable reforms, or of keeping up a distinct organization for each of them, or of transporting themselves to other places in search of sympathizers. Their own Newcastle can furnish coal for home-consumption, and some to supply the wants of its neighbors. Such is the Hopedale Community as a Universal Reform Association on Christian principles.

" *What are its Advantages ?*

" 1. It affords a theoretical and practical illustration of the way whereby all human beings, willing to adopt it, may become individually and socially happy. It clearly sets forth the principles to be received, the righteousness to be exemplified, and the social arrangements to be entered into, in order to this happiness. It is in itself a capital school for self-correction and improvement. No where else on earth is there a more explicit, understandable, practicable system of ways and means for those who really desire to enter into usefulness, peace and rational enjoyment. This will one day be seen and acknowledged by multitudes who now know nothing of it, or knowing, despise it, or conceding its excellence, are unwilling to bow to its wholesome requisitions. ' Yet the willing and the obedient shall eat the good of the land.'

" 2. It guarantees to all its members and dependents

employment, at least adequate to a comfortable subsistence ; relief in want, sickness or distress ; decent opportunities for religious, moral and intellectual culture ; an orderly, well regulated neighborhood ; fraternal counsel, fellowship and protection under all circumstances ; and a suitable sphere of individual enterprise and responsibility, in which each one may, by due self-exertion, elevate himself to the highest point of his capabilities.

" 3. It solves the problem which has so long puzzled Socialists, the harmonization of just individual freedom with social co-operation. Here exists a system of arrangements, simple and effective, under which all capital, industry, trade, talent, skill and peculiar gifts may freely operate and co-operate, with no restrictions other than those which Christian morality every where rightfully imposes, constantly to the advantage of each and all. All may thrive together as individuals and as a Community, without degrading or impoverishing any. This excellent system of arrangements in its present completeness is the result of various and wisely improved experiences.

" 4. It affords a peaceful and congenial home for all conscientious persons, of whatsoever religious sect, class or description heretofore, who now embrace practical Christianity, substantially as this Community holds it, and can no longer fellowship the popular religionists and politicians. Such need sympathy, co-operation and fraternal association, without undue interference in relation to non-essential peculiarities. Here they may find what they need. Here they may give and receive strength by rational, liberal Christian union.

" 5. It affords a most desirable opportunity for those

who mean to be practical Christians in the use of property, talent, skill or productive industry, to invest them. Here those goods and gifts may all be so employed as to benefit their possessors to the full extent of justice, while at the same time they afford aid to the less favored, help build up a social state free from the evils of irreligion, ignorance, poverty and vice, promote the regeneration of the race, and thus resolve themselves into treasure laid up where neither moth, nor rust, nor thieves can reach them. Here property is preëminently safe, useful and beneficent. It is Christianized. So, in a good degree, are talent, skill, and productive industry.

" 6. It affords small scope, place or encouragement for the unprincipled, corrupt, supremely selfish, proud, ambitious, miserly, sordid, quarrelsome, brutal, violent, lawless, fickle, high-flying, loaferish, idle, vicious, envious and mischief-making. It is no paradise for such ; unless they voluntarily make it first a moral penitentiary. Such will hasten to more congenial localities ; thus making room for the upright, useful and peaceable.

" 7. It affords a beginning, a specimen and a presage of a new and glorious social Christendom—a grand confederation of similar Communities—a world ultimately regenerated and Edenized. All this shall be in the forthcoming future.

" The Hopedale Community was born in obscurity, cradled in poverty, trained in adversity, and has grown to a promising childhood, under the Divine guardianship, in spite of numberless detriments. The bold predictions of many who despised its puny infancy have proved false. The fears of timid and compassionate friends that it would certainly fail have been put to rest. Even the repeated desertion of professed friends, disheartened by its imperfections, or alienated by too heavy trials of their patience, has scarcely retarded its progress. God willed otherwise. It has still many defects to outgrow, much impurity to put away, and a great deal of improvement to make—moral, intellectual and physical. But it will prevail and triumph. The Most High will be glorified in making it the parent of a numerous progeny of practical Christian Communities. Write, saith the Spirit, and let this prediction be registered against the time to come, for it shall be fulfilled."

In the large work subsequently published, Mr. Ballou goes over the whole ground of Socialism in a systematic and masterly manner. If the people of this country were not so bewitched with importations from England and France, that they can not look at home productions in this line, his scheme would command as much attention as Fourier's, and a great deal more than Owen's. The fact of practical failure is nothing against him in the comparison, as it is common to all of them.

For a specimen, take the following : Mr. Ballou finds all man's wants, rights and duties in seven spheres, viz.: 1, Individuality ; 2, Connubiality ; 3, Consanguinity ; 4, Congeniality ; 5, Federality ; 6, Humanity ; 7, Universality. These correspond very nearly to the series of spheres tabulated by Comtists. On the basis of this philosophy of human nature, Mr. Ballou proposes, not a mere monotony of Phalanxes or Communities, all alike, but an ascending series of four distinct kinds of Communities, viz.: 1, The Parochial Community, which is nearly the same as a common parish church ; 2, The Rural Community, which is a social body occupying a distinct territorial domain, but not other-

wise consolidated ; 3, The Joint-stock Community, con-
solidating capital and labor, and paying dividends and
wages ; of which Hopedale itself was a specimen ; and
4, The Common-stock Community, holding property in
common and paying no dividends or wages ; which is
Communism proper. Mr. Ballou provides elaborate
Constitutional forms for all of these social states, and
shows their harmonious relation to each other.   Then
he builds them up into larger combinations, viz. :
1, Communal Municipalities, consisting of two or more
Communities, making a town or city ; 2, Communal
States ; 3, Communal Nations ; and lastly, " the grand
Fraternity of Nations, represented by Senators in the
Supreme Unitary Council."   Moreover he embroiders
on all this an ascending series of categories for individual character.   Citizens of the great Republic are expected to arrange themselves in seven Circles, viz.:
1, The Adoptive Circle, consisting of members whose
connections with the world preclude their joining any
integral Community ; 2, The Unitive Circle, consisting
of those who join in building up Rural and Joint-stock
Communities ; 3, The Preceptive Circle, consisting of
persons devoted to teaching in any of its branches ;
4, The Communistic Circle, consisting of members of
common stock Communities ; 5, The Expansive Circle,
consisting of persons devoted to extending the Republic, by founding new Communities ; 6, The Charitive
Circle, consisting of working philanthropists ; and 7,
The Parentive Circle, consisting of the most worthy and
reliable counselors—the fathers and mothers in Israel.

This is only a skeleton.   In the book all is worked
into harmonious beauty.   All is founded on religion ; all
is deduced from the Bible.   We confess that if it were

our doom to attempt Community-building by paper
programme, we should choose Adin Ballou's scheme in
preference to any thing we have ever been able to find
in the lucubrations of Fourier or Owen.

To give an idea of the high religious tone of Mr.
Ballou and his Community, we quote the following
passage from his preface :

" Let each class of dissenting socialists stand aloof
from our Republic and experiment to their heart's
content on their own wiser systems. It is their right to
do so uninjured, at their own cost. It is desirable that
they should do so, in order that it may be demonstrated
as soon as possible which the true social system is.
When the radically defective have failed, there will be a
harmonious concentration of all the true and good
around the Practical Christian Standard. Meantime the
author confides this Cause calmly to the guidance,
guardianship and benediction of God, even that Heavenly Father who once manifested his divine excellency
in Jesus Christ, and who ever manifests himself through
the Christ-Spirit to all upright souls. He sincerely believes the movement to have been originated and thus
far supervised by that Holy Spirit. He is confident
that well-appointed ministering angels have watched
over it, and will never cease to do so. This strong
confidence has sustained him from the beginning, under
all temporary discouragements, and now animates him
with unwavering hopes for the future. The Hopedale
Community, the first constituent body of the new social
order, commenced the settlement of its Domain in the
spring of 1842, very small in numbers and pecuniary
resources. Its disadvantages were so multiform and
obvious, that most Associationists of that period re-

garded it as little better than a desperate undertaking, alike contracted in its social platform, its funds, and other fundamental requisites of success. Yet it has lived and flourished, while its supposed superiors have nearly all perished. Such was the will of God; such his promise to its founders; such their trust in him; such the realization of their hopes; and such the recompense of their persevering toils. And such is the benignant Providence which will bear the Practical Christian Republic onward through all its struggles to the actualization of its sublime destiny. Its citizens 'seek first the kingdom of God and his righteousness.' Therefore will all things needful be added unto them. Let the future demonstrate whether such a faith and such expectations are the dreams of a shallow visionary, or the divinely inspired, well-grounded assurances of a rightly balanced religious mind."

Let it not be thought that Ballou was a mere theorizer. Unlike Owen and Fourier, he worked as well as wrote. Originally a clergyman and a gentleman, he gave up his salary, and served in the ranks as a common laborer for his cause. In conversation with one who reported to us, he said, that often-times in the early days of Hopedale he would be so tired at his work in the ditch or on the mill-dam, that he would go to a neighboring haystack, and lie down on the sunny side of it, wishing that he might go to sleep and never wake again! Then he would recuperate and go back to his work. Nearly all the recreation he had in those days, was to go out occasionally into the neighborhood and preach a funeral sermon!

And this, by the way, is a fit occasion to say that in

our opinion there ought to be a prohibitory duty on the importation of socialistic theories, that have not been worked out, as well as written out, by the inventors themselves. It is certainly cruel to set vast numbers of simple people agog with Utopian projects that will cost them their all, while the inventors and promulgators do nothing but write and talk. What kind of a theory of chemistry can a man write without a laboratory? What if Napoleon had written out a programme for the battle of Austerlitz, and then left one of his aids-de-camp to superintend the actual fighting?

It will be noticed that Mr. Ballou, in his expositions, carries his assurance that his system is all right, and his confidence of success, to the verge of presumption. In this he appears to have partaken of a spirit that is common to all the socialist inventors. Fourier, without a laboratory or an experiment, was as dogmatic and infallible as though he were an oracle of God ; and Owen, after a hundred defeats, never doubted the perfection of his scheme, and never fairly confessed a failure. But in the end Ballou rises above these theorizers, even in this matter. Our informant says he manfully owns that Hopedale was a *total* failure.

As to the causes of the catastrophe, his account is the old story of general depravity. The timber he got together was not suitable for building a Community. The men and women that joined him were very enthusiastic, and commenced with great zeal ; their devotion to the cause seemed to be sincere ; but they did not know themselves.

The following details, given by Mr. Ballou, of the actual proceedings which brought Hopedale to its end, are very instructive in regard to the operation of the joint-stock principle.

Mr. Ballou was the first President of the Community; but was ultimately superseded by E. D. Draper. This gentleman came to Hopedale with great enthusiasm for the cause. He was not wealthy, but was a sharp, enterprising business man; and very soon became the managing spirit of the whole concern. He had a brother associated with him in business, who had no sympathy with the Community enterprise. With this brother Mr. Draper became deeply engaged in outside operations, which were very lucrative. They gained in wealth by these operations, while the inside interests were gradually falling into neglect and bad management. The result was that the Community sunk capital from year to year. Meanwhile Draper bought up three-fourths of the joint-stock, and so had the legal control in his own hands. At length he became dissatisfied with the way matters were tending, and went to Mr. Ballou and told him that "this thing must not go any further." Mr. Ballou asked him if that meant that the Community must come to an end. He replied, "Yes." "There was no other way," said Mr. Ballou, "but to submit to it." He then said to Mr. Draper that he had one condition to put to him; that was, that he should assume the responsibility of paying the debts. Mr. Draper consented; the debts were paid; and thus terminated the Hopedale experiment.

CHAPTER XIII.

THE RELIGIOUS COMMUNITIES.

WE have said that Brook Farm came very near being a religious Community; and that Hopedale came still nearer. In this respect these two stand alone among the experiments of the Fourier epoch. Here therefore is the place to bring to view in some brief way for purposes of comparison, the series of strictly religious Communities that we have referred to heretofore as colonies of foreigners. The following account of them first published in the *Social Record*, has the authority and freshness of testimony by an eye-witness. Of course it must not be taken as a view of the exotic Communities at the present time, but only at its date.

JACOBI'S SYNOPSIS.

"During the last eight years I have visited all the Communities in this country, except the Icarian and Oneida societies, staying at each from six months to two years, to get thoroughly acquainted with their practical workings. I will mention each society according to its age:

" 1. Conrad Beizel, a German, founded the colony of Ephrata, eight miles from Lancaster, Pennsylvania, in 1713. There were at times some thousands of members.

The Bible was their guide; they had all things in common; lived strictly a life of celibacy; increased in numbers, and became very rich. Conrad was at the head of the whole; he was the sun from which all others received the rays of life and animation. He lived to a very old age, but it was with him as with all other men; his sun was not standing in the zenith all the time, but went down in the afternoon. His rays had not power enough to warm up thousands of members, as in younger days: he as the head became old and lifeless, and the members began to leave. He appointed a very amiable man as his successor, but he could not stop the emigration. The property is now in the hands of trustees who belong to the world, and gives an income of about $1200 a year. Perhaps there are now twelve or fifteen members. Some of the grand old buildings are yet standing. This was the first Community in America.

" 2. Ann Lee, an English woman, came to this country in 1774, and founded the Shaker societies. I have visited four, and lived in two. In point of order, neatness, regularity and economy, they are far in advance of all the other societies. They are from nearly all the civilized nations of the globe, and this is one reason for their great temporal success. Other Communities do not prosper as well, because they are composed too much of one nation. In Ann Lee's time, and even some time after her departure, they had many spiritual gifts, as never a body of people after Christ's time has had ; and they were of such a nature as Christ said should be among his true followers ; but they have now lost them, so far as they are essential and beneficial. The ministry is the head. Too much attention is given to outward rules, that set up the ministers and elders as patterns, and keep all minds on the same plane. While limited by these rules there will be no progress, and their noble institutions will become dead letters.

" 3. George Rapp, a German, founded a society in the first quarter of this century. After several removals they settled at Economy, in Beaver County, Pennsylvania, eighteen miles from Pittsburg. They are all Germans ; live strictly a life of celibacy; take the Bible as their guide, as Rapp understood it. They numbered about eighteen hundred in their best times, but are now reduced to about three hundred, and most of them are far advanced in years. They are very rich and industrious. Rapp was their leader and head, and kept the society in prosperous motion so long as he was able to exercise his influence ; but as he advanced in years and his mental strength and activity diminished, the members fell off. He is dead; and his successor, Mr. Baker, is advanced in years. They are next to the Shakers in point of neatness and temporal prosperity ; but unlike them in being strict Bible-believers, and otherwise differing in their religious views.

" 4. Joseph Bimeler, a German, in 1816 founded the colony of Zoar, in Tuscorora County, Ohio, twelve miles from New Philadelphia, with about eight hundred of his German friends. They are Bible believers in somewhat liberal style. Bimeler was the main engine ; he had to do all the thinking, preaching and pulling the rest along. While he had strength all went on seemingly very well ; but as his strength began to fail the whole concern went on slowly. I arrived the week after his death. The members looked like a flock of sheep who had lost their shepherd. Bimeler appointed a well-meaning man for his successor, but as he was not Bimeler, he could not put his engine before the train. Every member pushed forward or pulled back just as he thought proper ; and their thinking was a poor affair, as they were not used to it. They live married or not, just as they choose ; are well off, a good moral people, and number about five hundred.

"5. Samuel Snowberger, an American, founded a society in 1820 at Snowhill, Pennsylvania, twenty miles from Harrisburg. He took Ephrata as his pattern in every respect. The Snowbergers believe in the Bible as explained in Beizel's writings. They are well off, and number about thirty. [This society should be considered an offshoot of No. 1.]

"6. Christian Metz, a German, with his followers, founded a society eight miles from Buffalo, New York, in 1846. They called themselves the inspired people, and their colony Ebenezer. They believe in the Bible, as it is explained through their mediums. Metz and one of the sisters have been mediums more than thirty years, through whom one spirit speaks and writes. This spirit guides the society in spiritual and temporal matters, and they have never been disappointed in his counsels for their welfare. They have been led by this spirit for more than a century in Germany. They permit marriage, when, after application has been made, the spirit consents to it; but the parties have to go through some public mortification. In 1851 they had some thousands of members. They have now removed to Iowa, where they have 30,000 acres of land. This is the largest and richest Community in the United States. One member brought in $100,000, others $60,000, $40,000, $20,000, etc. They are an intelligent and very kind people, and live in little comfortable cottages, not having unitary houses as the other societies. They are not anxious to get members, and none are received except by the consent of the controlling spirit. They have a printing-press for their own use, but do not publish any books.

"7. Erick Janson, a Swede, and his friends started a colony at Bishop Hill, Illinois, in 1846, and now number about eight hundred. They are Bible-believers according to their explanations. They believe that a life of celibacy is more adapted to develop the inner man, but marriage is not forbidden. Their minds are not closed against liberal progress, when they are convinced of the truth and usefulness of it. They began in very poor circumstances, but are now well off, and not anxious to get members ; do not publish any books about their colony. Janson died eight years ago. They have no head ; but the people select their preachers and trustees, who superintend the different branches of business. They are kept in office as long as the majority think proper. I am living there now.

"*August* 26 1858. A. JACOBI."

The connection between religion of some kind and success in these Communities, has come to be generally recognized, even among the old friends of non-religious Association. Thus Horace Greeley, in his "Recollections of a Busy Life," says :

"That there have been—nay, are—decided successes in practical Socialism, is undeniable ; but they all have that Communistic basis which seems to me irrational and calculated to prove fatal. * * *

"I can easily account for the failure of Communism at New Harmony, and in several other experiments ;

I can not so easily account for its successes. Yet the fact stares us in the face that, while hundreds of banks and factories, and thousands of mercantile concerns, managed by shrewd, strong men, have gone into bankruptcy and perished, Shaker Communities, established more than sixty years ago, upon a basis of little property and less worldly wisdom, are living and prosperous to-day. And their experience has been imitated by the German Communites at Economy, Zoar, the Society of Ebenezer, &c., &c. Theory, however plausible, must respect the facts.   *   *   *

" Religion often makes practicable that which were else impossible, and divine love triumphs where human science is baffled. Thus I interpret the past successes and failures of Socialism.

" With a firm and deep religious basis, any Socialistic scheme may succeed, though vicious in organization and at war with human nature, as I deem Shaker Communism and the antagonist or ' Free Love' Community of Perfectionists at Oneida. Without a basis of religious sympathy and religious aspiration, it will always be difficult, though I judge not impossible."

Also Charles A. Dana, in old times a Fourierist and withal a Brook Farmer, now chief of *The New York Sun*, says in an editorial on the Brocton Association (May 1 1869):

"Communities based upon peculiar religious views, have generally succeeded. The Shakers and the Oneida Community are conspicuous illustrations of this fact ; while the failure of the various attempts made by the disciples of Fourier, Owen, and others, who have not had the support of religious fanaticism, proves that without this great force the most brilliant social theories are of little avail."

It used to be said in the days of Slavery, that religious negroes were worth more in the market than the non-religious. Thus religion, considered as a working force in human nature, has long had a recognized commercial value. The logic of events seems now to be giving it a definite socialistic value. American experience certainly tends to the conclusion that religious men can hold together longer and accomplish more in close Association, than men without religion.

But with this theory how shall we account for the failure of Brook Farm and Hopedale? They certainly had, as we have seen, much of the "fanaticism" of the Shakers and other successful Communities—at least in their expressed ideals. Evidently some peculiar species of religion, or some other condition than religion, is necessary to insure success. To discover the truth in this matter, let us take the best example of success we can find, and see what other principle besides religion is most prominent in it.

The Shakers evidently stand highest on the list of successful Communities. Religion is their first principle; what is their second? Clearly the exclusion of marriage, or in other words, the subjection of the sexual relation to the Communistic principle. Here we have our clue; let us follow it. Can any example of success be found where this second condition is not present? We need not look for precisely the Shaker treatment of the sexual relation in other examples. Our question is simply this: Has any attempt at close Association ever succeeded, which took marriage into it substantially as it exists in ordinary society? Reviewing Jacobi's list, which includes all the Communities commonly reported to be successful, we find the following facts :

1. The Communists of Ephrata live strictly a life of celibacy.

2. The Rappites live strictly a life of celibacy ; though Williams says they did not adopt this principle till 1807, which was four years after their settlement in Pennsylvania.

3. The Zoarites marry or not as they choose, according to Jacobi ; but Macdonald, who also visited them, says : " At their first organization marriage was strictly forbidden, not from any religious scruples as to its propriety, but as an indispensable matter of economy. They were too poor to rear children, and for years their little town presented the anomaly of a village without a single child to be seen or heard within its limits. Though this regulation has been for years removed, as no longer necessary, their settlement still retains much of its old character in this respect."

4. The Snowbergers, taking Ephrata as their pattern, adhere strictly to celibacy.

5. The Ebenezers, according to Jacobi, permit marriage, when their guiding spirit consents to it ; but the parties have to go through some public mortification. Another account of the Ebenezers says: " They marry and are given in marriage ; but what will be regarded as most extraordinary, they are practically Malthusians when the economy of their organization demands it. We have been told that when they contemplated emigration to this country, in view of their then condition and what they must encounter in fixing a new home, they concluded there should be no increase of their popu-

lation by births for a given number of years ; and the regulation was strictly adhered to."

6. The Jansonists believe that a life of celibacy is more adapted to develop the life of the inner man ; but marriage is not forbidden.

Thus in all these Societies Communism evidently is stronger than marriage familism. The control over the sexual relation varies in stringency. The Shakers and perhaps the Ephratists exclude familism with religious horror ; the Rappites give it no place, but their repugnance is less conspicuous ; the Zoarites have no conscience against it, but exclude it from motives of economy ; the Ebenezers excluded it only in the early stages of their growth, but long enough to show that they held it in subjection to Communism. The Jansonists favor celibacy ; but do not prohibit marriage. The decreasing ratio of control corresponds very nearly to the series of dates at which these Communities commenced. The Ephratists settled in this country in 1713 ; the Shakers in 1774 ; the Rappites in 1804 ; the Zoarites in 1816 ; the Ebenezers in 1846 ; and the Jansonists in 1846. Thus there seems to be a tendency to departure from the stringent anti-familism of the Shakers, as one type of Communism after another is sent here from the Old World. Whether there is a complete correspondence of the fortunes of these several Communities to the strength of their anti-familism, is an interesting question which we are not prepared to answer. Only it is manifest that the Shakers, who discard the radix of old society with the greatest vehemence, and are most jealous for Communism as the prime unit of organization, have prospered most, and are making the longest and strongest mark on the history of Socialism. And in general it seems probable from the fact of success attending these forms of Communism to the exclusion of all others, that there is some rational connection between their control of the sexual relation and their prosperity.

The only case that we have heard of as bearing against the hypothesis of such a connection, is that of the French colony of Icarians. We have seen their example appealed to as proof that Communism may exist without religion, and *with* marriage Our accounts, however, of this Society in its present state are very meager. The original Icarian Community, founded by Cabet at Nauvoo, not only tolerated but required marriage ; and as it soon came to an end, its fate helps the anti-marriage theory. The present Society of Icarians is only a fragment of that Community—about sixty persons out of three hundred and sixty-five. Whether it retained its original constitution after separating from its founder, and how far it can fairly claim to be a success, we know not. All our other facts would lead us to expect that it will either subordinate the sexual relation to the Communistic, or that it will not long keep its Communism.

Of course we shall not be understood as propounding the theory that the negative or Shaker method of disposing of marriage and the sexual relation, is the only one that can subordinate familism to Communism. The Oneida Communists claim that their control over amativeness and philoprogenitiveness, the two elements of familism, is carried much farther than that of the Shakers ; inasmuch as they make those passions serve Communism, instead of opposing it, as they do under suppression. They dissolve the old dual unit of society, but take the constituent elements of it all back into Communism. The only reason why we do not name the Oneida Community among the examples of the connection between anti-marriage and success, is that we do not consider it old enough to be pronounced successful.

Let us now go back to Brook Farm and Hopedale, and see how they stood in relation to marriage.

We find nothing that indicates any attempt on the part of Brook Farm to meddle with the marriage relation. In the days of its original simplicity, it seems not to have thought of such a thing. It finally became a Fourier Phalanx, and of course came into more or less sympathy with the *expectations* of radical social changes which Fourier encouraged. But it was always the policy of the *Harbinger*, the *Tribune*, and all the organs of Fourierism, to indignantly protest their innocence of any *present* disloyalty to marriage. And yet we find in the *Dial* (January 1844), an article about Brook Farm by Charles Lane, which shows in the following significant passage, that there was serious thinking among the Transcendentalists, as to the possibility of a clash between old familism and the larger style of life in the Phalanx:

"The great problem of socialism now is, whether the existence of the marital family is compatible with that of the universal family, which the term 'Community' signifies. The maternal instinct, as hitherto educated, has declared itself so strongly in favor of the separate fireside, that Association, which appears so beautiful to the young and unattached soul, has yet accomplished little progress in the affections of that important section of the human race—the mothers. With fathers, the feeling in favor of the separate family is certainly less strong; but there is an undefinable tie, a sort of magnetic rapport, an invisible, inseverable, umbilical cord between the mother and child, which in most cases circumscribes her desires and ambition to her own immediate family. All the accepted adages and wise saws of society, all the precepts of morality, all the sanctions of theology, have for ages been employed to confirm this feeling. This is the chief corner-stone of present society; and to this maternal instinct have, till very lately, our most heartfelt appeals been made for the progress of the human race, by means of a deeper and more vital education. Pestalozzi and his most enlightened disciples are distinguished by this sentiment. And are we all at once to abandon, to deny, to destroy this supposed stronghold of virtue? Is it questioned whether the family arrangement of mankind is to be preserved? Is it discovered that the sanctuary, till now deemed the holiest on earth, is to be invaded by intermeddling skepticism, and its altars sacrilegiously destroyed by the rude hand of innovating progress? Here 'social science' must be brought to issue. The question of Association and of marriage are one. If, as we have been popularly led to believe, the individual or separate family is in the true order of Providence, then the associative life is a false effort. If the associative life is true, then is the separate family a false arrangement. By the maternal feeling it appears to be decided, that the co-existence of both is incompatible, is impossible. So also say some religious sects. Social science ventures to assert their harmony. This is the grand problem now remaining to be solved, for at least the enlightening, if not for the vital elevation of humanity. That the affections can be divided, or bent with equal ardor on two objects, so opposed as universal and individual love, may at least be rationally doubted. History has not yet exhibited such phenomena in an associate body, and scarcely perhaps in any individual. The monasteries and convents, which have existed in all ages, have been maintained solely by the annihilation of that peculiar affection on which the separate family is based. The Shaker families, in which the two sexes are not entirely dissociated, can yet only maintain their union by forbidding and preventing the growth of personal affection other than that of a spiritual character. And this in fact is not personal in the sense of individual, but ever a manifestation of universal affection. Spite of the speculations of hopeful bachelors and æsthetic spinsters, there is somewhat in the marriage bond which is found to counteract the universal nature of the affections, to a degree tending at least to make the considerate pause, before they assert that, by any social arrangements whatever, the two can be blended into one harmony. The general condition of married persons at this time is some evidence of the existence of such a doubt in their minds. Were they as convinced as the unmarried of the beauty and truth of associate life, the demonstration would be now presented. But might it not be enforced that the two family ideas really neutralize each other? Is it not quite certain that the human heart can not be set in two places? that man can not worship at two altars? It is only the determination to do what parents consider the best for themselves and their families, which renders the o'er populous world such a wilderness of self-hood as it is. Destroy this feeling, they say, and you prohibit every motive to exertion.

Much truth is there in this affirmation. For to them, no other motive remains, nor indeed to any one else, save that of the universal good, which does not permit the building up of supposed self-good, and therefore forecloses all possibility of an individual family.

"These observations, of course, equally apply to all the associative attempts, now attracting so much public attention; and perhaps most especially to such as have more of Fourier's designs than are observable at Brook Farm. The slight allusion in all the writers of the 'Phalansterian' class, to the subject of marriage, is rather remarkable. They are acute and eloquent in deploring Woman's oppressed and degraded position in past and present times, but are almost silent as to the future."

So much for Brook Farm. Hopedale was thoroughly conservative in relation to marriage. The following is an extract from its Constitution:

"ARTICLE VIII. Sec. 1. Marriage, being one of the most important and sacred of human relationships, ought to be guarded against caprice and abuse by the highest wisdom which is available. Therefore within the membership of this republic and the dependencies thereof, marriage is specially commended to the care of the Preceptive and Parentive circles. They are hereby designated as the confidential counselors of all members and dependents who may desire their mediation in cases of matrimonial negotiation, contract or controversy; and shall be held preëminently responsible for the prudent and faithful discharge of their duties. But no person decidedly averse to their interposition shall be considered under imperative obligation to solicit or accept it. And it shall be considered the perpetual duty of the Preceptive and Parentive Circles to enlighten the public mind relative to the requisites of true matrimony, and to elevate the marriage institution within this Republic to the highest possible plane of purity and happiness.

"Sec. 2. Marriage shall always be solemnized in the presence of two or more witnesses, by the distinct acknowledgment of the parties before some member of the Preceptive, or of the Parentive Circle, selected to preside on the occasion. And it shall be the imperative duty of the member so presiding, to see that every such marriage be recorded within ten days thereafter, in the Registry of the Community to which one or both of them shall at the time belong.

"Sec. 3. Divorce from the bonds of matrimony shall never be allowable within the membership of this Republic, except for adultery conclusively proved against the accused party. But separations for other sufficient reasons may be sanctioned, with the distinct understanding that neither party shall be at liberty to marry again during the natural lifetime of the other."

On this text Mr. Ballou comments in his book to the extent of thirty pages, and occupies as many more with the severest criticisms of "Noyesism" and other forms of sexual innovation.

The facts we have found stand thus: All the successful Communities, besides being religious, exercise control, more or less stringent, over the sexual relation; and this principle is most prominent in those that are most successful. But Brook Farm and Hopedale did not attempt any such control.

We incline therefore to the conclusion that the
Massachusetts Socialisms were weak, not altogether for
want of religion, but because they were too conservative
in regard to marriage, and thus could not digest and
assimilate their material. Or in more general terms,
the conclusion toward which our facts and reflections
point is, first, that religion, not as a mere doctrine, but
as an *afflatus* having in itself a tendency to make many
into one, is the first essential of successful Communism ;
and, secondly, that the *afflatus* must be strong enough
to decompose the old family unit and make Communism
the home-center

We will conclude with some observations that seem
necessary to complete our view of the religious Communities.

When we speak of these societies as successful, this
must not be understood in any absolute sense. Their
success is evidently a thing of *degrees*. All of them
appear to have been very successful at some period of
their career in *making money;* which fact indicates
plainly enough, that the theories of Owen and Fourier
about "compound economies " and "combined industry,"
are not moonshine, but practical verities. We may
consider it proved by abundant experiment, that it is
easy for harmonious Associations to get a living, and to
grow rich. But in other respects these religious Communities have had various fortunes. The oldest of
them, Beizel's Colony of Ephrata, in its early days
numbered its thousands ; but in 1858 it had dwindled
down to twelve or fifteen members. So the Rappites in
their best time numbered from eight hundred to a thousand ; but are now reduced to two or three hundred old
people. This can hardly be called success, even if the

money holds out. On the other hand, the Shakers appear to have kept their numbers good, as well as increased in wealth, for nearly a century; though Jacobi represents them as now at a stand-still. The rest of the Communities in his list, dating from 1816 to 1846, are perhaps not old enough to be pronounced permanently successful. Whether they are dwindling, like the Beizelites and Rappites, or at a stand-still, like the Shakers, or in a period of vigor and growth, Jacobi does not say; and we have no means of ascertaining. It is proper, however, to call them all successful in a relative sense; that is, as compared with the non-religious experiments. They have held together and made money for long periods; which is a success that the Owen and Fourier Communities have not attained.

If required here to define absolute success, we should say that at the lowest it includes not merely self-support, but also self-perpetuation. And this attainment is nearly precluded by the ascetic method of treating the sexual relation. The adoption of foreign children can not be a reliable substitute for home-propagation. The highest ideal of a successful Community requires that it should be a complete nursery of human beings, doing for them all that the old family-home has done, and a great deal more. Scientific propagation and universal culture should be its ends, and money-making only its means.

The causes of the comparative success which the ascetic Communities have attained, we have found in their religious principles and their freedom from marriage. Jacobi seems disposed to give special prominence to *leadership*, as a cause of success. He evidently attributes the decline of the Beizelites, the Rappites and

the Zoarites, to the old age and death of their founders.
But something more than skillful leadership is necessary
to account for the success of the Shakers. They had
their greatest expansion after the death of Ann Lee.
Jacobi recognizes, in his account of the Ebenezers,
another centralizing and controlling influence, coöpera-
ting with leadership, which has probably had more to do
with the success of all the religious Communities, than
leadership or anything else; viz., *inspiration.* He says
of the Ebenezers :

"They call themselves the inspired people. They
believe in the Bible, as it is explained through their
mediums. Metz, the founder, and one of the sisters,
have been mediums more than thirty years, through
whom *one* spirit speaks and writes. This spirit guides
the society in spiritual and temporal matters, and they
have never been disappointed in his counsels for their
welfare. They have been led by this spirit for more
than a century in Germany. No members are received
except by the consent of this controlling spirit."

Something like this must be true of all the Communities in Jacobi's list. This is what we mean by
afflatus. Indeed, this is what we mean by *religion,*
when we connect the success of Communities with their
religion. Mere doctrines and forms without afflatus are
not religion, and have no more power to organize successful Communities, than the theories of Owen and
Fourier.

Personal leadership has undoubtedly played a great
part in connection with afflatus, in gathering and
guiding the religious Communities. Afflatus requires
personal mediums ; and probably success depends on the
due adjustment of the proportion between afflatus and

medium. As afflatus is the permanent element, and personal leadership the transitory, it is likely that in the cases of the dwindling Communities, leadership has been too strong and afflatus too weak. A very great man, as medium of a feeble afflatus, may belittle a Community while he holds it together, and insure its dwindling away after his death. On the other hand, we see in the case of the Shakers, a strong afflatus, with an ordinary illiterate woman for its first medium ; and the result is success continuing and increasing after her death.

It is probably true, nevertheless, that an afflatus which is strong enough to make a strong man its medium *and keep him under*, will attain the greatest success ; or in other words, that the greater the medium the better, other things being equal.

In all cases of afflatus continuing after the death of the first medium, there seems to be an alternation of experience between afflatus and personal leadership, somewhat like that of the Primitive Christian Church. In that case, there was first an afflatus concentrated on a strong leader : then after the death of the leader, a distributed afflatus for a considerable period following the day of Pentecost : and finally another concentration of the afflatus on a strong leader in the person of Paul, who was the final organizer.

Compare with this the experience of the Shakers. The afflatus (issuing from a combination of the Quaker principality with the "French Prophets") had Ann Lee for its first medium, and worked in the concentrated form during her life. After her death, there was a short interregnum of distributed inspiration. Finally the afflatus concentrated on another leader ; and this time it was a man, Elder Meacham, who proved to be the final organizer. Each step of this progress is seen in the following brief history of Shakerism, from the American Cyclopædia:

"The idea of a community of property, and of Shaker families or unitary households, was first broached by Mother Ann, who formed her little family into a model after which the general organizations of the Shaker order, as they now exist, have been arranged. She died in 1784. In 1787 Joseph Meacham, formerly a Baptist preacher, but who had been one of Mother Ann's first converts at Watervliet, collected her adherents in a settlement at New Lebanon, and introduced both principles, together probably with some others not to be found in the revelations of their foundress. Within five years, under the efficient administration of Meacham, eleven Shaker settlements were founded, viz.: at New Lebanon, New York, which has always been regarded as the parent Society; at Watervliet, New York; at Hancock, Tyringham, Harvard, and Shirley, Massachusetts; at Enfield, Connecticut (Meacham's native town); at Canterbury and Enfield, New Hampshire; and at Alfred and New Gloucester, Maine."

Going beyond the Communities for examples (as the principles of growth are the same in all spiritual organizations), we may in like manner compare the development of Mormonism with that of Christianity. Joseph Smith was the first medium. After his death came a period of distributed inspiration. Finally the afflatus concentrated on Brigham Young as its second medium, and he has organized Mormonism.

For a still greater example, look at the Bonaparte dynasty. It can not be doubted that there is a persist-

ent afflatus connected with that power. It was concentrated on the first Napoleon. After his deposal and
death there was a long interregnum; but the afflatus
was only distributed, not extinguished. At length it
concentrated again on the present Napoleon; and he
proves to be great in diplomacy and organization, as the
first Napoleon was in war.

We have said that the general conclusion toward
which our facts and reflections point, is, first, that religion, not as a mere doctrine, but as an afflatus, is the
first essential to successful Communism; and secondly,
that the afflatus must be strong enough to make Communism the home-center. We may now add (if the law
we have just enunciated is reliable), that the afflatus must
also be strong enough to prevail over personal leadership
in its mediums, and be able, when one leader dies, to
find and use another.

We must note however that this law of apparent
transfer does not necessarily imply real change of leadership. In the case of Christianity, its adherents assume
that the first leader was not displaced, but only transferred from the visible to the invisible sphere, and thus
continued to be the administrative medium of the
original afflatus. And something like this, we understand, is claimed by the Shakers in regard to Ann Lee.

CHAPTER XIV.

THE NORTHAMPTON ASSOCIATION.

THIS Community, though its site was in a region where Jonathan Edwards and Revivalism reigned a hundred years before, could hardly be called religious. It seems to have represented a class sometimes called "Nothingarians." But like Brook Farm and Hopedale, it was an independent Yankee attempt to regenerate society, and a forerunner of Fourierism.

Massachusetts, the center of New England, the mother of school systems and factory systems, of Faneuil Hall revolutions and Anti-Slavery revolutions, of Liberalism, Literature, and Social Science, appears to have anticipated the advent of Fourierism, and to have prepared herself for or against the rush of French ideas, by throwing out three experiments of her own on her three avenues of approach:—Unitarianism, Universalism, and Nothingarianism.

The following neat account of the Northampton Community, is copied from a feminine manuscript in Macdonald's collection, on which he wrote in pencil:

"*By Mrs. Judson, for me, through G. W. Benson, Williamsburg, February* 14 1853."

MEMOIR.

"The Northampton Association of Education and Industry had its origin in the aspiration of a few individuals for a better and purer state of society—for freedom from the trammels of sect and bigotry, and an opportunity of carrying out their principles, socially, religiously, and otherwise, without restraint from the prevailing practices of the world around.

"The projectors of this enterprise were Messrs. David Mack, Samuel L. Hill, George W. Benson and William Adam. These, with several others who were induced to unite with them, in all ten persons, held their first meeting April 8 1842, organized the Association, and adopted a preamble, constitution and by-laws.

"This little band formed the nucleus, around which a large number soon clustered, all thinking, intelligent persons ; all, or nearly all, seeing and feeling the imperfections of existing society, and seeking a purer, more free and elevated position as regards religion, politics, business, &c. It would not be true to say that *all* the members of the Community were imbued with the true spirit of reform ; but the leading minds were sincere reformers, earnest, truthful souls, sincerely desiring to advance the cause of truth and liberty. Some were young persons, attracted thither by friends, or coming there to seek employment on the same terms as members, and afterwards applying for full membership.

"The Association was located about two and a half miles from the village and center of business of Northampton. The estate consisted of five hundred acres of land, a good water-privilege, a silk factory four stories in height, six dwelling-houses, a saw-mill and other property, all valued at about $31,000. This estate was formerly owned by the Northampton Silk Company; afterwards by J. Conant & Co., who sold it to the persons who originated the Association. The amount of stock paid in was $20,000. This left a debt of $11,000 upon the Community, which, in the enthusiasm of the new enterprise, they expected soon to pay by additions to their capital stock, and by the profits of labor. But by the withdrawal of members holding stock, and also by some further purchases of property, this debt was afterwards increased to nearly four times its original amount, and no progress was made toward its liquidation during the continuance of the Association.

"Labor was remunerated equally; both sexes and all occupations receiving the same compensation.

"It could not be expected that so many persons, bound by no pledges or 'Articles of Faith,' should agree in all things. They were never asked when applying for membership, 'Do you believe so and so?' On the contrary, a good life and worthy motives were the only tests by which they were judged. Of course it was necessary, before they could be admitted, to decide the question, 'Can they be useful to the Association?'

"The accommodations for families were extremely limited, and many times serious inconvenience was experienced, in consequence of small and few apartments. For the most part it was cheerfully sustained; at least, so long as there was any hope of success—that is, of paying the debts, and obtaining a livelihood. Most of the members had been accustomed to good, spacious houses, and every facility for comfortable living.

"To obviate the difficulty of procuring suitable tenements for separate families, a community family was
instituted, occupying a part of the silk-factory. Two
stories of this building were appropriated to the use of
such as chose to live at a common table and participate
in the labor of the family. This also formed the home
of young persons who were unconnected with families.

"There was always plenty of food, and no one suffered
for the necessaries or comforts of life. All were satisfied with simplicity, both in diet and dress.

"At the first annual meeting, held January 18 1843,
some important changes were made in the management
of the affairs of the Association, and a new 'Preamble
and Articles of Association,' tending toward consoli-
dation and communism, were adopted for the year.
This step was the occasion of dissatisfaction to some of
the stockholders—to one in particular, and probably led
to his withdrawal, before the expiration of the year.

"Previous to this time some of the early members
had become dissatisfied with life in a Community, and
had withdrawn from all connection with it. They were
persons who had been pleased with the avowed objects
and principles of the Association, and with the persons
composing it, and also looked upon it as a profitable
investment of money. Of course in this they were
disappointed, and they had no principles which would
induce them to make sacrifices for the cause.

"A department of education was organized, in which
it was designed to unite study with labor, on the ground
that no education is complete which does not combine
physical with mental development. Mr. Adam was the
first director of that department, and was an able and

efficient teacher.   He was succeeded by Mr. Mack and his wife, who were persons of much experience in teaching, and of superior attainments.   A boarding-school was opened under their auspices, and several pupils were received from abroad, who pursued the same course as those belonging to the Association.

"In the course of the third year a subscription was opened, for the purpose of relieving the necessities of the Association ; and people interested in the object of Social Reform were solicited to invest money in this enterprise, no subscription to be binding unless the sum of $25,000 was raised.   This sum never was subscribed, and of course no assistance was obtained in that way.

"Many troubles were constantly growing out of the pecuniary difficulties in which the Community was involved.   Many sacrifices were demanded, and much hard labor was required, and those whose hearts were not in the work withdrew.

"As might be inferred from what has been said, there was no religious creed, and no particular form of reli-gious worship enjoined.   A meeting was sustained on the first day of the week most of the time while the Association existed, in which various subjects were discussed, and all had the right and an opportunity of expressing their opinions or personal feelings.   Of course a great variety of views and sentiments were introduced. As the religious sentiment is strong in most minds, this introduction of every phase of religious belief was very exciting, producing in some dissatisfaction ; in others, the shaking of all their preconceived views ; and prob-ably resulting in greater liberality and more charitable feelings in all.

"The carrying out of different religious views was,

perhaps, the occasion of more disagreement than any other subject: the more liberal party advocating the propriety and utility of amusements, such as card-playing, dancing, and the like; while others, owing perhaps to early education, which had taught them to look upon such things as sinful, now thought them detrimental and wholly improper, especially in the impoverished state of the Community. This disagreement operated to general disadvantage; as in consequence of it several worthy people and valuable members withdrew.

"There was also a difference of opinion many times with regard to the management of business, which was principally in the hands of the trustees, viz., the President, Secretary, and Treasurer, and it is believed was honestly conducted.

"The whole number of persons ever resident there, as nearly as can be ascertained, was two hundred and twenty; while probably the number of actual members at any one time did not exceed one hundred and thirty.

"With regard to the dissolution of this organization, which took place November 1 1846, I can only quote from the official records. 'There being no business before the meeting, there was a general conversation among the members about the business prospects of the Association, and many were of the opinion that it was best to dissolve; as we were deeply in debt, and there was no prospect of any more stock being taken up, which was the only thing that could relieve us, as our earnings were not large, and those members who had left us, whose stock was due, were calling for it. Some spoke of the want of that harmony and brotherly feeling which were indispensable to the success of such an enterprise. Others spoke of the unwillingness to make sacrifices on the part of some of the members; also, of the lack of industry and the right appropriation of time.' At a subsequent meeting the Executive Council stated that 'in view of all the circumstances of the Association, they had decided upon a dissolution of the several departments as at present organized, and should proceed to close the affairs of the Association as soon as practicable.' So the Association ceased to exist.

"The spirit which prompted it can never die; and though, in the carrying out of the principles which led to its organization, a failure has been experienced, yet the spirit of good-will and benevolence, that all-embracing charity, which led them to receive among them some unworthy and unprofitable members, still lives and is developing itself in other situations and by other means.

"It is impossible to give a complete history of this Community—its changes—its trials—its failure, and in some respects, perhaps, its success. Much happiness was experienced there—much of trial and discipline. No doubt it had its influence on the surrounding world, leading them to greater liberality and Christian forbearance. It was a great innovation on the established order of things in the whole region, and was at first looked upon with horror and distrust. These prejudices in a great measure subsided, and gave way to a feeling of comparative respect. With other similar undertakings that have been abandoned, it has done its work; and may it be found that its influence has been for good and not for evil."

CHAPTER XV.

THE SKANEATELES COMMUNITY.

A WONDERFUL year was 1843. Father Miller's prophetic calculations had created a vast expectation that it
would be the year of the final conflagration. His confident followers had their ascension-robes ready; and
outside multitudes saw the approach of that year with
an uneasy impression that the advent of Christ, or
something equally awful, was about to make an end of
the world.

And indeed tremendous events did come in 1843.
If Father Miller and his followers had been discerning
and humble enough to have accepted a spiritual fulfillment of their prophecies, they might have escaped the
mortification of a total mistake as to the time. The
events that came were these:

The Anti-slavery movement, which for twelve years
had been gathering into itself all minor reforms and firing
the northern heart for revolution, came to its climax in
the summer of 1843, in a rush of one hundred National
Conventions! At the same time Brisbane had every
thing ready for his great socialistic movement, and
in the autumn of 1843 the flood of Fourierism broke
upon the country. Anti-slavery was destructive; Fourierism professed to be constructive. Both were ram-

pant against existing civilization. Perhaps it will be found that in the junction and triumphant sweep of these forces, the old world, in an important sense, did come to an end.

In 1843 Massachusetts, the great mother of notions, threw out in the face of impending Fourierism her fourth and last socialistic experiment. There was a mania abroad, that made common Yankees as confident of their ability to achieve new social machinery and save the world, as though they were Owens or Fouriers. The Unitarians at Brook Farm, the Universalists at Hopedale, and the Nothingarians at Northampton, had tried their hands at Community-building in 1841—2, and were in the full glory of success. It was time for Anti-slavery, the last and most vigorous of Massachusetts nurslings, to enter the socialistic field. This time, as if to make sure of out-flanking the French invasion, the post for the experiment was taken at Skaneateles (a town forty miles west of the present site of the Oneida Community), thus extending the Massachusetts line from Boston to Central New York.

John A. Collins, the founder of the Skaneateles Community, was a Boston man, and had been a working Abolitionist up to the summer of 1843. He was in fact the General Agent of the Massachusetts Anti-slavery Society, and in that capacity had superintended the one hundred National Conventions ordered by the Society for that year. During the latter part of this service he had turned his own attention and that of the Conventions he managed, so much toward his private schemes of Association, that he had not the face to claim his salary as Anti-slavery agent. His way was to get up a rousing Anti-slavery Convention, and conclude it by calling a socialistic Convention, to be held on the spot immediately after it. At the close of the campaign he resigned, and the Anti-slavery Board gave him the following certificate of character :

"Voted, That the Board, in accepting the resignation of John A. Collins, tender him their sincerest thanks, and take this occasion to bear the most cordial testimony to the zeal and disinterestedness with which, at a great crisis, he threw himself a willing offering on the altar of the Anti-slavery cause, as well as to the energy and rare ability with which for four years he has discharged the duties of their General Agent ; and in parting, offer him their best wishes for his future happiness and success."

In October Mr. Collins bought at Skaneateles a farm of three hundred and fifty acres for $15,000, paying $5,000 down, and giving back a mortgage for the remainder. There was a good stone farm-house with barns and other buildings on the place. Mr. Collins gave a general invitation to join. One hundred and fifty responded to the call, and on the first of January 1844 the Community was under way, and the first number of its organ, *The Communitist*, was given to the world.

The only document we find disclosing the fundamental principles of this Community is the following— which however was not ventilated in the *Communitist*, but found its way to the public through the *Skaneateles Columbian*, a neighboring paper. We copy *verbatim :*

Articles of Belief and Disbelief, and Creed prepared and read by John A. Collins, November 19, 1843.

"BELOVED FRIENDS : By your consent and advice, I am called upon to make choice of those among you to aid me in establishing in this place, a Community of property and interest, by which we may be brought into love relations, through which plenty and intelligence may be ultimately secured to all the inhabitants of this globe.   To accomplish this great work there are but very few, in consequence of their original organization, structure of mind, education, habits and preconceived opinions, who are at the present time adapted to work out this great problem of human redemption.   All who come together for this purpose, should be united in thought and feeling on certain fundamental principles ; for without this, a Community of property would be but a farce.   Therefore it may be said with great propriety that the success of the experiment will depend upon the wisdom exhibited in the choice of the materials as agents for its accomplishment.

"Without going into the detail of the principles upon which this Community is to be established, I will state briefly a few of the fundamental principles which I regard as essential to be assented to by every applicant for admission :

" 1. RELIGION.—A disbelief in any special revelation of God to man, touching his will, and thereby binding upon man as authority in any arbitrary sense ; that all forms of worship should cease ; that all religions of every age and nation, have their origin in the same great false-hood, viz., God's special Providences ; that while we admire the precepts attributed to Jesus of Nazareth, we do not regard them as binding because uttered by him, but because they are true in themselves, and best adapted to promote the happiness of the race : therefore we regard the Sabbath as other days ; the organized church as adapted to produce strife and contention rather than love and peace ; the clergy as an imposition ;

the Bible as no authority; miracles as unphilosophical; and salvation from sin, or from punishment in a future world, through a crucified God, as a remnant of heathenism.

" 2. GOVERNMENTS.—A disbelief in the rightful existence of all governments based upon physical force; that they are organized bands of banditti, whose authority is to be disregarded: therefore we will not vote under such governments, or petition to them, but demand them to disband; do no military duty; pay no personal or property taxes; sit upon no juries; refuse to testify in courts of so-called justice; and never appeal to the law for a redress of grievances, but use all peaceful and moral means to secure their complete destruction.

" 3. That there is to be no individual property, but all goods shall be held in common; that the idea of mine and thine, as regards the earth and its products, as now understood in the exclusive sense, is to be disregarded and set aside: therefore, when we unite, we will throw into the common treasury all the property which is regarded as belonging to us, and forever after yield up our individual claim and ownership in it; that no compensation shall be demanded for our labor, if we should ever leave.

" 4. MARRIAGE.—[Orthodox as usual on this head.] That we regard marriage as a true relation, growing out of the nature of things—repudiating licentiousness, concubinage, adultery, bigamy and polygamy; that marriage is designed for the happiness of the parties and to promote love and virtue; that when such parties have outlived their affections and can not longer contribute to each other's happiness, the sooner the separation takes place the better; and such separation shall not be a barrier to the parties in again uniting with any one, when they shall consider their happiness can be promoted thereby ; that parents are in duty bound to educate their children in habits of virtue and love and industry; and that they are bound to unite with the Community.

" 5. EDUCATION OF CHILDREN.—That the Community owes to the children a duty to secure them a virtuous education, and watch over them with parental care.

" 6. DIETETICS.—That a vegetable and fruit diet is essential to the health of the body, and purity of the mind, and the happiness of society ; therefore, the killing and eating of animals is essentially wrong, and should be renounced as soon as possible, together with the use of all narcotics and stimulants.

" 7. That all applicants shall, at the discretion of the Community, be put upon probation of three or six months.

" 8. Any person who shall force himself or herself upon the Community, who has received no invitation from the Community, or who does not assent to the views above enumerated, shall not be treated or considered as a member of the Community ; no work shall be assigned to him or her if solicited, while at the same time, he or she shall be regarded with the same kindness as all or any other strangers—shall be furnished with food and clothing ; that if at any time any one shall dissent from any or all of the principles above, he ought at once, in justice to himself, to the Community, and to the world, to leave the Association. To these views we hereby affix our respective signatures.

"Assented to by all, except Q. A. Johnson, of Syracuse ; J. Josephine Johnson, do. ; William Kennedy, do. ; Solomon Johnson, of Martinsburgh ; and William C. Besson, of Lynn, Massachusetts."

This was too strong, and had to be repudiated the next spring by the following editorial in the *Communitist:*

"CREEDS.—Our friends abroad require us to say a few words under this head.

"We repudiate all creeds, sects, and parties, in whatever shape or form they may present themselves. Our principles are as broad as the universe, and as liberal as the elements that surround us. They forbid the adoption and maintenance of any creed, constitution, rules of faith, declarations of belief and disbelief, touching any or all subjects ; leaving each individual free to think, believe and disbelieve, as he or she may be moved by knowledge, habit, or spontaneous impulses. Belief and disbelief are founded upon some kind of evidence, which may be satisfactory to the individual to-day, but which other or better evidence may change to-morrow. We estimate the man by his acts rather than by his peculiar belief. We say to all, Believe what you may, but act as well as you can.

"These principles do not deny to any one the right to draw out his peculiar views—his belief and disbelief—on paper, and present them for the consideration and adoption of others. Nor do we deny the fact that such a thing has been done even with us. But we are happy to inform all our friends and the world at large, that such a document was not fully assented to and was never adopted by the Community ; and that the authors were among the first to discover the error and retrace the step. The document, with all proceedings under it, or relating thereto, has long since been abolished and repudiated by unanimous consent ; and we now feel ourselves to be much wiser and better than when we commenced."

It will be noticed that there was a party in the Community, headed by Q. A. Johnson, who saw the error of the creed before Collins did, and refused to sign it.   This Johnson and his party made much trouble for Collins ; and the whole plot of the Community-drama turns on the struggle between these two men, as the reader will see in the sequel.

Macdonald says, " A calamitous error was made in the deeding of the property.   It appears that Mr. Collins, who purchased the property, and whose experiment it really was, permitted the name of another man [Q. A. J.] to be inserted in the deed, as a trustee, in connection with his own.   He did this to avoid even the suspicion of selfishness.   But his confidence was misplaced ; as the individual alluded to subsequently acted both selfishly and dishonestly.   Mr. Collins and his friends had to contend with the opposition of this person and one or two others during a great portion of the time."

Mr. Finch, an Owenite, writing to the *New Moral World*, August 16, 1845, says :

"Mr. Collins held to no-government or non-resistance principles : and while he claimed for the Community the right to receive and reject members, he refused to appeal to the government to aid him in expelling impostors, intruders and unruly members ; which virtually amounted to throwing the doors wide open for the reception of all kinds of worthless characters.   In consequence of his efforts to reduce that principle to practice, the Community soon swarmed with an indolent, unprincipled and selfish class of 'reformers,' as they termed themselves ; one of whom, a lawyer [Q. A. J.], got half the estate into his own hands, and well-nigh ruined the concern. Mr. Collins, from his experience, at length became convinced of his errors as to these new-fangled Yankee notions, and has now abandoned them, recovered the property, got rid of the worthless and dissatisfied members, restored the society to peace and harmony, and they are now employed in forming a new Constitution for the society, in agreement with the knowledge they have all gained by the last two years' experience.

"Owing to the dissensions that arose from their defective organization at the first, a considerable number of the residents have either been dismissed, or have withdrawn from the place. The population, therefore, at present numbers only eleven adult male members, eight female, and seven children. The whole number of members, male and female, labor most industriously from six till six ; and having large orders for their saw-mill and turning shop, they work them night and day, with two sets of men, working each twelve hours—the saw-mill and turning shop being their principal sources of revenue."

The Communitist, September 18, 1845, about two years after the commencement of the Community, and eight months before its end, gives the following picture of its experiences and prospects, from the lively pen of Mr. Collins :

" Most happy are we to inform our readers and the friends of Community in general, that our prospects of success are now cheering. The dark clouds which so long hung over our movement, and at times threatened not only to destroy its peace, but its existence, have at last disappeared. We now have a clear sky, and the genial rays of a brilliant sun once more are radiating upon us. Our past experience, though grievous, will be of great service to us in our future progress, and will no doubt ultimately work out the fruits of unity, industry, abundance, intelligence and progress. It has taught us how far we may, in safety to our enterprise, advance ; that some important steps may be taken, of the practicability of which we had doubts ; and others, in the success of which we had but little faith, have proved both safe and expedient. Our previous convictions have been confirmed, that all is not gold that glitters ; that not all who are most clamorous for reform are competent to become successful agents for its accomplishment ; that there is floating upon the surface of society, a body of restless, disappointed, jealous, indolent spirits, disgusted with our present social system, not because it enchains the masses to poverty, ignorance, vice and endless servitude ; but because they could not render it subservient to their private ends. Experience has convinced us that this class stands ready to mount every new movement that promises ease, abundance, and individual freedom ; and that when such an enterprise refuses to interpret license for freedom, and insists that members shall make their strength, skill and talent subservient to the movement, then the cry of tyranny and oppression is raised against those who advocate such industry and self-denial ; then the enterprise must become a scape-goat, to bear the fickleness, indolence, selfishness and envy of this class. But the above is not the only class of minds that our cause convened. From the great, noble, and disinterested principles which it embraces, from the high hopes which it inspires for progress, reform and, in a word, for human redemption, it has called many true reformers, genuine philanthropists, men and women of strong hands, brave hearts and vigorous minds.

" Our enterprise, the most radical and reformatory in its profession, gathers these two extremes of character, from motives diametrically opposite. When these are brought together, it is reasonable to expect that, like an acid and alkali, they will effervesce, or, like the two opposite poles of a battery, will repel each other. For the last year it has been the principal object of the Community to rid itself of its cumbersome material, knowing that its very existence hinged upon this point. In this it has been successful. Much of this material was hired to go at an expense little if any short of three thousand dollars. People will marvel at this. But the Community, in its world-wide philanthropy, cast to the winds its power to expel unruly and turbulent members, which gave our quondam would-be-called 'Reformers,' an opportunity to reduce to practice, their real principles. In this winnowing process it would be somewhat remarkable if much good wheat had not been carried off with the chaff.

"Communities and Associations, in their commencement too heavily charged with an impracticable, inexperienced, self-sufficient, gaseous class of mind, have generally exploded before they were conscious of the combustible material they embraced, or had acquired strength or experience sufficient to guard themselves against those elements which threaten their destruction.

With a small crew well acclimated, we have doubled the cape, and are now upon a smooth sea, heading for the port of Communism.

"The problem of social reform must be solved by its own members; by those possessed of living faith, indomitable perseverance, unflinching devotion and undying energy. The vicious, the sick, the infirm, the indolent, can not at present be serviceable to our cause. Community should neither be regarded in the light of a poor-house nor hospital. Our object is not so much to give a home to the poor, as to demonstrate to them their own power and resources, and thereby ultimately to destroy poverty. We make money no condition of membership; but poverty alone is not a sufficient qualification to secure admission. Stability of character, industrious habits, physical energy, moral strength, mental force, and benevolent feelings, are characteristics indispensable to a valuable Communist. A Community of such members has an inexhaustible mine of wealth, though not in possession of one dollar. Do not understand by this that we reject either men or money, simply because they happen to be united. The more wealth a good member brings, the better. It is, however, the smallest of all qualifications, in and of itself. There should be at first as few non-producers as possible. Single men and women and small families are best adapted to our condition and circumstances. In the commencement, the less children the better. It would be desirable to have none but the children born on the domain. Then they would grow up with an undivided Community feeling. Through the agency of such is our cause to be successfully carried forward. A man with a large family of non-producing children, must possess extraordinary powers, to justify his admission."

Macdonald thus concludes the tale: "After the experiment had progressed between two and three years, Mr. Collins became convinced that he and his fellow members could not carry out in practice the Community idea. He resolved to abandon the attempt; and calling the members together, explained to them his feelings on the subject. He resigned the deed of the property into their hands, and soon after departed from Skaneateles, like one who had lost his nearest and dearest friend. Most of the members left soon after, and the Community quietly dissolved.

"This experiment did not fail through pecuniary embarassment. The property was worth twice as much when the Community dissolved, as it was at first; and was much more than sufficient to pay all debts. So it may be truly said, that this experiment was given up through a conviction in the mind of the originator, that the theory of the Community could not be carried out in practice—that the attempt was premature, and the necessary conditions did not yet exist. The Community ended in May 1846."

Mr. Collins subsequently acknowledged in the public prints his abandonment of the schemes of philanthropy and social improvement in which he had been conspicuous; and returned, as a socialistic paper expressed it, "to the decencies and respectabilities of orthodox Whiggery."

For side-lights to this general sketch which we have collected from Macdonald, Finch and Collins, we have consulted the files of the *Phalanx* and the *Harbinger*. The following is all we find:

The Phalanx, September 7, 1844, mentions that the

Communitist has reached its seventh number—has been enlarged and improved—has changed its terms from *gratis* to $1.00 per year in advance—congratulates the Community on this improvement, but criticises its fundamental principle of Communism.

The Harbinger, September 14, 1845, quotes a Rochester paper as saying that "the Skaneateles concern has been sifted again and again of its chaff or wheat, we hardly know which, until, from a very wild republic, it appears verging toward a sober monarchy; i. e., toward the unresisted sway of a single mind." On this the *Harbinger* remarks:

" The Skaneateles Community, so far from being a Fourier institution, has been in open and bitter hostility with that system; no man has taken stronger ground against the Fourier movement than its founder, Mr. John Collins; and although of late it has somewhat softened in its opposition to the views of Fourier, it is no more in unison with them than it is with the doctrines of the Presbyterian Church, or the 'domestic arrangements' of South Carolina. We understand that Mr. Collins has essentially modified his ideas in regard to a true social order, since he commenced at Skaneateles; that he finds many principles to which he was attached in theory, untenable in practice; and that learning wisdom by experience, he is now aiming at results which are more practicable in their nature, than those which he had deeply at heart in the commencement. But with the most friendly feelings toward Mr. Collins and the Skaneateles Community, we declare that it has no connection with Association on the plan of Fourier; it is strictly speaking a Community of property—a system which we reject as the grave of liberty; though incomparably superior to the system of violence and fraud which is upheld in the existing order of society."

In the *Harbinger* of September 27, 1845, Mr. Ripley writes in friendly terms of the brightening prospects of the Skaneateles Community; objects to its Communistic principles and its hostility to religion; with these exceptions thinks well of it and wishes it success.

In the *Harbinger* of November 20, 1847, a year and more after the decease of the Community, an enthusiastic Associationist says that several defunct Phalanxes—the Skaneateles among the rest—"are not dead, but only asleep; and will wake up by and by to new and superior life!"

Several members of the Oneida Community had more or less personal knowledge of the Skaneateles experiment. At our request they have written what they remember; which we present in conclusion, as the nearest we can get to an "inside view."

RECOLLECTIONS OF H. J. SEYMOUR.

"My acquaintance with the Skaneateles Community was limited to what I gathered under the following circumstances: John A. Collins lectured on Association in Westmoreland, near where I lived, in 1843. His eloquence had some effect on my father and his family, and on me among the rest. In the fall, when the Community started, my father sent my brother, then eighteen years old, with a wagon and yoke of oxen, to the Community. He remained there till nearly the middle of winter, when he returned home, ostensibly by invitation of my mother, who had become alarmed by the reports and evidences of the infidelity of Collins and his associates; but I am inclined to think my brother was ready to leave, having satisfied his aspirations for that kind of Communism. The next summer I made a call of a few hours at the Community in company with my mother; but most of my information about it is derived from my brother.

"He spoke of Collins as full of fiery zeal, and a kind of fussy officiousness in business, but lacking in good judgment. To figure abroad as a lecturer was thought to be his appropriate sphere. The other most prominent leader was Q. A. Johnson of Syracuse. I have heard him represented as a long-headed, tonguey lawyer. The question to be settled soon after my brother's arrival, was, on which of the falls the saw-mill and machine-shop should be built. Collins said it should be on one; Johnson said it should be on the other; and the dispute waxed warm between them. I judge, from what my brother told me, that the conflict between these two men and their partisans raged through nearly the whole life of the Community, and was finally ended only by the withdrawal of Johnson, in consideration of a pretty round sum of money.

"My brother did not make a practice of attending their evening meetings, for the reason that he was one of the hard workers and could not afford it; as there was an amount of disputing going on that was very wearisome to the flesh.

"The question of diet was one about which the Community was greatly exercised. And there seems to have been an inner circle, among whom the dietetic furor worked with special violence. For the purpose of living what they considered a strictly natural life, they betook themselves to an exclusive diet of boiled wheat, and built themselves a shanty in the woods; hoping to secure long life and happiness by thus getting nearer to nature."

RECOLLECTIONS OF E. L. HATCH.

" I visited the Skaneateles Community twice, partly on business, and partly by request of a neighbor who was about to join, and wished me to join with him. I was received pleasantly and treated well. The first time, they gave me a cup of tea and bread and butter for supper. I told them I wished to fare as the rest did. They said it was usual for them to give visitors what they were accustomed to ; but they were looking forward to some reform in this respect. In the morning I noticed that some poured milk on their plates, laid a slice of bread in it, and cut it into mouthfuls before eating. Some used molasses instead of milk. There was not much of the home-feeling there. Every one seemed to be setting an example, and trying to bring all the others to it. The second time I was there I discovered there were two parties. One man remarked to another on seeing meat on the table, that he ' guessed they had been to some grave-yard.' The other said he 'did not eat dead creatures.' After supper I was standing near some men in the sitting-room, when one said to another, ' How high is your God ? ' The answer was, ' About as high as my head.' The first, putting his hand up to his breast, said, ' Mine is so high.' I concluded they were infidels."

RECOLLECTIONS OF L. VANVELZER.

" I attended a Convention of Associationists held near the Skaneateles Community in 1845, and became very much interested in the principles set forth by John A. Collins and his friends. There was much excitement at that time all through the country in regard to Association. Quite a number came from Boston and joined the Skaneateles Community. Johnson and Collins seemed to be the two leading spirits. Collins was a strong advocate of infidel principles, and was very intolerant to all religious sects; while Johnson advocated religious principles and general toleration. In becoming acquainted with these two men, I was naturally drawn toward Johnson; this created jealousy between them. Mrs. Vanvelzer and myself talked a great deal about selling out and going there; but before we had made any practical move, I began to see that there was not any unity among them, but on the contrary a great deal of bickering and back-biting. I became disgusted with the whole affair. But my wife did not see things as I did at that time. She was determined to go, and did go. At the expiration of three or four weeks I went to see her, and found she was becoming dissatisfied. In consequence of her joining them, there had been a regular quarrel detween the two parties, and it resulted in a rupture. They had a meeting that lasted nearly all night; Johnson and his party standing up for Mrs. Vanvelzer, and Collins and his party against her. Some went so far as to threaten Johnson's life. This state of things went on until they broke up, which was only a short time after Mrs. Vanvelzer left."

RECOLLECTIONS OF MRS. S. VANVELZER.

" In the winter of 1845 Mr. Collins and others associated with him lectured in Baldwinsville, where I then resided. My husband was interested in their teachings, and invited them to our house, where I had more or less conversation with them. They set forth their scheme in glowing colors, and professed that the doings of the day of Pentecost were their foundation ; and withal they flattered me considerably, telling me I was just the woman to go to the Community and help carry out their principles and build up a home for humanity.

"Well, I went ; but I was disappointed. Nothing was as represented ; but back-biting, evil-thinking, and quarreling were the order of the day. They set two tables in the same dining-room ; one provided with ordinary food, though rather sparingly ; the other with boiled wheat, rice and Graham mush, without salt or seasoning of any kind. They kept butter, sugar and milk under lock and key, and in fact almost every thing else. They had amusements, such as dancing, card-playing, checkers, etc. There were some 'affinity' affairs among them, which caused considerable gossiping. I remained there three weeks, and came away disgusted ; but firm in the belief that Christian Communism would be carried out sometime."

Allen and Orvis, the lecturing missionaries of Fourierism sent out by Brook Farm in 1847, passed through Central New York in the course of their tour, and in their reports of their experiences to the *Harbinger*, thus bewailed the disastrous effects of Collins's experiment :

"In Syracuse our meetings were almost a failure. Collins's Skaneateles 'Hunt of Harmony,' or fight to conquer a peace, his infidelity, his disastrous failure after making such an outcry in behalf of a better order of society, and the ignorance of the people, who have not intelligence enough to discriminate between a true Constructive Reform, and the No-God, No-Government, No-Marriage, No-Money, No-Meat, No-Salt, No-Pepper system of Community, but think that Collins was a 'Furyite' just like ourselves, has closed the ears of the people in this neighborhood against our words."

CHAPTER XVI.

SOCIAL ARCHITECTS.

THUS far we have been disposing of the preludes of Fourierism. Before commencing the memoirs of the regular PHALANXES (which is the proper name of the Fourier Associations), we will devote a chapter or two to general views of Fourierism, as compared with other forms of Socialism, and as it was practically developed in this country.

Parke Godwin was one of the earliest and ablest of the American expositors of Fourierism ; second only, perhaps, to Albert Brisbane. In his "*Popular View of the Doctrines of Charles Fourier*" (an octavo pamphlet of 120 pages published in 1844), he has a chapter on " Social Architects," in which he proposes the following classification :

" These daring and original spirits arrange themselves in three classes ; the merely Theoretical; the simply Practical ; and the Theoretico-Practical combined. In other words, the Social Architects whom we propose to consider, may be described as those who ideally plan the new structure of society ; those who set immediately to work to make a new structure, without any very large and comprehensive plan ; and those who have both devised a plan and attempted its actual execution.

" I. The Theoretical class is one which is most numerous, but whose claims are the least worthy of attention. [Under this head, Mr. Godwin mentions Plato, Sir Thomas More and Harrington, and discusses their imaginative projects—the Republic, Utopia and Oceana.]

" II. The Practical Architects of Society, or the Communities instituted to exemplify a more perfect state of social life. [The Essenes, Moravians, Shakers and Rappites are mentioned under this head.]

" III. The Theoretico-Practical Architects of Society, or those who have combined the enunciation of general principles of social organization with actual experiments, of whom the best representatives are St. Simon, Robert Owen and Charles Fourier. This class will extend the basis of our inquiries, and demand a more elaborate consideration."

This classification, if it had not gone beyond the popular pamphlet in which it was started, might have been left without criticism. But it is substantially reproduced in the New American Cyclopædia under the head of " Socialism," and thus has become a standard doctrine. We will therefore point out what we conceive to be its errors, and indicate a truer classification.

In the first place, from the account of St. Simon and Fourier which Mr. Godwin himself gives immediately after the last of his three headings, it is clear that they did *not* belong to the theoretico-practical class. St. Simon undertook to perfect himself in all knowledge, and for this purpose experimented in many things, good and bad ; but it does not appear that he ever tried his hand at Communism or Association of any kind. He published a book called "New Christianity," of which Godwin says:

"It was an attempt to show, what had been often before attempted, that the spirit and practice of religion were not at one; that there was a wide chasm separating the revelation from the commentary, the text from the gloss, the Master from the Disciples. Nothing could have been more forcible than its attacks on the existing church, in which the Pope and Luther received an equal share of the blows. He convicted both parties of errors without number, and heresies the most monstrous. But he did not carry the same vigor into the development of the positive portions of his thought. He ceased to be logical, that he might be sentimental. Yet the truth which he insisted on was a great one— perhaps the greatest, *viz.*, that the fundamental principle in the constitution of society, should be Love. Christ teaches all men, he says, that they are brothers; that humanity is one; that the true life of the individual is in the bosom of his race; and that the highest law of his being is the law of progress."

On the basis of this sentimentalism, St. Simon appealed most eloquently to all classes to unite—to march as one man—to inscribe on their banners, "Paradise on earth is before us!" but Godwin says:

"Alas! the magnanimous spirit which could utter these thrilling words was not destined to see their realization. The long process of starvation finally brought St. Simon to his end; but in the sufferings of death, as in the agony of life, his mind retained its calmness and sympathy, and he perished with these words of sublime confidence and hope on his lips: ' The future is ours!'

"The few devoted friends who stood round that death-bed, took up the words, and began the work of propagation. The doctrine rapidly spread; it received a more precise and comprehensive development under the expositions of Bazard and Enfantan; and a few years saw a new family, which was also a new church, gathered at Menilmontant. On its banner was inscribed, 'To each, according to his capacity, and to each capacity according to its work.' Its government took the form of a religious hierarchy, and its main political principle was the abolition of inheritance.

"It was evident that a society so constituted could not long be held together. Made up of enthusiasts, without definite principles of organization, trusting to feeling and not to science, its members soon began to quarrel, and the latter days of its existence were stained by disgusting license. St. Simon was one of the noblest spirits, but an unfit leader of any enterprise. He saw all things, says a friendly critic, through his heart. In this was his weakness; he wanted head; he wanted precise notions; he vainly hoped to reconstruct society by a sentiment; he laid the foundations of his house on sand."

What is there in all this that entitles St. Simon to a place among the theoretico-practicals? How does it appear that he "combined the enunciation of general principles of social organization with actual experiments?" His followers tried to do something; but St. Simon himself, according to this account, did absolutely nothing but write and talk; and far from being a theoretico-practical, was not even theoretical, but only sentimental!

Fourier was theoretical enough. But we look in vain through Mr. Godwin's account of him for any signs of the practical. He meditated much and wrote many books, and that is all. He was a student and a recluse to the end of his career. Instead of engaging in any practical attempt to realize his social theories, he quarreled with the only experiment that was made by his disciples during his life. Godwin says:

"A joint-stock company was formed in 1832, to realize the new theory of Association; and one gentleman, M. Baudet Dulary, member of parliament for the county of Seine and Oise, bought an estate, which cost him five hundred thousand francs (one hundred thousand dollars), for the express purpose of putting the theory into practice. Operations were actually commenced; but for want of sufficient capital to erect buildings and stock the farm, the whole operation was paralyzed; and notwithstanding the natural cause of cessation, the simple fact of stopping short after having commenced operations, made a very unfavorable impression upon the public mind. Success is the only criterion with the indolent and indifferent, who do not take the trouble to reason on circumstances and accidental difficulties.

"Fourier was very much vexed at the precipitation of his partisans, who were too impatient to wait until sufficient means had been obtained. They argued that the fact of having commenced operations would attract the attention of capitalists, and insure the necessary funds. He begged them to beware of precipitation; told them how he had been deceived himself in having to wait more than twenty years for a simple hearing, which, from the importance of his discovery, he had fully expected to obtain immediately.   All his entreaties were in vain.   They told him he had not obtained a hearing sooner because he was not accustomed to the duplicity of the world ; and confident in their own judgment, commenced without hesitation, and were taught, at the expense of their own imprudence, to appreciate more correctly the sluggish indifference of an ignorant public. "

Not only did Fourier thus wholly abstain from practical experiments himself and discourage those of others during his lifetime, but he condemned in advance all the experiments that have since been made in his name. He set the conditions of a legitimate experiment so high, that it has been thus far impossible to make a fair trial of Fourierism, and probably always will be.   How Mr. Godwin could imagine him to be one of the theoretico-practicals, we do not understand.   His system seems to us to have been as thoroughly separate from experiment, as it was possible for him to make it ; and in that sense, as far removed from the modern standards of science, as the east is from the west.   It can be defended only as a theory that came by inspiration or intuition, and therefore needs no experiment. Considered simply as the result of human lucubrations, it belongs with the *a priori* theories of the ancient world, of which Youmans says: " The old philosophers, disdaining nature, retired into the ideal world of pure meditation, and holding that the mind is the measure of the universe, they believed they could reason out all truths from the depths of the soul."

Owen, Mr. Godwin's third example, was really a theoretico-practical man ; i. e. he attempted to carry his theories into practice—with what success we have seen. Instead of classing St. Simon and Fourier with him, we should name Ballou and Cabet as his proper compeers.

Another error of Mr. Godwin is, in representing Plato as merely theoretical; meaning that the Republic, like the Utopia and Oceana, was "sketched as an exercise of the imagination or reason, rather than as a plan for actual experiment." It is recorded of Plato in the American Cyclopædia, that "he made a journey to Syracuse in the vain hope of realizing, through the new-crowned younger Dionysius, his ideal Republic." Thus, though he never made an actual experiment, he wished and intended to do so; which is quite as much as St. Simon and Fourier ever did.

Mr. Godwin seems also to underrate the Practical Architects: i. e. those that we have called the successful Communities. It is hardly fair to represent them as merely practical. The Shakers certainly have a theory which is printed in a book; and there is no reason to doubt that such thinkers as Rapp, and Bimeler of the Zoarites, and the German nobleman that led the Ebenezers, had socialistic ideas which they either worked by or worked out in their practical operations, and which would compare favorably at least with the sentimentalisms of the first French school. If St. Simon and Owen and Fourier are to be called the theoretico-practicals, such workers as Ann Lee, Elder Meacham, Rapp, and Bimeler ought at least to be called the practico-theoreticals.

Indeed these Practical Architects, who have actually given the world examples of successful Communism, have certainly contributed more to the great socialistic movement of modern times, than they have credit for in

Godwin's classification, or in public opinion.   We called attention, in the course of our sketch of the Owen movement, to the fact that Owen and his disciples studied the social economy of the Rappites, and were not only indebted to them for the village in which they made their great experiment, but leaned on them for practical ideas and hopes of success.   These facts came to us at the first without our seeking them.   But since then we have watched occasionally, in our readings of the socialistic journals and books, for indications that the Fourierist movement was affected in the same way by the silent successful examples; and we have been surprised to see how constantly the Shakers, Ebenezers &c., are referred to as illustrations of the possibilities and benefits of close Association.   We will give a few examples of what we have found.

The Dial, which was the nurse of Brook Farm and of the beginnings of Fourierism in this country, has two articles devoted to the Shakers.   One of them entitled "A Day with the Shakers," is an elaborate and very favorable exhibition of their doctrines and manner of life.   It concludes with the following observation :

"The world as yet but slightingly appreciates the domestic and humane virtues of this recluse people ; and we feel that in a record of attempts for the actualization of a better life, their designs and economies should not be omitted, especially as, during their first half century, they have had remarkable success.

The other article, entitled the "Millennial Church," is a flattering review of a Shaker book.   In it occurs the following paragraph :

"It is interesting to observe, that while Fourier in

France was speculating on the attainment of many advantages by union, these people have, at home, actually attained them. Fourier has the merit of beautiful words and theories; and their importation from a foreign land is made a subject for exultation by a large and excellent portion of our public; but the Shakers have the superior merit of excellent actions and practices; unappreciated, perhaps, because they are not exotic. 'Attractive Industry and Moral Harmony,' on which Fourier dwells so promisingly, have long characterized the Shakers, whose plans have always in view the passing of each individual into his or her right position, and of providing suitable, pleasant, and profitable employment for every one."

Miss Peabody, in the article entitled "Christ's Idea of Society," from which we quoted in a former chapter, thus refers to the practical Communities:

"The temporary success of the Hernhutters, the Moravians, the Shakers, and even the Rappites, has cleared away difficulties and solved problems of social science. It has been made plain that the material goods of life, 'the life that now is,' are not to be sacrificed (as by the anchorite) in doing fuller justice to the social principle. It has been proved, that with the same degree of labor, there is no way to compare with that of working in a Community, banded by some sufficient Idea to animate the will of the laborers. A greater quantity of wealth is procured with fewer hours of toil, and without any degradation of the laborer. All these Communities have demonstrated what the practical Dr. Franklin said, that if every one worked bodily three hours daily, there would be no necessity of any one's working more than three hours."

A writer in *The Tribune* (1845) at the end of a glowing account of the Ebenezers, says :

"The labor they have accomplished and the improvements they have made are surprising; it speaks well for the superior efficiency of combined effort over isolated and individual effort. A gentleman who accompanied me, and who has seen the whole western part of this State settled, observed that they had made more improvements in two years, than were made in our most flourishing villages when first settled, in five or six."

In *The Harbinger* (1845) Mr. Brisbane gives an account of his visit to the same settlement, and concludes as follows :

"It is amazing to see the work which these people have accomplished in two years; they have cleared large fields, and brought them under cultivation ; they have built, I should judge, forty comfortable houses, handsomely finished and painted white; many are quite large. They have the frame-work for quite an additional number prepared; they are putting up a large woolen manufactory, which is partly finished ; they have six or eight large barns filled with their crops, and others erecting, and some minor branches of manufactures. I was amazed at the work accomplished in less than two years. It testifies powerfully in favor of combined effort."

But enough for specimens. Such references to the works of the Practical Architects are scattered everywhere in socialistic literature. The conclusion toward which they lead is, that the successful religious Communities, silent and unconspicuous as they are, have been, after all, the specie-basis of the entire socialistic movement of modern times. A glimmering of this idea seems to have been in Mr. Godwin's mind, when he wrote the following:

"If, in spite of their ignorance, their mistakes, their imperfections, and their despotisms, the worst of these societies, which have adopted, with more or less favor, unitary principles, have succeeded in accumulating immeasurable wealth, what might have been done by a Community having a right principle of organization and composed of intellectual and upright men? Accordingly the discovery of such a principle has become an object of earnest investigation on the part of some of the most acute and disinterested men the world ever saw. This inquiry has given rise to our third divison, called theo-retico-practical architects of society."

The great facts of modern Socialism are these: From 1776—the era of our national Revolution—the Shakers have been established in this country; first at two places in New York; then at four places in Massachu-setts; at two in New Hampshire; two in Maine; one in Connecticut; and finally at two in Kentucky, and two in Ohio. In all these places prosperous religious Communism has been modestly and yet loudly preach-ing to the nation and the world. New England and New York and the great West have had actual Pha-lanxes before their eyes for nearly a century. And in all this time what has been acted on our American stage, has had England, France and Germany for its audience. The example of the Shakers has demon-strated, not merely that successful Communism is sub-jectively possible, but that this nation is free enough to let it grow. Who can doubt that this demonstration was known and watched in Germany from the beginning;

and that it helped the successive experiments and
emigrations of the Rappites, the Zoarites and the
Ebenezers? These experiments, we have seen, were
echoes of Shakerism, growing fainter and fainter, as the
time-distance increased. Then the Shaker movement
with its echoes was sounding also in England, when
Robert Owen undertook to convert the world to Communism; and it is evident enough that he was really a
far-off follower of the Rappites. France also had heard
of Shakerism, before St. Simon or Fourier began to
meditate and write Socialism. These men were nearly
contemporaneous with Owen, and all three evidently
obeyed a common impulse. That impulse was the
sequel and certainly in part the effect of Shakerism.
Thus it is no more than bare justice to say, that we are
indebted to the Shakers more than to any or all other
Social Architects of modern times. Their success has
been the solid capital that has upheld all the paper
theories, and counteracted the failures, of the French
and English schools. It is very doubtful whether
Owenism or Fourierism would have ever existed, or if
they had, whether they would have ever moved the practical American nation, if the facts of Shakerism had
not existed before them, and gone along with them.

But to do complete justice we must go a step further.
While we say that the Rappites, the Zoarites, the
Ebenezers, the Owenites, and even the Fourierites are
all echoes of the Shakers, we must also acknowledge
that the Shakers are the far-off echoes of the PRIMITIVE
CHRISTIAN CHURCH.

CHAPTER XVII.

FUNDAMENTALS OF SOCIALISM.

THE main idea on which Owen and Fourier worked was the same. Both proposed to reconstruct society by gathering large numbers into unitary dwellings. Owen had as clear sense of the compound economies of Association as Fourier had, and discoursed as eloquently, if not as scientifically, on the beauties and blessings of combined industry. Both elaborated plans for vast buildings, which they proposed to substitute for ordinary family dwellings. Owen's communal edifice was to be a great hollow square, somewhat like a city block. Fourier's phalanstery, on the other hand, was to be a central palace with two wings. In like manner their plans of reconstructing society differed in details, but the main idea of combination in large households was the same.

What they undertook to do may be illustrated by the history of bee-keeping. The usual way in this business is to provide hives that will hold only a few quarts of bees each, and so compel new generations to swarm and find new homes. But it has always been a problem among ingenious apiarians, how to construct compound hives, that will prevent the necessity of swarming, and either allow a single swarm to increase indefinitely, or

induce many swarms to live together in contiguous
apartments. We remember there was an invention of
this kind that had quite a run about the time of the
Fourier excitement. It was not very successful; and
yet the idea seems not altogether chimerical; for it is
known that wild bees, in certain situations, as in large
hollow trees and in cavities among rocks, do actually
accumulate their numbers and honey from generation to
generation. Owen and Fourier, like the apiarian inventors (who are proverbially unpractical), undertook to
construct, each in his own way, great compound hives
for human beings; and they had the example of the
Shakers (who may be considered the wild bees in the
illustration) to countenance their schemes.

The difference of their methods was this: Owen's
plan was based on *Communism;* Fourier's plan was
based on the *Joint-stock* principle. Both of these modes
of combination exist abundantly in common society.
Every family is a little example of Communism; and
every working partnership is an example of Joint-
stockism. Communism creates homes; Joint-stockism
manages business. Perhaps national idiosyncracies had
something to do with the choice of principles in these
two cases. *Home* is an English word for an English
idea. It is said there is no equivalent word in the
French language. Owen, the Englishman, chose the
home principle. Fourier, the Frenchman, chose the
business principle.

These two principles, as they exist in the world, are
not antagonistic, but reciprocal. Home is the center
from which men go forth to business; and business is
the field from which they go home with the spoil. Home
is the charm and stimulus of business; and business

provides material for the comfort and beauty of home. This is the present practical relation between Communism and Joint-stockism every-where. And these two principles, thus working together, have had a wonderful expansion in modern times. Every body knows what progress has been made in Joint-stockism, from the old-fashioned simple partnership, to the thousands of corporations, small and great, that now do the work of the world. But Communism has had similar progress, from the little family circle, to the thousands of benevolent institutions that are now striving to make a home of the world. Every hospital and free school and public library that is comforting and civilizing mankind, is an extension of the free, loving element, that is the charm of home. And it is becoming more and more the fashion for men to spend the best part of their lives in accumulating millions by Joint-stockism, and at last lay their treasures at the feet of Communism, by endowing great public institutions of mercy or education.

As these two principles are thus expanding side by side, the question arises, Which on the whole is prevailing and destined to prevail? and that means, which is primary in the order of truth, and which is secondary? The two great socialistic inventors seem to have taken opposite sides on this question. Owen believed that the grand advance which the world is about to make, will be into Communism. Fourier as confidently believed that civilization will ripen into universal Joint-stockism. In all cases of reciprocal dualism, there is manifestly a tendency to mutual absorption, coalescence and unity. Where shall we end? in Owenism or Fourierism? Or will a combination of both keep its place in the world hereafter, as it has done hitherto? and if so which will be primary and which secondary, and how will they be harmonized? We do not propose to answer these questions, but only to help the study of them, as we proceed with our history.

A few facts, however, may be mentioned in passing, which lead toward some solution of them. One is, that the changes which are going on in the laws of marriage, are in the direction of Joint-stockism. The increase of woman's independence and separate property, is manifestly introducing Fourierism into the family circle, which is the oldest sanctuary of Communism. But over against this is the fact, that all the successful attempts at Socialism go in the other direction, toward Communism. Providence has presented Shakerism, which is Communism in the concrete, and Owenism, which is Communism in theory, to the attention of this country in advance of Fourierism; and there are many signs that the third great socialistic movement, which many believe to be impending, will be a returning wave of Communism. All these facts together might be interpreted as indicating that Joint-Stockism is devouring the institutions of the past, while Communism is seizing the institutions of the future.

It must not be forgotten that, in representing Owen as the exponent of Communism, and Fourier as the exponent of Joint-stockism, we refer to their theoretical principles, and not at all to the experiments that have been made in their name. Those experiments were invariably compromises, and nearly all alike. We doubt whether there was ever an Owen Community that attempted unconditional Communism, even of worldly goods. Certainly Owen himself never got beyond provisional experiments, in which he held on to his land.

And on the other hand, we doubt whether there was ever a Fourier Association that came any where near carrying out Joint-stockism, into all the minutiæ of account-keeping which pure Fourierism requires. When we leave theories and attempt actual combinations, it is a matter of course that we should communize as far as we dare; that is, as far as we can trust each other; and beyond that manage things as well as we can by some kind of Joint-stockism. Experiments therefore always fall into a combination of Owenism and Fourierism.

If we could find out the metaphysical bases of the two principles represented respectively by Owen and Fourier, perhaps we should see that these practical combinations of them are, after all, scientifically legitimate. Let us search a little in this direction.

Our view is, that unity of *life* is the basis of Communism; and distinction of *persons* is the basis of Joint-stockism. Property belongs to life, and so far as you and I have consciously one life, we must hold our goods in common; but so far as distinct personalities prevail, we must have separate properties. This statement of course raises the old question of the Trinitarian controversy, viz., whether two or more persons can have absolutely the same life—which we will not now stop to discuss. All we need to say is that, according to our theory, if there is no such thing as unity of life between a plurality of persons, then there is no basis for Communism.

But the Communism which we find in families is certainly based on the assumption, right or wrong, that there is actual unity of life between husband and wife, and between parents and children. The common law of England and of most other countries recognizes only a unit in the male and female head of every family. The Bible declares man and wife to be "one flesh." Sexual intercourse is generally supposed to be a symbol of more complete unity in the interior life ; and children are supposed to be branches of the one life of their parents. This theory is evidently the basis of family Communism.

So also the basis of Bible Communism is the theory that in Christ, believers become spiritually one ; and the law, "Thou shalt love thy neighbor as thyself," is founded on the assumption that "thy neighbor" is, or should be, a part of "thyself."

In this view we can reduce Communism and Joint-stockism to one principle. The object of both is to secure property to life. Communism looks after the rights of the unitary life—call it *afflatus* if you please— which organizes families and spiritual corporations. Joint-stockism attends to the rights of individuals. Both these forms of life have rights ; and as all true rights can certainly be harmonized, Communism and Joint-stockism should find a way to work together. But the question returns after all, Which is primary and which is secondary? and so we are in the old quarrel again. Our opinion, however, is, that the long quarrel between afflatus and personality will be decided in favor of afflatus, and that personality will pass into the secondary position in the ages to come.

Practically, Communism is a thing of degrees. With a small amount of vital unity, Communism is possible only in the limited sphere of familism. With more unity, public institutions of harmony and benevolence make their appearance. With another degree of unity, Communism of external property becomes possible, as among the Shakers. With still higher degrees, Communism may be introduced into the sexual and propagative relations. And in all these cases the correlative principle of Joint-stockism necessarily takes charge of all property that Communism leaves outside.

Other differences of theory, besides this fundamental contrast of Communism and Joint-stockism, have been insisted upon by the respective partizans of Owen and Fourier; but they are less important, and we shall leave them to be exhibited incidentally in our memoirs of the Phalanxes.

CHAPTER XVIII.

LITERATURE OF FOURIERISM.

THE exposition of Fourierism in this country commenced with the publication of the "*Social Destiny of Man*," by Albert Brisbane, in 1840. It is very probable that the excitement propagated by this book, turned the thoughts of Dr. Channing and the Transcendentalists toward Association, and led to the Massachusetts experiments which we have reported. Other influences prepared the way. Religious Liberalism and Anti-slavery were revolutionizing the world of thought, and predisposing all lively minds to the boldest innovations. But it is evident that the positive scheme of reconstructing society came from France through Brisbane. Brook Farm, Hopedale, the Northampton Community and the Skaneateles Community struck out, each on an independent theory of social architecture; but they all obeyed a common impulse; and that impulse, so far as it came by literature, is traceable to Brisbane's importation and translation of the writings of Charles Fourier.

The second notable movement, preparatory to the great Fourier revival of 1843, was the opening of the *New York Tribune* to the teachings of Brisbane and the Socialists. That paper was in its first volume, but already popular and ascending towards its zenith of rivalry with the *Herald*, when one morning in the spring of 1842, it appeared with the following caption at the top of one of its columns:

"ASSOCIATION ; OR, PRINCIPLES OF A TRUE ORGANI-
ZATION OF SOCIETY.

"This column has been purchased by the Advocates of Association, in order to lay their principles before the public. Its editorship is entirely distinct from that of the *Tribune*."

By this contrivance, which might be called a paper within a paper, Brisbane became the independent editor of a small daily, with all the *Tribune's* subscribers for his readers ; and yet that journal could not be held responsible for his inculcations. It was known, however, that Horace Greeley, the editor-in-chief, was much in sympathy with Fourierism ; so that Brisbane had the help of his popularity ; though the stock-company of the *Tribune* was not implicated. Whether the *Tribune* lifted Fourierism or Fourierism lifted the *Tribune*, may be a matter of doubt ; but we are inclined to think the paper had the best of the bargain ; as it grew steadily afterward to its present dimensions, and all the more merrily for the *Herald's* long persistence in calling it "our Fourierite cotemporary ;" while Fourierism, after a year or two of glory, waned and disappeared.

Brisbane edited his column with ability for more than a year. Our file (which is defective), extends from March 28, 1842, to May 28, 1843. At first the socialistic articles appeared twice a week; after August 1842, three times a week ; and during the latter part of the series, every day.

This was Brisbane's great opportunity, and he im-

proved it. All the popularities of Fourierism—
"Attractive Industry," Compound Economies," "Democracy of Association," "Equilibrium of the Passions"
—were set before the *Tribune's* vast public from day to
day, with the art and zest of a young lawyer pleading
before a court already in his favor. Interspersed with
these topics were notices of socialistic meetings, reports
of Fourier festivals, toasts and speeches at celebrations
of Fourier's birthday, and all the usual stimulants of a
growing popular cause. The rich were enticed; the
poor were encouraged; the laboring classes were
aroused; objections were answered; prejudices were
annihilated; scoffing papers were silenced; the religious
foundations of Fourierism were triumphantly exhibited.
To show how gloriously things were going, it would
be announced on one day that "Mr. Bennett has promised us the insertion of an article in this day's *Herald*,
in vindication of our doctrines;" on the next, that "*The
Democratic* and *Boston Quarterly Reviews*, are publishing a series of articles on the system from the pen of
A. Brisbane;" on the next, that "we have obtained a
large Hall, seventy-seven feet deep by twenty-five feet
wide, in Broadway, for the purpose of holding meetings
and delivering lectures."

Perhaps the reader would like to see a specimen of
Brisbane's expositions. The following is the substance
of one of his articles in the *Tribune*, dated March, 1842;
subject—"Means of making a Practical Trial:"

"Before answering the question, How can Association
be realized? we will remark that we do not propose any
sudden transformation of the present system of society,
but only a regular and gradual substitution of a new

order by local changes or replacement. One Association must be started, and others will follow, without overthrowing any true institutions in state or church, such as universal suffrage or religious worship.

"If a few rich could be interested in the subject, a stock company could be formed among them with a capital of four or five hundred thousand dollars, which would be sufficient. Their money would be safe: for the lands, edifices, flocks, &c., of the Association, would be mortgaged to secure it. The sum which is required to build a small railroad, a steamship, to start an insurance company or a bank, would establish an Association. Could not such a sum be raised?

"A practical trial of Association might be made by appropriation from a State Legislature. Millions are now spent in constucting canals and railroads that scarcely pay for repairs. Would it endanger the constitution, injure the cause of democracy, or shock the consciences of politicians, if a Legislature were to advance for an Association, half a million of dollars secured by mortgage on its lands and personal estate? We fear very much that it might, and therefore not much is to be hoped from that source.

"The truth of Association and attractive industry could also be proved by children. A little Association or an industrial or agricultural institution might be established with four hundred children from the ages of five to fifteen. Various lighter branches of agriculture and the mechanical arts, with little tools and implements adapted to different ages, which are the delight of children, could be prosecuted These useful occupations could, if organized according to a system which we shall later explain, be rendered more pleasing and attractive than are their plays at present. Such an Association would prove the possibility of attractive industry, and that children could support themselves by their own labor, and obtain at the same time a superior industrial and scientific education. The Smithsonian bequest might be applied to such a purpose, as could have been Girard's noble donation, which has been so shamefully mismanaged.

"The most easy plan, perhaps, for starting an Association would be to induce four hundred persons to unite, and take each $1,000 worth of stock, which would form a capital of $400,000. With this sum, an Association could be established, which could be made to guarantee to every person a comfortable room in it and board for life, as interest upon the investment of $1,000; so that whatever reverses might happen to those forming the Association, they would always be certain of having two great essentials of existence—a dwelling to cover them, and a table at which to sit. Let us explain how this could be effected.

" The stockholders would receive one-quarter of the total product or profits of the Association ; or if they preferred, they would receive a fixed interest of eight per cent. At the time of a general division of profits at the end of the year, the stockholders would first receive their interest, and the balance would be paid over to those who performed the labor. A slight deviation would in this respect take place from the general law of Association, which is to give one-quarter of the profits to capital, whatever they may be; but additional inducements of security should be held out to those who organize the first Association.

" The investment of $1,000 would yield $80 annual

interest. With this sum the Association must guarantee
a person a dwelling and living; and this could be done.
The edifice could be built for $150,000, the interest
upon which, at 10 per cent., would be $15,000. Divide
this sum by 400, which is the number of persons, and
we have $37,50 per annum, for each person as rent.
Some of the apartments would consist of several rooms,
and rent for $100, others for $90, others for $80, and so
on in a descending ratio, so that about one-half of the
rooms could be rented at $20 per annum. A person
wishing to live at the cheapest rates would have, after
paying his rent, $60 left. As the Association would
raise all its fruit, grain, vegetables, cattle, &c., and as it
would economize immensely in fuel, number of cooks,
and every thing else, it could furnish the cheapest priced
board at $60 per annum, the second at $100, and the
third at $150. Thus a person who invested $1,000 would
be certain of a comfortable room and board for his interest, if he lived economically, and would have whatever
he might produce by his labor in addition. He would
live, besides, in an elegant edifice surrounded by beautiful fields and gardens.

"If one-half of the persons taking stock did not wish
to enter the Association at first, but to continue their
business in the world, reserving the chance of so doing
later, they could do so. Experienced and intelligent
agriculturists and mechanics would be found to take
their places; the buildings would be gradually enlarged,
and those who remained out, could enter later as they
wished. They would receive, however, in the mean
time their interest in cash upon their capital. A family
with two or three children could enter upon taking from
$2,000 to $2,500 worth of stock.

"We have not space to enter into full details, but we can say that the advantages and economies of combination and Association are so immense, that if four hundred persons would unite, with a capital of $1,000 each, they could establish an Association in which they could produce, by means of economical machinery and other facilities, four times as much by their labor as people do at present, and live far cheaper and better than they now can ; or which, in age or in case of misfortune, would always secure them a comfortable home.

"There are multitudes of persons who could easily withdraw $1,000 from their business and invest it in an establishment of this kind, and secure themselves against any reverses which may later overtake them. In our societies, with their constantly recurring revulsions and ruin, would they not be wise in so doing?"

With this specimen, we trust the imagination of the reader will be able to make out an adequate picture of Brisbane's long work in the *Tribune.* That work immediately preceded the rush of Young America into the Fourier experiments. He was beating the drum from March 1842 till May 1843 ; and in the summer of '43, Phalanxes by the dozen were on the march for the new world of wealth and harmony.

On the fifth of October 1843, Brisbane entered upon his third advance-movement by establishing in New York City, an independent paper called THE PHALANX, devoted to the doctrines of Fourier, and edited by himself and Osborne Macdaniel. It professed to be a monthly, but was published irregularly the latter part of its time. The volume we have consists of twenty-three numbers, the first of which is dated October 5, 1843,

and the last May 28, 1845. In the first number
Brisbane gives the following condensed statement of
practical experiments then existing or contemplated,
which may be considered the results of his previous
labors, and especially of his fourteen months *reveille* in
the *Tribune:*

"In Massachusetts, already there are three small
Associations, viz., the Roxbury Community near Boston,
founded by the Rev. George Ripley; the Hopedale Community, founded by the Rev. Adin Ballou; and the
Northampton Community, founded by Prof. Adam and
others. These Associations, or Communities, as they
are called, differ in many respects from the system of
Fourier, but they accept some of his fundamental practical principles, such as joint-stock property in real and
movable estate, unity of interests, and united domestic
arrangements, instead of living in separate houses with
separate interests. None of them have community of
property. They have been founded within the last three
years, and two of them at least, under the inspiration of
Fourier's doctrine.

"In the state of New York, there are two established
on a larger scale than those in Massachusetts : the
Jefferson County Industrial Association, at Watertown,
founded by A. M. Watson, Esq.; and another in
Herkimer and Hamilton Counties (on the line), called
the Moorhouse Union, and founded by Mr. Moorhouse. A larger Association, to be called the Ontario
Phalanx, is now organizing at Rochester, Monroe
County.

"In Pennsylvania there are several : the principal one
is the Sylvania in Pike County, which has been formed

by warm friends of the cause from the cities of New
York and Albany; Thomas W. Whitley, President, and
Horace Greeley, Treasurer. In the same county there
is another small Association, called the Social Unity,
formed principally of mechanics from New York and
Brooklyn. There is a large Association of Germans in
McKean County, Pennsylvania, commenced by the
Rev. George Ginal of Philadelphia. They own a very
extensive tract of land, over 30,000 acres we are informed, and are progressing prosperously: the shares,
which were originally $100, have been sold and are now
held at $200 or more. At Pittsburg steps are taking to
establish another.

"A small Association has been commenced in Bureau
County, Illinois, and preparations are making to establish another in Lagrange County, Indiana, which will
probably be done this fall, upon quite an extensive scale,
as many of the most influential and worthy inhabitants
of that section are deeply interested in the cause.

"In Michigan the doctrine has spread quite widely.
An excellent little paper called *The Future*, devoted
exclusively to the cause, published monthly, has been
established at Ann Arbor, where an Association is
projected to be called the Washtenaw Phalanx.

"In New Jersey an Association, projected upon a
larger scale than any yet started, has just been commenced in Monmouth County: it is to be called the
North American Phalanx, and has been undertaken by a
company of enterprising gentlemen of the city of
Albany.

"Quite a large number of practical trials are talked
of in various sections of the United States, and it is
probable that in the course of the next year, numbers

will spring into existence. These trials are upon so small a scale, and are commenced with such limited means, that they exhibit but a few of the features of the system. They are, however, very important commencements, and are small beginnings of a refoim in some of the most important arrangements of the present social order ; particularly its system of isolated households or separate families, its conflicts of interest, and its uncombined and incoherent system of labor."

The most important result of Brisbane's eighteen month's labor in the *Phalanx* was the conversion of Brook Farm to Fourierism. William H. Channing's magazine, the *Present*, which commenced nearly at the same time with the *Phalanx*, closed its career at the end of seven months, and its subscription list was transferred to Brisbane. In the course of a year after this, Brook Farm confessed Fourierism, changed its constitution, assumed the title of the *Brook Farm Phalanx*, and on the 14th of June 1845 commenced publishing the *Harbinger*, as the successor of the *Phalanx* and the heir of its subscription list. So that Brisbane's fourth advance was the transfer of the literary responsibilities of his cause to Brook Farm. This was a great move. A more brilliant attorney could not have been found. The concentrated genius of Unitarianism and Transcendentalism was at Brook Farm. It was the school that trained most of the writers who have created the newspaper and magazine literature of the present time. Their work on the *Harbinger* was their first drill. Fourierism was their first case in court. The *Harbinger* was published weekly, and extended to seven and a half semi-annual volumes, five of which were edited and printed at Brook Farm, and the last two and a half at

New York, but by Brook Farm men. Its issues at Brook Farm extend from June 14, 1845 to October 30, 1847; and at New York from November 6, 1847 to February 10, 1849. The *Phalanx* and *Harbinger* together cover a period of more than five years.

Other periodicals of a more provincial character, and of course a great variety of books and pamphlets, were among the issues of the Fourier movement; but the main vertebræ of its literature were the publications of which we have given account—Brisbane's *Social Destiny of Man*, his daily column in the *Tribune*, the monthly *Phalanx*, and the weekly *Harbinger*.

CHAPTER XIX.

THE PERSONNEL OF FOURIERISM.

ALBERT BRISBANE of course was the central man of
the brilliant group that imported and popularized
Fourierism. But the reader will be interested to see a
full tableau of the persons who were prominent in this
movement. We will bring them to view by presenting,
first, a list of the contributors to the *Phalanx* and *Harbinger*, and secondly, a condensed report of one of the
National Conventions of the Fourierists.

The indexes of the *Phalanx* and *Harbinger* (eight
volumes in all), have at their heads the names of the
principal contributors ; and their initials, in connection
with the articles in the indexes, enable us to give the
number of articles written by each contributor. Thus
the reader will see at a glance, not only the leading men
of the movement, but proximately the proportion of
influence, or at least of literature, that each contributed.
Several of the names on this list are now of world-
wide fame, and many of them have attained eminence

as historians, essayists, poets, journalists or artists. A few of them have reached the van in politics, and gained public station.

WRITERS FOR THE PHALANX AND HARBINGER.

Names.	No. of articles.	Names.	No. of articles.
John Allen,	2	Henry James,	32
Stephen Pearl Andrews,	1	Wm. H. Kimball,	1
Albert Brisbane,	56	Marx E. Lazarus,	52
Geo. H. Calvert,	1	James Russell Lowell,	2
Wm. E. Channing,	1	Osborne Macdaniel,	47
Wm. F. Channing,	1	Wm. H. Müller,	2
Wm. H. Channing,	39	C. Neidhardt,	1
Otis Clapp,	1	D. S. Oliphant,	1
J. Freeman Clarke,	1	John Orvis,	23
Joseph J. Cooke,	10	Jean M. Palisse,	16
Christopher P. Cranch,	9	E. W. Parkman,	1
George W. Curtis,	10	Mary Spencer Pease,	1
Charles A. Dana,	248	J. H. Pulte,	1
Hugh Doherty,	11	George Ripley,	315
A. J. H. Duganne,	3	Samuel D. Robbins,	1
John S. Dwight,	324	Lewis W. Ryckman,	5
George G. Foster,	7	J. A. Saxton,	1
Edward Giles,	3	James Sellers,	3
Parke Godwin,	152	Francis G. Shaw,	131
E. P. Grant,	4	Miss E. A. Starr,	5
Horace Greeley,	2	W. W. Story,	14
Frederic H. Hedge,	1	Edmund Tweedy,	7
T. W. Higginson,	10	John G. Whittier,	1
E. Ives, Jr.,	3	J. J. Garth Wilkinson,	12

Most of these writers were in the prime of youth, and Socialism was their first love. It would be interesting to trace their several careers in after time, when acquaintance with "stern reality" put another face on their early dream, and turned them aside to other pursuits. Certain it is, that the socialistic revival, barren as it was in direct fruit, fertilized in many ways the genius of these men, and through them the intellect of the nation.

NATIONAL CONVENTION.

Report from *The Phalanx* condensed.

Pursuant to a call published in the *Phalanx* and other papers, a Convention of Associationists assembled on Thursday morning, the 4th of April, 1844, at Clinton Hall, in the city of New York.

The following gentlemen were appointed officers of the Convention :

President,   George Ripley.

Vice Presidents.

A. B. Smolnikar,   Parke Godwin,   Horace Greeley,
Charles A Dana,   A. Brisbane,   Alonzo M. Watson.

Secretaries.

Osborne Macdaniel,   D. S. Oliphant.

Committee on the Roll and Finance.

John Allen,   James P. Decker,   Nathan Comstock, Jr.

Business Committee.

L. W. Ryckman,   John Allen,   Osborne Macdaniel,
George Ripley,   Horace Greeley, Albert Brisbane,
Parke Godwin,   James Kay,   Charles A. Dana,
W. H. Channing, A. M. Watson,   Solyman Brown.

Before proceeding to business, the secretary read letters addressed to the Convention by a number of societies and individuals in different parts of the United

States.   The style of these letters may be seen in a few brief extracts.   E. P. Grant wrote:

"The day is speedily coming when justice will be done to Fourier and his doctrines ; when monuments will rise from ten thousand hills, surmounted by his statue in colossal proportions, gazing upon a happy people, whose God will be truly the Lord, because they will live in spontaneous obedience to his eternal laws."

John White and others wrote:

"We behold in the science of associated industry, a new social edifice, of matchless and indescribable beauty, and true architectural symmetry!   Surely, it must be no other than that 'house not made with hands, eternal in the heavens ;' for its foundation is justice, and the superstructure, praise; in every department of which dwell peace and smiling plenty, and whose walls are every where inscribed with manifold representations of that highest Divine attribute—love."

H. H. Van Amringe wrote:

"Certainly all creation is a reflex of the mind of the Deity, and we cannot hesitate to believe that all the works of Divine wisdom are connected, as Fourier teaches, by laws of groups and series of groups.   To discover these, as observers of nature discover and combine the harmonies of astronomy, geology, botany and chemistry, should be our aim ; and this noble and heavenly employment, while it banishes want and misery from our present life—destroying the spiritual death and hell which now reign—will, under the Providence of the most High, open to us admission into the Kingdom of the Messiah, that the will of our Father may be done on earth as it is done in heaven."

And so on.   After the reading of the letters, Wm. H.

Channing, on behalf of the business committee, introduced a series of resolutions, prefacing them with a speech in the following vein :

"It is but giving voice to what is working in the hearts of those now present, and of thousands whose sympathies are at this moment with us over our whole land, to say this is a religious meeting. Our end is to do God's will, not our own ; to obey the command of Providence, not to follow the leadings of human fancies. We stand to-day, as we believe, amid the dawn of a new era of humanity ; and as from a Pisgah look down upon a promised land."

The resolutions (occupying nearly two pages of the *Phalanx*) commence with a long preamble of four *Whereases* about the designs of God in regard to universal unity, the call of Christendom and especially of the United States to forward these designs, the dreadful state of the world, &c., &c. The third resolution proposes Association on Fourier's principles of Joint-stockism, Guaranteeism, Combined Industry, Series and Groups, &c., as the panacea of human woes. The fourth resolution protests against "rash and fragmentary attempts," and advises Associationists not to undertake practical operations till they have secured the right sort of men and women and plenty of capital. The fifth resolution recommends that Associationists concentrate their efforts on experiments already commenced, in preference to undertaking new enterprises. The sixth resolution betrays a little distrust of Fourier, and an inclination to keep a certain independence of him—a symptom that the Brook Farm and Unitarian element prevailed in the business committee. They say:

"We do not receive all the parts of his theories

which in the publications of the Fourier school are denominated 'conjectural,' because Fourier gives them as
speculations, because we do not in all respects understand his meaning, and because there are parts which
individually we reject ; and we hold ourselves not only
free, but in duty bound, to seek and obey truth
wherever revealed, in the word of God, the reason of
humanity, and the order of nature. For these reasons
we do not call ourselves Fourierists ; but desire to be
always publicly designated as the Associationists of the
United States of America."

It must be borne in mind, in order to understand this
caveat, that the courtship between the Massachusetts
Socialists and the Brisbane propagandists, though very
warm, had not yet proceeded to coalescence. Brook
Farm was not yet a "Phalanx." The *Harbinger* was yet
in futuro. And Fourier's latitudinarian speculations
about marriage and sexual matters, made a difficulty for
men of Puritan blood, that was not yet disposed of. In
fact this difficulty always made a jar in the family of
American Fourierists, and probably helped on their disasters and hastened their dissolution.

The seventh resolution proposes that measures be
taken for forming a National Confederation of Associations. The eighth resolution expresses a wish for
concert of action with the Associationists of Europe,
and says :

"For this end we hereby appoint Albert Brisbane,
representative from this body, to confer with them as to
the best modes of mutual coöperation. And we assure
our brethren in Europe that the disinterestedness, ability
and perseverance with which our representative has
devoted himself to the promulgation of the doctrine of

Association in the United States, entitle him to their most cordial confidence. Through him we extend to them, with joy and trust, the right hand of fellowship; and may heaven soon bless all nations with a compact of perpetual peace."

The ninth and last resolution appoints the following gentlemen as an executive committee to edit the *Phalanx*, and to do many other things for carrying into effect the objects of the Convention:

Horace Greeley,   Parke Godwin,   James P. Decker,
Frederick Grain,   Albert Brisbane,   Wm. H Channing,
Edward Giles,   Chas. J. Hempel,   Osborne Macdaniel,
Rufus Dawes,   D. S. Oliphant,   Pierre Maroncelli,
                of the City of New York.

Solyman Brown, Leraysville Phalanx, Bradford County, Pennsylvania.

George Ripley, Brook Farm Association, West Roxbury, Massachusetts.

Alonzo M. Watson, Jefferson County Industrial Association, New York.

E. P. Grant, Ohio Phalanx, Belmont County, Ohio.

John White, Cincinnati Phalanx, Cincinnati, Ohio.

Nathan Starks, North American Phalanx, Monmouth County, New Jersey.

On the second evening of the Convention, Parke Godwin, on behalf of the business committee, reported a long address to the people of the United States. It is a powerful presentation of all the common-places of Fourierism: the defects of present society; organization of the townships into joint-stock companies; central unitary mansions and workshops; division of labor according to the law of groups and series; distribution of profit in the proportion of five-twelfths to labor, four-twelfths to capital, and three-twelfths to talent, &c. We quote the eloquent and pious conclusion, as a specimen of the whole :

"An important branch of the divine mission of our Savior Jesus Christ, was to establish the Kingdom of Heaven upon earth. He announced incessantly the practical reign of Divine wisdom and love among all men : and it was a chief aim of all his struggles and teachings to prepare the minds of men for this glorious consummation. He proclaimed the universal brotherhood of mankind ; he insisted upon universal justice, and he predicted the triumphs of universal unity. ' Thou shalt love,' he said, ' the Lord thy God with all thy mind and all thy heart, and all thy soul, and thy neighbour as thyself. On these two commandments hang all the law and the prophets.' Again : 'If ye love not one another, how can ye be my disciples ?' ' I have loved you, that you also may love one another.' ' Ye are all one, as I and my Father are one.' Again : he taught us to ask in daily prayer of our Heavenly Father, ' Thy Kingdom come, thy will be done on earth as it is in heaven.' Aye, it must be done, actually executed in all the details of life ! And again, in the same spirit his disciple said, ' Little children, love one another.' ' If you love not man, whom you have seen, how can you love God whom you have not seen ?' And in regard to the form which this love should take, the apostle Paul says, ' As the body is one, so also is Christ. For by one spirit we are all baptized into one body, whether we be Jews or Gentiles,' &c. ' That there should be no schism (disunity) in the body, but that the members should have the same care one for another ; and if one member suffer, all the members suffer with it ; or one member be honored, all the members rejoice with it.' 'Ye are members one of another.'

"These Divine truths must be translated into actual life. Our relations to each other as men, our business relations among others, must all be instituted according to this law of highest wisdom and love. In Association alone can we find the fulfillment of this duty ; and therefore we again insist that Association is the duty of every branch of the universal church. Let its views of points of doctrines be what they may ; let it hold to any creed as to the nature of man, or the attributes of God, or the offices of Christ ; we say that it can not fully and practically embody the spirit of Christianity out of an organization like that which we have described. It may exhibit, with more or less fidelity, some tenet of a creed, or even some phase of virtue ; but it can possess only a type and shadow of that universal unity which is the destiny of the church. But let the church adopt true associative organization, and the blessings so long promised it will be fulfilled. Fourier, among the last words that he wrote, describing the triumph of universal Association, exclaims, 'These are the days of mercy promised in the words of the Redeemer, Blessed are they which do hunger and thirst after righteousness, for they shall be filled.' It is verily in harmony, in Associative unity, that God will manifest to us the immensity of his providence, and that the Savior will come according to his word, in 'all the glory of his Father:' it is the Kingdom of Heaven that comes to us in this terrestrial world ; it is the reign of Christ ; he has conquered evil. *Christus regnat, vincit, imperat.* Then will the Cross have accomplished its two-fold destiny, that of consolation during the reign of sin, and that of universal banner, when human reason shall have accomplished the task imposed upon it by the Creator. ' Seek ye first the Kingdom of God and his righteousness'—the harmony of the passions in associative unity. Then will the banner of the Cross display with glory its device, the augury of victory, *In Hoc Signo Vinces;* for then it will have conquered evil, conquered the gates of hell, conquered false philosophy and national indigence and spurious civilization ; *et portæ inferi non prevalebunt.*

"To the free and Christian people of the United States, then, we commend the principle of Association ; we ask that it be fairly sifted ; we do not shrink from the most thorough investigation. The peculiar history of this nation convinces us that it has been prepared by Providence for the working out of glorious issues. Its position, its people, its free institutions, all prepare it for the manifestation of a true social order. Its wealth of territory, its distance from the political influences of older and corrupter nations, and above all the general intelligence of its people, alike contribute to fit it for that noble union of freemen which we call Association. That peculiar constitution of government, which, for the first time in the world's career, was established by our Fathers ; that signal fact of our national motto, *E Pluribus Unum*, many individuals united in one whole; that beautiful arrangement for combining the most perfect independence of the separate members with complete harmony and strength in the federal heart— is a rude outline and type of the more scientific and more beautiful arrangement which we would introduce into all the relations of man to man. We would give our theory of state rights an application to individual rights. We would bind trade to trade, neighborhood to neighborhood, man to man, by the ties of interest and affection which bind our larger aggregations called States; only we would make the ties holier and more indissoluble. There is nothing impossible in this; there is nothing unpractical! We, who are represented in this Convention have pledged our sleepless energies to its accomplishment. It may cost time, it may cost trouble, it may expose us to misconception and even to abuse; but it must be done. We know that we stand on sure and positive grounds; we know that a better time must come; we know that the hope and heart of humanity is with us—that justice, truth and goodness are with us; we feel that God is with us, and we do not fear the anger of man. *The future is ours—the future is ours.* Our practical plans may seem insignificant, but our moral aim is the grandest that ever elevated human thought. We want the love and wisdom of the Highest to make their daily abode with us; we wish to see all mankind happy and good; we desire to emancipate the human body and the human soul; we long for unity between man and man in true society, between man and nature by the cultivation of the earth, and between man and God, in universal joy and religion."

After this address, Mr. Ripley of Brook Farm made a speech, and Mr. Solyman Brown of the Leraysville Phalanx recited "a very beautiful pastoral, entitled, A Vision of the Future." Here occured a little episode that brought our old friends of the Owenite wing of Socialism on the scene; not, however, altogether harmonically. The report says:

"A delegation of English Socialists, from a society in

this city, presented itself. The gentlemen composing the delegation, demanded seats as members of the Convention. The call of the Convention was read, and they were asked if they could unite with the Convention according to the terms of the call, as 'friends of Association based on the principles of Charles Fourier.' This they said they could not do, as they differed with the partisans of Fourier in fundamental principles, and particularly in regard to religion and property. They held to community of property, and did not accept our views of a Providential and Divine social order. They were informed that the objects of the Convention were of a special and business character, and that a controversy and discussion of principles could not be entered into. Their claim to sit as members of the Convention was therefore denied: but they were allowed freely to express their opinions, and treated with the utmost courtesy, without reply."

Many "admirable addresses" continued to be delivered; among which one of Mr. Channing's is mentioned, and one of Charles A. Dana's is reported in full. He spoke as the representative of Brook Farm. We cull a few broken paragraphs:

" As a member of the oldest Association in the United States, I deem it my duty to make some remarks on the practical results of the system. We have an Association at Brook Farm, of which I now speak from my own experience. We have there abolished domestic servitude. This institution of domestic servitude was one of the first considerations ; it gave one of the first impulses to the movement at Brook Farm. It seemed that a continuance in the relations which it established, could not possibly be submitted to. It was a deadly sin—a thing to be escaped from. Accordingly it was escaped from, and we have now for three years lived at Brook Farm and have carried on all the business of life without it. At Brook Farm they are all servants of each other ; no man is master. We do freely, from the love of it, with joy and thankfulness, those duties which are usually discharged by domestics. The man who performs one of these duties—he who digs a ditch or executes any other repulsive work, is not at the foot of the social scale; he is at the head of it. Again we have in Association established a natural system of education ; a system of education which does justice to every one ; where the children of the poor receive the integral development of all their faculties, as far as the means of Association in its present condition will permit. Here we claim to have made an advance upon civilized society.

"Again, we are able already, not only to assign to manual labor its just rank and dignity in the scale of human occupations, but to insure to it its just reward. And here also, I think, we may humbly claim that we have made some advance upon civilized society. In the best society that has ever been in this world, with very small exceptions, labor has never had its just reward. Every where the gain is to the pocket of the employer. He makes the money. The laborer toils for him and is his servant. The interest of the laborer is not consulted in the arrangements of industry ; but the whole tendency of industry is perpetually to disgrace the laborer, to grind him down and reduce his wages, and to render deceit and fraud almost necessary for him. And all for the benefit of whom ? For the benefit of our excellent monopolists, our excellent companies, our excellent employers. The stream all runs into their pockets, and not one little rill is suffered to run into the pockets of those who do the work. Now in Association already we have changed all this ; we have established a true relation between labor and the people, whereby the labor is done, not entirely for the benefit of the capitalist, as it is in civilized society, but for the mutual benefit of the laborer and the capitalist. We are able to distribute the results and advantages which accrue from labor in a joint ratio.

"These, then, very briefly and imperfectly stated, are the practical, actual results already attained. In the first place we have abolished domestic servitude ; in the second place, we have secured thorough education for all ; and in the third place, we have established justice to the laborer, and ennobled industry. * * * Two or three years ago we began our movement at Brook Farm, and propounded these few simple propositions, which I say are here proven. All declared it to be a scheme of fanaticism. There was universal skepticism. No one believed it possible that men could live together in such relations. Society, it was said, had always lived in a state of competition and strife between man and man ; and when told that it was possible to live otherwise, no one received the proposition except with scorn and ridicule. But in the experience of two or three years, we maintain that we have by actual facts, by practical demonstration, proven this, viz.: that harmonious relations, relations of love and not of selfishness and mutual conflict, relations of truth and not of falsehood, relations of justice and not of injustice, are possible between man and man."

At noon on Saturday the last resolution was adopted,

and the Convention was about to adjourn, when Mr. Channing rose and addressed the assembly, as follows :

"Mr. President and brother Associationists: We began our meeting with calling to mind, as in the presence of God, our solemn privileges and responsibilities. We can not part without invoking for ourselves, each other, our friends everywhere, and our race, a blessing. If this cause in which we are engaged, is one of mere human device, the emanation of folly and self, may it utterly fail ; it will then utterly fail. But if, as we believe, it is of God, and, making allowance for human limitations, is in harmony with the Divine will, may it go on, as thus it must, conquering and to conquer. Those of us who are active in this movement have met, and will meet with suspicion and abuse. It is well! well that critical eyes should probe the schemes of Association to the core, and if they are evil, lay bare their hidden poison; well that in this fiery ordeal the sap of our personal vanities and weaknesses should be consumed. We need be anxious but on one account; and that is lest we be unworthy of this sublime reform. Who are we, that we should have the honor of giving our lives to this grandest of all possible human endeavors, the establishment of universal unity, of the reign of heaven on earth? Truly 'out of the mouths of babes and sucklings has the Lord ordained strength.' Kings and holy men have desired to see the things we see, and have not been able. Let our desire be, that our imperfections, our unfaithfulness, do not hinder the progress of love and truth and joy."

The Convention then united in prayer, and parted with the benediction, " Glory to God in the highest, and on earth, peace, good will toward men."

But this was not the end. That last day of the Convention was also the anniversary of Fourier's birthday, and in the evening the members held a festival at the Apollo Saloon. "The repast was plain and simple, but the intellectual feast and the social communion were delightful." The regular toasts, announced and probably prepared by Mr. Channing, were to the memory of Fourier, and to each of the twelve passions which, according to Fourier, constitute the active forces of human nature. "Soul-stirring speeches" followed each toast. Mr. Dana responded to the toast for friendship, and at the close of his speech Mr. Macdaniel proposed that the toast be repeated with clasped hands. "This proposition was instantly accepted, and with a burst of enthusiasm every man rose, and locking hands all round the table, the toast was repeated by the whole company, producing an electric thrill of emotion through every nerve."

Mr Godwin compared the present prospects of Association to the tokens of approaching land which cheered the drooping spirits of the crew of Columbus. The friends from Brook Farm were the birds, and those from other places the flowers that floated on the waves.

Mr. Ripley said, "Our friend has compared us to birds. Well, it is true we have a good deal of singing, though not a great deal to eat ; and we have very small nests. (Laughter.) Our most appropriate emblem is the not very beautiful or magnificent, but the very useful and respectable barn-yard fowl ! for we all have to scratch for a living !

"Mr. Brisbane pronounced an enthusiastic and hearty tribute of his gratitude, esteem and respect for Horace Greeley, for the manly, independent, and generous support he had given to the cause from its infancy to the present day; and closed by saying—

"He (Mr. Greeley), has done for us what we never could have done. He has created the cause on this continent. He has done the work of a century. Well then, I will give [as a toast], 'One Continent and One Man!'

Mr. Greeley returned his grateful thanks for what he said was the extravagant eulogium of his partial friend, and continued:

"When I took up this cause, I knew that I went in the teeth of many of my patrons, in the teeth of prejudices of the great mass, in the teeth of religious prejudices; for I confess I had a great many more clergymen on my list before, than I have now, as I am sorry to say, for had they kept on, I think I could have done them a little good. (Laughter.) But in the face of all this, in the face of constant advices, 'Don't have any thing to do with that Mr. Brisbane,' I went on. 'Oh!' said many of my friends, 'consider your position —consider your influence.' 'Well,' said I, 'I shall endeavor to do so, but I must try to do some good in the meantime, or else what is the use of the influence.' (Cheers.) And thus I have gone on, pursuing a manly and at the same time a circumspect course, treading wantonly on no man's prejudice, telling on the contrary, universal man, I will defer to your prejudices, as far as I can consistently with duty; but when duty leads me, you must excuse my stepping on your corn, if it be in the way." (Cheers.)

And so they went on with toasts and speeches and letters from distinguished outsiders—one, by the way, from Archbishop Hughes, courteously declining an invitation to attend—till the twelve o'clock bell warned them of the advent of holy time, and so they separated.

A notable thing in this great demonstration was the intense *religious* element that pervaded it. The Convention was opened and closed with prayers and Christian doxologies. The letters and addresses abounded in quotations from scripture, always laboring to identify Fourierism with Christianity. Even the jollities of the festival at the Apollo Saloon could not commence till a blessing had been asked.

These manifestations of religious feeling were mainly due to the presence of the Massachusetts men, and especially to the zeal of William H. Channing. He never forgot his religion in his enthusiasm for Socialism.

It would be easy to ridicule the fervor and assurance of the actors in this enthusiastic drama, by comparing their hopes and predictions with the results. But for our part we hold that the hopes and predictions were true, and the results were liars. Mistakes were made as to the time and manner of the blessings foreseen, as they have been made many times before and since: but the inspiration did not lie.

We have had a long succession of such enthusiasms in this country. First of all and mother of all, was the series of Revivals under Edwards, Nettleton and Finney, in every paroxysm of which the Millennium seemed to be at the door. Then came Perfectionism, rapturously affirming that the Millennium had already begun. Then came Millerism, reproducing all the excitements and hopes that agitated the Primitive Church just before the Second Advent. Very nearly coïncident with the crisis of this last enthusiasm in 1843, came this Fourier revival, with the same confident predictions of the coming of Christ's kingdom, and the same mistakes as to time and manner. Since then Spiritualism has gone through the same experience of brilliant prophecies and practical failures. We hold that all these enthusiasms are manifestations, in varied phase, of one great afflatus, that takes its time for fulfillment more leisurely than suits the ardor of its mediums, but inspires them with heart-prophecies of the good time coming, that are true and sure.

HORACE GREELEY'S POSITION.

The reader will observe that in the final passage of compliments between Messrs. Brisbane and Greeley at the Apollo festival, there is a clear answer to the question, Who was next in rank after Brisbane in the propagation of Fourierism in this country ? As there is much confusion in the public memory on this important point in the *personnel* of Fourierism, we will here make a note of the principal facts in the Fourieristic history of the *Tribune:*

A prominent New England journal in an elaborate obituary on the late Henry J. Raymond, after mentioning that he was an efficient assistant of Mr. Greeley on the *Tribune,* from the commencement of that paper in 1841 till he withdrew and took service on the *Courier and Enquirer,* went on to say :

" It was at the time of Mr. Raymond's withdrawal from it, that the *Tribune,* which was speedily joined by George Ripley and Charles A. Dana, fresh from Brook Farm, had its Fourieristic phase."

The mistakes in this paragraph are remarkable, and ought not to be allowed any chance of getting into history.

In the first place Ripley and Dana did not thus immediately succeed Raymond on the *Tribune*. The American Cyclopædia says that Raymond left the *Tribune* and joined Webb on the *Courier and Enquirer* in 1843. But Ripley and Dana retained their connection with Brook Farm till October 30, 1847, and continued to edit the *Harbinger* in New York till February 10, 1849, as we know by the files of that paper in our possession. They could not have joined the *Tribune* before the first of these dates, and probably did not till after the last; so that there was an interval of from three to six years between Raymond's leaving and their joining the *Tribune*.

But the most important error of the above quoted paragraph is its implication that the " Fourieristic phase" of the *Tribune* was after Raymond left it, and was owing to the advent of Ripley and Dana "fresh from Brook Farm." The truth is, that the *Tribune* had become the organ of Mr. Brisbane, the importer of Fourierism, in March 1842, less than a year from its commencement (which was on April 10, 1841); and of course had its " Fourieristic phase" while Raymond was employed on it, and in fact before Ripley and Dana had been converted to Fourierism. Brook Farm, be it ever remembered, was originally an independent Yankee experiment, started in 1841 by the suggestion of Dr. Channing, and did not accept Fourierism till the winter of 1843—4. During the entire period of Brisbane's promulgations in the *Tribune*, which lasted more than a year, and which manifestly caused the great Fourier excitement of 1843, Brook Farm had nothing to do with Fourierism, except as it was being carried away with the rest of the world, by Brisbane and the *Tribune*. Thus it is certain that Ripley and Dana did not bring Fourierism into the *Tribune*, but on the contrary received Fourierism from the *Tribune*, during the very period when Raymond was assisting Greeley. When they joined the *Tribune* in 1847—9, Fourierism was in the last stages of defeat, and the most that they or Greeley or any body else did for it after that, was to help its retreat into decent oblivion.

The obituary writer probably fell into these mistakes by imagining that the controversy between Greeley and Raymond, which occurred in 1846, while Raymond was employed on the *Courier and Enquirer*, was the principal "Fourieristic phase" of the *Tribune*. But this was really an after-affair, in which Greeley fought on the defensive as the rear-guard of Fourierism in its failing fortunes ; and even this controversy took place before Brook Farm broke up; so that Ripley and Dana had nothing to do with it.

The credit or responsibility for the original promulgation of Fourierism through the *Tribune*, of course does not belong to Mr. Raymond ; though he was at the time (1842) Mr. Greeley's assistant. But neither must it be put upon Messrs. Ripley and Dana. It belongs exclusively to Horace Greeley. He clearly was Brisbane's other and better half in the propagation of Fourierism. For practical devotion, we judge that he deserves even the *first* place on the roll of honor. We doubt whether Brisbane himself ever pledged his property to Association, as Greeley did in the following address, published in the *Harbinger*, October 25, 1845 :

"As one Associationist who has given his efforts and means freely to the cause, I feel that I have a right to speak frankly. I know that the great number of our believers are far from wealthy; yet I know that there is wealth enough in our ranks, if it were but devoted to it, to give an instant and resistless influence to the cause. A few thousand dollars subscribed to the stock of each existing Association would in most cases extinguish the mortgages on its property, provide it wlth machinery and materials, and render its industry immediately productive and profitable. Then manufacturing invention and skill would fearlessly take up their abode with our infant colonies; labor and thrift would flow thither, and a new and brighter era would dawn upon them. Fellow Associationists! *I* shall do whatever I can for the promotion of our common cause; to it whatever I have or may hereafter acquire of pecuniary ability is devoted: may I not hope for a like devotion from you?

"H. G."

CHAPTER XX.

THE SYLVANIA ASSOCIATION.

THIS was the first of the PHALANXES. The North American was the last. These two had the distinction of metropolitan origin; both being colonies sent forth by the socialistic schools of New York and Albany. The North American appears to have been Mr. Brisbane's *protege*, if he had any. Mr. Greeley seems to have attached himself to the Sylvania. His name is on its list of officers, and he gives an account of it in his "Recollections," as one of the two Phalanxes that issued from New York City. In the following sketch we give the rose-color first, and the shady side afterward. Indeed this will be our general method of making up the memoirs of the Phalanxes.

The first number of Brisbane's paper, the *Phalanx*, (October 5, 1843) gives the following account of the Sylvania :

"This Association has been formed by warm friends of the cause from the cities of New York and Albany. Thomas W. Whitley is President, and Horace Greeley, Treasurer. Operations were commenced in May last, and have already proved incontestably the great advantages of Association ; having thus far more than fulfilled the most sanguine hopes of success of those engaged in the enterprise. Temporary buildings have been erected, and the foundation laid of a large edifice; a great deal of land has been cleared, and a saw- and grist-mill on the premises when purchased, have been put in excellent repair ; several branches of industry, shoe-making particularly, have been established, and the whole concern is now in full operation. Upwards of one hundred and fifty persons, men, women and children, are on the domain, all contented and happy, and much gratified with their new mode of life, which is new to most of the members as a country residence, as well as an associated household ; for nearly all the mechanics formerly resided in cities, New York and Albany principally. In future numbers we will give more detailed accounts of this enterprising little Association. The following is a description of its location and soil :

"The Sylvania domain consists of 2,300 acres of arable land, situated in the township of Lackawaxen, County of Pike, State of Pennsylvania. It lies on the Delaware river, at the mouth of the Lackawaxen creek, fourteen miles from Milford, about eighty-five miles in a straight line west by north of New York City (by stage route ninety-four, and by New York and Erie Railroad to Middletown, one hundred and ten miles ; seventy-four of which are now traversed by railroad). The railroad will certainly be carried to Port Jervis, on the Delaware, only fifteen miles below the domain ; certainly if the Legislature of the State will permit. The Delaware and Hudson Canal now passes up the Delaware directly across from the domain, affording an unbroken water communication with New York City ; and the turnpike from Milford, Pennsylvania, to Owego,

New York, bounds on the south the lands of the Association, and crosses the Delaware by a bridge about one mile from the dwellings. The domain may be said, not very precisely, to be bounded by the Delaware on the north, the Lackawaxen on the west, the Shoholy on the east, and the turnpike on the south.

"The soil of the domain is a deep loam, well calculated for tillage and grazing. About one hundred acres had been cleared before the Association took possession of it ; the remainder is thinly covered with the primitive forest; the larger trees having been cut off of a good part of it for timber. Much of it can be cleared at a cost of six dollars per acre. Abundance of timber remains on it for all purposes of the Association. The land lies in gentle sloping ridges, with valleys between, and wide, level tables at the top. The general inclination is to the east and south. There are very few acres which can not be plowed after clearing.

"Application for membership, to be made (by letter, post paid), to Thomas W. Whitley, Esq., President, or to Horace Greeley, Esq., New York."

The Executive officers issued a pamphlet soon after the commencement of operations, from which we extract the following:

"This Association was formed early in 1843, by a few citizens of New York, mainly mechanics, who, deeply impressed with the present defective, vice-engendering and ruinous system of society, with the wasteful complication of its isolated households, its destructive competition and anarchy in industry, its constraint of millions to idleness and consequent dependence or famine for want of employment, and its failure to secure education and devolopment to the children growing up all around and among us in ignorance and vice, were impelled to immediate and energetic action in resistance to these manifold and mighty evils. Having earnestly studied the system of industrial organization and social reform propounded by Charles Fourier, and been led to recognize in it a beneficent, expansive and practical plan for the melioration of the condition of man and his moral and intellectual elevation, they most heartily adopted that system as the basis and guide of their operations. Holding meetings from time to time, and through the press informing the public of their enterprise and its objects, their numbers steadily increased; their organization was perfected; explorations with a view to the selection of a domain were directed and made; and in the last week of April a location was finally determined on and its purchase effected. During the first week in May, a pioneer division of some forty persons entered upon the possession and improvement of the land. Their number has since been increased to nearly sixty, of whom over forty are men, generally young or in the prime of life, and all recognizing labor as the true and noble destiny of man on earth. The Sylvania Association is the first attempt in North America to realize in practice the vast economies, intellectual advantages and social enjoyments resulting from Fourier's system.

" Any person may become a stockholder by subscribing for not less than one share ($25); but the council, having as yet its head-quarters in New York, is necessarily entrusted with power to determine at what time and in what order subscribers and their families can be admitted to resident membership on the domain. Those who are judged best calculated to facilitate the progress of the enterprise must be preferred; those with large

families unable to labor must await the construction of
buildings for their proper accommodation; while such as
shall, on critical inquiry, be found of unfit moral character or debasing habits, can not be admitted at all.
This, however, will nowise interfere with their ownership in the domain; they will be promptly paid the
dividends on their stock, whenever declared, the same
as resident members.

"The enterprise here undertaken, however humble in
its origin, commends itself to the respect of the
skeptical and the generous coöperation of the philanthropic. Its consequences, should success (as we can
not doubt it will) crown our exertions, must be far-
reaching, beneficent, unbounded. It aims at no
aggrandizement of individuals, no upbuilding or overthrow of sect or party, but at the founding of a new,
more trustful, more benignant relationship between
capital and labor, removing discord, jealousy and hatred,
and replacing them by concord, confidence and mutual
advantage. The end aimed at is the emancipation of
the mass; of the depressed toiling millions, the slaves of
necessity and wretchedness, of hunger and constrained
idleness, of ignorance, drunkenness and vice; and their
elevation to independence, moral and intellectual development; in short, to a true and hopeful manhood. This
enterprize now appeals to the lovers of the human race
for aid; not for praises, votes or alms, but for coöperation in rendering its triumph signal and speedy. It
asks of the opulent and the generous, subscriptions to its
stock, in order that its lands may be promptly cleared
and improved, its buildings erected, &c.; as they must be
far more slowly, if the resident members must devote
their energies at once and henceforth to the providing,

under the most unfavorable circumstances, of the entire means of their own subsistence. Subscriptions are solicited, at the office of the Association, 25 Pine street, third story.

"THOS. W. WHITLEY, President; J. D. PIERSON, Vice President; HORACE GREELEY, Treasurer; J. T. S. SMITH, Secretary."

After this discourse, the pamphlet presents a constitution, by-laws, bill of rights, &c., which are not essentially different from scores of joint-stock documents which we find, not only in the records of the Fourier epoch, but scattered all along back through the times of Owenism. The truth is, the paper constitutions of nearly all the American experiments, show that the experimenters fell to work, only under the *impulse*, not under the *instructions*, of the European masters. Yankee tinkering is visible in all of them. They all are shy, on the one hand, of Owen's flat Communism (as indeed Owen himself was,) and on the other, of Fourier's impracticable account-keeping and venturesome theories of "passional equilibrium." The result is, that they are all very much alike, and may all be classed together as attempts to solve the problem, How to construct a *home* on the joint-stock principle; which is much like the problem, How to eat your cake and keep it too.

For the shady side, Macdonald gives us a Dialogue which, he says, was written by a gentleman who was a member of the Sylvania Association from beginning to end. It is not very artistic, but shrewd and interesting. We print it without important alteration. The curious reader will find entertainment in comparing its descriptions of the Sylvania domain with those given in the official documents above. In this case as in many others, views taken before and after trial, are as different as summer and winter landscapes.

TALK ABOUT THE SYLVANIA ASSOCIATION.

B.—Good morning, Mr. A. I perceive you are busy among your papers. I hope we do not disturb you?

A.—Not in the least, sir. I am much pleased to meet you.

B.—I wish to introduce to you my friend Mr. C. He is anxious to learn something concerning the experiment in which you were engaged in Pike County, Pennsylvania, and I presumed that you would be willing to furnish him with the desired information.

A.—I suppose, Mr. C., like many others, you are doubtful about the correctness of the reports you have heard concerning these Associations.

C.—Yes, sir: but I am endeavoring to discover the truth, and particularly in relation to the causes which produce so many failures. I find thus far in my investigations, that the difficulties which all Associations have to contend with, are very similar in their character. Pray, sir, how and where did the Sylvania Association originate?

A.—It originated partly in New York City and partly in Albany, in the winter of 1842—3. We first held meetings in Albany, and agitated the subject of Socialism till we formed an Association. Our original object was to read and explain the doctrines of Charles Fourier, the French Socialist; to have lectures delivered, and arouse public attention to the consideration of those social questions which appeared to us, in our new-born zeal, to have an important bearing upon the present, and more especially upon the future welfare of the human family. In this we partly succeeded, and had arrived at the point where it appeared necessary for us to think of practically carrying out those splendid views which we had hitherto been dreaming and talking about. Hearing of a similar movement going on in New York City, we communicated with them and ascertained that they thought precisely as we did concerning immediate and practical operations. After several communications the two bodies united, with a determination to vent their enthusiasm upon the land. Our New York friends appointed a committee of three persons to select a desirable location, and report at the next meeting of the Society.

C.—What were the qualifications of the men who were appointed to select the location? I think this very important.

A.—One was a landscape painter, another an industrious cooper, and the third was a homœopathic doctor!

C.—And not a farmer among them! Well, this must have been a great mistake. At what season did they go to examine the country?

A.—I think it was in March; I am sure it was before the snow was off the ground.

C.—How unhappy are the working classes in having so little patience. Every thing they attempt seems to fail because they will not wait the right time. Had you any capitalists among you?

A.—No; they were principally working people, brought up to a city life.

C.—But you encouraged capitalists to join your society?

A.—Our constitution provided for them as well as

laborers. We wished to combine capital and labor, according to the theory laid down by Charles Fourier.

C.—Was his theory the society's practice?

A.—No; there was infinite difference between his theory and our practice. This. is generally the case in such movements, and invariably produces disappointment and unhappiness.

C.—Does this not result from ignorance of the principles, or a want of faith in them?

A.—To some extent it does. If human beings were passive bodies, and we could place them just where we pleased, we might so arrange them that their actions would be harmonious. But they are not so. We are active beings; and the Sylvanians were not only very active, but were collected from a variety of situations least likely to produce harmonious beings. If we knew mathematically the laws which regulate the actions of human beings, it is possible we might place all men in true relation to each other.

C.—Working people seem to know no patience other than that of enduring the everlasting toil to which they are brought up. But about the committee which you say consisted of an artist, mechanic and a doctor ; what report did they make concerning the land?

A.—They reported favorably of a section of land in Pike County, Pennsylvania, consisting of about 2,394 acres, partly wooded with yellow pine and small oak trees, with a soil of yellow loam without lime. It was well watered, had an undulating surface, and was said to be elevated fifteen hundred feet above the Hudson river. To reach it from New York and Albany, we had to take our things first to Rondout on the Hudson, and thence by canal to Lackawanna ; then five miles up hill on a

bad stony road.   [In the description on p. 234 the canal
is said to be "*directly across from* the domain."]   There
was plenty of stone for building purposes lying all over
the land.   The soil being covered with snow, the
committee did not see it, but from the small size of
the trees, they probably judged it would be easily
cleared, which would be a great advantage to city-
choppers.   Nine thousand dollars was the price demanded for this place, and the society concluded to
take it.

C.—What improvements were upon it, and what were
the conditions of sale ?

A.—There were about thirty acres planted with rye,
which grain, I understood, had been successively planted
upon it for six years without any manure.   This was
taken as a proof of the strength of the soil ; but when we
reaped, we were compelled to rake for ten yards on each
side of the spot where we intended to make the bundle,
before we had sufficient to tie together.   There were
three old houses on the place ; a good barn and cow-
shed ; a grist-mill without machinery, with a good stream
for water-power ; an old saw-mill, with a very indifferent
water-wheel.   These, together with several skeletons of
what had once been horses, constituted the stock and
improvements.   We were to pay $1,000 down in cash ;
the owner was to put in $1,000 as stock, and the balance
was to be paid by annual instalments.

C.—How much stock did the members take ?

A.—To state the exact amount would be somewhat
difficult ; for some who subscribed liberally at first,
withdrew their subscriptions, while others increased
them.   On examining my papers, I reckon that in
Albany there were about $4,500 subscribed in money

and useful articles for mechanical and other purposes. In New York I should estimate that about $6,000 were subscribed in like proportions.

C.—When did the members proceed to the domain, and how did they progress there?

A.—They left New York and Albany for the domain about the beginning of May; and I find from a table I kept of the number of persons, with their ages, sex and occupations, that in the following August there were on the place twenty-eight married men, twenty-seven married women, twenty-four single young men, six single young women, and fifty-one children; making a total of one hundred and thirty-six individuals. These had to be closely packed in three very indifferent two-story frame houses. The upper story of the grist-mill was devoted to as many as could sleep there. These arrangements very soon brought trouble. Children with every variety of temper and habits, were brought in close contact, without any previous training to prepare them for it. Parents, each with his or her peculiar character and mode of educating children, long used to very different accommodations, were brought here and literally compelled to live like a herd of animals. Some thought their children would be taken and cared for by the society, as its own family; while others claimed and practiced the right to procure for their children all the little indulgences they had been used to. Thus jealousies and ill-feelings were created, and in place of that self-sacrifice and zealous support of the constitution and officers, to which they were all pledged (I have no doubt by some in ignorance), there was a total disregard of all discipline, and a determination in each to have the biggest share of all things going, except hard labor, which was very unpopular with a certain class. Aside from the above, had we been carefully selected from families in each city, and had we been found capable of giving up our individual preferences to accomplish the glorious object we had in view, what had we to experiment upon? In my opinion, a barren wilderness; not giving the slightest prospect that it would ever generously yield a return for the great sacrifices we were making upon it. The land was cold and sterile, apparently incapable of supporting the stunted pines which looked like a vast collection of barbers' poles upon its surface. I will give you one or two illustrations of the quality of the soil: We cut and cleared four and a half acres of what we thought might be productive soil; and after having plowed and cross-plowed it, we sowed it with buckwheat. When the crop was drawn into the barn and threshed, it yielded eleven and a-half bushels. Again, we toiled hard, clearing the brush and picking up the stones from seventeen acres of new land: we plowed it three different ways, and then sowed and harrowed it with great care. When the product was reaped and threshed, it did not yield more than the quantity of seed planted. Such experiences as these made me look upon the whole operation as a suicidal affair, blasting forever the hopes and aspirations of the few noble spirits who tried so hard to establish in practice, the vision they had seen for years.

C.—How long did the Association remain on the place?

A.—About a year and a half, and then it was abandoned as rapidly as it was settled.

C.—They made improvements while there. What were they, and who got them when the society left?

A.—We cleared over one hundred acres and fenced it in; built a large frame-house forty feet by forty, three stories high; also a two-story carpenter's-shop, and a new wagon-house. We repaired the dam and saw-mill, and made other improvements which I can not now particularize. These improvements went to the original owner, who had already received two thousand dollars on the purchase; and (as he expressed it) he generously agreed to take the land back, with the improvements, and release the trustees from all further obligations!

C.—It appears to me that your society, like many others, lacked a sufficient amount of intelligence, or they never would have sent such a committee to select a domain; and after the domain was selected, sent so many persons to live upon it so soon. Your means were totally inadequate to carry out the undertaking, and you had by far too many children upon the domain. There should have been no children sent there, until ample means had been secured for their care and education under the superintendence of competent persons.

A.—It is difficult to get any but married men and women to endure the hardships consequent on such an experiment. Single young men, unless under some military control, have not the perseverance of married men.

C.—But the children! What have you to say of them?

A.—I am not capable of debating that question just now; but I am satisfied that a very different course from the one we tried must be pursued. Better land and more capital must be obtained, and a greater degree of intelligence and subordination must pervade the people, before a Community can be successful.

Macdonald moralizes as usual on the failure. The following is the substance of his funeral sermon :

" There were too many children on the place, their number being fifty-one to eighty-five adults. Some persons went there very poor, in fact without anything, and came away in a better condition ; while others took all they could with them, and came back poor. Young men, it is stated, wasted the good things at the commencement of the experiment ; and besides victuals, dry-goods supplied by the Association were unequally obtained. Idle and greedy people find their way into such attempts, and soon show forth their character by burdening others with too much labor, and, in times of scarcity, supplying themselves with more than their allowance of various articles, instead of taking less.

" Where such a failure as this occurs, many persons are apt to throw the blame upon particular individuals as well as on the principles ; but in this case, I believe, nearly all connected with it agree that the inferior land and location was the fundamental cause of ill success.

" It was a loss to nearly all engaged in it. Those who subscribed and did not go, lost their shares ; and those who subscribed and did go, lost their valuable time as well as their shares. The sufferers were in error, and were led into the experiment by others, who were likewise in error. Working men left their situations, some good and some bad, and, in their enthusiasm, expected, not only to improve their own condition, but the condition of mankind. They fought the fight and were defeated. Some were so badly wounded that it took them many years to recover ; while others, more fortunate, speedily regained their former positions, and now thrive well in the world again. The capital expended on this experiment was estimated at $ 14,000."

The exact date at which the Sylvania dissolved is not given in Macdonald's papers, but the *Phalanx* of August 10, 1844, indicates in the following paragraph, that it was dying at that time :

" We are requested to state that the Sylvania Association, having become satisfied of its inability to contend successfully against an ungrateful soil and ungenial climate, which unfortunately characterize the domain on which it settled, has determined on a dissolution. Other reasons also influence this step, but these, and the fact that the domain is located in a thinly inhabited region, cut off almost entirely from a market for its surplus productions, are the prominent reasons. A grievous mistake was made by those engaged in this enterprise, in the selection of a domain ; but as a report on the matter is forthcoming, we shall say no more at present."

It is evident enough that this was not Fourierism. Indeed, Mr. A., the respondent in the Dialogue, frankly admits, for himself and doubtless for his associates, that their doings had in them no semblance of Fourierism. But then the same may be said, without much modification, of all the experiments of the Fourier epoch. Fourier himself would have utterly disowned every one of them. We have seen that he vehemently protested against an experiment in France, which had a cash basis of one hundred thousand dollars, and the advantage of his own possible presence and administration. Much more would he have refused responsibility for the whole brood of unscientific and starveling " picnics," that followed Brisbane's excitations.

Here then arises a distinction between Fourierism as a theory propounded by Fourier, and Fourierism as a practical movement administered in this country by Brisbane and Greeley. The constitution of a country is one thing; the government is another. Fourier furnished constitutional principles; Brisbane was the working President of the administration. We must not judge Fourier's theory by Brisbane's execution. We can not conclude or safely imagine, from the actual events under Brisbane's administration, what would have been the course of things, if Fourier himself had been President of the American movement. It might have been worse; or it might have been better. It certainly would not have been the same; for Brisbane was a very different man from Fourier. For one thing, Fourier was practically a cautious man; while Brisbane was a young enthusiast. Again, Fourier was a poor man and a worker; while Brisbane was a capitalist. Our impression also is, that Fourier was more religious than Brisbane. From these differences we might conjecture, that Fourier would not have succeeded so well as Brisbane did, in getting up a vast and swift excitement; but would have conducted his operations to a safer end. At all events, it is unfair to judge the French theory by the American movement under Brisbane. The value of Fourier s ideas is not determined, nor the hope of good from them foreclosed, merely by the disasters of these local experiments.

And, to deal fairly all round, it must further be said, that it is not right to judge Brisbane by such experiments as that of the Sylvania Association. Let it be remembered that, with all his enthusiasm, he gave warning from time to time in his publications of the

deficiencies and possible failures of these hybrid ventures; and was cautious enough to keep himself and his
money out of them. We have not found his name in
connection with any of the experiments, except the North
American Phalanx; and he appears never to have been
a member even of that; but only was recommended for
its presidency by the Fourier Association of New York,
which was a sort of mother to it.

What then shall we say of the rank-and-file that
formed themselves into Phalanxes and marched into the
wilderness to the music of Fourierism? Multitudes of
them, like the poor Sylvanians, lost their all in the
battle. To them it was no mere matter of theory or
pleasant propagandism, but a miserable "Bull Run."
And surely there was a great mistake somewhere. Who
was responsible for the enormous miscalculation of
times, and forces, and capabilities of human nature, that
is manifest in the universal disaster of the experiments?
Shall we clear the generals, and leave the poor soldiers
to be called volunteer fools, without the comfort even of
being in good company?

After looking the whole case over again, we propose
the following distribution of criticism:

1. Fourier, though not responsible for Brisbane's
administration, was responsible for tantalizing the world
with a magnificent theory, without providing the means
of translating it into practice. Christ and Paul did no
such thing. They kept their theory in the back-ground,
and laid out their strength mainly on execution. The
mistake of all "our incomparable masters" of the French
school, seems to have been in imagining that a supreme
genius is required for developing a theory, but the
experimenting and execution may be left to second-rate

men. One would think that the example of their first Napoleon might have taught them, that the place of the supreme genius is at the head of the army of execution and in the front of the battle with facts.

2. Brisbane, though not altogether responsible for the inadequate attempts of the poor Sylvanians and the rest of the rabble volunteers, must be blamed for spending all his energy in drumming and recruiting; while, to insure success, he should have given at least half his time to drilling the soldiers and leading them in actual battle. One example of Fourierism, carried through to splendid realization, would have done infinitely more for the cause in the long run, than all his translations and publications. As Fourier's fault was devotion to theory, Brisbane's fault was devotion to propagandism.

3. The rank-and-file, as they were strictly volunteers, should have taken better care of themselves, and not been so ready to follow and even rush ahead of leaders, who were thus manifestly devoting themselves to theorizing and propagandism without experience.

It may be a consolation to all concerned—officers, privates, and far-off spectators of the great "Bull Run" of Fourierism—that the cause of Socialism has outlived that battle, and has learned from it, not despair, but wisdom. We have found by it at least *what can not be done*. As Owenism, with all its disasters, prepared the way for Fourierism, so we may hope that Fourierism, with all its disasters, has prepared the way for a third and perhaps final socialistic movement. Every lesson of the past will enter into the triumph of the future.

CHAPTER XXI.

OTHER PENNSYLVANIA EXPERIMENTS.

OUR memoirs of the Phalanxes and other contemporary Associations, may as well be arranged according to the States in which they were located. We have already disposed of the Sylvania, which was the most interesting of the experiments in Pennsylvania during the Fourier epoch. Our accounts of the remaining half-dozen are not long. The whole of them may be dispatched at a sitting.

THE PEACE UNION SETTLEMENT.

This was a Community founded by Andreas Bernardus Smolnikar, whose name we saw among the Vice Presidents of the National Convention. Macdonald says nothing of it; but the *Phalanx* of April 1844, has the following paragraph :

" This colony of Germans is situated in Limestown township, Warren County, Pennsylvania; it is founded upon somewhat peculiar views and associative principles, by Andreas Bernardus Smolnikar, who was Professor of Biblical Study and Criticism in Austria, and perceiving by the signs of the times compared with prophecies of the Bible, that the time was at hand for the foundation of the universal peace which was promised to all nations, and feeling called to undertake a mission to aid in carrying out the great work thus disclosed to him, he came to America.   In the years 1838 and 1842, he published at Philadelphia five volumes in explanation of his views ; and gathering around him a body of his countrymen, during the last summer he commenced with them the Peace Union Settlement, on a tract of fertile wild land of 10,000 acres, which had been purchased."

That is all we find.   Smolnikar begun, but, we suppose, was not able to finish.   In 1845 he was wandering about the country, professing to be the "Ambassador extraordinary of Christ, and Apostle of his peace."   He called on us at Putney ; but we heard nothing of his Community.

THE MCKEAN COUNTY ASSOCIATION.

The *Phalanx*, in its first number (October 1843), announced this experiment among many others, in the following terms :

" There is a large Association of Germans in McKean County, Pennsylvania, commenced by the Rev. George Ginal of Philadelphia.   They own a very extensive tract of land, over thirty thousand acres we are informed, and are progressing prosperously.   The shares, which were originally $100, have been sold and are now held at $200 or more."

This is the first and the last we hear of the Rev. George Ginal and his thirty thousand acres.

THE ONE—MENTIAN COMMUNITY.

The name of this Community, Macdonald says, was derived from Scripture ; probably from the expression of Paul, "Be of one mind."   The *New Moral World* claimed it as an Owenite Association, "with a constitution slightly altered from Owen's outline of rational society, i. e., made a little more theological." It originated at Paterson, New Jersey, but the sect of One-Mentianists appears to have had branches in Newark, New York, Brooklyn, Philadelphia and other cities. The prominent men were Dr. Humbert and Messrs. Horner, Scott, and Hudson.

The *Regenerator* of February 12, 1844, published a long epistle from John Hooper, a member of the One-Mentian Community, giving an account in rather stilted style, of its origin, state and prospects. We quote the most important paragraphs:

"In the beginning of last year a few humble but sincere persons resolved to raise the standard of human liberty, and though limited indeed in their means, yet such as they could sacrifice they contributed for that purpose; believing that the tree being once planted, other generous spirits, filled with the same sympathy, enlightened by the same knowledge, and kindled by the same resolve. would, from time to time step forward, unite in the same holy cause, and nurture this tree, until its redeeming unction shall shed a kindred halo through the length and breadth of the land. Having made this resolve, they looked not behind them, but freely contributed of their hard-earned means, and purchased eight hundred acres of fertile wood-land, in Monroe County, Pensylvania. Their zeal perhaps overpacing their judgment, they located upon their domain several families before organizing sufficient means for their support, which necessarily produced much privation and disappointment, and which placed men and women, good and true, in a position to which human nature never ought to be exposed. But their undying faith in the truth and grandeur of social Community, strengthened them in their endeavor to overcome their disasters, and they have passed the fiery ordeal chastened and purified. Do I censure their want of foresight? Do I regret this trial? Oh, no! It but the more forcibly confirms me in my persuasion of the practicability of our system. It but the more clearly shows how persons united in a good and just cause, can and will surmount unequaled privations, withering disappointments, and unimagined difficulties, if their impulse be as pure as their object is sacred and magnificent. It shows, too, most clearly, how the humblest in society can work out their redemption, when true to one another. And moreover, it is a security that blessings so dearly purchased, will be guarded by as judicious watchfulness and jealous care, as the labor was severe and trying in producing them.

"But the land has been bought, and better still, it is paid for; and the Society stands at this moment free from debt. We have no interest nor rent to pay, no mortgage to dread; but we are free and unincumbered. The land is good, as can be testified by several persons in the city of New York, who well know it, and who are willing to bear witness of this fact to any who may or have questioned it. About sixteen acres of this land are cleared and cultivated. We have implements, some stock, and some machinery. But what is better than all, we have honest hearts, clear heads, and hardy limbs, which have passed the severest tests, battling with the huge forest, struggling with the hitherto sterile glebe, fostering the generous seed, that they may build suffering humanity a home. Who after this can be so cold as not to bid them good speed? Who so ungenerous as to

speak to their disparagement? Who so niggardly as
to withhold from them their mite? Having a fine
water-power on their domain, they are yearning for the
creation of a mill, which, at a small cost, can and will be
soon accomplished," etc.

Macdonald reports the progress and *finale* of this
experiment, with some wholesome criticisms, as follows:

"The committee appointed to select a domain, chose
the location when the ground was covered with snow.
The land was wild and well timbered, but the region is
said to be cold. Some of the soil is good, but generally
it is very rocky and barren. The society paid five
hundred dollars for some six or seven hundred acres.
Cheap enough, one would say; but it turned out to be
dear enough.

"Enthusiasm drove between thirty and forty persons
out to the spot, and they commenced work under very
unfavorable circumstances. The accommodations were
very inferior, there being at first only one log cabin on
the place; and what was worse, there was an insufficiency
of food, both for men and animals. The members
cleared forty acres of land and made other improvements; and for the number of persons collected, and the
length of time spent on the place, the work performed is
said to have been immense.

"As the land was paid for and assistance was being
rendered by the various branches of the society, there
were great anticipations of success. But it appears that
an individual from Philadelphia visited the place, constituted himself a committee of inspection, and reported
unfavorably to the Philadelphia branch; which quenched
the Philadelphia ardor in the cause. A committee was

sent on from the New York branch, and they likewise
reported unfavorably of the domain. This speedily
caused the dissolution of the Community.

"The parties located on the domain reluctantly
abandoned it, and returned again to the cities. I am
informed that one of the members still lives on the
place, and probably holds it as his own. Who has got
the deeds, it seems difficult to determine.

"This failure, like many others, is ascribed to ignorance. Disagreements of course took place ; and one
between Mr. Hudson and the New York branch, caused
that gentleman to leave the One-Mentian, and start
another Community a few miles distant. This probably
broke up the One-Mentian. It lasted scarcely a year."

THE SOCIAL REFORM UNITY.

"This Association," says Macdonald, "originated in
Brooklyn, Long Island, among some mechanics and
others, who were stimulated to make a practical attempt
at social reform, through the labors of Albert Brisbane
and Horace Greeley. Business was dull and the times
were hard ; so that working-men were mostly unem-
ployed, and many of them were glad to try any
apparently reasonable plan for bettering their condition."

Mr. C. H. Little and Mr. Mackenzie were the leading men in this experiment. They framed and printed
a very elaborate constitution ; but as Macdonald says
they never made any use of it, we omit it. One or
two curiosities in it, however, deserve to be rescued from
oblivion.

The 14th article provides that "The treasury of the
Unity shall consist of a suitable metallic safe, secured by
seven different locks, the keys of which shall be de-

posited in the keeping and care of the following officers, to wit: one with the president of the Unity, one with the president of the Advisory Council, one with the secretary general, one with the accountant general, one with the agent general, one with the arbiter general, and one with the reporter general The monies in said treasury to be drawn out only by authority of an order from the Executive Council, signed by all the members of the same in session at the time of the drawing of such order, and counter-signed by the president of the Unity. All such monies thus drawn shall be committed to the care and disposal of the Executive Council."

The 62d Article says , " The question or subject of the dissolution of this Unity shall never be entertained, admitted or discussed in any of the meetings of the same."

" Land was offered to the society by a Mr. Wood, in Pike County, Pennsylvania, at $ 1,25 per acre, and the cheapness of it appears to have been the chief inducement to accepting it. They agreed to take two thousand acres at the above rate, but only paid down $ 100. The remainder was to be paid in installments within a certain period.

" A pioneer band was formed of about twenty persons, who went on to the property : their only capital being their subscriptions of $ 50 each. The journey thither was difficult, owing to the bad roads and the ruggedness of the country.

" The domain was well-timbered land near the foot of a mountain range, and was thickly covered with stones and boulders. A half acre had been cleared for a garden by a previous settler. A small house with about four rooms, a saw-mill, a yoke of oxen, some pigs, poultry, etc., were on the place; but the accommodations and provisions were altogether insufficient, and the circumstances very unpleasant for so many persons, and especially at such a season of the year; for it was about the middle of November when they went on the ground.

"At the commencement of their labors they made no use of their constitution and laws to regulate their conduct, intending to use them when they had made some progress on their domain, and had prepared it for a greater number of persons. All worked as they could, and with an enthusiasm worthy of a great cause, and all shared in common whatever there was to share. They commenced clearing land, building bridges over the 'runs,' gathering up the boulders, and improving the habitation. But going on to an uncultivated place like that, without ample means to obtain the provisions they required, and at such a season, seems to me to have been a very imprudent step; and so the sequel proved.

"None of the leading men were agriculturists; and although it may be quite true that the soil under the boulders was excellent, yet a band of poor mechanics, without capital, must have been sadly deluded, if they supposed that they could support themselves and prepare a home for others on such a spot as that; unless, indeed, mankind can live on wood and stone.

"They depended upon external support from the Brooklyn Society, and expected it to continue until they were firmly established on the domain. In this they were totally disappointed; the promised aid never came; and indeed the subscriptions ceased entirely on the departure of the pioneers to the place of experiment.

"They continued struggling manfully with the rocks, wood, climate and other opposing circumstances, for about ten months ; and agreed pretty well till near the close, when the legislating and chafing increased, as the means decreased.

" Occasionally a new member would arrive, and a little foreign assistance would be obtained.   But this did not amount to much ; and finally it was thought best to abandon the enterprise.   Want of capital was the only cause assigned by the Community for its failure ; but there was evidently also want of wisdom and general preparation."

GOOSE-POND COMMUNITY.

It was mentioned at the close of the account of the One-Mentian Community, that a Mr. Hudson seceded and started another Association.   That Association took the domain left by the Social Reform Unity.   The locality was called " Goose Pond," and hence the name of this Community.   About sixty persons were engaged in it.   After an existence of a few months it failed.

THE LERAYSVILLE PHALANX.

Several notices of this Association occur in The *Phalanx*, from which we quote as follows :

[From the *Phalanx*, February 5, 1844.]

" An Industrial Association, which promises to realize immediately the advantages of united interests, and ultimately all the immense economies and blessings of a true, brotherly social order, is now in progress of organization near the village of Leraysville, town of Pike, county of Bradford, in the State of Pennsylvania.

" Nearly fifty thousand dollars have been subscribed to its stock, and a constitution nearly identical with that of the North American Phalanx, has received the signatures of a number of heads of families and others, who are preparing to commence operations early in the spring. Thus the books are fairly open for subscription to the capital stock, only a few thousand dollars more of cash capital being needed for the first year's expenditures.

"About fifteen hundred acres of land have already been secured for the domain, consisting of adjacent farms in a good state of cultivation, well fenced and watered, and as productive as any tract of equal dimensions in its vicinity.

"As Dr. Lemuel C. Belding, the active projector of this enterprise, and several other gentlemen who have united their farms to form the domain, are members of the New Jerusalem church, it may be fairly presumed that the Leraysville Phalanx will be owned mostly by members of that religious connection; although other persons desirous of living in charity with their neighbors, will by no means be excluded, but on the contrary be freely admitted to the common privileges of membership.

"We are very much pleased with this little Phalanx, which is just starting into existence. Rev. Dr Belding, the clergyman at the head of it, is a man of sound judgment, great practical energy, and clear views—not merely a theologian, talking only of abstract faith and future salvation. He knows that 'work is worship;' that order, economy and justice must exist on earth in the practical affairs of men, as they do wherever God's laws are carried out ; and that if men would pray in *deed*, as they do in *word*, those principles would soon be realized in this world.

"He enjoys the confidence of the people around him, and unites with them practically in the enterprise, setting an example by putting in his own land and other property, and doing his share of the LABOR."

[From the *Phalanx* March 1, 1844.]

"We learn that this Association is proceeding with its organization under favorable auspices. The most interesting practical step that has been taken is, throwing down the division fences of the farms which have been united to form the domain. How significant a fact is this! The barricades of selfishness and isolation are overthrown!

"Buried deep in the mountains of Pennsylvania, in a secluded, and as is said, beautiful valley, some honest farmers are living on their separate farms. In general they are thrifty; but they feel sensibly many evils and disadvantages to which they are subjected. The doctrines of Association reach them, and as intelligent, sincere minded men, they come together and discuss their merits. They are satisfied of their truth, and that they can live together as brethren with united interests, far better than they can separated, under the old system of divided and conflicting interests. They resolve to carry out their convictions, and to form an Association. Now how is this to be done? Simply by uniting their farms, and forming of them one domain. They do not sacrifice any interest in their property; the tenure of it only is changed. Instead of owning the acres themselves, they own the shares of stock which represent the acres, and the individual and collective interests are at once united. They are now joint-partners in a noble domain, and the interest of each is the interest of all, and the interest of all the interest of each. From unity of interests at once springs unity of feeling and unity of design; and the first sign is a destructive one; they throw down the old land-marks of division. The next will be constructive ; they will build them a large and comfortable edifice in which they can reside in true social relations.

"Now what do we gather from this? Plainly that the social transformation from isolation to Association, is a simple and easy thing, a peaceful and a practical thing, which neither violates any right nor disturbs any order.

"We understand that as soon as the spring opens, the Leraysville Phalanx is to be joined by a number of enterprising men and skillful mechanics from this city and other places."

[From the *Phalanx*, April 1, 1844.]

"The cash resources of the Phalanx, in addition to its local trade, will consist of sales of cattle, horses, boots, shoes, saddles and harness, woolen goods, hats, books of its own manufacture, paper, umbrellas, stockings, gloves, clothing, cabinet-wares, piano-fortes, tin-ware, nursery-trees, carriages, bedsteads, chairs, oil-paintings and other productions of skill and art, together with the receipts from pupils in the schools and boarders from abroad, residing on the domain.

"It need not be concealed that the intention of the founders of the Leraysville Association, is to keep up, if possible, a prevailing New Church influence in the Phalanx, in order that its schools may be conducted consistently with the views of that religious connection."

SOLYMAN BROWN, General Agent.

13 Park Place, New York.

[From the *Phalanx*, September 7, 1844.]

"We have received a paper containing an oration delivered on the Fourth of July, by Dr. Solyman Brown, late of this city, at the Leraysville Phalanx, which institution he has joined."

So far the *Phalanx* carries us pleasantly ; but here it leaves us. Macdonald tells the unpleasant part of the story thus :

"There were about forty men, women and children in the Association. Among them were seven farmers, two or three carpenters, one cabinet maker, two or three shoemakers, one cooper, one lawyer, and several doctors of physic and divinity, together with some young men who made themselves generally useful. The majority of the members were Swedenborgians, and Dr. Belding was their preacher.

"The land (about three hundred acres) and other property belonged to Dr. Belding, his sons, his brother, and other relatives. It was held as stock, at a valuation made by the owners.

"In addition to the families who were thus related, and who owned the property, individuals from distant places were induced to go there ; but for these outsiders the accommodations were not very good. Each of the seven persons owning the land had comfortable home-steads on which they lived, the estimated value of which gave them controlling power and influence. But the associates from a distance (some even from the State of Maine) were compelled to board with Dr. Belding and others, until the associative buildings could be con-structed—which in fact was never done. No doubt these invidious arrangements produced disagreements, which led to a speedy dissolution. The outsiders very soon became discontented with the management, con-ceiving that those who held the most stock, i. e., the original owners of the soil, after receiving aid from without, endeavored so to rule as to turn all to their own advantage.

" The circumstances of the property owners were improved by what was done on the place ; but the associates from a distance, whose money and labor were expended in cultivating the land and in rearing new buildings, were not so fortunate. Their money speedily vanished, and their labor was not remunerated. The land and the buildings remained, and the owners enjoyed the improvements. The whole affair came to an end in about eight months."

We hope the reader will not fail to notice how powerfully the land-mania raged among these Associations. Let us recapitulate. The Pennsylvania Associations, including the Sylvania, are credited with real estate as follows :

Acres.

The Sylvania Association had	2,394
The Peace Union Settlement "	10,000
The McKean Co. Association "	30,000
The Social Reform Unity "	2,000
The Goose-Pond Community "	2,000
The Leraysville Phalanx "	1,500
The One-Mentian Community "	800

Total for the seven Associations 48,694

It is to be observed that Northern Pennsylvania, where all these Associations were located, is a paradise of cheap lands. Three great chains of mountains and not less than eight high ridges run through the State, and spread themselves abroad in this wild region. Any one who has passed over the Erie railroad can judge of the situation. It is evident from the description of the soil of the above domains, as well as from the prices paid for them, that they were, almost without exception, mountain deserts, cold, rocky and remote from the world of business. The Sylvania domain in Pike County, was elevated 1,500 feet above the Hudson river. Its soil was " yellow loam," that would barely support stunted pines and scrub-oaks ; price, four dollars per acre. Smolnikar's Peace Union Settlement was on the ridges of Warren County, a very wild region. The Rev. George Ginal's 30,000 acres were among the mountains of McKean County, which adjoins Warren, and is still wilder. The Social Reform Unity was located in Pike County, near the site of the Sylvania. Its domain was thickly covered with stones and boulders ; price, one dollar and a quarter per acre. The Goose Pond Community succeeded to this domain of the Social Reform Unity, with its stones and boulders. The Leraysville Association appears to have occupied some respectable land ; but the *Phalanx* speaks of it as " deep buried in the mountains of Pennsylvania." The One-Mentian Community, like the Sylvania, selected its domain while covered with snow; the soil is described as wild, cold, rocky and barren ; price, five hundred dollars for seven or eight hundred acres, or about sixty-five cents per acre.

Such were the domains on which the Fourier enthusiasm vented itself. An illusion, like the *mirages* of the desert, seems to have prevailed among the Socialists, cheating the hungry mechanics of the cities with the fancy, that, if they could combine and obtain vast tracts of land, no matter where or how poor, their fortunes were made. Whereas it is well known to the wise that the more of worthless land a man has the poorer he is, if he pays taxes on it, or pays any attention to it; and that agriculture anyhow is a long and very uncertain road to wealth.

We can not but think that Fourier is mainly responsible for this *mirage*. He is always talking in grand style about vast domains—three miles square, we believe, was his standard—and his illustrations of attractive industry are generally delicious pictures of fruit-raising and romantic agriculture. He had no scruple in assigning a series of twelve groups of amateur laborers to raising twelve varieties of the Bergamot pear! And his staunch disciples are always full of these charming impracticable ruralities.

CHAPTER XXII.

THE VOLCANIC DISTRICT.

WESTERN New York was the region that responded most vigorously to the gospel of Fourierism, proclaimed by Brisbane, Greeley, Godwin and the Brook Farmers.

Taking Rochester for a center, and a line of fifty miles for radius, we strike a circle that includes the birth-places of nearly all the wonderful excitements of the last forty years. At Palmyra, in Wayne County, twenty-five miles east of Rochester, Joseph Smith in 1823 was visited by the Angel Moroni, and instructed about the golden plates from which the book of Mormon was copied; and there he began the gathering which grew to be a nation and settled Utah. Batavia, about thirty miles west of Rochester, was the scene of Morgan's abduction in 1820; which event started the great Anti-Masonic excitement, that spread through the country and changed the politics of the nation. At Acadia, in Wayne County, adjoining Palmyra, the Fox family first heard the mysterious noises which were afterward known as the "Rochester rappings," and were the beginning of the miracles of modern Spiritualism. The Rochester region has also been famous for its Revivals, and borders on what Hepworth Dixon has celebrated as the "Burnt District."

In this same remarkable region around Rochester, occurred the greatest Fourier excitement in America. T. C. Leland, writing from that city in April 1844, thus described the enthusiasm: "I attended the socialistic Convention at Batavia. The turn-out was astonishing. Nearly every town in Genesee County was well represented. Many came from five to twelve miles on foot. Indeed all western New York is in a deep, a shaking agitation on this subject. Nine Associations are now contemplated within fifty miles of this city. From the astonishing rush of applications for membership in these Associations, I have no hesitation in saying that twenty thousand persons, west of the longitude of Rochester in this State, is a low estimate of those who are now ready and willing, nay anxious, to take their place in associative unity."

Mr. Brisbane traveled and lectured in this excited region a few months before Mr. Leland wrote the above. The following is his report to the *Phalanx:*

" It will no doubt be gratifying to those who take an interest in the great idea of a Social Reform, to learn that it is spreading very generally through the State of New York. I have visited lately the central and western parts of the State, and have been surprised to see that the principles of a reform, based upon Association and unity of interests, have found their way into almost every part of the country, and the farmers are beginning to see the truth and greatness of a system of dignified and attractive industry, and the advantages of Association, such as its economy, its superior means of education, and the guaranty it offers against the indirect and legalized spoliation by those intermediate classes who now live upon their labor.

"The conviction that Association will realize Christianity practically upon earth, which never can be done in the present system of society, with its injustice, frauds, distrust, and the conflict and opposition of all interests, is taking hold of many minds and attracting them strongly to it. There is a very earnest desire on the part of a great number of sincere minds to see that duplicity which now exists between theory and practice in the religious world, done away with ; and where this desire is accompanied with intelligence, Association is plainly seen to be the means. It is beginning to be perceived that a great social reformation must take place, and a new social order be established, before Christianity can descend upon earth with its love, its peace, its brotherhood and charity. The noble doctrine propounded by Fourier, is gaining valuable disciples among this class of persons.

"I lectured at Utica, Syracuse, Seneca Falls, and Rochester, and although the weather was very unfavorable, the audiences were large. At Rochester I attended a convention of the friends of Association, interested in the establishment of the Ontario Phalanx. Men of intelligence, energy and strong convictions, are at the head of this enterprise, and it will probably soon be carried into operation. A very heavy subscription to the stock can be obtained in Rochester and the vicinity, in productive farms and city real estate, for the purpose of organizing this Association ; but, owing to the scarcity of money, it is difficult to obtain the cash capital requisite to commence operations. From the perseverance and determination of the men at the head of the undertaking, it is presumed, however, that this difficulty will be overcome. Those persons in the western part of the

State of New York, who wish to enter an Association, can not be too strongly recommended to unite with the Ontario Phalanx.

"It is very advisable that the friends of the cause should not start small Associations. If they are commenced with inadequate means, and without men who know how to organize them, they may result in failures, which will cast reproach upon the principles. The American people are so impelled to realize in practice any idea which strikes them as true and advantageous, that it will of course be useless to preach moderation in organizing Associations; still I would urgently recommend to individuals, for their own interest, to avoid small and fragmental undertakings, and unite with the largest one in their section of the country.

"Four gentlemen from Rochester and its vicinity will be engaged this winter in propagating the principles of Association by lectures etc., in western New York. At Rochester they have commenced the publication of tracts upon Association, which we trust will be extensively circulated. That city is becoming an important center of propagation, and will, we believe, exercise a very great influence, as it is situated in a flourishing region of country, inhabited by a very intelligent population.

"It must be deeply gratifying to the friends of Association to see the unexampled rapidity with which our principles are spreading throughout this vast country. Would it not seem that this very general response to, and acceptance of, an entirely new and radically reforming doctrine by intelligent and practical men, prove that there is something in it harmonizing perfectly with the ideas of truth, justice, economy and order, and those higher sentiments implanted in the soul of man, which, although so smothered at present, are awakened when the correspondences in doctrine or practice are presented to them clearly and understandingly?

"The name of Fourier is now heard from the Atlantic to the Mississippi; from the remotest parts of Wisconsin and Louisiana responsive echoes reach us, heralding the spread of the great principles of universal Association; and this important work has been accomplished in a few years, and mainly within two years, since Horace Greeley, Esq., the editor of the *Tribune*, with unprecedented courage and liberality, opened the columns of his widely-circulated journal to a fair exposition of this subject. What will the next ten years bring forth?"

Mr. John Greig of Rochester, a participator in this socialistic excitement and in the experiments that went with it, contributed the following sketch of its beginnings to Macdonald's collection of manuscripts:

"We in western New York received an account of the views and discoveries of (the to-be-illustrious) Fourier, through the writings of Brisbane, Greeley, Godwin and the earnest lectures of T. C. Leland. Those ideas fell upon willing ears and hearts then (1843), and thousands flocked from all quarters to hear, believe, and participate in the first movement.

"This excitement gathered itself into a settled purpose at a convention held in Rochester in August 1843, which was attended by several hundred delegates from the city and neighboring towns and villages. A great deal of discussion ensued as a matter of course, and some little amount of business was done. The nucleus of a society was formed, and committees for several purposes were appointed to sit in permanence, and call together future conventions for further discussions.

"I was one of the Vice Presidents of that convention, and took a decided interest in the whole movement. As there existed from the very beginning of the discussions some diversity of opinion on several points of doctrine and expediency, there arose at least four different Associations out of the constituents of said convention. Those who were most determined to follow as near the letter of Fourier as possible, were led off chiefly by Dr. Theller (of 'Canadian Patriot' notoriety), Thomas Pond (a Quaker), Samuel Porter of Holly, and several others of less note, including the writer hereof. They located at Clarkson, in Monroe County. The other branches established themselves at Sodus Bay in Wayne County, at Hopewell near Canandaigua in Ontario County, at North Bloomfield in Ontario County, and at Mixville in Alleghany County."

The Associations that thus radiated from Rochester, hold a place of peculiar interest in the history of the Fourier movement, from the fact that they made the first, and, we believe, the only practical attempt, to organize a *Confederation* of Associations. The National Convention, as we have seen, recommended general Confederation ; and its executive committee afterward, through Parke Godwin, made suggestions in the *Phalanx* tending in the same direction. The movement, however, came to nothing, and at the subsequent National Convention in October, was formally abandoned. But the Rochester group of Associations, attracted together by their common origin, actually formed a league, called the "American Industrial Union," and a Council of their delegates held a session of two days at the domain of the North Bloomfield Association, commencing on the 15th of May, 1844. The *Phalanx* has an interesting report of the doings of this Confederate Council, from which we give below a liberal extract, showing how heartily these western New Yorkers abandoned themselves to the spirit of genuine Fourierism :

FROM THE REPORT OF THE SESSION OF THE INDUSTRIAL UNION.

" *Resolved*, That it be recommended to the several institutions composing this Confederacy to adopt, as far as possible, the practice of mutual exchanges between each other ; and that they should immediately take such measures as will enable them to become the commercial agents of the producing classes in the sections of the country where the Associations are respectively located.

Classification of Industry.

" *Resolved*, That in the opinion of the council, the first step towards organization should be an arrangement of the different branches of agricultural, mechanical and domestic work, in the classes of necessity, usefulness and attractiveness. The exact category in which an occupation shall be placed, will be influenced more or less by local circumstances, and is, at best, somewhat conjectural. It will be indicated, however, with certainty, by observation and experience. In the meantime, the council take the liberty to express an opinion, that to the

Class of Necessity

belong, among others, the following, viz. : ditching, masonry, work in woolen and cotton factories, quarrying stone, brickmaking, burning lime and coal, getting out manure, baking, washing, ironing, cooking, tanning and

currier business, night-sawing and other night work,
blacksmithing, care of children and the sick, care of
dairy, flouring, hauling seine, casting, chopping wood,
and cutting timber.

Class of Usefulness.

"All mechanical trades not mentioned in the class
of necessity ; agriculture, school-teaching, book-keeping,
time of directors while in session, other officers acting in
an official capacity, engineering, surveying and mapping,
store-keeping, gardening, rearing silk-worms, care of
stock, horticulture, teaching music, housekeepers (not
cooks), teaming.

Class of Attractiveness.

"Cultivation of flowers, cultivation of fruit, portrait-
and landscape-painting, vine-dressing, poultry-keeping,
care of bees, embellishing public grounds.

Groups and Series.

" The Council recommend to the different Associations the following plan for the organization of groups
and series, viz.:

" 1. Ascertain, for example, the whole number of
members who will attach themselves to, or at any time
take part in, the agricultural line. From this number,
organize as many groups as the business of the line will
admit.

" 2. We recommend the numbers 30, 24, 18, as the
maximum rank of the classes of necessity, usefulness
and attractiveness.

" The series should then be numbered in the order in
which they are formed, and the groups in the same
manner, begining 1, 2, 3, &c., for each series.

" Mechanical series can be organized, embracing all

the different trades employed by the Association, in the same manner ; and if the groups can not be filled up at once with adults, we would recommend to the institutions to fill them sufficiently for the purpose of organization, with apprentices.

" Each group should have a foreman, whose business it should be to keep correct accounts of time, superintend and direct the performance of work, and maintain an oversight of working-dresses, etc.

" There should be one individual elected as superintendent of the series, whose business it should be to confer with the farming committee of the board, and inform the different foremen of groups, of the work to be done, and inspect the same afterwards.

" The council is thoroughly satisfied that all the labor of an Association should be performed by groups and series, and although the combined order can not be fully established at once, the adoption of this arrangement will avoid incoherence, and be calculated to impress on each member a sense of his personal responsibility.

Time and Rank.

" The time, rank and occupation should be noted daily, and oftener,. if a change of employment is made. The sum of the products of the daily time of each individual, as multiplied by his daily rank, should be carried to the time-ledger, weekly or monthly, to his or her credit. Each of the several amounts, whether performed in the classes of necessity, usefulness, or attractiveness, will thus be made to bear an equal proportion to the value of the services rendered.

A. M. Watson, President.

E. A. Stillman, Secretary."

The reader may be curious to see how these instructions were carried out in actual account-keeping. Fortunately the *Phalanx* furnishes a specimen of what, we suppose, may be called, unmitigated Fourierism.

"The following tables," says a subsequent report, "exhibit the mode of keeping the account of a group at the Clarkson domain. The total number of hours that each individual has been employed during the week, is multiplied by the degree in the scale of rank, which gives an equation of rank and time of the whole group. At Clarkson, for every thousand of the quotient, each member is allowed to draw on his account for necessaries, to the value of seventy-five cents:

SERIES OF TAILORESSES—GROUP NO. I.

Maximum Rank 25.

1844 Rank		Mo.	Tue.	We.	Thu.	Fri.	Sat.	Total hours	Hours & rank.
20	M. Weed,	6	10	3	—	—	5	24	480
25	J. Peabody,	10	10	10	12	10	10	62	1550
20	S. Clark,	10	10	10	10	8	—	48	960
25	E. Clark,	2	10	10	Sick	—	—	22	550
18	H. Lee,	6	4	10	6	4	4	34	612
15	J. Folsom,	3	3	2	6	5	3	22	330
12	Eliza Mann,	4	4	2	2	6	4	22	264

The above is a true account of the time and rank of the whole group, working under my direction for the past week.   JULIA PEABODY. Foreman.

Entered on the books of the Association, by

WM. SEAVER, Clerk.

Clarkson Domain, July 6, 1844.

SERIES OF WORKERS IN WOOD—GROUP NO. II.

Maximum Rank 30.

1844 Rank		Mo.	Tue.	We.	Thu	Fri.	Sat.	Total hours	Hours & rank.
24	Chas. Odell,	10	9	10	10	8	9	56	1344
30	John Allen,	10	10	2	6	10	8	46	1380
20	Jas. Smith,	Sick	—	—	—	—	3	3	120
30	Wm. Allen,	10	12	10	10	10	10	62	1860
30	Jas. Griffith,	10	10	10	10	10	10	60	1800

The above is a true account of the time and rank of the whole group, working under my direction for the past week.   JAMES GRIFFITH, Foreman.

Entered on the books of the Association, by

WM. SEAVER, Clerk.

Clarkson Domain, July 6, 1844."

For the sake of keeping in view the various religious influences that entered into the Fourier movement, it is worth noting here that Edwin A. Stillman, the Secretary of the Union, was one of the early Perfectionists ; intimately associated with the writer of this history at New Haven in 1835. We judge from the frequent occurrence of his official reports in the *Phalanx* and *Harbinger*, that he was the working center of the socialist revival at Rochester, and of the incipient confederacy of Associations that issued therefrom. In like manner James Boyle, another New Haven Perfectionist, was a very busy writer and lecturer among the Socialists of New England in the excitements 1842—3, and was a member of the Northampton Community.

CHAPTER XXIII.

THE CLARKSON PHALANX.

THIS Association appears to have been the first and most important of the Confederated Phalanxes. Mr. John Greig (before referred to) is its historian, whose account we here present with few alterations:

"Our Association commenced at Clarkson on the shore of Lake Ontario, in the county of Monroe, about thirty miles from Rochester, in February 1844. We adopted a constitution and bye-laws, but I am sorry to say that I have not a copy of them. The reason why no copies have been preserved is, that after a year's experience in the associative life, we all became so wise (or smart, as the phrase is), that we thought we could make much better constitutions, and ceased to value the old ones.

"We had no property qualifications. All male and female members over eighteen years of age were voters upon all important matters, excepting the investment and outlay of capital. No religious or political tests were required. The chief principle upon which we endeavored to found our Association, was to establish justice and judgment in our little earth at Clarkson domain, and as much further as possible.

"Our means were ample; but, as it proved, unavailable. The beginning and ending of our troubles was this—and let all readers consider it—we were without the pale and protection of law, for want of incorporation. Consequently we could do no business, could not buy or sell land or other property, could not sue or be sued, could neither make ourselves responsible, nor compel others to become so; and as a majority of us were never able to adopt the dreamy abstractions of non-resistance and no-law, we were unable to live and prosper in that kingdom of smoke 'above the world.'

"The members, in different proportions, had placed in the hands of trustees, after the manner of religious societies in this State, ninety-five thousand dollars worth of choice landed property, to be sold, turned into cash, and invested in Clarkson domain. We purchased of a Mr Richmond Church and others, over two thousand acres of first-rate land, all on trust, excepting twenty acres bought for cash. The rise in value of our large purchase since our dispersion, has exceeded fifty thousand dollars. We probably took on to the domain some ten thousand dollars worth of goods and chattels.

"Our property was not considered common stock; we only recognized a common cause. Our agreement gave capital to labor for less than half of the world's present interest, and gave to labor its full reward, according to merit, that is, skill, strength, and time; establishing 'Do as you would be done by' first; and attending to the questions of brotherhood afterward, such as home for life, respect, comfort, and all needful or desirable things to the old, the infant, the disabled, etc. This was the extent of our Communism. Our company stock was divided into twenty-five dollar shares. About one-third of the members owned none at all at first, although their rights were considered equal; and that point, be it said to the glory of the domain, was never mooted and scarcely mentioned.

"We commenced our new life at Clarkson in March, April and May, 1844; building our temporary, and enlarging our established, houses, and beginning to marshal our forces of toil. In April we 'numbered Israel,' and found we were four hundred and twenty souls, as happy and joyous a family as ever thronged to an Independence dinner. If, in our fiscal affairs we were not Communists, in our moral and social feelings we were a house not divided against itself.

"In relation to education, natural intelligence, and morality, I candidly think we were a little above the average of common citizens at large in the State, and no more. Trades and occupations were multiform. Our doctor and minister were academical scholars merely. We had one ripe merchant (a great rogue, too), some first-rate mechanics of all the substantial trades, and a noble lot of common farmers.

"As for religion, we had seventy-four praying Christians, including all the sects in America, excepting Millerites and Mormons. We had one Catholic family (Dr. Theller's), one Presbyterian clergyman, and one Universalist. One of our first trustees was a Quaker. We had one Atheist, several Deists, and in short a general assortment; but of Nothingarians, none; for being free for the first time in our lives, we spoke out, one and all, and found that every body did believe something. All the gospels were preached in harmony and good fellowship. We early got up a committee on preaching the gospel, placing one of each known denomination upon said committee, including a Deist, who being a liberal soul, and no bigot in his infidelity, was chosen chairman on the gospel; and allow him modestly to say, he did acquit himself to the entire satisfaction of his more fortunate brethren in the faith. One word about our Atheist—our poor unfortunate Atheist; he was beloved by every soul on the domain, and was an intimate friend of our orthodox minister. We had no difficulties on the score of religion, and had we remained, we should have been nearer to love to God and love to man, than we are now, scattered as we are, broadcast over the continent. For membership, we required a decent character—no more. No oaths nor fines were required. Honorable pledges were given and generally kept.

"Our domain was located at the mouth of Sandy Creek, on Lake Ontario. It was a slightly rolling plain, and the best soil in the world. On account of so much water (Lake, Bay and Creek), it was rather unhealthy, but would improve in time by cultivation. We had one good flour-mill, two saw-mills, one machine-shop, some good farm buildings and barns, and about half a mile in length of temporary rows of board buildings; a dry goods store for a portion of the time, and over 400 acres of land, under fair cultivation. At one period of our career, we had about four hundred sheep, forty cows, twenty-five span of horses, twelve yoke of oxen, swine, guinea fowls, barn fowls, geese, ducks, bees, etc., etc., in great abundance. We cultivated several acres of vegetable garden, reaped one hundred acres of wheat, and had corn, potatoes, peas, etc., to a large amount—I should think seventy-five acres. We had abundance of pasture, and must have cut two hundred tons of hay. Of wild berries there must have been gathered hundreds of bushels.

"Our regularly elected officers managed the receipts and expenditures ; and they were, I believe, honestly managed up to a certain time.

"The four hundred and twenty members kept together until the autumn of the first year, and then were forced to break up and divide property, having but little to sustain themselves, because our capital was wrongfully tied up, in the hands of trustees : this course having been pursued by advice of certain great lawyers, who, when our legal troubles commenced, appeared in the courts against us. No purchasers could be found to buy the lands in the hands of the trustees ; so we had come to a dead lock, and were obliged to break up or down, as the fact may be estimated. The associates did not disagree at all save in one thing, and that was, as to these bad property arrangements, which compelled them to break up. They staid or went by lots cast. Two hundred persons staid on the domain some four months longer, and then, the hope of a legal foundation having entirely died out, the whole matter was necessarily thrown into the court of Chancery, and the lawyers, as usual, took the avails of the hard earnings of the disappointed members.

"The regularly organized Association kept together nearly one year. A remnant of the band remained after the court of chancery had adjudged a transfer of the estate back into the hands of the original owners. That remnant tried every little scheme and new contrivance that imagination could devise (except Fourierism), to stick together in a joint-stock capacity for a year longer or so, and then broke and ran all over the world, proclaiming Fourierism a failure. The Heavens may fall, and Fourier's industrial science may fail; but it must be tried first; till then it can not fail.

"In short the reason why the attempt at Clarkson failed, and the only reason, was, that the founders missed the entrance door, viz., a legal foundation; by which they would have made friends with the old world, and begun the new in a constructive way, obtaining the right men and plenty of the 'mammon of unrighteousness.' They should have got incorporated under a general law like our manufacturing law, and obtained a suitable domain of at least 5760 acres of land or three miles square, and should have built and furnished a sufficient portion of a phalanstery to accommodate at least 400 persons, at the outset of organization. I boldy pronounce all partial attempts, short of such a beginning, a waste, and worse than a waste, of time and brain, blood and muscle, soul and body.

JOHN GREIG."

A writer in the *Phalanx* (July 1844), viewing things from a standpoint a little further off than Mr. Greig's, gave the following more probable account of the Clarkson failure:

"The original founders of this Association, no doubt actuated by good motives, but lacking discretion, held out such a brilliant prospect of comfort and pleasure in the very infancy of the movement, that hundreds, without any correct appreciation of the difficulties to be undergone by a pioneer band, rushed upon the ground, expecting at once to realize the heaven they so ardently desired, and which the eloquent words of the lecturers had warranted them to hope for. Thus, ignorant of Association, possessed, for the most part, of little capital, without adequate shelter from the inclemency of the weather, or even a sufficient store of the most common articles of food, without plan, and I had almost said, without purpose, save to fly from the ills they had already experienced in civilization, they assembled together such elements of discord as naturally in a short time led to their dissolution."

One feature of Mr. Greig's entertaining sketch deserves notice in passing, viz., his cheerful boast of the multiplicity of religions in the Clarkson Association, and the wonderful harmony that prevailed among them. The meaning of the boast undoubtedly is, that religious belief was so completely a secondary and insignificant matter, that it did not prevent peaceful family relations, even between the atheists and the orthodox. This kind of harmony is often spoken of in the accounts of other Associations, and seems to have been a general characteristic, or at least a *desideratum*, of the Owen and Fourier schools. It is this harmonious indifference, which we refer to when we speak of the Associations of those schools as *non-religious*.

The primary Massachusetts Communities, however, were hardly so free from religious limitations, though they issued from the sects commonly called liberal. The Brook Farmers, we have seen, covered the National Convention all over with the mantle of piety, insisting that they were at work as devout Christians, and that Fourierism, as they held it, was Christianity. And Hopedale was even more zealous for Christianity than Brook Farm. Collins's Community at Skaneateles, on the other hand, went clear over to exclusive anti-religion; and actually barred out by its original creed, all kinds of

Christians, tolerating nobody but sound Atheists and Deists.

The Northampton Association, which we have termed Nothingarian, seems to have invented the happy medium of the Clarkson platform, and in that respect may be regarded as the prototype of the whole class of Fourier Associations. The mixture of religions, however, at Northampton, was not so harmonious as at Clarkson. The historian of the Northampton Community says: "The carrying out of different religious views was perhaps the occasion of more disagreement than any other subject ; and this disagreement operated to general disadvantage, as in consequence of it several valuable members withdrew." We shall meet with similar disagreements and disasters in the Sodus Bay Phalanx and other Associations, to be reported hereafter. So that it does not seem altogether safe to huddle a great variety of contradictory religions together in close Association, notwithstanding the apparent results in the Clarkson case. And it occurs, as a natural suggestion, that possibly the Clarkson Association did not last long enough to fairly test the results of a general mixture of religions.

CHAPTER XXIV.

THE SODUS BAY PHALANX.

THIS Association originated about the same time as the Clarkson Association (February 1844), and in the same place (Rochester). The following description of its domain is from the *Herald of Freedom:*

"We have at this place about 1,400 acres of choice land, three hundred of which are under improvement. It borders on Sodus Bay, the best harbor on Lake Ontario, and for beauty of scenery, is not surpassed by any tract in the State. We have on the domain two streams of water, which can both be used for propelling machinery. We number at present about three hundred men, women and children. The buildings on the place were nearly enough to accommodate the whole, the place having formerly been occupied by the Shakers, who had erected good buildings for their own accommodation."

The editor of the *Phalanx* visited this Association in the autumn of 1844, and wrote of it as follows:

"The advantages of the location seemed to us very rare, and it was with great pain that we discovered that the internal condition of the Phalanx was not encouraging. We did not find that unity of purpose, without which a small and imperfectly provided Association can not be held together until it has attained the necessary perfection in its mechanism. At the commencement, as it appeared to us, there was not sufficient caution in the admission of members. A large number of persons were received without proper qualification, either in character or industrial abilities. Sickness unfortunately soon arose in the new Phalanx, and increased the confusion which resulted from a want of unity of feeling and systematic organization. Religious differences, pressed in an intolerant manner on both sides, had at the time of our visit produced entire uncertainty as to future operations, and carried disorder to its height. We left the domain with the conviction, which reflection has strengthened, that without an entire reörganization under more efficient leaders, the Association must fall entirely to pieces ; a fact which is greatly to be deplored on account of the cause in general, as well as on account of the excellence of the location, and the real worth of several individuals who have passed unshaken through such trying circumstances. We have, however, in the case of this Phalanx, a striking example of the folly of undertaking practical Association without sufficient means, and without men of proper character. No other advantages can compensate for the want of these."

Nearly a year later (September 1845), a member of the Sodus Bay Phalanx wrote to the *Harbinger* in the following dubious vein:

" We have only about twelve or fifteen adult males, and we believe we may safely say (from the amount of labor performed the present season), not many unprofitable ones. We have learned wisdom from the many difficulties and privations of last year, and there is now evidently a settled and determined will to succeed in our enterprise. There is, however, a debt which is very discouraging ; $7,000 principal (besides $2,450 interest), which will come due next spring, and an ability on our part of paying no more than the interest."

About the beginning of 1846 John A. Collins of the Skaneateles Community, visited Sodus Bay, and sent to his paper, the *Communitist*, the following mournful report :

" Experience has taught them that but little confidence can be placed on calculations which are predicated upon a newly-organized, or more properly disorganized, body of heterogeneous materials, during the first and second years of its existence. There is not the least doubt, but that an energetic and efficient individual, with sufficient capital to erect with the least possible delay the saw-mill, lath, shingle, broom-handle, tub and pail, fork and hoe-handle, last, and general turning machinery, and employ as many first-class workmen as the business would require, could in three years, pay both principal and interest, and have the entire farm and several thousand dollars besides. But an Association composed of inexperienced, restless, indolent, feeble and selfish individuals, would perish beneath the pressure of interest, ere they could construct their mills, get their machinery in operation, and become organized and systematized, so that all things could be carried forward with that system and perfection which characterize isolation and the older established Communities.

" But had not capital stepped forth to crush this movement, other elements equally poisonous and deadly were introduced, which would have sealed its ruin. A great portion of its members were brought together, not

by a strong feeling or sympathy for the poor, noble philanthropy, or self-denying enthusiasm, but by the most
narrow selfishness. Add to this, that bane of all that is
meek, pure, noble and peaceful, religious bigotry was
carried in and incorporated into the constitution of the
Phalanx. Soon the body was divided into the religious
and liberal portions, both of which carried their views,
we think, to extremes.

" We were present at a business meeting, in the early
part of the fall of 1844. Each party, it seemed, felt
bound to oppose the wishes, plans and movements of
the other. We advised the more liberal portion of the
society quietly to withdraw, and allow the other party to
succeed if it possibly could. But they did not feel at
liberty to do so ; and soon after the religious body left,
taking with them what of their property they could find,
leaving those who remained (the liberal portion of the
society), comparatively destitute They felt determined
to succeed, and nobly have they combated, to the present time, the hostile elements which have warred against
them with terrible force. United in sympathy and feeling, they re-organized last spring ; but the interest was
too much for them to meet, and now there is no prospect
of their remaining as an Association longer than the
approaching April. Could those now upon the domain
purchase three or four hundred acres of the land, we
have not the least doubt but that they would succeed,
and ultimately come into possession of the valuable
wood-land adjoining. But this is impossible. In the
evening all the adults convened together, and at their
earnest request, we spoke for the space of an hour or
more upon the signs of the times, the evidences of social
progress, and the various minor difficulties that the

pioneers in this movement must necessarily have to experience; proving to the satisfaction of most of them, we think, that Fourier's plan of distributing wealth, was both arbitrary and superficial; that it was a useless effort to unite two opposite and hostile elements, which have no more affinity for each other than water and oil, or fire and gunpowder; that inasmuch as individual and separate interests are the cause or occasion of nearly all the crime, poverty, and suffering in civilized society, it follows that the cause and occasion must be removed, ere the effects will disappear. Still the difference between Communists and Associationists is not so great, that they should be opposed and alienated. It should be our object to see the points of agreement, rather than seek for points of disagreement. In the former we have been too active and earnest. Association is a great school for Communism. It will develop the false, and point out the good.

"As we left this interesting spot the following morning, it was painful to think that those men and women, who for nearly two years had struggled against great odds, with their philanthropic, manly and heroic spirit, with all their enthusiasm, zeal and confidence in the beauty and practicability of the principles of social co-operation, must soon be dispersed and thrown back again, to act upon the selfish and beggarly principles of strife and competition."

Macdonald ends the story in his usual sombre style as follows:

"This experiment was a total failure. I have been unable to gather many particulars concerning its last days, and those I have obtained are of a very unfavorable character.

"The chief cause of failure was religious difference. Persons of various religious creeds could not agree. There were some among them who thought it no sin to labor on the Sabbath, and others who looked upon it as an outrage, which the Phalanx should take action to prevent. A committee was appointed to settle such differences, but in this they failed. Sickness was another of their troubles. They were severely afflicted with typhoid erysipelas, and at one time forty-nine of their members were upon the sick list.

"After laboring a year or two under these difficulties, there was a hasty and disorderly retreat. It is said that each individual helped himself to the movable property, and that some decamped in the night, leaving the remains of the Phalanx to be disposed of in any way which the last men might choose. The fact that mankind do not like to have their faults and failings made public, will probably account for the difficulty in obtaining particulars of such experiments as the Sodus Bay Phalanx."

Allen and Orvis, the lecturing missionaries of Brook Farm, in that same letter from which we quoted some time since a maledictory paragraph on the memory of the Skaneateles Community, mention also the bad odor of the defunct confederated Phalanxes of Western New York, in the following disrespectful terms. Their letter is dated at Rochester, September 1847:

"The prospect for meetings in this city is less favorable than that of any place where we have previously visited. It is the nest wherein was hatched that anomalous brood of birds, called the 'Sodus Bay Phalanx,' 'The Clarkson Phalanx,' the 'Bloomfield Phalanx,' and the 'Ontario Union.' The very name of Association is odious with the public, and the unfortunate people who went into these movements in such mad haste, have been ridiculed till endurance is no longer possible, and they have slunk away from the sight and knowledge of their neighbors."

The experience of the Sodus Bay Phalanx in regard to religion, suggests reflections. Let us improve the opportunity to study some of the practical relations of religion to Association.

The object and end of Association in all its forms, as we have frequently said, is to gather men, women and children into larger and more permanent HOMES than those established by marriage. The advantages of partnership, incorporation and cooperation have become so manifest in modern affairs, that an unspeakable long- ing has arisen in the very heart of civilization for the extension of those advantages to the dearest of all hu- man interests—family affairs—the business of home. The charm that drew the western New Yorkers together in such rushing multitudes, was simply the prospect of home on the large scale, which indeed is heaven.

Now if we consider the laws which govern the forma- tion of homes on the small scale, we shall be likely to get some wisdom in regard to their formation on the large scale.

And in the first place, it is evident that homes formed by the conjunction of pairs in the usual way, are not all harmonious—perhaps we might say, are not generally harmonious. Families quarrel and break up, as well as Associations; and if husbands and wives were as free to separate as the members of Association are, possibly marriage would not make much better show than Social- ism has made. Human nature, as we have seen it in the Communities and Phalanxes—discordant, centrifugal—is the same in marriage. Now, as experience has developed something like a code of rules that govern prudent people in venturing on marriage, our true way is to study that code, and apply it as far as possible to the vastly greater venture of Association.

Fourier's dream that two or three thousand discordant centrifugal individuals in one great home, would fall, by natural gravitation, into a balance of passions, and realize a harmony unattainable on the small scale of familism, has not been confirmed by experience, and seems to us the wildest opposite of truth. We should expect, *a priori*, that with discordant materials, the greater the formation, the worse would be the hell: and this is just what has been proved by all the experiments. Let us go back, then, and study the rules of harmony in the formation of common families.

Probably there is not one among those rules so familiar and so universally approved by the prudent, as that which advises men and women not to marry without agreement in religion This rule has nothing to do with bigotry. It does not look at the supposed truth or falsehood of different religious creeds. It simply says: Let the Catholic marry the Catholic; the Orthodox, the Orthodox; the Deist, the Deist; the Nothingarian, the Nothingarian; but don't match these discords together, if you wish for family peace. Now this is the precept which the Fourier Associations, as we see, deliberately violated; and yet they expected peace, and complained dreadfully because they did not get it! There is latent quarrel enough in the religious opposition of a single pair, to spoil a family; and yet these Socialists ventured on hundred-fold complications of such oppositions, with a heroism that would be sublime, if it were not desperately unwise.

It is useless to say that religion is an affair of the inner man and need not disturb external relations. It did disturb the external relations of the Socialists at Sodus Bay, and could not do otherwise. They quarreled about the Sabbath. It did disturb the external relations of the Northampton Socialists. They quarreled about amusements. Religion always extends from the inner man to such external things.

It is useless to say, as Collins evidently wished to insinuate, that the bigoted sort of religionists, those of the orthodox order, were alone to blame. In the first place this is not true. All the witnesses say, Collins among the rest, that both parties pushed and hooked. And in the next place, if it were true, it would only show the importance of excluding the orthodox from Associations, and the value of the rule that forbids marrying religious discords.

Even Collins, with all his liberality, had originally too much good sense to attempt Association in the promiscuous way of the Fourierists. His first idea was to make his Community a sort of close-communion church of infidelity ; and, as it turned out, this was his brightest idea ; for in abandoning it he succumbed to his more religious rival, Johnson, and admitted quarreling and weakness that ruined the enterprise. His advice also to the liberal party at Sodus Bay to withdraw, shows that his judgment was opposed to the heterogeneous mixtures that were popular among the Fourierists.

On the whole it seems to us that it should be considered settled by reason and experience, that the rule we have found governing the prudential theory of marriage on the small scale, should be transferred to the theory of Association, which is really marriage on the large scale. Better not marry at all, than marry a religious quarrel. Better have no religion, than have a dozen different religions, as they had at Clarkson. If you mean to found a Community for peace and permanence, first of all find associates that agree with you in religion, or at least in no-religion, and if possible bar out all others. Remember that all the successful Communities are harmonious, and the basis of their harmony is unity in religion. If you think you can find a way to secure harmony in no-religion, try it. But do n't be so foolish as to enter on the tremendous responsibilities of Community-building, with a complication of religious quarrels lurking in your material.

CHAPTER XXV.

OTHER NEW YORK EXPERIMENTS.

THE next on the list of the Confederated Associations of western New York, was

THE BLOOMFIELD ASSOCIATION.

We have but meager accounts of this experiment. Macdonald does not mention it. The *Phalanx* of June 15, 1844, says that it commenced operations on the 15th of March in that year, on a domain of about five hundred acres, mostly improved land, situated one mile east of Honeoye Falls, in the Counties of Monroe, Livingston and Ontario; that it was in debt for its land about $ 11,000, and had $ 35,000 of its subscriptions actually paid in; that it had one hundred and forty-eight resident members, and a large number more expecting to join, as soon as employment could be found for them. Two or three allusions to this Association occur afterward in the *Phalanx*, congratulating it on its prospects, and mentioning good reports of its progress. Finally in the *Harbinger*, volume 1, page 247, we find a letter from E. D. Wight and E. A. Stillman, dated August 20, 1845, defending the Association against newspaper charges, and asserting its continued prosperity ; but giving us the following peep into a complication of troubles, that probably brought it to its end shortly afterwards :

" We are not fully satisfied with the tenor by which our real estate, under the existing laws, is obliged to be held. Conveyances, pursuant to legal advice, were made originally by the owners of each particular parcel, to the committee of finance, in trust for the stockholders and members ; and a power was executed by the stockholders to the committee, by which, under certain regulations, they were to have authority to sell and convey the same. The absurdity of the Statute of Trusts never having been licked into shape by judicial decisions, a close and unavailing search has since been instituted for the fugitive legal title.

" Some counselors, learned in the law, find it in the committee of finance, as representatives of the Association ; others have discovered that it is vested in them as individuals ; others still, of equal eminence, and equally intent on arriving at a true solution, find perhaps that it is in the committee and stockholders jointly ; while there are those who profess to find it in neither of these parties, but in the persons of whom the property was purchased, and to whom has been paid its full valuation !

" In order to educe order out of this confusion of opinions, and to enable us to acquire, if possible, a less objectionable title, it has been proposed to petition the Chancellor for a sale, as a title from the court would be free from doubt."

If this may be considered the end (as it probably was), it shows that the Bloomfield Association died, as the

Clarkson did, in a quarrel about its titles, and in the hands of the lawyers.

"This Association" says the *Phalanx* of June 1844, "commenced operations about two weeks since, in Hopewell, Ontario County, five miles from Canandaigua. They have purchased the mills and farm formerly owned by Judge Bates, consisting of one hundred and fifty acres of land, a flouring mill with five run of burr stones, and saw-mill, at $16,000. They have secured by subscription, about one hundred and thirty acres of land in the immediate vicinity, which they are now working. To meet their liabilities for the original purchase, I am informed they have already a subscription which they believe can be relied on, amounting to over $40,000. They have now upon the domain about seventy-five members. This institution has been able already to commence such branches of industry as will produce an immediate return, and as a consequence, will avoid the necessity of living upon their capital. There is danger that their enthusiasm will get the better of their judgment in admitting members too fast."

The editor of the *Phalanx* visited this Association among others, in the fall of 1844, and gave the following cheerful account of it:

"The whole number of resident members is one hundred and fifty; fifty of whom are men, and upward of sixty children. We were greatly pleased with the earnest spirit which seemed to pervade this little Community. We thought we perceived among them a really religious devotion to the great cause in which they have embarked. This gave an unspeakable charm to their rude, temporary dwellings, and lent a grace to their plain manners, far above any superficial elegance. We have no doubt that they will succeed in establishing a state of society higher even than they themselves anticipate. Of their pecuniary success their present condition gives good assurance. We should think that, with ordinary prudence, it was entirely certain."

We find nothing after this in the *Phalanx* about this Association. Macdonald merely mentions a few such items as the date, place, etc., and concludes with the following terse epitaph: " It effected but little, and was of brief duration. No further particulars."

THE MIXVILLE ASSOCIATION

was one of the group that radiated from Rochester, according to Mr. Greig ; but we can find no account of it anywhere, except that it had not commenced operations at the time of the session of the Confederated Council; though a delegate from it was a member of that Council. How long it lived, or whether it lived at all, does not appear.

THE JEFFERSON COUNTY PHALANX.

This Association, though not properly a member of the group that radiated from Rochester, and somewhat remote from western New York, was named among the confederated Associations, and sent a delegate to the Bloomfield Council. Three notices of it occur in the *Phalanx*, which we here present.

[From the *Phalanx* October 5, 1843.]

" This Association has been commenced through the efforts, principally, of A. M. Watson, Esq., the President, who for some years past has been engaged in advocating and disseminating the principles of Association in Watertown and that section of the State. There are over three hundred persons now on the domain, which consists of twelve or fifteen hundred acres of superior land, finely watered, and situated within two or three miles of Watertown. It is composed of several farms, put in by farmers, who have taken stock for their lands, and joined the Association. Very little cash capital has been paid in; the enterprise was undertaken with the subscription of property, real estate, provisions, tools, implements, &c., brought in by the members, who were principally farmers and mechanics in the neighborhood; and the result is an interesting proof of what can be done by union and combined effort among the producing classes. Different branches of manufactures have been established, contracts for building in Watertown have been taken, and an organization of labor into groups or squads, with their foremen or leaders, has been made to some extent. The agricultural department is prosecuted with vigor, and when last heard from, the Association was flourishing. We hope from this Association that perseverance and constancy—for it of course has many difficulties to contend with—which will insure success, and give another proof of the truth of the great principles of combined effort and united interests."

[From the *Phalanx*, November 4, 1843.]

"The following statement from the *Black River Journal* of October 6th, exhibits the affairs of the Jefferson County Association in a gratifying light, and shows that so far it has been extremely prosperous and successful. The fact alone of a profit having been made, whether much or little, affords a strong proof of the advantages of associated effort, for we apprehend that either farmers or mechanics working separately, would generally find it difficult to show a balance in their favor upon the settlement of their accounts. But a net profit of nearly thirteen thousand dollars, or twenty-five per cent. upon the capital invested, for the first six months that a small Association has been in operation, under circumstances by no means the most favorable, is striking and incontestable evidence of real prosperity. Before a great while we shall have many such cases to record.

ABSTRACT OF SEMI-ANNUAL REPORT.

The first Semi-Annual Report of the property, expenditures and proceeds of labor of the Jefferson County Industrial Association, was submitted to a meeting of the stockholders on Monday the 2d inst.

Since the organization of the Association in April last, the real and personal property acquired by purchase and subscription, has reached the amount of $ 54,832.10

This is subject to reduction by the amount of subscribed property applied to the purchase of real estate   .   .   .   5,458.28

Total property on hand   .   .   .   .   .   . $ 49,373.82
The aggregate product of the several departments of business, to Sept. 23d $ 20,301.67
Expense of same, including all purchases of goods and supplies 7,331.95

Net proceeds   .   .   .   . $ 12,969.72
Of this has been expended in improvement of buildings, making a brick-yard, and preparing summer fallows 1,365.00

Balance on hand   .   .   .   . $ 11,604.72
This balance consists of agricultural products in store,

brick manufactured and now on hand, proceeds of jobbing contracts, earnings of mechanics' shops, etc.

Published by order of the President and Board of Directors.

Report of A. M. Watson to the Confederate Council, May 15, 1844.

" The Jefferson County Association has made its first annual statement, by which it appears that capital in that institution will receive a fraction over six per cent. interest. Owing to inattention to the principles of Association, and a defective and incomplete organization of industry into groups and series, as well as to the fact that in the commencement much time is lost, labor in this institution fails to obtain its fair remuneration. Another circumstance which has operated to the disadvantage of labor, is, that no allowance has been made in its favor, in the annual settlement, for working dresses. These facts are conclusive, to my mind, that the disadvantages of improper or inadequate organization in all institutions, will be even more injurious to labor than to capital.

" This institution commenced operations without the investment of much, if any, cash capital, and they now are somewhat embarrassed for want of such means. A subscription to their stock of two thousand dollars in cash, or a loan of that amount for a reasonable time, for which good security could be given, would, in my opinion, place them in a situation to carry on a very profitable business the ensuing year. If this obstacle can be surmounted, I know of no institution of better promise than this. This would seem to be but a small matter ; but when the fact is considered that they are located in the midst of a community which sympathizes but little in the movement, while many exert themselves

to increase the embarrassment by decrying their responsibility, it will readily be seen that their situation is
unenviable. Their responsibility, when compared with
that of most business concerns in the country, is more
real than that of a majority of business men who are
considered perfectly solvent. Considering the difficulties and embarrassments through which they have
already struggled, I have strong confidence in their ultimate success. The whole number of members will not
vary much at this time, from one hundred and fifty.
They have reduced, by sale, their lands to about eight
hundred acres, and I refer you to the annual report for
further information as to their liabilities."

We perceive in the depressed tone of this report, as
well as in the reduction of numbers and land which it
exhibits, that decline had begun and failure was impending. Nothing more is said in the *Phalanx* about this
Association, except that it sent a delegate to a socialistic
convention that met in New York City on the 7th of
October, 1844. We have to fall back, as usual, on
Macdonald, for the summing-up and final moral. He
says:

"After a few months, disagreements among the
members became general. Their means were totally
inadequate; they were too ignorant of the principles of
Association; were too much crowded together, and had
too many idlers among them. There was bad management on the part of the officers, and some were
suspected of dishonesty. As times grew better, many
of those who joined on account of hard times, got
employment and left; and many more thought they
could do better in the world again, and did the same

thing. The only aid they could get in their difficulties, was from stock subscriptions, and that was not much. Men who invested actual property sustained heavy losses. One farmer who involved his farm, lost nearly all he possessed. After existing about twelve months the land was sold to pay the debts, and the Association disbanded."

THE MOORHOUSE UNION

is mentioned in the first number of the *Phalanx*, October 1843, as one among the many Associations just starting at that time. Macdonald gives the following account of it:

"This experiment originated in the offer of a grant of land by A. K. Moorhouse, of Moorhouseville, Hamilton County, New York, who owned 60,000 acres of land in the counties of Hamilton, Herkimer and Saratoga. As most of this land was situated in what is called the 'wilderness of New York,' he could find few persons who were willing to purchase and settle the inhospitable wild. Under these circumstances he offered to the Socialists as much of 10,000 acres as they might clear in three years, hoping that an Association would build up a village and form a nucleus around which individuals and Associations might settle and purchase his lands.

"The offer was accepted by an Association formed in New York City, and several capitalists promised to take stock in the enterprise; but none was ever paid for. In May 1843, Mr. Moorhouse arrived at Piseco from New York, with a company of pioneers, who were soon followed by others, and the work commenced. The locality chosen at Lake Piseco was situated about five miles from Lake Pleasant, the county seat, a village of

eight or nine houses and a court-house. On the arrival
of the party it was found that Mr. Moorhouse had made
some improvements, which he was willing to exchange
for $2,000 of stock in the Association. This was agreed
to. He also engaged to furnish provisions, tools etc.,
and take his pay in stock. The land on which the
Association commenced its labors was a gift from Mr
Moorhouse; but the improvements which consisted of
120 acres of cleared land with a few buildings, was
accepted as stock at the above valuation.

"The money, property and labor were put into
common stock. Labor was rated at fifty cents per day,
no matter of what kind. A store was kept on the
premises, in which articles were sold at prime cost, with
an allowance for transportation, &c. By the constitution
the members were entitled to scrip representing the
excess of wages over the amount of goods received from
the store; or, in other words, laborers became stockholders in proportion to that excess. No dividends
were to be declared for the first five years.

"The persons thus congregated to carry out the
principles of Association [number not stated], belonged
to a variety of occupations; but it appears that but few
of them were adapted to the wants of the Community.
Some of the members were intelligent and moral people;
put the majority were very inferior. No property
qualifications were necessary to admission. It appears
that members were obtained by an agent, who took
indiscriminately all he could get. The most common
religious belief among them was Methodist; but a large
proportion of them did not profess any religion, and
some were what is commonly called infidels.

"Though the persons congregated here had left but

humble homes and poor circumstances generally, yet the
circumstances now surrounding them were worse than
those they had left, and as a natural consequence there
was a deterioration of character.   Not having formed
any organization in the city, as is customary in such
experiments, they received no aid from without ; and the
want of this aid does not appear to have insured success,
as some enthusiastic Socialists have imagined that it
would ; but on the contrary a most signal failure
ensued.

"The leading persons were Mr. Moorhouse and a
relative of his named Brown.   The former furnished
every thing and turned it in as stock.   The latter kept
the store and the accounts.   The members do not
appear to have been acquainted with the mode in which
either the store or books were kept.

" At the commencement, when they were sufficiently
supplied from the store, they agreed tolerably well; but
during the latter period of the experiment, when Mr.
Moorhouse began to be slack in buying things for the
members, there was a good deal of disagreement.   The
store was nearly always empty, and when anything was
brought into it, there was a general scramble to see who
should get the most.   This, as a matter of course,
produced much jealousy and quarreling.   All kinds of
suspicions were afloat, and it was generally reported
that the executive, including the store-keeper, fared
better than the rest.

" Some work was done, and some improvements were
made upon the land.   Rye and potatoes were planted,
and probably consumed.   The experiment existed a few
months, and then by degrees died away."

The following from a person who took part in the experiment, will give the reader a nearer view of the causes of the failure:

"The population congregated at Piseco was composed of all nations, characters and conditions; a motley group of ill-assorted materials, as inexperienced as it was heterogeneous. We had some specimens of the raw material of human nature, and some of New York manufacture spoiled in the making. There were philosophers and philanthropists, bankrupt merchants and broken-down grocery-keepers ; officers who had retired from the Texan army on half-pay ; and some who had retired from situations in the New York ten-pin alleys. There were all kinds of ideas, notions, theories, and whims ; all kinds of religions ; and some persons without any. There was no unanimity of purpose, or congeniality of disposition ; but there was plenty of discussion, and an abundance of variety, which is called the spice of life. This spice however constituted the greater part of the fare, as we sometimes had scarcely anything else to eat.

" At first we were pretty well off for provisions ; but soon the supplies began to be reduced ; and in November the list of luxuries and necessaries commenced with rye and ended with potatoes, with nothing between ! As the supplies were cut off, the number of members decreased. They were starved out. But of course the starving process was slower in those cases where the individuals had not the means of transportation back to the white settlements. When I left the 'promised land' in March 1844, there were only six families remaining. I had determined to see it out ; but the state of things was so bad, and the prospects ditto, that I could stand it no longer. I thought the whole would soon fall into the hands of Mr. Moorhouse, and I could not afford to spend any more time in a cause so hopeless. I had given nine months' time, was half starved, got no pay, had worn out my clothes, and had my best coat borrowed without leave, by a man who went to New York some time before. This I thought might suffice for one experiment. I left the place less sanguine than when I went there that Associations could succeed without capital and without a good selection of members. Yet my belief was as firm as ever in the coming abolition of conflicting interests, and the final harmonious reconstruction of society."

Here ends the history of the Fourier Associations in the State of New York. The Ohio experiments come next.

CHAPTER XXVI.

THE MARLBORO ASSOCIATION.

As in New England, so in Ohio, the general socialistic excitement of 1841 and afterwards, gave rise to several experiments that had nothing to do with Fourier's peculiar philosophy. We begin with one of these indigenous productions.

Mrs. Esther Ann Lukens, a member of the Marlboro Community, answered Macdonald's inquiries about its history. We copy the greater part of her story:

Mrs. Lukens's Narrative.

" The Marlboro Community seems, as I think of it, to have had its existence so entirely in dreams of human advancement and the generous wish to promote it, and also in ignorance of all but the better part of human nature, that it is hard to speak of it as a *bona fide* portion of our plodding work-a-day world.

"It was originated by a few generous and ardent spirits, who were disgusted with the oppressive and antagonistic conditions of ordinary labor and commerce. The only remedy they saw, was a return to the apostolic manner of living—that of 'having all things common.'

"The Association was first talked of and its principles

generally discussed in Clinton County, some years before anything was done. Many in all parts of Ohio participated in this discussion, and warmly urged the scheme; but only a few were found who were hopeful and courageous enough to dare the final experiment.

"The gathering commenced in 1841 on the farm of Mr. E. Brooke, and consisted at first of his family and a few other persons. Gradually the number increased, and another farm was added by the free gift of Dr. A. Brooke, or rather by his resigning all right and title to it as an individual, and delivering it over to the joint ownership of the great family.

"As may be supposed, the majority of those who gathered around this nucleus, were without property, and very slenderly gifted with the talent of acquiring it, but thoroughly honest, philanthropic, warmly social, and willing to perform what appeared to them the right amount of labor belonging to freemen in a right state of society. They forgot in a few instances, that this right state did not exist, but was only dreamed about, and had yet to be realized by more than common labor with the hands.

"The Community had but little property of any value but land, and that was in an uncultivated, half-wild state. There were a few hundred dollars in hand ; I can not say how many ; but certainly not half the amount required for purchases that seemed immediately necessary. There was a good house and barn on each farm, each house capable of accommodating comfortably three families, besides three small tenant houses of logs, capable of accommodating one family each. There were also on the premises four or five horses and a few cattle and sheep.

" It became necessary, as the numbers increased, to purchase the farm intervening between the one first owned by E. Brooke, and the one given by Dr. A. Brooke, both for convenience in passing and repassing, and for the reason that more land was needed to give employment to all. The owner asked an exorbitant price, knowing our necessities ; but it was paid, or rather promised, and so a load of debt was contracted.

" The members generally were eminently moral and intellectual. As to religious belief, they were what people called, and perhaps justly, Free-thinkers. In our conferences for purposes of improvement and domestic counsel, which were held on Sundays, religion, as a distinct obligation, was never mentioned.

" Provisions were easily procured. One of the farms had a large orchard, and our living was confined to the plainest vegetable diet ; so that much time was left for social and mental improvement. All will join with me in saying that love and good fellowship reigned paramount ; so that all enjoyed good care during sickness, and kindly sympathy at all times.

" About a year and a-half after its foundation, the Community sustained a great loss by the death of one of its most efficient and ardent supporters, Joseph Lukens. It was after this period that a constitution or form of Association was framed, and many persons were admitted who had different views of property and the basis of rights, from what were generally held at the beginning.

" The existence of the Community, from first to last, was nearly four years. If I should say there was perfect unanimity of feeling to the last, it would not be true. Yet there were no quarrels, and all discussions among us were temperate and kind. As to our breaking up, there was no cause for it clear to my mind, except the complicated state of the business concerns, the amount of debt contracted, and the feeling that each one would work with more energy, for a time at least, if thrown upon his own resources, with plenty of elbow-room and nothing to distract his attention."

Mr. Thomas Moore, also a member of this Community, gave his opinion of the cause of its decease in a separate paper, as follows :

Mr. Moore's Post Mortem.

" The failure of this experiment may be traced to the fact that the minds of its originators were not homogeneous. They all agreed that in a properly organized Community, there should be no buying and selling between the members, but that each should share the common products according to his necessity. But while Dr. A. Brooke held that this principle should govern our conduct in our interchange with the whole world, the others believed it right for any number of individuals to separate themselves from the surrounding world, and form themselves into a distinct Community ; and while they had every thing free among themselves, continue to traffic in the common way with those outside. And again, while many believed they were prepared to enter into a Community of this kind, Mr. Edward Brooke had his doubts, fearing that the time had not yet arrived when any considerable number of individuals could live together on these principles ; that though some might be prompted to enter into such relations through principles of humanity and pure benevolence, others would come in from motives altogether selfish ; and that discord would be the result. Dr. A. Brooke, not being willing to be confined in any Community that did not embrace the whole world, stepped out at the start, but left the Community in possession of his property during his life ; believing that to be as long as he had any right to dispose of it. But Edward Brooke yielded to the views of others, and went on with the Community.

" For some time the members who came in from abroad added nothing of consequence to the common stock. Some manifested by their conduct that their objects were selfish, and being disappointed, left again. Others, who perhaps entered from purer motives, also became dissatisfied for various reasons and left ; and so the Community fluctuated for some time. At length three families were admitted as members, who had property invested in farms, and who were to sell the farms and devote the proceeds to the common stock. Two of these, after having tried community life a year, concluded to leave before they had sold their farms ; and the third not being able to sell, there was a lack of capital to profitably employ the members ; and the consequence was, there was not quite enough produced to support the Community. Discovering this to be the case, several of the persons who originally owned the property became dissatisfied ; and although according to the principles of the Community they had no greater interest in that property than any other members, yet it was no less a fact that they had donated it nearly all (excepting Dr. A. Brooke's lease), and that now they would like to have it back. This placed the true Socialists in delicate circumstances. Being without pecuniary means of their own, they could not exercise the power that had voluntarily been placed in their

hands, to control these dissatisfied ones, so as to cause
them, against their will, to leave their property in the
hands of the Community. The property was freely
yielded up, though with the utmost regret. My opinion
therefore is that the experiment failed at the time it did,
through lack of faith in those who had the funds, and
lack of funds in those who had the faith."

Dr. A. Brooke, who devoted his land to the Marlboro
Community, but stepped out himself, because he would
not be confined to anything less than Communism with
the world, afterwards tried a little experiment of his own,
which failed and left no history.   Macdonald visited him
in 1844, and reports some curious things about him,
which may give the reader an idea of what was probably
the most radical type of Communism that was developed
in the Socialistic revival of 1841—3.

" Dr. Brooke" says Macdonald, "was a tall, thin man,
with gray hair, and beard quite unshaven. His face
reminded me of the ancient Philosophers. His only clothing was a shirt and pantaloons ; nothing else on either
body, head, or feet. He invited us into his comfortable
parlor, which was neatly furnished and had a good
supply of books and papers. Our breakfast consisted of
cold baked apples, cold corn bread, and I think potatoes.

" We questioned him much concerning his strange
notions, and in the course of conversation I remarked,
that such men as Robert Owen, Charles Fourier, Josiah
Warren and others, had each a certain number of
fundamental principles, upon which to base their
theories, and I wished to understand definitely what
fundamental principles he had, and how many of them.
He replied that he had only one principle, and that was

to do what he considered right. He said he attended the sick whenever he was called upon, for which he made no charge. When he wanted anything which he knew one of his neighbors could supply, he sent to that neighbor for it. He shewed me a brick out-building at the back of his cottage, which he said had been put up for him by masons in the vicinity. He made it known that he wanted such work done, and no less than five men came to do it for him.

Macdonald adds the following story:

"I remember when in Cincinnati, one Sunday afternoon at a Fourier meeting I heard Mr. Benjamin Urner read a letter from Dr. A. Brooke to some hardware merchants in Cincinnati (the Brothers Donaldson in Main street, I believe), telling them that his necessities required a variety of agricultural tools, such as a plow, harrow, axes, etc., and requesting that they might be sent on to him. He stated that he had given up the use of money, that he gave his professional services free of cost to those whose necessities demanded them, and for any thing his necessities required he applied to those whom he thought able to give. Mr. Urner stated that this strange individual had been the post-master of the place where he now lived, but that he had given up the office so that he might not have to use money. He also informed us that the hardware merchants very kindly sent on the articles to Dr. Brooke free of cost; which announcement gave great satisfaction to the meeting."

CHAPTER XXVII.

PRAIRIE HOME COMMUNITY.

THIS Association (another indigenous production) with several like attempts, originated with Mr. John O. Wattles, Valentine Nicholson and others, who, after attending a socialistic convention in New York in 1843, lectured on Association at various places on their way back to the West. Orson S. Murray, the editor of the *Regenerator*, was also interested in this Community, and was on his way with his printing establishment to join it and publish his paper under its auspices, when he was wrecked on Lake Erie, and lost nearly every thing but his life.

Prairie Home is a beautiful location near West Liberty in Logan County, Ohio. The domain consisted of over five hundred acres; half of which on the hills was well-timbered, and the remainder was in fine rich fields stretching across the prairie.

The members numbered about one hundred and thirty, nearly all of whom were born and bred in the West. Of foreigners there were only two Englishmen and one German. Most of the members were agriculturists. Many of them had been Hicksite Quakers. A few were from other sects, and some from no sect at all. There were but few children.

A few months before the dissolution of this Community Macdonald visited it, and staid several days. His gossiping report of what he saw and heard gives as good an inside view of the transitory species of Associations as any we find in his collections.   We quote the most of it :

Macdonald's visit at Prairie Home.

" On arriving at West Liberty I inquired eagerly for the Community ; but when very coldly and doubtfully told that it was somewhere down the Urbana road, and seeing that folks in the town did not seem to know or care much where it was, my ardor sensibly abated, and I began to doubt whether it was much of an affair after all ; but I pushed on, anxious at once to see the place.

" On reaching the spot where I was told I should find the Community, I turned off from the main road up a lane, and soon met a gaunt-looking individual, rough but very polite, having the look of a Quaker, which I afterwards found he was. He spoke kindly to me, and directed me where to go. There was a two-story frame house at the entrance of the lane, which belonged to the Community ; also a log cabin at the other corner of the lane. After walking a short distance I arrived at another two-story frame house, opposite to which was a large flour-mill on a little stream, and an old saw-mill, looking very rough. At the door of the dwelling-house there was a group of women and girls, picking wool ; and as it was just noon, many men came in from various parts of the farm to take their dinner. At the back of the house there was a long shed, with a rough table down the center, and planks for seats on each side, on which thirty or forty people sat. I was kindly received by them, and invited to dinner; and a good dinner it was, consisting of coarse brown bread piled up in broken lumps, dishes of large potatoes unpeeled, some potato-soup, and a supply of melons for a second course.

"I sat beside a Dr. Hard, who noticed that I took a little salt with my potatoes, and remarked to me that if I abstained from it, I would have my taste much more perfect. There was but little salt on the table, and I saw no person touch it. There was no animal food of any kind except milk, which one or two of them used. They all appeared to eat heartily. The women waited upon the table, but the variety of dishes being small, each person so attended to himself that waiting was rendered almost unnecessary. All displayed a rude politeness.

"After dinner I fell in with a cabinet-maker, a young man from Bond street, London, and had quite a chat with him; also an elderly man from England, John Wood by name, who was acquainted with the socialistic movement in that country. I then went to see the man work the saw-mill, and was much pleased with his apparent interest and industry.

"Not finding the acquaintance I was in search of at this place, and hearing that he was at another Community or branch of Prairie Home, about nine miles distant in a northerly direction (which they called the Upper Domain or Highland Home or Zanesfield), I determined to see him that night, and after obtaining necessary information I started on my journey.

"The walk was long, and it was dark before I reached the Community farm. At length the friendly bow-wow of a dog told of the habitable dwelling, and soon I was in the comfortable and pretty looking farm house at

Highland Home. This Community consisted of only ten or twelve persons. Here I found my friend, and after a wholesome Grahamite supper of corn-bread, apple-pie and milk, I had a long conversation with him and others on Community matters. I put many questions to them, all of which were answered satisfactorily. Here is a specimen of our dialogue:

"Do you make laws? No. Does the majority govern the minority? No. Have you any delegated power? No. Any kind of government? No. Do you express opinions and principles as a body? No. Have you any form of society or test for admission of members? No. Do you assist runaway slaves? Yes. Must you be Grahamites? No. Do you object to religionists? No. What are the terms of admission? The land is free to all; let those who want, come and use it. Any particular trades? No. Can persons take their earnings away with them when they leave? Yes.

"Their leading principle, they repeatedly told me, was to endeavor to practice the golden rule, 'Do as you would be done by.'

"The next morning I took a walk round the farm. It was a nice place, and appeared to have been well kept formerly, but now there was some disorder. The workmen appeared to be without clear ideas of the duties they were to perform. It seemed as if they had not made up their minds what they could do, or what they intended to do. Some of them were feeble-looking men, and in conversation with them I ascertained that several, both here and at Prairie Home, had adopted the present mode of Grahamite living to improve their health.

"Phrenology seemed to be pretty generally understood, and I was surprised to hear rude-looking men, almost ragged, ploughing, fence-making, and in like employments, converse so freely upon Phrenology, Physiology, Magnetism, Hydropathy, &c. The *Phrenological Journal* was taken by several of them.

"I visited a neighboring farm, said to belong to the Community, the residence, I believe, of Horton Brown, with whom I had an interesting conversation on religion and Community matters. He said they took the golden rule as their guide, 'Do unto others as ye would have others do unto you.' I reminded him that even the golden rule was subject to individual interpretation, and might be misinterpreted.

"*Saturday, August* 25, 1844.—I noticed several persons here were sick with various complaints, and those who were not sick labored very leisurely. During the day four men arrived from Indiana to see the place and 'join the Community;' but there were no accommodations for them. They reported quite a stir in Indiana in regard to the Community.

"In the afternoon my friend was ready to return to Cincinnati, whither he was going to try and induce his family to come to Zanesfield. We walked to Prairie Home that evening. At night we were directed to sleep at the two-story frame house at the entrance of the lane. At that place there seemed to be much confusion ; too many people and too many idlers among them. The young women were most industrious, attending to the supper table and the provisions in a very steady, business-like manner ; but the young men were mostly lounging about doing nothing. At bed-time there were too many persons for each to be accommodated with a bed ; so the females all went up stairs and slept as they could ; and the males slept below, all spread out in rows upon the floor. This was unpleasant, and as the sequel proved, could not long be endured.

" *Prairie Home, Sunday, August 26.*—In the morning, there was a social meeting of all the members. The weather was too wet and cold for them to meet on the hills, as was intended ; so they adjourned to the flour-mill, and seated themselves as best they could, on chairs and planks, men and women all together. Such a meeting as this was quite a novel sight for me. There was no chairman, no secretary and no constitution or by-laws to preserve order. Yet I never saw a more orderly meeting. The discussions seemed chiefly relating to agricultural matters. One man rose and stated that there was certain plowing to be done on the following day, and if it was thought best by the brothers and sisters, he would do it. Another rose and said he would volunteer to do the plowing if the first one pleased, and he might do something else. There appeared to be some competition in respect to what each should do, and yet a strong non-resistant principle was manifest, which seemed to smooth over any difficulty. There was some talk about money and the lease of the property, and several persons spoke, both male and female, apparently just as the spirit moved them. At the close of the meeting some singing was attempted, but it was very poor indeed. The folks scattered to the houses for dinner, and as usual took a pretty good supply of the potatoes, potato-soup, brown bread, apples and apple butter, together with large quantities of melons of various kinds.

"Owing to the cold weather the people were all huddled together inside the houses. The rooms were too

small, and many of the young men were compelled to
sleep in the mill. Altogether there were too many persons brought together for the scanty accommodations
of the place.

"*Monday, August 27.*—The wind blew hard, and
threw down a large stack of hay. It was interesting to
see the rapidity with which a group of volunteers put it
in order again. The party seemed to act with perfect
union.

"Several persons arrived to join the Community ;
among the rest a farmer and his family in a large wagon,
with a lot of household stuff.

"I watched several men at work in different places,
and to one party I could not help expressing myself
thus : 'If you fail, I will give it up; for never did I see
men work so well or so brotherly with each other.' But
all were not thus industrious; for I saw some who
merely crawled about (probably sick), just looking on
like myself, at any thing which fell in their way. There
was evident disorder, showing a transition state toward
either harmony or anarchy. I am sorry to say, it too
soon proved to be the latter.

"After dinner some one suggested having a meeting
to talk about a plow. With some little exertion they
managed to get ten or twelve men together. Then they
sat down and reasoned with each other at great length.
But it was very uneconomical, I thought, to bring so
many persons together from their work, to talk so much
about so small a matter. A plow had to be repaired ;
some one must and did volunteer to go to the town with
it ; he wanted money to pay for it ; there was no money ;
he must take a bag of corn or wheat, and trade that off

to pay for the repairs; a wagon had to be got out; two horses put to it, and a journey of some miles made, and nearly a day of time expended about such a trifling job.

"I went to see the saw-mill at work; found one or two men engaged at it. They were working for customers, and got a certain portion of the lumber for what they sawed. I then went into an old log cabin and found my acquaintance, the cabinet-maker. On my inquiring how he liked Community, he told me the following story: He came from London to find friends in Indiana, and brought with him a fine chest of tools. On his arrival, he found his friends about to start for Community; so he came with them. He brought his tools with him, but left them at Zanesfield, and came down here. The folks at Zanesfield, wanting a plane, a saw and chisels, and knowing that his box was there, having no key, actually broke open the box, and under the influence of the common-property idea, helped themselves to the tools, and spoiled them by using them on rough work. He had got his chest away from there. He said he had no objection to their using the tools, if they knew how and did not spoil them. I saw one or two large chisels with pieces chipped out of them and planes nicked by nails, all innocently and ignorantly done by the brothers, who scarcely saw any wrong in it.

"It was interesting to see the groups of unshaven men. There were men between forty and fifty years of age, who had shaved all their lives before, but now they let their beards grow, and looked ferocious. The young men looked well, and some of them rather handsome, with their soft beards and hair uncut; but the elderly ones did certainly look ugly. There was a German of a thin, gaunt figure, about fifty years of age, with a

large, stubby, gray beard, and an ill-tempered countenance.

"John Wood, the Englishman, a pretty good specimen,
blunt, open hearted and independent, had got three pigs
in a pen, which he fed and took care of. They were the
only animals on the place, except the horses. But
exercising his rights, he said, 'If the rest of them did
not want meat, he *did*—for he liked a bit o'meat.'

"I was informed that all the animals on the place,
when the Community took possession of the domain,
were allowed to go where they pleased; or those who
wanted them were free to take them.

"Before the meeting on Sunday, groups of men stood
round the house talking; some two or three of them,
including John Wood and the Dutchman (as he was
called) were cleaning themselves up a bit; and John
had blackened and polished his boots; after which he
carefully put the blacking and brushes away. Out
came the Dutchman and looked round for the same
utensils. Not seeing them, he asked the Englishman
for the 'prushes.' So John brings them out and hands
them to him. Whereupon the Dutchman marches to
the front of the porch, and in wrathful style, with the
brushes uplifted in his hand, he addresses the assembled
crowd: 'He-ar! lookee he-ar! Do you call dis Community? Is dis common property? See he-ar! I ask
him for de prushes to placken mine poots, and he give
me de prushes, and *not give me de placking!*' This
was said with great excitement. 'He never saw such
community as dat; he could not understand; he tought
every ting was to be common to all!' But John Wood
good-humoredly explained that he had bought a box of
blacking for himself, and if· he gave it to every one who

wanted to black boots, he would very soon be without
any ; so he shut it up for his own use, and those who
wanted blacking must buy it for themselves.

" I noticed there was some carelessness with the farm
tools. There was a small shed in which all the scythes,
hoes, axes, &c., were supposed to be deposited when not
in use. But they were not always returned there. It
appeared that these tools were used indiscriminately by
any one and every one, so that one day a man would
have one ax or scythe, and the next day another. This
was evidently not agreeable in practice ; for every
working-man well knows that he forms attachments for
certain tools, as much as he does for friends, and his
hand and heart get used to them, as it were, so that he
can use them better than he can strange ones.

" With these few notices of failings, I must say I never
saw a better-hearted or more industrious set of fellows.
They appeared to struggle hard to effect something, yet
it seemed evident that something was lacking among
them to make things work well. It might have been
organized laws, or government of some kind ; it might
have been a definite bond of union, or a prominent
leader. It is certain there was some power or influence
needed, to direct the force mustered there, and make it
work economically and harmoniously.

" People kept coming and going, and were ready to do
something ; but there was nobody to tell them what to
do, and they did not know what to do themselves. They
had to eat, drink and sleep ; and they expected to obtain
the means of doing so ; but they seemed not to reflect
who was going to supply these means, or where they
were to come from Some seemed greedy and reckless,
eating all the time, cutting melons out of the garden and

from among the corn, eating them and throwing the peels and seeds about the foot-paths and door-ways.

" There was an abundance of fine corn on the domain, abundance of melons of all kinds, and, I believe, plenty of apples at the upper Community. Much provision had been brought and sent there by farmers who had entered into the spirit of the cause. For instance there were some wagon-loads of potatoes and apples sent, as well as quantities of unbolted wheat meal, of which the bread was made.

" On my asking about the idlers, the reply was, ' Oh ! they will not stop here long ; it is uncongenial to lazy people to be among industrious ones ; and for their living, it do'nt cost much more than fifty cents per week, and they can surely earn that.'

" At the Sunday meeting before mentioned, the enthusiasm of some was great. One man said he left his home in Indiana ; he had a house there, which he thought at first to reserve in case of accident ; but he finally concluded that if he had any thing to fall back upon, he could not give his heart and soul to the cause as he wanted to ; so he gave up every thing he possessed, and put it into Community. Others did the same, while some had reserved property to fall back upon. Some said they had lands which they would put into the Community, if they could get rid of them ; but the times were so hard that there was much scarcity of money, and the lands would not sell.

" From all I saw I judged that the Community was too loosely put together, and that they had not entire confidence in each other ; and I left them with forebodings.

" The experiment lasted scarcely a year. On the 25th

of October, about two months after my visit, they had a meeting to talk over their affairs. More than three thousand dollars had been paid on the property; but the land owner was pressed with a mortgage, and so pressed them. One man sold his farm and got part of the required sum ready to pay. Others who owned farms could not sell them; and the consequence was, that according to agreement they were obliged to give up the papers; so they surrendered the domain and all upon it, into the hands of the original proprietor.

" The members then scattered in various directions. Several were considerable losers by the attempt, while many had nothing to lose. At the present time I learn that there are men and women of that Community who are still ready with hands and means to try the good work again. The cause of failure assigned by the Communists was their not owning the land they settled upon; but I think it very doubtful whether they could have kept together if the land had been free; for as I have before said, there was something else wanted to make harmony in labor."

CHAPTER XXVIII.

THE TRUMBULL PHALANX.

THIS experiment originated among the Socialist enthusiasts of Pittsburg, Pennsylvania Its domain at Braceville, Trumbull County, Ohio, was selected and a commencement was made in the spring of 1844. From this date till its failure in the latter part of 1847, we find in the *Phalanx* and *Harbinger* some sixteen notices of it, long and short, from which we are to gather its history. We will quote the salient parts of these notices ; and so let the friends of the experiment speak for themselves. The rose-color of their representations will be corrected by the ultimate facts. This was one of the three most notable experiments in the Fourier epoch—the North American and the Wisconsin Phalanxes being the other two.

[From a letter of Mr. Jehu Brainerd, June 29, 1844.]

" The location which this society has chosen, is a very beautiful one and is situated in the north-west quarter of Braceville township, eight miles west of Warren, and five miles north of Newton Falls.

" The domain was purchased of Mr. Eli Barnum, at twelve dollars per acre, and consists of two hundred and eighty acres of the choicest land, about half of which is under good cultivation. There is a valuable and durable mill privilege on the domain, valued at three thousand six hundred dollars ; and at the time the purchase was made, there were in successful operation, a grist-mill with two run of stones, an oil-mill, saw-mill, double carding-machine, and cloth-dressing works.

"The principal buildings on the domain are a large two story brick house, grist-mill and oil-mill, very large, substantial, and entirely new, framed and well painted, and a large barn ; the other buildings, though sufficient for present accommodation, are old and somewhat decayed.

"There has been already subscribed in real estate stock, most of which is within two miles and less of the domain, nine hundred and fifty-seven acres of land, mostly improved farms, which were valued (including neat stock, grain, &c) at sixteen thousand one hundred and fifty dollars. Five hundred dollars cash capital has also been subscribed and paid in ; and about six hundred dollars in lathes, tools, machinery, &c., including one hundred thousand feet of lumber, have been received.

"There are thirty-five families now belonging to the Association, in all one hundred and forty persons ; of this number forty-three are males over twenty-one years of age. Until accommodations can be prepared on the domain, some of the families will reside on the farms subscribed as stock. It is the intention to commence an edifice of brick this present summer, and extend it from time to time, as the increase of members may require, or the funds of the society admit. For present necessity, temporary buildings are erected.

[From a letter of N. C. Meeker, August 10, 1844.]

"The number of persons belonging to the Phalanx is about two hundred ; some reside on the domain proper ;

others on more distant farms belonging to the Phalanx. Indeed as regards room, they are much crowded, residing in loose sheds. Nevertheless, on no consideration would they exchange present conditions for former ones. More convenient residences are to be erected forthwith, but it is not contemplated to erect the Phalanstery or final edifice for a year or so, or until they are possessed of sufficient means. Then the magnificent palace of the Combined Order will equally shame the temples of antiquity and the card-houses of modern days.

"For the present year hard work and few of the attractions of Association are expected. Almost everything is unfitted for the use of Associations, being too insignificant, or characteristic of present society ; made to sell rather than to use. The members of the Trumbull Phalanx, knowing how to work truly, and fully understanding that it is a gigantic labor to overturn the despair which has been accumulating so long in men's bosoms, have nerved themselves manfully, showing the true dignity of human nature.

" Labor is partially organized by the instituting of groups, and to much advantage. Boys who were idle and unproductive, have become producers, and a very fine garden is the work of their hands. They are under the charge of a proper person, who permits them to choose their foreman from among themselves, and at certain hours, in grounds laid out for the purpose, to engage in sports. Even the men themselves, at the close of the work, find agreeable and salutary exercise in a game of ball. Some going to school, earn six or seven shillings a week, and where they work in the brick-yard, from three to four shillings a day. These sums are not final wages, but *permits;* for when a dividend is declared there will be an additional remuneration.

"On the Sabbath I attended their social meeting, in which those of all persuasions participated. The liberal views and kindly feelings manifested by the various speakers were such as I had never heard before. They spoke of the near relations they sustained to each other, and of the many blessings they look to receive in the future; meanwhile the present unity gave them an idea of heaven. One spirit of joy and gladness seemed to animate them, viz; that they had escaped from the wants, cares, and temptations of civilization, and instead were placed where public good is the same as individual good; hence nothing save pre-conceived prejudices, fast giving away, prevent their loving their neighbors as themselves. This is the spirit of Christianity. Their position calls for union. No good can arise from divers sects; no good ever did arise. They will all unite, Presbyterians, Disciples, Baptists, Methodists, and all; and if any name be needed, under that of Unionism. After meeting the sacrament was administered; then followed a Bible-class, and singing exercises closed the day. [It would seem from this description, that the religion of the Trumbull was more orthodox than any we have found in other Phalanxes.]

"Those not accustomed to view the progress of combined labor will be astonished to see aggregates. A vast brick-kiln is raised in a short time; a touch plants a field of corn, and a few weeks turns a forest into a farm. Only a few of such results can be seen now; but enough has been done at this Phalanx since last spring, to give one an idea of the vast results which will arise in the days of the new industrial world.

Seating myself in the venerable orchard, with the temporary dwellings on the opposite side, the joiners at their benches in their open shops under the green boughs, and hearing on every side the sound of industry, the roll of wheels in the mills, and merry voices, I could not help exclaiming mentally: Indeed my eyes see men making haste to free the slave of all names, nations and tongues, and my ears hear them driving, thick and fast, nails into the coffin of despotism. I can but look on the establishment of this Phalanx as a step of as much importance as any which secured our political independence; and much greater than that which gained the Magna Charta, the foundation of English liberty.

"But as yet there is nothing clearly demonstrated save by faith. That which remains to be seen is, whether families can be made to associate in peace, enjoying the profits as well as pleasures arising from public tables, granaries, store-houses, libraries, schools, gardens, walks and fountains ; or, briefer, whether a man will be willing that he and his neighbor should be happy together. Are men forever to be such consummate fools as to neglect even the colossal profits of Association? Am I to be astonished by hearing sensible men declare, because mankind have been the victims of false relations, that these things are impracticable? No, no! We have been shown by the Columbus of the new industrial world how to solve the problem of the egg, and a few caravels have adventured across the unknown ocean, and are now, at the dawn of a new day, drawing nigh unto strange shores, covered with green, and loading the breeze with the fragrance of unseen flowers.

"Nathan C. Meeker."

[From an official letter to a Convention of Associations in New York, signed by B. Robins and H. N. Jones, President and Secretary of the Trumbull Phalanx, dated October 1, 1844.]

"We should have sent a delegate to your Convention or written sooner, were not the assistance of all of our members daily demanded, as also all our time, in the building up of Humanity's Home. In common with the inhabitants of the region round about (it is supposed on account of the dry season), we have had many cases of fever and ague, a disease which has not been known here for many years. This has prevented our executing various plans for organization, etc., which we are now entering upon. And now, with each day, we have abundant cause to hope for a joyous future. We have harmony within and sympathy without; and being persuaded that these are sure indications of success, we toil on, 'heart within and God o'erhead.'

"Further, our pecuniary prospects brighten. Late arrangements add to our means of paying our debt, which is light; and accumulations of landed estate make us quite secure. Nevertheless we feel that we are in the transition period, using varied and noble elements not the most skillfully, and that we need more than man's wisdom to guide us.

"The union of the Associations we look upon as a great and noble idea, without which the chain of universal unity were incomplete. When we shall have emerged from the sea of civilization, so that we can do our own breathing, we shall be able to coöperate with our friends throughout the world, as members of the grand Phalanx. Meanwhile our hearts will be with you, urging you not to falter in the work in which all the noble and healthy spirit of the age is engaged.

"Accompanying is a copy of our constitution. Our number is over two hundred. We have 1,500 acres of land, half under cultivation, and a capital stock of $100,000. The branches of industry are sufficiently varied, but mostly agricultural.

[Letter to the Pittsburg *Spirit of the Age*, July 1845.]

"I have just returned from a visit to the Trumbull Phalanx, and I can but express my astonishment at the condition in which I found the Association. I had never heard much of this Phalanx, and what little had been said, gave me no very favorable opinion of either location or people, and in consequence I went there somewhat prejudiced against them. I was pleased, however, to find that they have a beautiful and romantic domain, a rich soil, with all the natural and artificial advantages they can desire. The domain consists of eleven hundred acres in all. The total cost of the real estate of the Phalanx is $18,428 ; on which they have paid $8,239, leaving a debt of $10,189. The payments are remarkably easy ; on the principal, $1,000 are to be paid in September next, and the same sum in April 1846, and $1,133 in April 1847, and the same sum annually thereafter. They apprehend no difficulty in meeting their engagements. Should they even fail in making the first payments, they will be indulged by their creditor. From this it will be seen that the pecuniary condition of the Trumbull Phalanx is encouraging.

"The Phalanx has fee simple titles to many tracts of land, and a house in Warren, with which they will secure capitalists who choose to invest money, for the purpose of establishing some branches of manufacturing

"There are about two hundred and fifty people on the domain at present, and weekly arrivals of new mem-

bers.   The greater portion of them are able-bodied men,
who are industrious and devoted to the cause in which
they are engaged.   The ladies perform their duties in
this pioneer movement in a manner deserving great praise.
The educational department of the Phalanx is well organized.   The children from eight to fourteen attend a
manual-labor school, which is now in successful operation.   The advantages of Association are realized in the
boarding department.   The cost per week for men,
women and children, is not more than forty cents.

" They soon expect to manufacture their own clothing.
Carders, cloth-dressers, weavers etc., are now at work.
These branches will be a source of profit to the Association.   A good flouring-mill with two run of stone is
now in operation, which more than supplies the bread-
stuffs.   They expect shortly to have four run of stone,
when this branch will be of immense profit to the Association.   The mill draws the custom of the neighborhood
for a number of miles around.   Two saw-mills are now in
operation, which cut six hundred thousand feet per year,
worth at least $ 3,000.   The lumber is principally sent to
Akron.   A shingle-machine now in operation, will yield
a revenue of $ 3,000 or $ 4,000 per annum.   Machinery
for making wooden bowls has been erected, which will
also yield a revenue of about $ 3,000.   An ashery will
yield the present season about $ 500.   The blacksmiths,
shoemakers, and other branches are doing well.   A
wagon-shop is in progress of erection, and a tan-yard will
be sunk and a house built, the second story of which is
intended for a shoe-shop.

"*Crops:* thirty acres of wheat, fifty acres of oats,
seventy acres of corn, twelve acres of potatoes, five
acres of English turnips, ten acres of buckwheat, five

acres of garden truck, one and a-half acres of broom corn. There are five hundred young peach trees in the nursery ; two hundred apple trees in the old orchard ; (fruit killed this year). *Live Stock:* forty-five cows, twelve horses, five yoke of oxen, twenty-five head of cattle.

" From the above hasty sketch (for I can not find time to speak of this flourishing Association as I should), it will be seen that it stands firm. Under all the disadvantages of a new movement, the members live together, in perfect harmony ; and what is gratifying, Mr. Van Amringe is there, cheering them on in the great cause by his eloquence, and setting them an example of devotion to the good of humanity. J. D. T.

[Editorial in the *Harbinger* August 23 1845.]

" TRUMBULL PHALANX.—We rejoice to learn by a letter just received from a member of this promising Association, that they are going forward with strength and hope, determined to make a full experiment of the great principles which they have espoused. Have patience, brothers, for a short season ; shrink not under the toils of the pioneer ; let nothing daunt your courage, nor cloud your cheerfulness ; and soon you will joy with the 'joy of harvest.' A few years will present the beautiful spectacle of prosperous, harmonic, happy Phalanxes, dotting the broad prairies of the West, spreading over its luxuriant valleys, and radiating light to the whole land that is now in ' darkness and the shadow of death ' The whole American people will yet see that the organization of industry is the great problem of the age ; that the spirit of democracy must expand in universal unity ; that coöperation in labor and union of interest alone can realize the freedom and equality which have been made the basis of our national institutions.

" We trust that our friends at the Trumbull Phalanx will let us hear from them again at an early date. We shall always be glad to circulate any intelligence with which they may favor us. Here is what they say of their present condition: 'Our crops are now coming in ; oats are excellent, wheat and rye are about average, while our corn will be superior. We are thankful that we shall raise enough to carry us through the year ; for we know what it is to buy every thing. We are certain of success, certain that the great principles of Association are to be carried out by us ; if not on one piece of ground, then on another. Literally we constitute a Phalanx, a Phalanx which can not be broken, let what will oppose. And this you are authorized to say in any place or manner.' "

[Letter of N. C. Meeker to the *Pittsburg Journal.*]

" *Trumbull Phalanx, September* 13, 1845.

" R. M. RIDDLE—Sir : I have the pleasure of inform- ing the public, through the columns of the *Commercial Journal*, that we consider the success of our Association as entirely certain. We have made our fall payment of five hundred dollars, and, what is perhaps more encouraging, we are at this moment engaged in indus- trial operations which yield us thirty dollars cash, each week. The waters are now rising, and in a few days, in addition to these works which are now in operation, we shall add as much more to the above revenue. The Trumbull Phalanx may now be considered as an entirely successful enterprise.

" Our crops will be enough to carry us through. Last

year we paid over a thousand dollars for provisions. We have sixty-five acres of corn, fifty-five of oats, twenty-four of buckwheat, thirty of wheat, twenty of rye, twelve of potatoes, and two of broom-corn. Our corn, owing to the excellent soil and superior skill of the foreman of the farming department, is the best in all this region of country. Thus we have already one of the great advantages of Association, in securing the services of the most able and scientific, not for individual, selfish good, but for public good. We are fortunate, also, that we shall be able to keep all our stock of fifty cows, etc., and not be obliged to drive them off or kill them, as the farmers do around us, for we have nearly fodder enough from our grains alone. Thus we are placed in a situation for building up an Association, for establishing a perfect organization of industry by means of the groups and series, and in education by the monitorial manual-labor system, and shall demonstrate that order, and not civilization, is heaven's first law.

"Some eight or ten families have lately left us, one-fourth because they had been in the habit of living on better food (so they said), but the remainder because they were averse to our carrying out the principles of Association as far as we thought they ought to be carried. On leaving, they received in return whatever they asked of us. They who enter Association ought first to study themselves, and learn which stage of Association they are fitted for, the transitional or the perfect. If they are willing to endure privations, to eat coarse food, sometimes with no meat, but with milk for a substitute (this is a glorious resort for the Grahamites), to live on friendly terms with an old hat or coat, rather than have the society run in debt, and to have patience when many things go wrong, and are willing to work long and late to make them go right, they may consider themselves fitted for the transition-period. But if they sigh for the flesh-pots and leeks and onions of civilization, feel melancholy with a patch on their back, and growl because they can not have eggs and honey and warm biscuit and butter for breakfast, they had better stay where they are, and wait for the advent of perfect industrial Association. I am thus trifling in contrast; for there is nothing so serious, hearty, and I might add, sublime, as the building up of a Phalanx, making and seeing it grow day by day, and anticipating what fruits we shall enjoy when a few years are past. Why, the heart of man has never yet conceived what are the to-be results of the equilibrial development of all the powers and faculties of man. It is like endeavoring to comprehend the nature and pursuits of a spiritual and superior race of beings.

"We are prepared to receive members who are desirous of uniting their interests with us, and of becoming truly devoted to the cause of industrial Association.

"Yours truly, N. C. MEEKER."

[From a letter to the *Tribune*, September 29, 1846.]

"The progress made by the Trumbull Phalanx is doing great good. People begin to say, 'If they could hang together under such bad circumstances for so long a time, and no difficulties occur, what must we hope for, now that they are pecuniarily independent?' You have heard, I presume, that the Pittsburghers have furnished money enough to place that Association out of debt. I may be over-sanguine, but I feel confident of their complete success. I fear our Eastern friends have not sufficient faith in our efforts. Well, I trust we may dis-

appoint them.   The Trumbull, so far as means amount
to any thing, stands first of any Phalanx in the United
States ; and as to harmony among the members, I can
only say that there has been no difficulty yet.

"Yours truly,   J. D. S."

[From the Harbinger, January 2, 1847.]

"We have received the following gratifying account
of the Trumbull Phalanx.   Every attempt of the kind
here described, though not to be regarded as an experiment of a model Phalanx, is in the highest degree
interesting, as showing the advantages of combined
industry and social union.   Go forward, strong-hearted
brothers, assured that every step you take is bringing us
nearer the wished-for goal, when the redemption of
humanity shall be fully realized.   This is what they say :

"'We are getting along well.   Our Pittsburg friends
have lately sent us two thousand dollars, and are to send
more during the winter.   We are also adding to our
numbers.   We have an abundance to eat of our own
raising ; but aside from this, our mill brings sufficient
for our support.   We have put up a power-loom at our
upper works, and are about prepared to produce thereby
sufficient to clothe us.   Hence, by uniting capital,
labor and skill in two mechanical branches, we secure,
with ordinary industry, what no equal number of families
in civilization can be said to possess entirely, a sufficient
amount of food and clothing.   And these are items
which practical men know how to value ; and we know
how to value them too, because they are the results of
our own efforts.

"'We have two schools, one belonging to the district,
that is, a State or public school, and the other to the

Phalanx, both taught by persons who are members. In the latter school, among other improvements, there are classes in Phonography and Phonotopy, learning the new systems embraced by the writing and printing reformation, the progress of which is highly satisfactory.

" 'On the whole, we feel that our success is ensured beyond an earthly doubt. Not but that we have yet to pass through trying scenes. But we have encountered so many difficulties that we are not apprehensive but that we are prepared to meet others equally as great. Indeed we feel that if we had known at the commencement what fiery trials were to surround us, we should have hesitated to enter upon the enterprise. Now, being fairly in, we will brave it through, and we think you may look to see us grow with each year, adding knowledge to wealth, and industrious habits to religious precepts and elevated sentiments, till we shall be prepared to enter upon the combined order, and, with our co-partners, who are now breast and heart with us, lead the kingdoms of the earth into the regions of light, liberty and love.' "

[From the *Pittsburg Post*, January 1847.]

"TRUMBULL PHALANX.—Several Pittsburgers have joined the above-named Association : and a sufficient amount of money has been contributed to place it upon a solid foundation. It is pecuniarily independent, as we are informed ; and the members are full of faith in complete success. Several letters have been received by persons in this city from resident members of the Phalanx. We should like to have one of them for publication, to show the feelings which pervade those who are working out the problem of social unity. They write in substance, ' The Association is prosperous, and we are all happy.'

" The Trumbull Phalanx is now in its third or fourth year, and so far has met with but few of the difficulties anticipated by the friends or enemies of the cause. The progress has been slow, it is true, owing to a variety of causes, the principal one of which has been removed, viz.: debt. Much sickness existed on the domain during the last season, but no fears are felt for the future, as to the general health of the neighborhood.

[From a letter of C. Woodhouse, July 3, 1847.]

" This Phalanx has been in existence nearly four years, and has encountered many difficulties and submitted to many privations. Difficulties still exist and privations are not now few or small; but so great is the change for the better in less than four years, that they are fully impressed with the promise of success. At no time, indeed, have they met with as many difficulties as the lonely settler in a new country meets with; for in all their poverty they have been in pleasant company and have aided one another. They are now surrounded by all the necessaries and some of the comforts of life. Each family has a convenient dwelling, and so far as I can judge from a short visit, they enjoy the good of their labor, with no one to molest or make them afraid. Several branches of mechanical industry are carried on there, but agriculture is the staff on which they principally lean. Their land is very good, and of their thousand acres, over three hundred are improved. Their stock--horses, cattle and cows--look very well, as the farmers say. The improvements and condition of the domain bespeak thrift, industry and practical skill. The Trumbullites are workers. I saw no dainty-fingered theorists there. When such do come, I am informed, they do not stay long. Work is the order of the day. They would be glad of more leisure ; but at this stage of the enterprise they put forth all their powers to redeem themselves from debt, and make such improvements as will conduce to this end and at the same time add to their comforts. Not a cent is expended in display or for knicknacks. The President lives in a log house and drives team on the business of the Association. Whatever politicians may say to the contrary, I think he is the only veritable ' log-cabin President' the whole land can show."

[From a letter of the Women of the Trumbull Phalanx to the Women of the Boston Union of Associationists, July 15, 1847.]

"It is plain that our efforts must be different from yours. Yours is the part to arouse the idle and indifferent by your conversation, and by contributing funds to sustain and aid publications. Ours is the part to organize ourselves in all the affairs of life, in the best manner that our imperfect institution will permit ; and, not least, to have faith in our own efforts. In this last particular we are sometimes deficient, for it is impossible for us with our imperfect and limited capacities, clearly and fully to foresee what faith and confidence in God's providence can accomplish. We have been brought hither through doubts and dangers, and through the shadows of the future we have no guide save where duty points the way.

"Our trials lie in the commonest walks. To forego conveniences, to live poorly, dress homely, to listen calmly, reply mildly, and wait patiently, are what we must become familiar with. True, these are requirements by no means uncommon ; but imperfect beings like ourselves are apt to imagine that they alone are called upon to endure. Yet, perhaps, we enjoy no less than the most of our sex; nay, we are in truth, sisters the world round; if one suffers, all suffer, no matter whether she tends her husband's dogs amidst the Polar snows, or mounts her consort's funeral pile upon the banks of the Ganges. Together we weep, together we rejoice. We rise, we fall together.

"It would afford us much pleasure could we be associated together. Could all the women fitted to engage in Social Reform be located on one domain, one can not imagine the immense changes that would ensue. We pray that we, or at least our children, may live to see the day when kindred souls shall be permitted to coöperate in a sphere sufficiently extensive to call forth all our powers."

(From a letter of N. C. Meeker, August 11, 1847.)

"Our progress and prosperity are still continued. By this we only mean that whatever we secure is by overcoming many difficulties. Our triumphs, humble though they be, are achieved in the same manner that the poet or the sculptor or the chemist achieves his, by labor, by application; and we believe that to produce the most useful and beautiful things, the most labor and pains are necessary.

"Our present difficulties are, first, want of a sufficient number to enable us to establish independent groups, as Fourier has laid down. The present arrangement is as though we were all in one group; what is earned by the body is divided among individuals according to the amount of labor expended by each. Were our branches of business fewer (for we carry on almost every branch of industry necessary to support us) we could organize with less danger of interruption, which at present must be incessant ; yet, at the same time there would be less choice of employment. Our number is about two hundred and fifty, and that of laboring men not far from fifty. This want of a greater number is by no means a serious difficulty ; still, one we wish were corrected by an addition of scientific and industrious men, with some capital.

" Again, when the season is wet, we have the fever and ague among us to some extent, though previous to our locating here the place was healthy. Whether it will be healthy in future we of course can not determine, but see no reason why it may not. The ague is by no means dangerous, but it is quite disagreeable, and during its continuance, is quite discouraging. Upon the approach of cold weather it disappears, and we recover, feeling as strong and hopeful as ever. Other diseases do not visit us, and the mortality of the place is low, averaging thus far, almost four years, less than two annually, and these were children. We are convinced, however, that all cause of the ague may be removed by a little outlay, which of course we shall make.

" These are our chief incumbrances at present ; others have existed equally discouraging, and have been surmounted. The time was when our very existence for a period longer than a few months, was exceedingly doubtful. Two or three heavy payments remained due, and our creditor was pressing. Now we shall not owe him a cent till next April. By the assistance of our Pittsburg friends and Mr. Van Amringe, we have been put in this situation. About half of our debt of about $ 7,000 is paid. All honor to Englishmen (William Bayle in particular), who have thus set an example to the 'sons of '76.'

[From a report of a Socialist Convention at Boston, October 1847.]

"The condition and prospects of the experiments now in progress in this country, especially the North American, Trumbull and Wisconsin Phalanxes, were discussed. Mr. Cooke has lately visited all these Associations, and brings back a large amount of interesting information. The situation of the North American is decidedly hopeful; as to the other two, his impressions were of a less sanguine tone than letters which have been recently published in the *Harbinger* and *Tribune*. Yet it is not time to despair."

The reader will hardly be prepared for the next news we have about the Trumbull; but we have seen before that Associations are apt to take sudden turns.

[Letter to the *Harbinger* announcing failure.]

"*Braceville, Ohio, December* 3, 1847.

To the Editors of the Harbinger,

"GENTLEMEN: You and your readers have no doubt heard before this of the dissolution of this Association, and the report is but too true; we have fallen. But we wish civilization to know that in our fall we have not broken our necks. We have indeed caught a few pretty bad scratches; but all our limbs are yet sound, and we mean to pick ourselves up again. We will try and try again. The infant has to fall several times before he can walk; but that does not discourage him, and he succeeds; nor shall we be so easily discouraged.

"Some errors, not intentional though fatal, have been committed here; we see them now, and will endeavor to avoid them. I believe that it may be said of us with

truth, that our failure is a triumph. Our fervent love
for Association is not quenched; we are not dispersed;
we are not discouraged; we are not even scared. We
know our own position. What we have done we have
done deliberately and intentionally, and we think we
know also what we have to do. There are, however,
difficulties in our way: we are aware of them. We
may not succeed in reörganizing here as we wish to do;
but if we fail, we will try elsewhere. There is yet room
in this western world. We will first offer ourselves, our
experience, our energies, and whatever means are left
us, to our sister Associations. We think we are worth
accepting; but if they have the inhumanity to refuse,
we will try to build a new hive somewhere else, in the
woods or on the prairies. God will not drive us from his
own earth. He has lent it to all men; and we are men,
and men of good intentions, of no sinister motives.
Our rights are as good in his eyes as those of our
brothers.

"We do not deem it necessary here to give a detailed
account of our affairs and circumstances. It will be
sufficient to say that, however unfavorable they may be
at present, we do not consider our position as desperate.
We think we know the remedy; and we intend to use
our best exertions to effect a cure. It may be proper
also to state that we have not in any manner infringed
our charter.

"I do not write in an official capacity, but I am
authorized to say, gentlemen, that if you can con-
veniently, and will, as soon as practicable, give this
communication an insertion in the *Harbinger*, you will
serve the cause, and oblige your brothers of the late
Trumbull Phalanx.   G. M. M."

After this decease, an attempt was made to resuscitate the Association ; as will be seen in the following paragraphs :

[From a letter in the *Harbinger*, May 27, 1848.]

"With improvident philanthropy, the Phalanx had admitted too indiscriminately ; so that the society was rather an asylum for the needy, sick and disabled, than a nucleus of efficient members, carrying out with all their powers and energies, a system on which they honestly rely for restoring their race to elevation and happiness.   They also had accepted unprofitable capital, producing absolutely nothing, upon which they were paying interest upon interest.   All this weighed most heavily on the efficient members.   They made up their minds to break up altogether.

" A new society has been organized, which has bought at auction, and very low, the domain with all its improvements.   We, the new society, purpose to work on the following foundation : Our object is to try the system of Fourier, so far as it is in our power, with our limited means, etc."

[From a letter in the *Harbinger*, July 15, 1848.]

"With respect to our little society here, we wish at present to say only that it is going on with alacrity and great hopes of success.   We are prepared for a few additional members with the requisite qualifications ; but we do not think it expedient to do or say much to induce any body to come on until we see how we shall fare through what is called the sickly season.   To the present date, however, we may sum up our condition in these three words :   We are healthy, busy and happy."

This is the last we find about the new organization.

So we conclude it soon passed away. As it is best to hear all sides, we will conclude this account with some extracts from a grumbling letter, which we find among Macdonald's manuscripts.

[Account by a Malcontent.]

" A great portion of the land was swampy, so much so that it could not be cultivated. It laid low, and had a creek running through it, which at times overflowed, and caused a great deal of sickness to the inhabitants of the place. The disease was mostly fever and ague; and this was so bad, that three-fourths of the people, both old and young, were shaking with it for months together. Through the public prints, persons favorable to the Association were invited to join, which had the effect of drawing many of the usual mixed characters from various parts of the country. Some came with the idea that they could live in idleness at the expense of the purchasers of the estate, and these ideas they practically carried out; whilst others came with good hearts for the cause. There were one or two designing persons, who came with no other intent than to push themselves into situations in which they could impose upon their fellow members; and this, to a certain extent, they succeeded in doing.

"When the people first assembled, there was not sufficient house room to accommodate them, and they were huddled together like brutes; but they built some log cabins, and then tried to establish some kind of order, by rules and regulations. One of their laws was, that all persons before becoming members must pay twenty-five dollars each. Some did pay this, but the majority had not the money to pay. I think most persons came there for a mere shift. Their poverty and their quarrelling about what they called religion (for there were many notions about which was the right way to heaven), were great drawbacks to success. Nearly all the business was carried on by barter, there was so little money. Labor was counted by the hour, and was booked to each individual. Booking was about all the pay they ever got. At the breaking up, some of the members had due to them for labor and stock, five or six hundred dollars; and some of them did not receive as many cents.

"To give an idea of the state of things, I may mention that there was a shrewd Yankee there, who established a boarding-house and pretended to accommodate boarders at very reasonable charges. He was poor, but he made many shifts to get something for his boarders to eat, though it was but very little. There was seldom any butter, cheese, or animal food upon the table, and what he called coffee was made of burnt bread. He had no bedding for the boarders; they had to provide it for themselves if they could; if not, they had to sleep on the floor. For this board he charged $1.62 per week, while it was proved that the cost per week for each individual was not more than twenty cents. This man professed to be a doctor, (though I believe he really knew no more of medicine than any other person there); and as there were so many persons sick with the ague, he got plenty of work. Previous to the breaking up, he brought in his bills to the patients (whom he had never benefited), charging them from ten to thirty dollars each, and some even higher. But the people being very poor, he did not succeed in recovering much of what he called his 'just dues;' though by threats of the law he scared some of them out of a trifle. There was another keen fellow, a preacher and lawyer, who got into office as secretary and treasurer, and kept the accounts. When there was any money he had the management of it; and I believe he knew perfectly well how to use it for his own advantage, which many of the members felt to their sorrow. The property was supposed to have been held by stockholders. Those who had the management of things know best how it was finally disposed of. For my part I think this was the most unsatisfactory experiment attempted in the West.

"J. M., member of the Trumbull Phalanx."

What a story of passion and suffering can be traced in this broken material! Study it. Think of the great hope at the beginning; the heroism of the long struggle; the bitterness of the end. This human group was made up of husbands and wives, parents and children, brothers and sisters, friends and lovers, and had two hundred hearts, longing for blessedness. Plodding on their weary march of life, Association rises before them like the *mirage* of the desert. They see in the vague distance, magnificent palaces, green fields, golden harvests, sparkling fountains, abundance of rest and romance ; in one word, HOME—which also is HEAVEN. They rush like the thirsty caravan to realize their vision., And now the scene changes. Instead of reaching palaces, they find themselves huddled together in loose sheds—thirty-five families trying to live in dwellings built for one. They left the world to escape from want and care and temptation; and behold, these hungry wolves follow them in fiercer packs than ever. The gloom of debt is over them from the beginning. Again and again they are on the brink of bankruptcy.   It is a constant question and doubt whether they will "SUCCEED," which means, whether they will barely keep soul and body together, and pacify their creditors.   But they cheer one another on.   "They *must* succeed ; they *will* succeed ; they *are* already succeeding!"   These words they say over and over to themselves, and shout them to the public.   Still debt hangs over them.   They get a subsidy from outside friends.   But the deficit increases.   Meanwhile disease persecutes them.   All through the sultry months which should have been their working time, they lie idle in their loose sheds, or where they can find a place, sweating and shivering in misery and despair.   Human parasites gather about them, like vultures scenting prey from afar.   Their own passions torment them. They are cursed with suspicion and the evil eye. They quarrel about religion.   They quarrel about their food.   They dispute about carrying out their principles. Eight or ten families desert.   The rest worry on through the long years.   Foes watch them with cruel exultation. Friends shout to them, "Hold on a little longer!" They hold on just as long as they can, insisting that they are successful, or are just going to be, till the last. Then comes the "break up;" and who can tell the agonies of that great corporate death !

If the reader is willing to peer into the darkest depths of this suffering, let him read again and consider well that suppressed wail of the women where they speak of the "polar snows" and the "funeral pile;" and let him think of all that is meant when the men say, "If we had known at the commencement what fiery trials were to surround us, we should have hesitated to enter on the enterprise. *But now being fairly in, we will brave it*

through!" See how pathetically these soldiers of despair, with defeat in full view, offer themselves to other
Associations, and take comfort in the assurance that
God will not drive them from the earth! See how the
heroes of the "forlorn hope," after defeat has come, turn
again and reörganize, refusing to surrender! The end
came at last, but left no record.

This is not comedy, but direst tragedy. God forbid
that we should ridicule it, or think of it with any feeling
but saddest sympathy. We ourselves are thoroughly
acquainted with these heights and depths. These men
and women seem to us like brothers and sisters. We
could easily weep with them and for them, if it would do
any good. But the better way is to learn what such
sufferings teach, and hasten to find and show the true
path, which these pilgrims missed; that so their illusions
may not be repeated forever.

CHAPTER XXIX.

THE OHIO PHALANX.

THIS Association, originally called the American Phalanx, commenced with a very ambitious programme and
flattering prospects ; but it did not last so long as many
of its contemporaries. It belonged to the Pittsburg group
of experiments. The founder of it was E. P. Grant.
Mr. Van Amringe was one of its leaders, whom we
saw busy at the Trumbull. The first announcement
of it we find in the third number of the *Phalanx*, as
follows :

[From the *Phalanx*, December 5, 1843.]

" GRAND MOVEMENT IN THE WEST.—The friends of
Association in Ohio and other portions of the West, have
undertaken the organization of a Phalanx upon quite
an extended scale. They have secured a magnificent
tract of land on the Ohio, have framed a constitution, and taken preliminary steps to make an early
commencement.

The projectors say : " We feel pleasure in announcing
that the American Phalanx has contracted for about
two thousand acres of land in Belmont County, Ohio,
known as the Pultney farm, lying along the Ohio river,
seven or eight miles below Wheeling ; and that sufficient
means are already pledged to remove all doubts as to

the formation of an Association, as soon as the domain can be prepared for the reception of the members. The land has been purchased of Col. J. S. Shriver, of Wheeling, Virginia, at thirty dollars per acre, payable at the pleasure of the Association, in sums not less than $ 5,000. The payment of six per cent. interest semi-annually, is secured by a lien on the land.

" The tract selected is two and a-half miles in length from north to south, and of somewhat irregular breadth, by reason of the curvatures of the Ohio river, which forms its eastern boundary. It contains six hundred acres of bottom land, all cleared and under cultivation ; the residue is hill land of a fertility truly surprising and indeed incredible to persons unacquainted with the hills of that particular neighborhood. Of the hill lands, about two hundred and fifty acres are cleared, and about three hundred acres more have been partially cleared, so as to answer imperfectly for sheep pasture. The residue is for the most part well-timbered.

" There are upon the premises two frame dwelling-houses, and ten log houses, mostly with shingle roofs ; none of them, however, are of much value, except for temporary purposes.

" The domain is singularly beautiful, as well as fertile ; and when it is considered, in connection with the advantages already enumerated, that it is situated on one of the greatest thoroughfares in the world, the charming Ohio, along which from six to ten steamboats pass every day for eight or nine months in the year ; that it is immediately accessible to several large markets, and a multitude of small ones ; and that it is within seven miles of that great public improvement, the National Road, leading through the heart of the Western States, we think we are authorized to affirm that the broad territory of our country furnishes but few localities more favorable for an experiment in Association, than that which has been secured by the American Phalanx.

" From eighty to one hundred laborers are expected to be upon the ground early in the spring, and it is hoped that in the fall a magnificent edifice or Phalanstery, on Fourier's plan, will be commenced, and will progress rapidly, until it shall be of sufficient extent to accommodate one hundred families.

"Our object can not be more intelligibly explained than by stating that it is proposed to organize an industrial army, which, instead of ravaging and desolating the earth, like the armies of civilization, shall clothe it luxuriantly and beautifully with supplies for human wants; to distribute this army into platoons, companies, battalions, regiments, in which promotion and rewards shall depend, not upon success in spreading ruin and woe, but upon energy and efficiency in diffusing comfort and happiness; in short, to invest labor the creator, with the dignity which has so long impiously crowned labor the destroyer and the murderer, so that men shall vie with each other, not in devastation and carnage, but in usefulness to the race."

Applicants for admission or stock were referred to E. P. Grant, A. Brisbane, H. Greeley and others.

[From the *Phalanx*, February 5, 1844.]

" E. P. Grant, Esq,. of Canton, Ohio, a gentleman of high standing, superior talents, and indefatigable energy, who is at the head of the movement to establish the American Phalanx, which is to be located on the banks of the beautiful Ohio, informs us by letter, that 'the prospect is truly cheering: even that greatest of wants, capital, is likely to be abundantly supplied. There will indeed be some deficiency during the ensuing spring and summer; but the amount already pledged to be paid by the end of the first year, is not, I think, less than $40,000, and by the end of the second year, probably not less than $100,000; and these amounts, from present appearances, can be almost indefinitely increased. Besides, the proposed associates are devoted and determined, resenting the intimation of possible failure, as a reflection unworthy of their zeal.'"

[From the *Phalanx*, March 1, 1844.]

"The Ohio Phalanx (heretofore called the American), is now definitely constituted, and the first pioneers are already upon the domain. More will follow in a few days to assist in making preliminary preparations. A larger company will be added in March, and by the end of May the Phalanx is expected to consist of 120 resident members, of whom the greater part will be adult males. They will be received from time to time as rapidly as temporary accommodations can be provided. The prospects of the Phalanx are cheering beyond the most sanguine anticipations of its friends.

E. P. GRANT.

[From the *Phalanx*, July 13, 1844.]

"Our friends of the Ohio Phalanx appear to have celebrated the Fourth of July with much hilarity and enthusiasm. About ten o'clock the members of the Association with their guests, were seated beneath the shade of spreading trees, near the dwelling; when Mr. Grant, the President, announced briefly the object of the assemblage and the order to be observed, which was, first, prayer by Dr. Rawson, then an address by Mr. Van Amringe, in which the present condition of society, its inevitable tendencies and results, were contrasted with the social system as delineated by Fourier. It is not doing full justice to the orator to say merely that his address was interesting and able. It was lucid, cogent, religious and highly impressive. This portion of the festival was closed by prayer and benediction by Rev. J. P. Stewart, and adjournment for dinner. After a good and plentiful repast, the social party resumed their seats for the purpose of hearing (rather than drinking) toasts and whatsoever might be said thereupon."

The topics of the regular toasts were, *The day we celebrate; The memory of Fourier; The Associationists of Pittsburg;* and so on through a long string. The volunteer toasters liberally complimented each other and the socialistic leaders generally, not forgetting Horace Greeley. Somebody in the name of the Phalanx gave the following:

" *The Bible*, the book of languages, the book of ideas, the book of life. May its pages be the delight of Associationists, and its precepts practiced by the whole world."

Our next quotation hints that something like a dissolution and reörganization had taken place.

[From the *Phalanx*, May 3, 1845.]

" We notice in a recent number of the *Pittsburg Chronicle*, an article from the pen of James D. Thornburg, on the present condition of the Ohio Phalanx, from which it appears that the report of its failure which has gone the rounds of the papers, is premature; and that although it has suffered embarrassment and difficulties from various causes, it is still in operation under new arrangements that authorize the hope of its ultimate success. We know nothing of the internal obstacles of which Mr. Thornburg speaks, and have no means of forming an opinion on the merits of the questions which, it would seem, have given rise to divided counsels and inefficient action. For the founder of the Ohio Phalanx, E. P. Grant, we cherish the most unqualified respect, believing him to be fitted as few men are, by his talents, energy and scientific knowledge, for the station of leader of the great enterprise, which demands no less courage and practical vigor, than wisdom and magnanimity.

"We learn from Mr. Thornburg's statement that to those who chose to leave the Phalanx, it was proposed to give thirty-three per cent. on their investments, which is all they could be entitled to, in case of a forfeiture of the title to the domain, in which case all the improvements, buildings, crops in ground, etc., would be a total loss to the members. But there is no depreciation in the stock, when these improvements are estimated. The rent has been reduced to one-half the former amount. The proprietor is expected to furnish a large number of sheep, the profits of which, it is believed, will be nearly or quite sufficient to pay the rent. At the end of two years, $ 30,000 in bonds, mortgages, etc., is to be raised, for which the Phalanx will receive a fee-simple title to the domain. A large share of the balance will be invested in stock, and whatever may remain will be apportioned in payments at two and a-half per cent. interest, and fixed at a date so remote that no difficulty will result. There are buildings on the domain sufficient for the accommodation of forty families, in addition to a number of rooms suitable for single persons. The movable property on the domain is at present worth three thousand dollars.

"In view of all the facts in the case, as set forth by Mr. Thornburg, we see no reason to dissent from the conclusion which he unhesitatingly expresses, that the future success of the Phalanx is certain. We trust that we have not been inspired with too flattering hopes by the earnestness of our wishes. For we acknowledge that we have always regarded the magnificent material resources of this Phalanx with the brightest anticipations ; we have looked to it with confiding trust, for the commencement of a model Association ; and we can not now permit ourselves to believe that any disastrous circumstance will prevent the realization of the high hopes which prompted its founders to engage in their glorious enterprise.

"The causes of difficulty in the Ohio Phalanx, as stated in the article before us, are as follows : Want of experience ; too much enthusiasm ; unproductive members ; want of means. These causes must always produce difficulty and discouragement ; and at the same time, can scarcely be avoided in the commencement of every attempt at Association.

" The harmonies of the combined order are not to be arrived at in a day or a year. Even with the noblest intentions, great mistakes in the beginning are inevitable, and many obstacles of a formidable character are incident to the very nature of the undertaking. A want of sufficient means must cripple the most strenuous industry. Ample capital is essential for a complete organization, for the necessary machinery and fixtures, for the ordinary conveniences, to say nothing of the elegancies of the household order ; and this in the commencement can scarcely ever be obtained. Restriction, retrenchment, more or less confusion, are the necessary consequences ; and these in their turn beget a spirit of impatience and discontent in all but the heroic ; and few men are heroes. The transition from the compulsory industry of civilization to the voluntary, but not yet attractive, industry of Association, is not favorable to the highest industrial effects. Men who have been accustomed to shirk labor under the feeling that they had poor pay for hard work, will not be transformed suddenly into kings of industry by the atmosphere of a Phalanx. There will be more or less loafing, a good deal of exertion unwisely applied, a certain waste of strength in random and unsystematic efforts, and a want of the business-like precision and force which makes every blow tell, and tell in the right place. Under these circumstances many will grow uneasy, at length become discouraged, and perhaps prove false to their early love. But all these, we are fully persuaded, are merely temporary evils. They will soon pass away. They are like the thin mists of the valley, which precede, but do not prevent, the rising of the sun. The principles of Association are founded on the eternal laws of justice and truth ; they present the only remedy for the appalling confusion and discord of the present social state ; they are capable of being carried into practice by just such men and women as we daily meet in the usual walks of life ; and as firmly as we believe in a Universal Providence, so sure we are that their practical accomplishment is destined to bless humanity with ages of abundance, harmony, and joy, surpassing the most enthusiastic dream."

[Editorial in the *Harbinger*, June, 14, 1845.]

"We learn from a personal interview with Mr. Thornburg, whose letter on the Ohio Phalanx was alluded to in a recent number of the *Phalanx*, that the affairs of that Association wear a very promising aspect, and that there can be no reasonable doubt of its success. He gives a very favorable description of the soil and general resources of the domain, and from all that we have learned of its character, we believe there are few localities at the West better adapted for the purposes of an experimental Association on a large scale. We sincerely hope that our friends in that vicinity will concentrate their efforts on the Ohio Phalanx, and not attempt to multiply Associations, which, without abundant capital and devoted and experienced men, will, almost to a certainty, prove unsuccessful. The true policy for all friends of Associative movements, is to combine their resources, and give an example of a well-organized Phalanx, in complete and harmonic operation. This will do more for the cause than any announcement of theories, however sound and eloquent, or ten thousand abortive attempts begun in enthusiasm and forsaken in despair."

[From the correspondence of the *Harbinger*, July 19, 1845, announcing the final dissolution.]

"On the 24th of June last, the Ohio Phalanx again dissolved. The reason is the want of funds. Since the former dissolution they have obtained no accession of numbers or capital worth considering. The members, I presume, will now disperse. They all retain, I believe, their sentiments in favor of Association ; but they have not the means to go on."

Madconald contributes the following summary, to close the account :

[From the Journal of a Resident Member of the Ohio Phalanx.]

"At the commencement of the experiment there was general good-humor among the members. There seemed to be plenty of means, and there was much profusion and waste. There was no visible organization according to Fourier, most of the members being inexperienced in Association. They were too much crowded together, had no school nor reading-room, and the younger members, as might be expected, were at first somewhat unruly. The character of the Association had more of a sedate and religious tone, than a lively or social one. There was too much discussion about Christian union, etc., and too little practical industry and business talent. No weekly or monthly accounts were rendered.

"About ten months after the commencement of the Association, a partial scarcity of provisions took place, and other difficulties occurred, which may in part be attributed to neglect in keeping the accounts. At this juncture Mr. Van Amringe started on a lecturing tour in aid of the Association; and the Phalanx had a meeting at which Mr. Grant, who was then regent, stated that between $7,000 and $8,000 had been expended since they came together; but no accounts were shown giving the particulars of this expenditure. From the difficult position in which the Phalanx was placed, Mr. Grant advised the breaking-up of the concern, which was agreed to, with two or three dissentients. [This was probably the first dissolution, referred to in a previous extract from the *Harbinger*.]

"On December 26 a new constitution was proposed which caused much discontent and confusion; and with the commencement of 1845 more disagreements took place, some in relation to the social amusements of the people, and some regarding the debts of the Phalanx, the empty treasury, the depreciation of stock, Mr. Van Amringe's possession of the lease of the property, and the bad prospect there was for raising the interest upon the cost of the domain, which was about $4,140, or six per cent on $69,000, the price of twenty-two hundred acres.

"On January 20th, 1845, another attempt at re-organization was made by persons who had full confidence in the management of Mr. Grant, and on February 28th still another re-organization was considered. On March 10th a general meeting of the Phalanx took place. Three constitutions were read, and the third (attributed, I believe, to Mr. Van Amringe), was adopted by a majority of one. After this there was a meeting of the minority, and the constitution of Mr. Grant was adopted with some slight alterations. Difficulties now took place between the two parties, which led to a suit at law by one of the members against the Ohio Phalanx. [These fluctuations remind us of the experience of New Harmony in its last days.]

"In such manner did the Association progress until August 27, 1845, when it was whispered about, that the Phalanx was defunct, although no notification to that effect was given to the members. Colonel Shriver, who held the mortgage on the property, took alarm at the state of affairs, and placed an agent on the premises to look after his interests. This agent employed persons to work the farm, and the members had to shift for themselves as best they could. Col. S. proposed an asssignment of the whole property over to him, requiring entire possession by the 1st of October. This was assented to, though the value of the property was more than enough to cover every claim.

"On September 9th advertisements were issued for the public sale of the whole property, and on the 17th of that month the sale took place before two or three hundred persons. After this the members dispersed, and the Ohio Phalanx was at an end. The lease of the property had been made out in the name of Mr. Grant for the Phalanx. It was afterward given up to him by Mr. Van Amringe, who had possession of it, and by Mr. Grant was returned to Colonel Shriver.

"Much space might be occupied in endeavoring to show the right and the wrong of these parties and proceedings, which to the reader would be quite unprofitable. The broad results we have before us, viz., that certain supposed-to-be great and important principles were tried in practice, and through a variety of causes failed. The most important causes of failure were said to be the deficiency of wealth, wisdom, and goodness; or if not these, the fallacy of the principles."

CHAPTER XXX.

THE CLERMONT PHALANX.

THIS Association originated in Cincinnati. An enthusiastic convention of Socialists was held in that city on the 22d of Februrary, 1844, at which interesting letters were read from Horace Greeley, Albert Brisbane, and Wm. H. Channing, and much discussion of various practical projects ensued. A committee was appointed to find a suitable domain; and at a second meeting on the 14th of March, the society adopted a constitution, elected officers, and opened books for subscription of stock. Mr. Wade Loofbourrow, a gentleman of capital and enterprise, took the lead in these proceedings, and was chosen president of the future Phalanx. A domain of nine hundred acres was soon selected and purchased on the banks of the Ohio, in Clermont County, about thirty miles above Cincinnati. On the 9th of May a large party of the members proceeded from Cincinnati on a steamer chartered for the occasion, to take possession of the domain with appropriate ceremonies, and leave a pioneer band to commence operations. Macdonald accompanied this party, and gives the following account of the excursion :

"There were about one hundred and thirty of us. The weather was beautiful, but cool, and the scenery on the river was splendid in its spring dress. The various parties brought their provisions with them, and toward noon the whole of it was collected and spread upon the table by the waiters, for all to have an equal chance. But alas for equality! On the meal being ready, a rush was made into the cabin, and in a few minutes all the seats were filled. In a few minutes more the provisions had all disappeared, and many persons who were not in the first rush, had to go hungry. I lost my dinner that day; but improved the opportunity to observe and criticise the ferocity of the Fourieristic appetite. We reached the domain about two o'clock P. M., and marched on shore in procession, with a band of music in front, leading the way up a road cut in the high clay bank; and then formed a mass meeting, at which we had praying, music and speech-making. I strolled out with a friend and examined the purchase, and we came to the conclusion that it was a splendid domain. A strip of rich bottom-land, about a quarter of a mile wide, was backed by gently rolling hills, well timbered all over. Nine or ten acres were cleared, sufficient for present use. Here then was all that could be desired, hill and plain, rich soil, fine scenery, plenty of first-rate timber, a maple-sugar camp, a good commercial situation, convenient to the best market in the West, with a river running past that would float any kind of boat or raft; and with steamboats passing and repassing at all hours of the day and night, to convey passengers or goods to any point between New Orleans and Pittsburg. Here was wood for fuel, clay and stone to make habitations, and a rich soil to grow food. What more could be asked from nature? Yet, how soon all this was found insufficient!

"The land was obtained on credit; the price was

$ 20,000. One thousand was to be paid down, and the rest in installments at stated periods. The first installment was paid; enthusiasm triumphed; and now for the beginning! On my return to the landing, I found a band of sturdy men commencing operations as pioneers. They were clearing a portion of the wood away with their axes, and preparing for building temporary houses, the materials for which they brought with them. A temporary tent was put up, and it would surprise any one to hear how many things were going to be done.

"We left the domain on our return at about five P. M., and I noticed that the president, Mr. Loofbourrow, and the secretary, Mr. Green, remained with the workmen. There were about a dozen persons left, consisting, I believe, of carpenters, choppers and shoemakers. They all seemed in good spirits, and cheered merrily on our departure."

A second similar excursion of Socialists from Cincinnati came off on the 4th of July following, which also Macdonald attended, and reports as follows:

"We left Cincinnati triumphantly to the sound of martial music, and took our journey up the river in fine spirits, the young people dancing in the cabin as we proceeded. We arrived at the Clermont Phalanx about one o'clock. On landing, we formed a procession and marched to a new frame building, which was being erected for a mill. Here an oration was delivered by a Mr. Whitly, who, I noticed, had the Bible open before him. After this we formed a procession again and marched to a lot of rough tables enclosed within a line of ropes, where we stood and took a cold collation.

After this the folks enjoyed themselves with music and dancing, and I took a walk about the place to see what progress had been made since my last visit. The frame building before mentioned was the only one in actual progress. A steam-boiler had been obtained, and preparations had been made to build other houses. A temporary house had been erected to accommodate the families then on the domain, amounting as I was informed, to about one hundred and twenty persons. This building was made exactly in the manner of the cabin of a Western steamboat; i. e., there was one long narrow room the length of the house, and little rooms like state-rooms arranged on either side. Each little room had one little window, like a port-hole; and was intended to accommodate a man and his wife, or two single men temporarily. It was at once apparent that the persons living there were in circumstances inferior to what they had been used to; and were enduring it well, while the enthusiastic spirit held out. But it seldom lasts long. It is said that people will endure these deprivations for the sake of what is soon to come. But experience shows that the endurance is generally brief, and that if they are able, they soon return to the circumstances to which they have been accustomed. They either find that their patience is insufficient for the task, or that being in inferior circumstances, *they* are becoming inferior. Be the cause what it may, the result is nearly always the same. This Association had been on the ground only a few months; but I was told that disagreements had already commenced. The persons brought together were strangers to each other, of many different trades and habits, and discord was the result, as might have been anticipated. From one of the shoemakers I gained considerable information as to their state and prospects. In the afternoon we returned to the city."

[From the *Phalanx*, May 3, 1845.]

"We are glad to learn by the following notice, taken from a Cincinnati paper, that the *Clermont Phalanx* still lives, and is in a fair way of going on successfully. We have received no account of it lately, and as the last that we had was not very flattering in respect to its pecuniary condition, we should not have been surprised to hear of its dissolution. The indiscretion of starting Associations without sufficient means and a proper selection of persons, has been shown to be disastrous in some other cases, and that we should fear for the fate of this one was quite natural. But if our Clermont friends can, by their devotion, energy and self-sacrificing spirit, overcome the trying difficulties of a pioneer state, rude and imperfect as it must be, they will deserve and will receive an abundant reward. We bid them God speed! They say:

"'The pioneer band, with their friends, took possession of the domain on the 9th day of May last year, since which time we have been engaged in cultivating our land, clearing away the forest, and erecting buildings of various kinds for the use of the Phalanx.

"'The amount of capital stock paid in is about $10,000; $3,000 of which has been paid for the domain. We have a stock of cattle, hogs and sheep, and sufficient teams and agricultural utensils of various kinds; also a steam saw- and grist-mill. Shoe, brush, tin and tailor's shops are in active operation. There are on the ground thirty-five able-bodied men, with a sufficient number of women and children.

"'When we first entered on our domain, there were no buildings of any description, except three log-cabins, which were occupied by tenants. We have since erected a building for a saw- and grist-mill, a frame building forty by thirty feet, two stories high, and another, one story high, eighty by thirty-six feet, and one thirty-six by thirty feet, together with a kitchen, wash-house, etc. These buildings are of course slightly built, being temporary. We have also commenced a brick building eighty by thirty feet, three stories high, which is ready for the roof; all the timbers are sawed for that purpose; and we expect soon to put them on.

"'There are about two thousand cords of wood chopped, part of which is on the bank of the river. There are thirty acres of wheat in the ground, in excellent condition, and it is intended to put in good spring crops. We are also preparing to plant large orchards this spring, Mr. A. H. Ernst having made us the noble donation of one thousand selected fruit-trees.'"

[From the *Harbinger*, June 14, 1845.]

"George Sampson, Secretary of the Phalanx, says, in an address soliciting funds: 'The members of the Association have the satisfaction of announcing that they have just paid off this year's installment due for their domain, amounting to $4,505, and have also advanced nearly $1,000 on their next year's payment. With increased zeal and confidence we now look forward to certain success.'"

[Letter from a member, in the *Harbinger*, October 4, 1845.]

"*Clermont Phalanx, September* 13, 1845.

"I am pleased to have to inform you, that we are improving since you were among us. We have had an accession of members, three single men, and two with families.   One of them attends the saw-mill, which he understands, and the others are carpenters and joiners, whom we much needed.

" We are now hard at work on our large brick edifice. We are fitting up a large dining-hall in the rear of it, with kitchen, wash-house, bakery, etc.   We think we shall get into it in about five weeks from this time.   We now all sit down to the Phalanx table, and have done so for about six weeks, and all goes on harmoniously.   How much better is this system than for each family to have their own table, their own dining-room, kitchen, etc. We have admitted several other members, who have not yet arrived.   We have applications before us from several members of the Ohio Phalanx.   How much I regret that these people were compelled to abandon so beautiful a location as Pultney Bottom, merely for want of money to carry on their operations.   Their experience is the same as ours.   Though their movement failed, they have become confirmed Associationists ; they know that living together is practicable ;   that the Phalanstery is man's true home ; and the only one in which he can enjoy all the blessings of earthly existence, without those evils which flesh is heir to in false civilization."

Macdonald concludes his account with the following observations :

" The Phalanx continued to progress, or to exist, till the fall of 1846, when it was finally abandoned.   During its existence various circumstances concurred to hasten its termination ; among them the following : Stock to the amount of $17,000 was subscribed, but scarcely $6,000 of it was ever paid ; consequently the Associ-

ation could not meet its liabilities. An installment
of $3,000 had been paid at the purchase of the property,
but as the after installments could not be met, a portion
of the land had to be sold to pay for the rest. A little
jealousy, originating among the female portion of the
Community, eventually led to a law-suit on the part of
one of the male members against the Association, and
caused them some trouble. I have it also on good
authority, that an important difficulty took place between Mr. Loofbourrow and the Phalanx, relative to the
deed of the property which he held for the Phalanx.

"At one time there were about eighty persons on the
domain, exclusive of children. They were of various
trades and professions, and of various religious beliefs.
There was no common religious standard among them.

"Some of the friends of this experiment say it failed
from two causes, viz., the want of means and the want
of men ; while others attribute the failure to jealousy
and the law-suit, and also to losses they sustained by
flood."

The fifth volume of the *Harbinger* has a letter from
one who had been a member of the Clermont Phalanx,
giving a curious account of certain ghosts of Associations that flitted about the Clermont domain, after the
decease of the original Phalanx. Here is what it says:

[Letter in the *Harbinger*, October 2, 1847.]

"It was well known that our frail bark would strand
about a year ago. I need not say from what cause, as
the history of one such institution is the history of all ;
but it is commonly said and believed that it was owing
to our large indebtedness on our landed property. Persons of large discriminating powers need not inquire

how and why such debt was contracted ; suffice it to say, it was done, and under such burden the Clermont Phalanx went down about the first of November, 1856. The property of the concern was delivered up to our esteemed friends, B. Urner and C. Donaldson of Cincinnati, who disposed of the land in such a way as to let it fall into the hands of our friends of the Community school, of which John O. Wattles, John P. Cornell and Hiram S. Gilmore are conspicuous members, and who seem to have all the pecuniary means and talents for carrying on a grand and notable plan of reform. They are now putting up a small Community building, spaciously suited for six families, which for beauty, convenience and durability, probably is not surpassed in the western country.

"Of the old members of the Clermont, many returned again to the city where the institution was first started, but a goodly number still remain about the old domain, making various movements for a re-organization. After the break-up, a deep impression seemed to pervade the whole of us that something had been wrong at the outset, in not securing individually a permanent place *to be*, and then procuring the things *to be with*. Had that been the case, a permanent and happy home would have been here for us ere this time. But I will add with gratitude that such is the case now. We have a home ! we have a place to be ! After various plans for uniting our energies in the purchase of a small tract of land, we were visited during the past summer by Mr. Josiah Warren of New Harmony, Indiana, who laid before us his plan for the use of property, in the rudimental re-organization of society. Mr. Warren is a man of no ordinary talents. In his investigations of human character his experience has been of the most rigorous kind, having begun with Mr. Owen in 1825, and been actively engaged ever since ; and being an ingenious mechanic and artist, an inventor of several kinds of printing-presses and a new method of stereotyping and engraving, and an excellent musician, and combining withal a character to do instead of say, gives us confidence in him as a man. His plan was taken up by one of our former members, who has an excellent tract of land lying on the bank of the Ohio river, within less than a mile of the old domain. He has had it surveyed into lots, and sells to such of us as wish to join in the cause. An extensive brick-yard is in operation, stone is being quarried and lumber hauled on the ground, and buildings are about to go up 'with a perfect rush.' Mr. Warren will have a press upon the ground in a few weeks that will tell something. So you see we have a home, we have a place. But by no means is the cause at rest. We call upon philanthropists and all men who have means to invest for the cause of Association, to come and see us, and understand our situation, our means and our intentions. We are ready to receive capital in many forms, but not to hold it as our own. The donor only becomes the lender, and must maintain a strict control over every thing he possesses. [Here Warren's Individual Sovereignty protrudes.] Farms and farming utensils, mechanical tools, etc., can be received only to be used and not abused ; and in the language of the 'Poughkeepsie seer,' of whose work we have lately received a number of copies, this all may be done without seriously depreciating the capital or riches of one person in society. On the contrary, it will enrich and advance all to honor and happiness."

Here we come upon the trail of two old acquaintances. John O. Wattles was one of the founders of the Prairie Home Community. It seems from the above, that after the failure of that experiment, he set up his tent among the *debris* of the Clermont Phalanx. And Josiah Warren came from the failure of his New Harmony Time-store to the same favored or haunted spot, and there started his Utopia. These intersections of the wandering Socialists are intricate and interesting. Note also that the ideas of the "Poughkeepsie seer," A. J. Davis, whose star was then only just above the horizon, had found their way to this queer mixture of all sorts of Socialists.

CHAPTER XXXI.

THE INTEGRAL PHALANX.

THIS Association was founded in the early part of 1845 by John S. Williams of Cincinnati, who is spoken of by the *Phalanx*, as one of the most active adherents of Fourierism in the West. It settled first in Ohio, and afterwards in Illinois.

[From the *Ohio State Journal*, June 14, 1845.

"An Association of citizens of Ohio, calling themselves the 'Integral Phalanx,' have recently purchased the valuable property of Mr. Abner Enoch, near Middletown, Butler County, in this State, known by the name of Manchester Mills, twenty-three miles north of Cincinnati, on the Miami Canal. This property embraces about nine hundred acres of the most fertile land in Ohio, or perhaps in the world; six hundred acres of which lie in one body, and are now in the highest state of cultivation, according to the usual mode of farming; three hundred acres in wood and timber land. There are now in operation on the place a large flouring-mill, saw-mill, lath-factory and shingle-cutter, with water-power which is abundantly sufficient to propel all necessary machinery that the company may choose to put in operation. The property is estimated to be worth $75,000, but was sold to the Phalanx for $45,000. As Mr. Enoch is himself an Associationist and a devoted friend of the cause, the terms of sale were made still more favorable, by the subscription, on the part of Mr. Enoch, of $25,000 of purchase money, as capital stock of the Phalanx. Entire possession of the domain is to be given as soon as existing contracts of the proprietor are completed.

"Arrangements are already made for the vigorous prosecution of the plans of the Phalanx. A press is to be established on the domain, devoted to the science of industrial Association generally, and the interests of the Integral Phalanx particularly. Competent agents are appointed to lecture on the science, and receive subscriptions of stock and membership; and it is contemplated to erect, as soon as possible, one wing of a unitary edifice, large enough to accommodate sixty-four families, more than one-half of which number are already in the Association."

[From the *Harbinger*, July 19, 1845.]

"We have received the first number of a new paper, entitled, the '*Plowshare and Pruning-Hook*,' which the Integral Phalanx proposes to publish semi-monthly at the rate of one dollar per year.

"The reasons presented for the establishment of the Integral Phalanx are to our minds quite conclusive, and we feel great confidence that its affairs will be managed with the wisdom and fidelity which will insure success. We earnestly desire to witness a fair and full experiment of Association in the West. The physical advantages which are there enjoyed, are far too great to be lost. With the fertility of the soil, the ease with which it is cultivated, the abundance of water-power, and the comparative mildness of the climate, a very few years of judicious and energetic industry would place an Association in the West in possession of immense material resources. They could not fail to accumulate wealth rapidly. They could live in great measure within themselves, without being compelled to sustain embarrassing relations with civilization ; and with the requisite moral qualities and scientific knowledge, the great problem of social harmony would approximate, at least, toward a solution. We trust this will be done by the Integral Phalanx. And to insure this, our friends in Ohio should not be eager to encourage new experiments, but to concentrate their capital and talent, as far as possible, on that Association which bids fair to accomplish the work proposed. The advantages possessed by the Integral Phalanx will be seen from the following statement in their paper :

"'To say that our prospects are not good, would be to say what we do not believe; or to say that the Phalanx, so far, is not composed of the right kind of materials, would be to affect a false modesty we desire not to possess. One reason why our materials are superior is, that young Phalanxes generally are known to be in doubtful, difficult circumstances, and therefore the inducement to rush into such movements merely from the pressure of the evils of civilization, without a full convincement of the good of Association, is not so great as it was. We are composed of men whose reflective organs, particularly that of caution, seem to be largely developed. We believe in moving slowly, cautiously, safely ; giving our Phalanx time to grow well, that permanence may be the result. The members already enrolled on the books of the *Phalanx*, are, in their individual capacities, the owners of property to an amount exceeding one hundred thousand dollars, clear of all incumbrances ; and they are all persons of industrial energy and skill, fully capable of compelling the elements of earth, air and water, to yield them abundant contributions for that harmonic unity with which their souls are deeply inspired. In view of all these advantages we can, with full confidence, invite the accession of numbers and capital, and assure them of a safe investment in the Integral Phalanx.'"

[From the *Harbinger*, August 16, 1845.]

"We have received the second number of the *Plowshare and Pruning-Hook*. Besides a variety of interesting articles on the subject of Association, this number contains the pledges and rules of the Integral Phalanx, together with an explanation of some parts of the instrument, which have been supposed to be rather obscure. It is an elaborate document, exhibiting the fruits of deep reflection, and aiming at the application of scientific principles to the present condition of Association. We do not feel ourselves called on to criticise it ; as every written code for the government of a Phalanx must necessarily be imperfect, of the nature of a compromise, adapted to special exigences, and taking its character, in a great measure, from the local or personal circumstances of the Association for which it is intended. In a complete and orderly arrangement of groups and series, with attractive industry fully organized, with a sufficient variety of character for the harmonious development of the primary inherent passions of our nature, and a corresponding abundance of material resources, we conceive that few written laws would be necessary ; everything would be regulated with spontaneous precision by the pervading common sense of the Phalanx ; and the law written on the heart, the great and holy law of attraction, would supersede all others. But for this blessed condition the time is not yet. Years may be required, before we shall see the first red streaks of its dawning. Meanwhile, we must make the wisest provisional arrangements in our power. And no constitution recognizing the principles of distributive justice and the laws of universal unity, will be altogether defective ; while time and experience will suggest the necessary improvements.

" Three attorneys-at-law have left that profession and joined the Integral Phalanx, not, as they say, that they could not make a living, if they would stick to it and do their share of the dirty work, but because by doing so they must sacrifice their consciences, as the practice of the law, in many instances, is but stealing under another name. They are elevating themselves by learning honest and useful trades, so as to become producers in Association. A wise resolution."

Here comes a sudden turn in the story of this Phalanx, for which the previous assurances of caution and prosperity had not prepared us, and of which we can find no detailed account. We skip from Ohio to Illinois, with no explanation except the dark hints of trouble, defeat, and partial dissolution, contained in the following document. The Sangamon Phalanx, which seems to have taken in the Integral (or was taken in by it), is one of the Associations of which we have no account either from Macdonald or the Fourier Journals.

[From the New York *Tribune.*]

"*Home of the Integral Phalanx,*
Sangamon Co., Illinois, Oct. 20, 1845.

"*To the Editor of the New York Tribune:*

"We wish to apprise the friends of Association that the Integral Phalanx, having for the space of one year wandered like Noah's dove, finding no resting place for the sole of its foot, has at length found a habitation. A union was formed on the 16th of October inst., between it and the Sangamon Association; or rather the Sangamon Association was merged in the Integral Phalanx; its members having abandoned its name and constitution, and become members of the Integral Phalanx, by placing their signatures to its pledges and rules: the Phalanx adopting their domain as its home. We were defeated, and we now believe, very fortunately for us, in securing a location in Ohio. We have, during the time of our wanderings, gained some experience which we could not otherwise have gained, and without which we were not prepared to settle down upon a location. Our members have been tried. We now know what kind of stuff they are made of. Those who have abandoned us in consequence of our difficulties, were 'with us, but not of us,' and would have been a hindrance to our efforts. They who are continually hankering after the 'flesh-pots of Egypt,' and are ready to abandon the cause upon the first appearance of difficulties, had better stay out of Association. If they will embark in the cause, every Association should pray for difficulties sufficient to drive them out. We need not only clear heads, but also true hearts. We are by no means sorry for the difficulties which we have encountered, and all we fear is that we have not yet had sufficient difficulties to try our souls, and show the principles by which we are actuated.

"We have now a domain embracing five hundred and eight acres of as good land as can be found within the limits of Uncle Sam's dominions, fourteen miles southwest from Springfield, the capital of the State, and in what is considered the best county and wealthiest portion of the State. This domain can be extended to any desired limit by purchase of adjoining lands at cheap rates. We have, however, at present, sufficient land for our purposes. It consists of high rolling prairie and woodlands adjoining, which can not be excelled in the State, for beauty of scenery and richness of soil, covered with a luxuriant growth of timber, of almost every description, oak, hickory, sugar-maple, walnut, etc. The land is well watered, lying upon Lick Creek, with springs in abundance, and excellent well-water at the depth of twenty feet. The land, under proper cultivation, will produce one hundred bushels of corn to the acre, and every thing else in proportion. There are five or six comfortable buildings upon the property ; and a temporary frame-building, commenced by the Sangamon Association (intended, when finished, to be three hundred and sixty feet by twenty-four), is now being erected for the accommodation of families.

"The whole domain is in every particular admirably adapted to the industrial development of the Phalanx. The railroad connecting Springfield with the Illinois river, runs within two miles of the domain. There is a steam saw- and flouring-mill within a few yards of our present eastern boundary, which we can secure on fair terms, and shall purchase, as we shall need it immediately.

"But we will not occupy more time with description, as those who feel sufficiently interested, will visit us and examine for themselves. We 'owe no man,' and although we are called infidels by those who know not what constitutes either infidelity or religion, we intend to obey at least this injunction of Holy Writ. The Sangamon Association had been progressing slowly, prudently and cautiously, determined not to involve themselves in pecuniary difficulties ; and this was one great inducement to our union with them. We want those whose 'bump of caution' is fully developed. Our knowledge of the progressive movement of other Associations has taught us a lesson which we will try not to forget. We are convinced that we can never succeed with an onerous debt upon us. We trust those who attempt it may be more successful than we could hope to be.

"We are also convinced that we can not advance one step toward associative unity, while in a state of anarchy and confusion, and that such a state of things must be avoided. We will therefore not attempt even a unitary subsistence, until we have the number necessary to enable us to organize upon scientific principles, and in accordance with Fourier's admirable plan of industrial organization. The Phalanx will have a store-house, from which all the families can be supplied at wholesale prices, and have it charged to their account. It is better that the different families should remain separate for five years, than to bring them together under circumstances worse than civilization. Such a course will unavoidably create confusion and dissatisfaction, and we venture the assertion that it has done so in every instance where it has been attempted. Under our rules of progress, it will be seen that until we are prepared to organize, we shall go upon the system of hired labor. We pay to each individual a full compensation for all assistance rendered in labor or other services, and charge him a fair price for what he receives from the Phalanx; the balance of earnings, after deducting the amount of what he receives, to be credited to him as stock, to draw interest as capital. To capital, whether it be money or property put in at a fair price, we allow ten per cent. compound interest. This plan will be pursued until our edifice is finished and we have about four hundred persons, ready to form a temporary organization. Fourier teaches us that this number is necessary, and if he has taught the truth of the science, it is worse than folly to pursue a course contrary to his instructions. If there is any one who understands the science better than Fourier did himself, we hope he will make the necessary corrections and send us word. We intend to follow Fourier's instructions until we find they are wrong ; then we will abandon them.

"As to an attempt to organize groups and series until we have the requisite number, have gone through a proper system of training, and erected an edifice sufficient for the accommodation of about four hundred persons, every feature of our Rules of Progress forbids it. We believe that the effort will place every Phalanx that attempts it, in a situation worse than civilization itself. The distance between civilization and Association can not be passed at one leap. There must necessarily be a transition period ; and any set of rules or constitution (hampered and destroyed by a set of by-laws), intended for the government of a Phalanx, during the transition period, and which have no analogical reference to the human form, will be worse than useless. They will be an impediment instead of an assistance to the progressive movement of a Phalanx. The child can not leap to manhood in a day nor a month, and unless there is a system of training suited to the different states through which he must pass in his progress to manhood, his energies can never be developed. If Associations will violate every scientific principle taught by Fourier, pay no regard to analogy, and attempt organisms of groups and series before any preparation is made for it, and then run into anarchy and confusion, and become disgusted with their efforts, we hope they will have the honesty to take the blame upon themselves, and not charge it to the science of Association.

"We are ready at all times to give information of our situation and progress, and we pledge ourselves to give a true and correct statement of the actual situation of the Phalanx. We pledge ourselves that there shall not be found a variance between our written or published statements, and the statements appearing upon our records. Those of our members now upon the ground are composed principally of the former members of the Sangamon Association. We expect a number of our members from Ohio this fall, and many more of them in the spring. We have applications for information and membership from different directions, and expect large accession in numbers and capital during the coming year. We can extend our domain to suit our own convenience, as, in this land of prairies and pure atmosphere, we are not hemmed in by civilization to the same extent as Socialists in other States. We have elbow-room, and there is no danger of treading on each other's toes and then fighting about it.

"The *Plowshare and Pruning-Hook* will be continued from its second number, and published from the home of the Integral Phalanx in a few weeks, as soon as a press can be procured.

"SECRETARY OF INTEGRAL PHALANX."

Here all information in the *Harbinger* about the Integral comes to an end, and Macdonald breaks off short with, "No further particulars."

CHAPTER XXXII.

THE ALPHADELPHIA PHALANX.

THIS Association was commenced in the winter of 1843—4, principally by the exertions of Dr. H. R. Schetterly of Ann Arbor, Michigan, a disciple of Brisbane and the *Tribune.* The *Phalanx* of February 5, 1844, publishes its prospectus, from which we take the following paragraph :

"Notice is hereby given, that a Fourier industrial Association, called the Alphadelphia Phalanx, has been formed in this State, under the most flattering prospects. A constitution has been adopted and signed, and a domain selected on the Kalamazoo river, which seems to possess all the advantages that could be desired. It is extremely probable (judging from the information possessed), that only half the applicants can be received into one Association, because the number will be too great : and if such should be the case, two Associations will doubtless be formed ; for such is the enthusiasm in the West that people will not suffer themselves to be disappointed."

[From the *Phalanx*, March 1, 1844.]

" THE ALPHADELPHIA ASSOCIATION.—We have received the constitution of this Association, a notice of the formation of which was contained in our last. In most respects the constitution is similar to that of the North American Phalanx. It will be seen by the description of the domain selected, which we publish below, that the location is extremely favorable. The establishment of this Association in Michigan is but a pioneer movement, which we have no doubt will soon be followed by the formation of many others. Our friends are already numerous in that State, and the interest in Association is rapidly growing there, as it is throughout the West generally. The West, we think, will soon become the grand theater of action, and ere long Associations will spring up so rapidly that we shall scarcely be able to chronicle them. The people, the farmers and mechanics particularly, have only to understand the leading principles of our doctrines, to admire and approve of them; and it would therefore be no matter of surprise to see in a short time their general and simultaneous adoption. Indeed, the social transformation from a state of isolation with all its poverty and miseries, to a state of Association with its immense advantages and prosperity, may be much nearer and proceed more rapidly than we now imagine. The signs are many and cheering."

History and Description of the Alphadelphia Association.

" In consequence of a call of a convention published in the *Primitive Expounder*, fifty-six persons assembled in the school-house at the head of Clark's lake, on the fourteenth day of December last, from the Counties of Oakland, Wayne, Washtenaw, Genesee, Jackson, Eaton, Calhoun and Kalamazoo, in the State of Michigan; and after a laborious session of three days, from morning to midnight, adopted the skeleton of a constitution, which was referred to a committee of three, composed of Dr. H. R. Schetterly, Rev. James Billings and Franklin Pierce, Esq., for revision and amendment. A committee consisting of Dr. Schetterly, John Curtis and William Grant, was also elected to view three places, designated by the convention as possessing the requisite qualifications for a domain. The convention then adjourned to meet again at Bellevue, Eaton County, on the third day of January, to receive the reports of said committees, to choose a domain from those reported on by the committee on location, and to revise, perfect and adopt said constitution. This adjourned convention met on the day appointed, and selected a location in the town of Comstock, Kalamazoo County, whose advantages are described by the committee on location, in the following terms :

"The Kalamazoo river, a large and beautiful stream, nine rods wide, and five feet deep in the middle, flows through the domain. The mansion and manufactories will stand on a beautiful plain, descending gradually toward the bank of the river, which is about twelve feet high. There is a spring, pouring out about a barrel of pure water per minute, half a mile from the place where the mansion and manufactories will stand. Cobble-stone more than sufficient for foundations and building a dam, and easily accessible, are found on the domain ; and sand and clay, of which excellent brick have been made, are also abundant. The soil of the domain is exceedingly fertile, and of great variety, consisting of prairie, oak openings, and timbered and bottom-land along the river. About three thousand acres of it have been tendered to our Association, as stock to be appraised at the cash value, nine hundred of which are under cultivation, fit for the plow; and nearly all the remainder has been offered in exchange for other improved lands belonging to members at a distance, who wish to invest their property in our Association."

[Letter from H. R. Schetterly.]

"*Ann Arbor, May* 20, 1844.

" GENTLEMEN :—Your readers will no doubt be pleased to learn every important movement in industrial Association; and therefore I send you an account of the present condition of the Alphadelphia Association, to the organization of which all my time has been devoted since the beginning of last December.

" The Association held its first annual meeting on the second Wednesday in March, and at the close of a session of four days, during which its constitution and by-laws were perfected, and about eleven hundred persons, including children and adults, admitted to membership, adjourned to meet on the domain on the first of May. Its officers repaired immediately to the place selected last winter for the domain, and after overcoming great difficulties, secured the deeds of 2,814 acres of land, (927 of which is under cultivation), at a cost of $32,000. This gives us perfect control over an immense water-power ; and our land-debt is only $5,776 (the greater portion of the land having been invested as stock), to be paid out of a proposed capital of $240,000, $14,000 of which is to be paid in cash during the summer and autumn. More land adjoining the domain has since been tendered as stock ; but we have as much as we can use at present, and do not wish to increase our taxes and diminish our first annual dividend too much. It will all come in as soon as wanted. At our last meeting the number of members was increased to upwards of 1,300, and more than one hundred applicants were rejected, because there seemed to be no end, and we became almost frightened at the number. Among our members are five mill-wrights, six machinists, furnacemen, printers, manufacturers of cloth, paper, etc., and almost every other kind of mechanics you can mention, besides farmers in abundance.

" Farming and gardening were commenced on the domain about the middle of April, and two weeks since, when I came away, there were seventy-one adult male and more than half that number of adult female laborers on the ground, and more constantly arriving. We shall not however be able to accommodate more than about 200 resident members this season.

" There is much talk about the formation of other Associations in this State (Michigan), and I am well convinced that others will be formed next winter. The fact is, men have lost all confidence in each other, and those who have studied the theory of Association, are desirous of escaping from the present hollow-hearted state of civilized society, in which fraud and heartless competition grind the more noble-minded of our citizens to the dust.

" The Alphadelphia Association will not commence building its mansion this season ; but several groups have been organized to erect a two-story wooden building, five hundred and twenty-three feet long, including the wings, which will be finished the coming Fall, so as to answer for dwellings till we can build a mansion, and afterwards may be converted into a silk establishment or shops. The principal pursuit this year, besides putting up this building, will be farming and preparing for erecting a furnace, saw-mill, machine-shop, etc. We have more than one hundred thousand feet of lumber on hand; and a saw-mill, which we took as stock, is running day and night.

"I do not see any obstacle to our future prosperity. Our farmers have plenty of wheat on the ground. We have teams, provisions, all we ought to desire on the domain; and best of all, since the location of the buildings has been decided, we are perfectly united, and have never yet had an angry discussion on any subject. We have religious meetings twice a week, and preaching at least once, and shall have schools very soon. If God be for us, of which we have sufficient evidence, who can prevail against us?

"Our domain is certainly unrivaled in its advantages in Michigan, possessing every kind of soil that can be found in the State. Our people are moral, religious, and industrious, having been actually engaged in manual labor, with few exceptions, all their days. The place where the mansion and out-houses will stand, is a most beautiful level plain, of nearly two miles in extent, that wants no grading, and can be irrigated by a constant stream of water flowing from a lake. Between it and the river is another plain, twelve feet lower, on which our manufactories may be set in any desirable position. Our mill-race is half dug by nature, and can be finished, according to the estimate of the State engineer, for eighteen hundred dollars, giving five and a-half feet fall without a dam, which may be raised by a grant from the Legislature, adding three feet more, and affording water-power sufficient to drive fifty pair of mill-stones. A very large spring, brought nearly a mile in pipes, will rise nearly fifty feet at our mansion. The

Central railroad runs across our domain.   We have a great abundance of first-rate timber, and land as rich as any in the State.

"Our constitution is liberal, and secures the fullest individual freedom and independence.   While capital is fully protected in its rights and guaranteed in its interests, it is not allowed to exercise an undue control, or in the least degree encroach on personal liberty, even if this too common tendency could possibly manifest itself in Association.   As we proceed I will inform you of our progress.   H. R. SCHETTERLY."

The *Harbinger* of January 17, 1846, mentions the Alphadelphia as still existing and in hopeful condition ; but we find no further notice of it in that quarter. Macdonald tells the following story of its fortunes and failure, the substance of which he obtained from Dr. Schetterly :

"At the commencement a disagreement took place between a Mr. Tubbs and the rest of the members. Mr. Tubbs wanted to have the buildings located on the land he had owned ; but the Association would not agree to that, because the digging of a mill-race on the side of the river proposed by Mr. Tubbs would have cost nearly $18,000 ; whereas on the railroad side of the river, which was supposed to be a much better building-place, the race would have cost only $1,800.   The consequence was that all but Mr. Tubbs voted for the rail-road side, and Mr. Tubbs left, no doubt in disgust, at the same time cautioning every person against investing property in the Phalanx.   This disagreement at the commencement of the experiment threw a damper on it, from which it never entirely recovered.

"There were a number of ordinary farm-houses on the domain, and a beginning of a Phalanstery seventy feet long was erected to accommodate those who resided there the first winter. The rooms were comfortable but small. A large frame-house was also begun. During the warm weather a number of persons lived in a large board shanty.

"The members of the Association were mostly farmers, though there were builders, shoemakers, tailors, blacksmiths and printers, and one editor; all tolerably skillful and generally well informed; though but few could write for the paper called the *Tocsin*, which was published there. The morality of the members is said to have been good, with one exception. A school was carried on part of the time, and they had an exchange of some seventy periodicals and newspapers. No religious tests were required in the admission of members. They had preaching by one of the printers, or by any person who came along, without asking about his creed.

"All lived in clover so long as a ton of sugar or any other such luxury lasted; but before provisions could be raised, these luxuries were all consumed, and most of the members had to subsist afterward on coarser fare than they were accustomed to. No money was paid in, and the members who owned property abroad could not sell it. The officers made bad bargains in selling some farms that lay outside the domain. Laborers became discouraged and some left; but many held on longer than they otherwise would have done, because a hundred acres of beautiful wheat greeted them in the fields. In the winter some of the influential members went away temporarily, and thus left the real friends of the Association in the minority ; and when they returned after two or three months absence, every thing was turned up-side-down.   There was a manifest lack of good management and foresight.   The old settlers accused the majority of this, and were themselves elected officers ; but it appears that they managed no better, and finally broke up the concern."

CHAPTER XXXIII.

LA GRANGE PHALANX.

THE first notice of this Association is the following announcement in the *Phalanx*, October 5, 1843:

"Preparations are making to establish an Association in La Grange County, Indiana, which will probably be done this fall, upon quite an extensive scale, as many of the most influential and worthy inhabitants of that section are deeply interested in the cause."

[From a letter of W. S. Prentise, Secretary of the La Grange Phalanx, published in the Phalanx, February 5, 1844.]

"We have now about thirty families, and I believe might have fifty, if we had room for them. We have in preparation and nearly completed, a building large enough to accommodate our present members. They will all be settled and ready to commence business in the spring. They leave their former homes and take possession of their rooms as fast as they are completed. The building, including a house erected before we began by the owner of a part of our estate, is one hundred and ninety-two feet long, two stories high, divided so as to give each family from twelve to sixteen feet front and twenty-six feet depth, making a front room and one or two bed-rooms. One hundred and twenty feet of this building is entirely new. We commenced it in September, and have had lumber, brick and lime to haul from five to twelve miles. All these materials can be hereafter furnished on our domain. Notwithstanding the disadvantages and waste attendant on hasty action without previous plan, we shall have our tenements at least as cheap again as they would cost separately. Our farm consists of about fifteen hundred acres of excellent land, four hundred of which is improved, about three hundred of rich meadow, with a stream running through it, falling twelve feet, and making a good water-power. We are about forty miles from Fort Wayne, on the Wabash and Erie canal. Our land, including one large new house and three large new barns, and a saw-mill in operation, cost us about $8.00 per acre. It was put in as stock, at $10.31 for improved, and $2.68 for unimproved. We have about one hundred head of cattle, two hundred sheep, and horse and ox teams enough for all purposes: also farming tools in abundance; and in fact every thing necessary to carry on such branches of business as we intend to undertake at present, except money. This property was put in as stock, at its cash value; cows at $10.00, sheep $1.50, horses $50.00, wheat fifty cents, corn twenty-five cents.

"We shall have about one hundred and fifty persons when all are assembled; probably about half of this number will be children. Our school will commence in a few days. We have a charter from the Legislature, one provision of which, inserted by ourselves, is, that we shall never, as a society, contract a debt. We are located in Springfield, La Grange County, Indiana. The nearest post-office is Mongoquinong. We think our location a good one. Our members are seventy-three of them practical farmers, and the rest mechanics, teachers, etc. We shall not commence building our main edifice at present. When our dwelling rooms, now in progress, are completed, and such work-shops as are necessary to accommodate our mechanics, we shall stop building until more capital flows in, either from abroad or from our own labors. It is a pity that the mechanics of the city and farmers of the country could not be united. They would do far better together than separate. We have two of the best physicians in the country in our number."

[From the *Harbinger*, July 4, 1846.]

" LA GRANGE PHALANX.—This Association has been in operation some two years, and has been incorporated since the first of June, 1845. It commenced on the sure principle of incurring no debts, which it has adhered to, with the exception of some fifteen hundred dollars yet due on its domain. We find in the *True Tocsin* a statement of the operations of this Association for the last fifteen months, and of its present condition, by Mr. Anderson, its Secretary, from which we make the following extracts:

"*Annual Statement of the condition of La Grange Phalanx, on the 1st day of April, 1846.*

" Total valuation of the real and personal estate of the Phalanx, including book accounts, due from members and others . . . .$ 19,861.61

Deduct capital stock . . . . . $ 14,668.39
 " debts 1,128.82 15,797.21

 Total product for fifteen months previous to
  the above date . . . . $ 4,064 40

Being a net increase of property on hand (since our settlement on the 1st of January, 1845), of $ 1,535.63, the balance of the total product above having been consumed (namely, $2,531.72) in the shape of rent, tuition, fuel, food and clothing. The above product forms a dividend to labor of sixty-one cents eight mills per day of ten hours, and to the capital stock four and eleven-twelfths per cent. per annum.

"Our domain at present consists of ten hundred and forty-five acres of good land, watered by living springs. The land is about one-half prairie, the balance openings, well timbered, We have four hundred and ninety-two acres improved, and two hundred and fifty acres of meadow. The improvements in buildings are three barns, some out-houses, blacksmith's-shop, and a dwelling house large enough to accommodate sixteen families; besides a school-room twenty-six by thirty-six feet, and a dining-room of the same size. All our land is within fences. We consider our condition bids fair for the realization of at least a share of happiness, even upon the earth.

"The rule by which this Association makes dividends to capital is as follows: When labor shall receive seventy-five cents per day of ten hours at average or common farming labor, then capital shall receive six per cent. per annum, and in that ratio, be the dividend what it may; in other words, an investment of one hundred dollars for one year will receive the same amount which might be paid to eight days average labor.

"There are now ten families of us at this place, busily engaged in agriculture. We are rather destitute of mechanics, and would be very much pleased to have a good blacksmith and shoemaker, of good moral character and steady habits, and withal Associationists, join our number.

"Since our commencement in the fall of 1843, our school has been in active operation up to the present time, with the exception of some few vacations. It is our most sincere desire to have the very best instruction in school, which our means will enable us to procure."

The *Harbinger* adds : "The preamble to the constitution of this little band of pioneers in the cause of human elevation, shows that their enterprise is animated by the highest purposes. We trust that they will not be disheartened by any discouragements or obstacles. These must of necessity be many ; but it should be borne in mind that they can not be equal to the burdens which the selfishness and antagonism of the existing order of things lay upon every one who toils through its routine. The poorest Association affords a sphere of purer, more honest, and heartier life than the best society that we know of in the civilized world. Let our friends persevere ; they are on the right track, and whatever mistakes they may make, we do not doubt that they will succeed in establishing for themselves and their children a society of united interests."

[Communication in the *Harbinger*.]

Springfield, June, 14, 1846.

"We hope our humble effort here to establish a Phalanx, will in due time be crowned with success. Our prospects since we got our charter have been very cheering, notwithstanding the difficulties attendant upon so weak an attempt to form a nucleus, around which we expect to see truth and happiness assembled in perpetual union, and that too at no very distant period. Our numbers have lately been increased by some members from the Alphadelphia Association, whose faith has outlived that of others in the attempt to establish an Association at that place.

"Agriculture has been our main and almost only employment since we came together. We have ten hundred and forty-five acres of excellent land, four hundred and ninety-two acres of which are improved, and two hundred and fifty acres of it are natural meadow. We are preparing this fall to sow three hundred acres of wheat. Our domain is as yet destitute of water-power except on a very limited scale. Our location in other respects is all that could be wished. We have a very fine orchard of peach- and apple-trees, set out mostly a year ago last spring, and many of the trees will soon bear, they having been moved from orchards which were set out for the use of families on different points of what we now call our domain. We shall have this season a considerable quantity of apples and peaches from old trees which have not been moved. The wheat crop promises to be very abundant in this part of the country. Oats and corn are rather backward on account of the late dry weather. We have at present on the ground one hundred and forty acres of wheat, fifty-two acres of oats, thirty-eight acres of corn, besides buckwheat, potatoes, beans, squashes, pumpkins, melons and what not.

"WILLIAM ANDERSON, Secretary."

Macdonald gives the following meager account of the decease of this Phalanx:

"A person named Jones owned nearly one-half of the stock, and it appears that his influence was such that he managed trading and money matters all in his own way,

whether he was an officer or not. This gave great dissatisfaction to the members, and has been assigned as
the chief cause of their failure. They possessed about
one thousand acres of land, with plenty of buildings of
all kinds. The members were mostly farmers, tolerably
moral, but lacking in enterprise and science. They
maintained schools and preaching in abundance, and
lived as well as western farmers commonly do. But
they fully proved that, though hard labor is important in
such experiments, yet without the right kind of genius
to guide, mere labor is vain."

CHAPTER XXXIV.

OTHER WESTERN EXPERIMENTS.

A HALF dozen obscure Associations, begun or contemplated in the Western States, will be disposed of
together in this chapter ; and then all that will remain
of the experiments on our list, will be the famous
trio with which we propose to conclude our history
of American Fourierism—the Wisconsin, the North
American and the Brook Farm Phalanxes.

One of the experiments mentioned by Macdonald, but
about which he gives very little information, was

THE COLUMBIAN PHALANX.

This Association turns up twice in the pages of the
Harbinger; but we can not ascertain when it started,
how long it lasted, nor even where it was located, except
that it was in Franklin County, Ohio.   Nevertheless it
crowed cheerily in its time, as the following paragraphs
testify :

[Letter to the *Harbinger*, August 15, 1845.]

" It is reported all through the country, and currently
within thirty miles of the location, that the Columbian
Phalanx have disbanded and broken up; and that those
who remain are in a constant state of discontent and bickering, owing to want of food and comforts of life.   Now,

sir, having visited this spot, and viewed for myself, I can safely say, that in no one thing is this true. In fact only one family has left, and it is supposed that they can't stay away; while five families are now entering or about to enter, from Beverly, Morgan County, all of good, substantial character. As good a state of harmony exists in the Phalanx as could possibly be expected in so incipient a state. On Saturday last, having the required number of families (thirty-two), they went into an inceptive organization; and all feel that at no time have the prospects been as fair as at this moment. In proof of this, it need only be stated, that they are about four thousand dollars ahead of their payments, and no interest due till spring, with no other debts that they are not able to meet. They have one hundred and thirty-seven acres of wheat, and thirteen of rye, all of a most excellent quality, decidedly the best that I have seen this year; not more than ten or fifteen acres at all injured. On a part of it they calculate to get twenty-five bushels to the acre. They have one hundred and fifty acres of corn, much better than the corn generally in Franklin County; one hundred acres of oats, all of the largest kind; fifteen acres of potatoes, in the most flourishing condition; four acres of beans; five acres of vines; besides forty acres of pumpkins! (won't they have pies!) one acre of sweet potatoes; ten thousand cabbage plants; and are preparing ground for five acres of turnips; six acres of buckwheat; five acres of flax, and ten acres of garden. I had the pleasure of taking dinner with them to-day at the public table, furnished as comfortably as we generally find. They have provisions enough growing to supply three times their number, and they are calculating on a large increase this season. They are fully satisfied of the validity of their deed, which they are soon to secure."

[A letter from a Member, in the *Harbinger*.]

"*Columbian Phalanx, October* 4, 1845.

"If I have said aught in high-toned language of our future prospects, preserve it as truth, sacred as Holy Writ. We are in a prosperous condition. The little difficulties which beset us for a time, arising from lack of means, and which the world magnified into destruction and death, have been dissipated.

"Our crops of grain are the very best in the State of Ohio, a very severe drought having prevailed in the north of the State. We could, if we wished, sell all our corn on the ground. We have one hundred and fifty acres, every acre of which will yield one hundred bushels. We have cut one hundred acres of good oats. Potatoes, pumpkins, melons, etc., are also good. We are now getting out stuff to build a flouring-mill in Zanesville, for a Mr. Beaumont; two small groups of seven persons each, make twenty-five dollars per day at the job. We have the best hewed timber that ever came to Zanesville; and it is used in all the mills and bridges in this region. We have purchased fixtures for a new steam saw-mill, with two saws and a circulator, and various other small machinery, all entirely new, which we shall get into operation soon. Plenty to eat, drink, and wear, with three hundred dollars per week coming in, all from our own industry, imparts to us a tone of feeling of a quite different zest, to an abundance obtained in any other way. The world has watched with anxious solicitude our capacity to survive alone. Now that we have gained shore, we find extended to us the right hand of the capitalist and the laboring man; they beg permission to join our band.

"You are already aware, no doubt, that the Beverly Association has joined us. The Integral having failed to obtain the location they had selected, some of the members have united their efforts with us. Tell Mr. W., of Alleghany, to come here; tell him for me that all danger is out of the question. Please by all means tell Mr. M. to come here; tell him what I have written. Tell H., of Beaver, to come and see us, and say to him that you have alway failed in depicting the comforts and pleasures of Association. And in fine, say to all the Associationists in Pittsburg, that we are doing well, even better than we ourselves ever expected; and if they wish to know more and judge for themselves, let them come and see us.   Yours,   J. R. W."

These are all the memorials that remain of the Columbian Phalanx. Another experiment of some note and enterprise, but with scanty history, was

THE SPRING FARM ASSOCIATION, WISCONSIN.

"In the year 1845," says Macdonald, "there was quite an excitement in the quiet little village of Sheboygan Falls, Wisconsin, on the subject of Fourier Association, stimulated by the energetic mind of Dr. P. Cady of Ohio. Meetings were held and Socialism was discussed, until ten families agreed to attempt an Association somewhere in the wilds of Sheboygan County. In making a selection of a suitable place, they divided into two parties, the one wishing to settle on the shore of Lake Michigan, and the other about twenty miles from the lake and six miles from any habitation. So strong were the opinions and prejudices of each, that the tents were pitched in both places. The following brief account relates to the one which was commenced in February, 1846, on Government land about twenty miles from the lake shore, and was named 'Spring Farm' from the lovely springs of water which were found there. (The other company was less successful.) The objects proposed to be carried out by this little band, were 'Union, Equal Rights, and Social Guaranties.'

"The pecuniary means, to begin with, amounted to only $ 1,000, put in as joint stock. The members consisted of six families, including ten children. Among them were farmers, blacksmiths, carpenters and joiners. They were tolerably intelligent, and with religious opinions various and free. They possessed an unfinished two-story frame building, twenty feet by thirty. They cultivated thirty acres of the prairie, and a small opening in the timber ; but they appear to have made very little progress ; though they worked in company for three years.

One of the members thus answered Macdonald's questions concerning the general course and results of the experiment:

"Mr. B. C. Trowbridge was generally looked up to as leader of the society. The land was bought of Government by individual resident members. We had nothing to boast of in improvements ; they were only anticipated. We obtained no aid from without ; what we did not provide for ourselves, we went without. The frost cut off our crops the second year, and left us short of provisions. We were not troubled with dishonest management, and generally agreed in all our affairs. We dissolved by mutual agreement. The reasons of failure were poverty, diversity of habits and dispositions, and disappointments through failure of harvest. Though we failed in this attempt, yet it has left an indelible impression on the minds of one-half the members at least, that a harmonious Association in some form is the way, and the only way, that the human mind can be fully and properly developed; and the general belief is, that community of property is the most practicable form."

THE BUREAU COUNTY PHALANX.

In the first number of the *Phalanx*, October 5, 1843, it is mentioned that a small Association had been commenced in Bureau County, Illinois. Macdonald repeats the mention, and adds, "No further particulars."

THE WASHTENAW PHALANX

was projected at Ann Arbor, Michigan, and a monthly paper called the *Future*, was started in connection with it; but it appears to have failed before it got fairly into operation; as the *Phalanx* barely refers to it once, and Macdonald dismisses it as a mere abortive excitement.

GARDEN GROVE COMMUNITY, IOWA,

was projected by D. Roberts, W. Davis, and others. The plan was to settle a colony of the "right sort" on contiguous lots, each family with its separate farm and dwelling, but all having a common pleasure-ground, dancing-hall, lecture-room and seminary. What came of it is not known.

THE IOWA PIONEER PHALANX

is mentioned twice in the *Phalanx*, as a Fourierist colony about to emigrate from Jefferson County, New York, to

Iowa. It issued a paper ; but whether it ever emigrated or what became of it, does not appear.

If there were any more of these feeble experiments— as there may have been many—they escaped the sharp eyes of Macdonald and the *Harbinger*, and left no memorials.

CHAPTER XXXV.

THE WISCONSIN PHALANX.

THIS was one of the most conspicuous experiments of the Fourier epoch. The notices of it in the *Phalanx* and *Harbinger* are quite voluminous. We shall have to curtail them as much as possible, and still our patchwork will be a long one. The Wisconsin had the advantage of most other Phalanxes in the skill of its spokesman. Mr. Warren Chase, a gentleman at present well known among Spiritualists, was its founder and principal manager. Most of the important communications relating to it in the socialistic Journals and other papers, were from his ready pen. We will do our best to save all that is most valuable in them, while we omit what seems to be irrelevant or repetitious. It may be understood that we are indebted to the *Phalanx* and *Harbinger* for nearly all our quotations from other papers.

[From the *Green Bay Republican*, April 30, 1844.]

"WISCONSIN PHALANX.—We have just been informed by the agent of the above Association, that the *locale* has been chosen, and ten sections of the finest land in the Territory entered at the Green Bay Land Office. The location is on a small stream near Green Lake,

Marquette county. The teams conveying the requisite implements, will start in a week, and the improvements will be commenced immediately. We are in favor of Fourier's plan of Association, although we very much fear that it will be unsuccessful on account of the selfishness of mankind, this being the principal obstacle to be overcome : yet we are pleased to see the commendable zeal manifested by the members of the Wisconsin Phalanx, who are mostly leading and influential citizens of Racine County. The feasibility of Association will now be tested in such a manner that the question will be decided, at least so far as Wisconsin is concerned.

[From a letter in the *Southport Telegraph*,]

Wisconsin Phalanx, May 27, 1844.

"We left Southport on Monday, the 20th inst., and arrived on the proposed domain, without accident, on Saturday last at five o'clock P. M. This morning (Monday) the first business was to divide into two companies, one for finding the survey stakes, and the other for setting up the tent on the ground designed for building and gardening purposes. Eight men, with ox-teams and cattle, arrived between nine and ten A. M. After dinner the members all met in the tent and proceeded to a regular organization, Mr. Chase being in the chair and Mr. Rounds Secretary.

"A prayer was offered, expressing thanks for our safe protection and arrival, and invoking the Divine blessing for our future peace and prosperity. The list of resident members was called (nineteen in number), and they divided themselves into two series, viz., agricultural and mechanical (each appointing a foreman), with a miscellaneous group of laborers, under the supervision of the resident directors.

"A letter was read by request of the members, from Peter Johnson, a member of the board of directors, relating to the proper conduct of the members in their general deportment, and reminding them of their obligations to their Creator.

"The agricultural series are to commence plowing and planting to-morrow, and the mechanical to excavate a cellar and prepare for the erection of a frame building, twenty-two feet by twenty, which is designed as a central wing for a building twenty-two feet by one hundred and twenty. There are nineteen men and one boy now on the domain. The stock consists of fifty-four head of cattle, large and small, including eight yoke of oxen and three span of horses. More men are expected during the week, and others are preparing to come this summer. Families will be here as the building can be sufficiently advanced to accommodate them.

"A few words in regard to the domain: There is a stream which, from its clearness, we have denominated Crystal Creek; it has sufficient fall and water supplied by springs, for one or two mill-seats. It runs over a bed of lime-stone, which abounds here, and can be had convenient for fences and building. There is a good supply of prairie and timber. Every member is well pleased with the location, and also the arrangements for business. Up to this time no discordant note has sounded in our company.

"We have begun without a debt, which is a source of great satisfaction to each member; and we are certain of success, provided that the same union prevails which has hitherto, and the company incur no debt by loan or otherwise, in the transaction of business. We expect to be prepared this summer or fall to issue the prospectus of a paper to be published on the ground

" GEO. H. STEBBINS."

[From a letter of Warren Chase.]

" *Wisconsin Phalanx, September* 12, 1844.

" Our first company, consisting of about twenty men, arrived here and commenced improvements on the 27th of May last. We put in about twenty acres of spring crops, mostly potatoes, buckwheat, turnips, etc., and have now one hundred acres of winter wheat in the ground. We have erected three buildings (designed for wings to a large one to be erected this fall), in which there are about twenty families snugly stored, yet comfortable and happy and busy, comprising in all about eighty persons, men, women, and children. We have also erected a saw-mill, which will be ready to run in a few days, after which we shall proceed to erect better dwellings. We do all our cooking in one kitchen, and all eat at one table. All our labor (excepting a part of female labor, on which there is a reduction), is for the present deemed in the class of usefulness, and every member works as well as possible where he or she is most needed, under the general superintendence of the directors. We adhere strictly to our constitution and by-laws, and adopt as fast as possible the system of Fourier. We have organized our groups and series in a simple manner, and thus far every thing goes admirably, and much better than we could have expected in our embryo state. We have regular meetings for business and social purposes, by which means we keep a harmony of feeling and concert of action. We have a Sunday-school,

Bible-class, and Divine service every Sabbath by different denominations, who occupy the Hall (as we have but
one) alternately ; and all is harmony in that department,
although we have many members of different religious
societies. They all seem determined to lay aside metaphysical differences, and make a united social effort,
founded on the fundamental principles of religion.

" WARREN CHASE."

[From a letter in the *Ohio American*, August, 1845.]

" I wish, through the medium of your columns, to
correct a statement which has been going the rounds of
the newspapers in this vicinity and in other parts, that
the Wisconsin Phalanx has failed and dispersed. I am
prepared to state, upon the authority of a letter from
their Secretary, dated July 31, 1845, that the report is
entirely without foundation. They have never been in
a more prosperons condition, and the utmost harmony
prevails. They are moving forward under a charter ;
own two thousand acres of fine land, with water-power ;
twenty-nine yoke of oxen, thirty-seven cows, and a
corresponding amount of other stock, such as horses,
hogs, sheep, etc. ; are putting in four hundred acres of
wheat this fall ; have just harvested one hundred acres
of the best of wheat, fifty-seven acres of oats, and other
grains in proportion. They have been organized a little
more than a year, and embrace in their number about
thirty families.

" One very favorable feature in this institution is, that
they are entirely out of debt, and intend to remain so ;
they do not owe, and are determined never to owe, a
single dollar. An excellent free school is provided for
all the members ; and as they have no idle gentlemen

or ladies to support, all have time to receive a good education."

[From a letter of Warren Chase.]

" *Wisconsin Phalanx, August,* 13, 1845.

"We are Associationists of the Fourier school, and intend to reduce his system to practice as fast as possible, consistently with our situation. We number at this time about one hundred and eighty souls, being the entire population of the congressional township. We are under the township government, organized similar to the system in New York. Our town was set off and organized last winter by the Legislature, at which time the Association was also incorporated as a joint-stock company by a charter, which is our constitution. We had a post-office and weekly mail within forty days after our commencement. Thus far we have obtained all we have asked for.

"We have religious meetings and Sabbath-schools, conducted by members of some half-a-dozen different denominations of Christians, with whom creeds and modes of faith are of minor importance compared with religion. All are protected, and all is harmony in that department. We have had no deaths and very little sickness. No physician, no lawyer or preacher, yet resides among us ; but we expect a physician soon, whose interest will not conflict with ours, and whose presence will consequently not increase disease. In politics we are about equally divided, and vote accordingly ; but generally believe both parties culpable for many of the political evils of the day.

"The Phalanx has a title from Government to fourteen hundred and forty acres of land, on which there is one of the best of water-powers, a saw-mill in operation and a grist-mill building; six hundred and forty acres under improvement, four hundred of which is now seeding to winter wheat. We raised about fifteen hundred bushels the past season, which is sufficient for our next year's bread; have about seventy acres of corn on the ground, which looks well, and other crops in proportion. We have an abundance of cattle, horses, crops and provisions for the wants of our present numbers, and physical energy enough to obtain more. Thus, you see, we are tolerably independent ; and we intend to remain so, as we admit none as members who have not sufficient funds to invest in stock, or sufficient physical strength, to warrant their not being a burden to the society. We have one dwelling-house nearly finished, in which reside twenty families, with a long hall conducting to the dining-room, where all who are able, dine together. We intend next summer to erect another for twenty families more, with a hall conducting to another dining-room, supplied from the same cook-room. We have one school constantly, but have as yet been unable to do much toward improving that department, and had hoped to see something in the *Harbinger* which would be a guide in this branch of our organization. We look to the Brook Farm Phalanx for instruction in this branch, and hope to see it in the *Harbinger* for the benefit of ourselves and other Associations.

" We have a well-regulated system of grouping our laborers, but have not yet organized the series. We have no difficulty in any department of our business, and thus far more than our most sanguine expectations have been realized. We commenced with a determination to avoid all debts, and have thus far adhered to our resolution ; for we believed debts would disband more

Associations than any other one cause ; and thus far, I believe it has, more than all other causes put together.

" WARREN CHASE."

From the Annual Statement of the Condition and Progress of the Wisconsin Phalanx, for the fiscal year ending December 1, 1845.

" The four great evils with which the world is afflicted, intoxication, lawsuits, quarreling, and profane swearing, never have, and with the present character and prevailing habits of our members, never can, find admittance into our society. There is but a very small proportion of the tattling, backbiting and criticisms on character, usually found in neighborhoods of as many families. Perfect harmony and concert of action prevail among the members of the various churches, and each individual seems to lay aside creeds, and strive for the fundamental principles of religion. Many have cultivated the social feeling by the study and practice of vocal and instrumental music. In this there is a constant progress visible. Our young gentlemen and ladies have occasionally engaged in cotillions, especially on wedding occasions, of which we have had three the past summer.

" Our convenience for schools, their diminished expense, &c., is known only to those acquainted with Association. We have done but little in perfecting this branch of our new organization ; but having erected a school-house, we are prepared to commence our course of moral, physical and intellectual education. For want of a convenient place, we have not yet opened our reading-room or library, but intend to do so during the present month.

" The family circle and secret domestic relations are not intruded on by Association ; each family may gather around its family altar, secluded and alone, or mingle with neighbors without exposure to wet or cold. In our social and domestic arrangements we have approximated as far toward the plan of Fourier, as the difficulties incident to a new organization in an uncultivated country would permit. Owing to our infant condition and wish to live within our means, our public table has not been furnished as elegantly as might be desirable to an epicurean taste. From the somewhat detached nature of our dwellings, and the consequent inconveniencies attendant on all dining at one table, permission was given to such families as chose, to be furnished with provisions and cook their own board. But one family has availed itself of this privilege.

"In the various departments of physical labor, we have accomplished much more than could have been done by the same persons in the isolated condition. We have broken and brought under cultivation, three hundred and twenty-five acres of land; have sown four hundred acres to winter wheat; harvested the hundred acres which we had on the ground last fall; plowed one hundred and seventy acres for crops the ensuing spring; raised sixty acres of corn, twenty of potatoes, twenty of buckwheat, and thirty of peas, beans, roots, etc. ; built five miles of fence ; cut four hundred tons of hay ; and expended a large amount of labor in teaming, building sheds, taking care of stock, etc.

"We have nearly finished the long building commenced last year (two hundred and eight feet by thirty-two), making comfortable residences for twenty families ; built a stone school-house, twenty by thirty ; a dining-room eighteen by thirty ; finished one of the twenty-by-thirty dwellings built last year; expended about two hundred days' labor digging a race and foundation for a grist-mill thirty by forty, three stories high, and for a shop twenty by twenty-five, one story, with stone basements to both, and erected frames for the same; built a wash-house sixty by twenty-two; a hen-house eleven by thirty, of sun-dried brick; an ash-house ten by twenty, of the same material; kept one man employed in the saw-mill, one drawing logs, one in the blacksmith shop, one shoe-making, and most of the time two about the kitchen.

"The estimated value of our property on hand is $27,725.22, wholly unincumbered; and we are free from debt, except about $600 due to members, who have advanced cash for the purchase of provisions and land. But to balance this, we have over $1,000 coming from members, on stock subscriptions not yet due.

"The whole number of hours' labor performed by the members during the past year, reduced to the class of usefulness, is 102,760; number expended in cooking, etc., and deducted for the board of members, 21,170; number remaining after deducting for board, 81,590, to which the amount due to labor is divided. In this statement the washing is not taken into account, families having done their own.

"Whole number of weeks board charged members (including children graduated to adults) forty-two hundred and thirty-four. Cost of board per week for each person, forty-four cents for provisions, and five hours labor.

"Whole amount of property on hand, as per invoice, $27,725.22. Cost of property and stock issued up to December 1, $19,589.18. Increase the past year, being the product of labor, etc., $8,136.04; one-fourth of which, or $2,034.01, is credited to capital, being twelve per cent. per annum on stock, for the average time invested; and three-fourths, or $6,102.03 to labor, being seven and one-half cents per hour.

"The property on hand consists of the following items:

1,553 acres of land, at $3.00	$4,659.00
Agricultural improvements	1,522.47
Mechanical improvements	8,405.00
Personal property	10,314.01
Advanced members in board, etc.	2,824.74
Amount	$27,725.22

"W. CHASE, *President.*"

[From a letter of Warren Chase,]

Wisconsin Phalanx, March 3, 1846.

"Since our December statement, our course and progress has been undeviatingly onward toward the goal. We have added eighty acres to our land, making one thousand six hundred and thirty-three acres free of incumbrance. We are preparing to raise eight hundred acres of crops the coming season, finish our grist-mill, and build some temporary residences, etc. We have admitted but one family since the 1st of December, although we have had many applications. In this department of our organization, as well as in that of contracting debts, we are profiting by the experience of many Associations who preceded or started with us.

"We pretend to have considerable knowledge of the serial law, but we are not yet prepared, mentally or physically, to adopt it in our industrial operations. We have something in operation which approaches about as near to it as the rude hut does to the palace. Even this is better than none, and saves us from the merciless peltings of the storm.

"Success with us is no longer a matter of doubt. Our questions to be settled are, How far and how fast can we adopt and put in practice the system and principle which we believe to be true, without endangering or retarding our ultimate object. We feel and know that our condition and prospects are truly cheering, and to the friends of the cause we can say, Come on, not to join us, but to form other Associations; for we can not receive one-tenth of those who apply for admission. Nothing but the general principles of Association are lawful tender with us. Money will not buy admission for those who have no faith in the principles, but who merely believe, as most of our neighbors do, that we shall get rich; this is not a ruling principle here. With our material, our means, and the principles of eternal truth on our side, success is neither doubtful nor surprising.

We expect at our next annual statement, to be able to represent ourselves as a minimum Association of forty families, not fully organized on Fourier's plan, but approaching to, and preparing for it.   W. CHASE."

From the Annual Statement of the Condition and Progress of the Wisconsin Phalanx, for the fiscal year ending December 7, 1846.

"The study and adoption of the principles of industrial Association, have here, as elsewhere, led all reflecting minds to acknowledge the principles of Christianity, and to seek through those principles the elevation of man to his true condition, a state of harmony with himself, with nature and with God. The Society have religious preaching of some kind almost every Sabbath, but not uniformly of that high order of talent which they are prepared to appreciate.

"The educational department is not yet regulated as it is designed to be ; the Society have been too busily engaged in making such improvements as were required to supply the necessaries of life, to devote the means and labor necessary to prepare such buildings as are required. We have not yet established our reading-room and library, more for the want of room, than for a lack of materials.

"The social intercourse between the members has ever been conducted with a high-toned moral feeling, which repudiates the slanderous suspicions of those enemies of the system, who pretend that the constant social intercourse will corrupt the morals of the members ; the tendency is directly the reverse.

"We have now one hundred and eighty resident members ; one hundred and one males, seventy-nine females ; fifty-six males and thirty-seven females over the age of twenty-one years. About eighty have boarded at a public table during the past year, at a cost of fifty cents per week and two and a half hours' labor ; whole cost sixty-three cents. The others, most of the time, have had their provisions charged to them, and done their own cooking in their respective families, although their apartments are very inconvenient for that purpose. Most of the families choose this mode of living, more from previous habits of domestic arrangement and convenience, than from economy. We have resident on the domain, thirty-six families and thirty single persons ; fifteen families and thirty single persons board at the public table : twenty-one families board by themselves, and the remaining five single persons board with them.

" Four families have left during the past year, and one returned that had previously left. One left to commence a new Association : one, after a few weeks' residence, because the children did not like; and two to seek other business more congenial with their feelings than hard work. The Society has increased its numbers the past year about twenty, which is not one-fourth of the applicants. The want of room has prevented us from admitting more.

"There has been 96,297 hours' medium class labor performed during the past year (mostly by males), which, owing to the extremely low appraisal of property, and the disadvantage of having a new farm to work on, has paid but five cents per hour, and six per cent. per annum on capital.

"The amount of property in joint-stock, as per valuation, is $30,609.04; whole amount of liabilities, $1,095.33. The net product or income for the past year is $6,341.84, one-fourth of which being credited to capital, makes the six per cent.; and three-fourths to labor, makes the five cents per hour. We have, as yet, no machinery in operation except a saw-mill, but have a grist-mill nearly ready to commence grinding. Our wheat crop came in very light, which, together with the large amount of labor necessarily expended in temporary sheds and fences, which are not estimated of any value, makes our dividend much less than it will be when we can construct more permanent works. We have also many unfinished works, which do not yet afford us either income or convenience, but which will tell favorably on our future balance-sheets.

"The Society has advanced to the members during the past year $3,293, mostly in provisions and such necessary clothing as could be procured.

"The following schedule shows in what the property of the Society consists, and its valuation:

1,713 acres of land, at $ 3.00 . ·	$ 5,139.00
Agricultural improvements	3,206.00
Agricultural products	4,806.76
Shops, dwellings, and out-houses	6,963.61
Mills, mill-race and dam	5,112.90
Cattle, horses, sheep, hogs, &c.	3,098.45
Farming tools, &c	1,199.36
Mechanical tools, &c.	367.26
Other personal property	715.70
Amount	$ 30,609.04

"W. Chase, President."

In the *Harbinger* of March 27, 1847, there is a letter from Warren Chase giving eighteen elaborate reasons why the Fourierists throughout the country should concentrate on the Wisconsin, and make it a great model Phalanx; which we omit.

[From a letter of Warren Chase.]

"*Wisconsin Phalanx, June* 28, 1847.

"We have now been a little more than three years in operation, and my most sanguine expectations have been more than realized. We have about one hundred and seventy persons, who, with the exception of three or four families, are contented and happy, and more attached to this home than to any they ever had before. Those three or four belong to the restless, discontented spirits, who are not satisfied with any condition of life, but are always seeking something new. The Phalanx will soon be in a condition to adopt the policy of purchasing the amount of stock which any member may have invested, whenever he shall wish to leave. As soon as this can be done without embarrassing our business, we shall have surmounted the last obstacle to our onward progress. We have applications for admission constantly before us, but seldom admit one. We require larger amounts to be invested now when there is no risk, than we did at first when the risk was great. We have borne the heat and burden of the day, and now begin to reap the fruits of our labor. We also must know that an applicant is devoted to the cause, ready to endure for it hardships, privations and persecution, if necessary, and that he is not induced to apply because he sees our physical or pecuniary prosperity. We shall admit such as, in our view, are in all respects prepared for Association and can be useful to themselves and us ; but none but practical workingmen need apply, for idlers can not live here. They seem to be out of their element, and look sick and lean. If no accident befalls us, we shall declare a cash dividend at our next annual settlement.

"W. Chase."

[From a letter in the New York Tribune.]

" Wisconsin Phalanx, July 20, 1847.

"I have been visiting this Association several days, looking into its resources, both physical and moral. Its physical resources are abundant. In a moral aspect there is much here to encourage. The people, ninety of whom are adults, are generally quite intelligent, and possess a good development of the moral and social faculties. They are earnest inquirers after truth, and seem aware of the harmony of thought and feeling that must prevail to insure prosperity. They receive thirty or forty different publications, which are thoroughly perused. The females are excellent women, and the children, about eighty, are most promising in every respect. They are not yet well situated for carrying into effect all the indispensable agencies of true mental development, but they are not idle on this momentous subject. They have an excellent school for the children, and the young men and women are cultivating music. Two or three among them are adepts in this beautiful art. While writing, I hear good music by well-trained voices, with the Harmonist accompaniment.

"I do believe something in human improvement and enjoyment will soon be presented at Ceresco, that will charm all visitors, and prove a conclusive argument against the skepticism of the world as to the capability of the race to rise above the social evils that afflict mankind, and to attain a mental elevation which few have yet hoped for. I expect to see here a garden in which shall be represented all that is most beautiful in the vegetable kingdom. I expect to see here a library and reading-room, neatly and plentifully furnished, to which rejoicing hundreds will resort for instruction and amusement. I expect to see here a laboratory, where the chemist will unfold the operations of nature, and teach the most profitable mode of applying agricultural labor. I expect to see here interesting cabinets, where the mineral and animal kingdoms will be presented in miniature. And I expect to see all the arts cultivated, and every thing beautiful and grand generally appreciated. HINE."

On which the editor of the *Tribune* observes : "We trust the remark will be taken in good part, that the writers of letters from these Associative experiments are too apt to blend what they desire or hope to see, with what they actually do see."

[From a letter of J. J. Cooke in the *Tribune*.]

" *Wisconsin Phalanx, August* 28, 1847.

"*Editor of the New York Tribune:*

"DEAR SIR: I have just perused in your paper, a letter from Mr. Hine, dated at this place. Believing that the letter is calculated to leave an erroneous impression on the mind of the reader, as to the true condition of this Association, I deem it to be my duty to notice it, for the reason of the importance of the subject, and the necessity of true knowledge in reference to correct action.

" It is now twelve days since I arrived here, with the intention of making a visit sufficiently long to arrive at something like a critical knowledge of the experiment now in progress in this place. As you justly remark in your comments on Mr. Hine's letter, 'the writers of letters from these associative experiments are too apt to blend what they desire or hope to see, with what they actually do see.' So far as such a course might tend to induce premature and ill-advised attempts at practical Association, it should be regarded as a serious evil, and as such, should, if possible, be remedied. I presume no one here would advise the commencement of any Association, to pass through the same trials which they themselves have experienced. I have asked many of the members this question, ' Do you think that the reports and letters which have been published respecting your Association, have been so written as to leave a correct impression of your real existing condition on the mind of the reader?' The answer has invariably been, 'No.'"

The writer then criticises the water-power, climate, etc., and proceeds to say:

"The probability now is, that corn will be almost a total failure. 'Their present tenements,' says Mr. Hine, 'are such as haste and limited means forced them to erect.' This is undoubtedly true, and I will also add, that they are such as few at the East would be contented to live in. With the exception of the flouring-mill, blacksmith's-shop and carpenter's-shop, there are no arrangements for mechanical industry. This is not surprising, in view of the small means in their possession. 'In a moral aspect,' Mr. Hine says, 'there is much to encourage.' It would not be incorrect to say, that there is also something to fear. The most unpleasant feelings which I have experienced since I have been here, have been caused by the want of neatness around the dwellings, which seems to be inconsistent with the individual character of the members with whom I have become acquainted. This they state to be owing to their struggles for the necessaries of life; but I have freely told them that I considered it inexcusable, and calculated to have an injurious influence upon themselves and upon their children. 'They are earnest inquirers after truth,' says Mr. Hine, 'and seem aware of the harmony of thought and feeling that must prevail, in order to insure prosperity.' This I only object to so far as it is calculated to produce the impression that such harmony really exists. That there is a difference of feeling upon, at least, one important point, I know. This is in reference to the course to be pursued in relation to the erection of dwellings. I believe that a large majority are in favor of building only in reference to a combined dwelling; but there are some who think that this generation are not prepared for it, and who wish to erect comfortable dwellings for isolated households. A portion of the members go out to labor for hire; some, in order to procure those necessaries which the means of the Association have been inadequate to provide; and others, for want of occupation in their peculiar branches of industry. Mr. Hine says, 'They have an excellent school for the children.' I had thought that the proper education of the children was a want here, and members have spoken of it as such. They have no public library or reading-room for social re-union, excepting the school-room; and no room which is convenient for such purposes. There are no Associational guarantees in reference to sickness or disability in the charter (which is the constitution) of this Phalanx.

"From the above statement, you can judge somewhat of the present foundation of Mr. Hine's hopes of 'soon' seeing the realization of the beautiful picture which he has drawn.   JOSEPH J. COOKE."

In the *Harbinger* of January 8, 1848, Warren Chase replied to Mr. Cooke's criticisms, admitting the general truth of them, but insisting that it is unfair to judge the Association by eastern standards. In conclusion he says:

"There is a difference of opinion in regard to board, which, under the law of freedom and attraction, works no harm. Most of our families cook their board in their rooms from choice under present circumstances; some because they use no meat and do not choose to sit at a table plentifully supplied with beef, pork and mutton: others because they choose to have their children sit at the table with them, to regulate their diet, etc., which our circumstances will not yet permit at our public table ; others because they want to ask a blessing, etc. ; and others because their manner of cooking and habits of living have become so fixed as to have sufficient influence to require their continuance. Some of our members think all these difficulties can not be speedily removed, and that cheap and comfortable dwellings should be built, adapted to our circumstances, with a unitary work-house, bakery and dairy, by which the burdens should be removed as fast as possible, and the minds prepared by combined effort, co-operative labor, and equitable distribution, for the combined dwelling and unitary living, with its variety of tables to satisfy all tastes. Others think our devotion to the cause ought to induce us to forego all these attachments and prejudices, and board at one table and improve it, building none but unitary dwellings adapted to a unitary table. We pursue both ways in our living with perfect freedom, and probably shall in our building; for attraction is the only law whose force we acknowledge in these matters. We have passed one more important point in our progress since I last wrote you. We have adopted the policy to refund all investments to any member when he chooses to leave. W. CHASE."

[From a letter of Warren Chase.]

"*Wisconsin Phalanx, August* 21, 1847.

"We are in the enjoyment of an excellent state of health, owing in part to our healthy location, and in part to the diet and regimen of our members. There is a prevailing tendency here to abandon the use of animal food ; it has been slowly, but steadily increasing for some time, and has been aided some by those excellent and interesting articles from the pen of Dr. Lazarus on 'Cannibalism.' When we have to resort to any medical treatment, hydropathy is the system, and the *Water-cure Journal* very good authority. Our society will soon evince symptoms of two conditions of Associative life, viz.: physical health and material wealth. By wealth I do not mean burdensome property, but an ample supply of the necessaries of life, which is real wealth.

"I fully believe that nine out of ten organizations and attempts at Association would finally succeed, even with small means and few members, if they would adhere strictly to the following conditions:

"First, keep free from debt, and live within their means ; Second, not attempt too much in the commencement.

"Great changes require a slow movement. All pioneers should remember to be constructive, and not merely destructive ; not to tear down faster than they can substitute something better. Every failure of Association which has come to my knowledge, has been in consequence of disregarding these conditions ; they have all been in debt, and depended on stock subscriptions to relieve them ; and they have attempted too much. Having, in most cases, torn down the isolated household and family altar (or table), before they had even science enough to draft a plan of a Phalanstery or describe a unitary household, they seemed in some cases to imagine that the true social science, when once discovered, would furnish them, like the lamp of Aladdin, with all things wished for. They have awakened from their dreams ; and now is the time for practical attempts, to start with, first, the joint-stock property, the large farm or township, the common home and joint property of all the members; second, cooperative labor and the equitable distribution of products, the large fields, large pastures, large gardens, large dairies, large fruit orchards, etc., with their mills, mechanic shops, stores, common wash-houses, bake-houses, baths, libraries, lectures, cabinets, etc.; third, educational organization, including all, both children and adults, and through that the adoption of the serial law, organization of groups and series; (at this point labor, without reference to the pay, will begin to be attractive;) fourth, the Phalansterian order, unitary living. As this is the greatest step, it requires the most time, most capital, and most mental preparation, especially for persons accustomed to country life. In most cases many years will be required for the adoption of the second of these conditions, and more for the third, and still more for the fourth. Hence the necessity of commencing, if the present generation is to realize much from the discovery of the science.

" Let no person construe these remarks to indicate an advanced state of Association for the Wisconsin Phalanx. We have taken the first step, which required but little time, and are now barely commencing the second. We have spent three years, and judging from our progress thus far, it will doubtless take us from five to ten more to get far enough in the second to commence the third. We have made many blunders for the want of precedents, and in consequence of having more zeal than knowledge. Among the most serious blunders was an attempt at unitary living, without any of the surrounding circumstances being adapted to it. With this view we built, at a cost of more than $ 3,000, a long double front building, which can not be ventilated, and is very uncomfortable and extremely inconvenient for families to live in and do their cooking. But in this, bad as it is, some twenty of our families are still compelled to live, and will be for some time to come. This, with some other mistakes, will be to us a total loss, for the want of more knowledge to commence with. But these are trifling in comparison with the importance of our object and the result for a series of years. No true Associationist has been discouraged by these trials and losses ; but we have a few among us who never were Associationists, and who are waiting a favorable opportunity to return to civilization ; and we are waiting a favorable opportunity to admit such as we want to fill their places.   W. CHASE."

From the Annual Statement of the Condition and Progress of the Wisconsin Phalanx, for the fiscal year ending December 6, 1847.

" The number of resident members is one hundred and fifty-seven ; eighty-four males and seventy-three females. Thirty-two males and thirty-nine females are under twenty-one years, fifty-two males and thirty-four females over twenty-one years, and eighteen persons above the age of twenty-one unmarried. The whole number of resident families is thirty-two. We have resident with us who are not members, one family and four single persons. Four families and two single persons have left during the year, the stock of all of whom has been purchased, except of one family, and a single person ; the former intends returning, and the latter owns but $25.00.

" The number of hours' labor performed during the year, reduced to the medium class, is 93,446. The whole amount of property at the appraisal is $32,564.18. The net profits of the year are $9,029.73 ; which gives a dividend to stock of nearly 7 3-4 per cent., and 7 3-10 cents per hour to labor.

"The Phalanx has purchased and cancelled during the year $2,000 of stock; we have also, by the assistance of our mill (which has been in operation since June), and from our available products, paid off the incumbrance of $1,095.33 with which we commenced the year; made our mechanical and agricultural improvements, and advanced to members, in rent, provisions, clothing, cash, etc., $5,237.07. The annexed schedule specifies the kinds and valuation of the property on hand:

1,713 acres of land at $3.00	$5,139.00
Agricultural improvements	3,509.77
Agricultural products	5,244.16
Mechanical improvements	12,520.00
Live stock	2,983.50
Farm and garden tools	1,219.77
Mechanical tools	380.56
Personal property, miscellaneous . . .	1,567.42
Amount	$32,564.18

"BENJ. WRIGHT, President."

In June, 1848, Warren Chase sent a letter to the *Boston Investigator*, complaining of the *Harbinger's* indifference to the interests of the Wisconsin Phalanx; and another writer in the *Investigator* suggested that this indifference was on account of the irreligious character of the Phalanx; all of which the *Harbinger* denied. To the charge of irreligion, a member of the Phalanx indignantly replied in the *Harbinger*, as follows:

"Some of us are and have been Methodists, Baptists, Presbyterians, Congregationalists, etc. Others have never been members of any church, but (with a very few exceptions) very readily admit the authenticity and moral value of the Scriptures. The ten commandments are the sum, substance and foundation of all true law. Add to this the gospel law of love, and you have a code of laws worthy of the adoption and practice of any man or set of men, and upon which Associationists must base themselves, or they can never succeed. There are many rules, doctrines and interpretations of Scripture among the (so denominated) Orthodox churches, that any man of common sense can not assent to. Even they can not agree among themselves; for instance the Old and New School Presbyterians, the Baptists, Methodists, etc. If this difference of faith and opinion is infidelity or irreligion, we to a man are infidels and irreligious; but if faith in the principles and morality of the Bible is the test, I deny the charge. I can scarcely name an individual here that dissents from them.

"I have been a member of the Methodist Episcopal Church for about twenty years, and a Methodist local preacher for over three years, and am now Secretary of the Association. I therefore should know somewhat about this matter."

[From the New York *Tribune*, July, 1848.]

"WISCONSIN PHALANX.—Having lately seen running around the papers a statement that the last remaining 'Fourier Association,' somewhere in Illinois, had just given up the ghost, we gladly give place to the following extracts from a private letter we have just received from a former fellow citizen, who participated in two of the earlier attempts (Sylvania and Leraysville) to establish something that ultimately would or might become an Association after the idea of Fourier. After the second

failure he attached himself to the communistic undertaking near Skaneateles, New York, and when this too
ran aground, he went back perforce to the cut-throat
system of civilized competition. But this had become
unendurably hateful to him, and he soon struck off for
Ceresco, and became a member of the Wisconsin
Phalanx at that place, whereof he has now for some
months been a resident. Of this Association he writes:

"I have worked in the various groups side by side
with the members, and I have never seen a more persevering, practical, matter-of-fact body of people in any
such movement. Since I came here last fall, I see a
great improvement, both externally and internally. Mr.
Van Amringe, the energetic herald of national and social
reform, did a good work by his lectures here last winter;
and the meetings statedly held for intellectual and social
improvement, have an excellent effect. All now indicates unity and fraternity. The Phalanx has erected
and enclosed a new unitary dwelling, one hundred feet
long, two stories high, with a spacious kitchen, belfry,
etc. They have burnt a lime-kiln, and are burning a
brick-kiln of one hundred thousand bricks as an experiment, and they bid fair to be first-rate. All this has
been accomplished this spring in addition to their agricultural and horticultural operations. Their water-power
is small, being supplied from springs, which the drought
of the last three seasons has sensibly affected. In adding to their machinery, they will have to resort to steam.

"The location is healthy and pleasant. The atmosphere is uniformly pure, and a good breeze is generally
blowing. I doubt whether another site could be found
combining so many natural advantages. I have visited
nearly all the associative experiments in the country,

and I like this the best.   I think it already beyond the
possibility of failure.   D.   S."

Mr. Van Amringe spent considerable time at Ceresco,
and sent several elaborate articles in favor of the Phalanx to the *Harbinger*.   One of the members wrote to
him as follows :

"Since you left here a great change has taken place
in the feelings and tastes of the members, and that too
for the better.   You will recollect the black and dirty
appearance of the buildings, and the wood-work inside
scrubbed until it had the appearance of a dirty white.
About the first of May they made a grand rally to alter
the appearance of things.   The long building was white-
washed inside and out, and the wood-work of nearly all
the houses has been painted.   The school-house has
been white-washed and painted, the windows white, the
panels of the wood-work a light yellow, carvings around
a light blue, the seats and desks a light blue ; this has
made a great change in its appearance.   You will recollect the frame of a new building that stood looking so
distressed ; about as much more was added to it, and all
covered and neatly painted.   The corridor is now finished ; a handsome good kitchen has been put up in the
rear of the old one, with a bakery underneath ; a beautiful cupola is on the top, in which is placed a small bell,
weighing one hundred and two pounds, about the size
of a steamboat bell; it can be heard on the prairie.
The blinds in the cupola windows are painted green.
Were you to see the place now you would be surprised,
and agreeably so, too.   Some four or five have left since
spring ; new members have been taken in their stead,
and a good exchange, I think, has been made.   Two or

three tailors, and the same number of shoemakers, are expected shortly."

From the Annual Statement of the Condition and progress of the Wisconsin Phalanx, for the fiscal year ending December 4, 1848.

"Religious meetings are sustained by us every Sabbath, in which the largest liberty is extended to all in the search for truth. In the educational department we do no more than sustain a common school; but are waiting, anxiously waiting, for the time when our condition will justify a more extended operation. In the absence of a reading-room and library, one of our greatest facilities for knowledge and general information is afforded by a great number and variety of newspapers and periodical publications, an interchange of which gives advantages in advance of the isolated family. The number of resident members is one hundred and twenty, viz.: sixty-three males and fifty-seven females. The number of resident families is twenty-nine. We have resident with us, who are not members, one family and twelve single persons. Six families and three single persons have left during the year, a part of whose stock we have purchased. We have lost by death the past year seven persons, viz.: one married lady (by consumption), one child two years of age, and five infants. The health of the members has been good, with the exception of a few cases of remittent and billious fevers. The Phalanx has sustained a public boarding-house the past year, at which the majority of the members have boarded at a cost not exceeding seventy-five cents per week. The remaining families board at their own apartments.

"The number of hours' labor performed during the year, reduced to the medium class, is 97,036. The whole amount of property at the appraisal, is $33,527.77. The net profits of the year are, $8,077.02 ; which gives a dividend to stock of 6 1-4 per cent., and 6 1-4 cents per hour to labor. The annexed schedule specifies the kinds and valuation of property on hand :

Real estate 1,793 acres at $3.00	$5,379.00
Live Stock	3,117.00
Mechanical tools	1,866.34
Farming tools	1,250.75
Mechanical improvements	14,655.00
Agricultural improvements	2,298.90
" products	3,161.56
Garden products	1,006.13
Miscellaneous property	793.09
Total amount	$33,527.77

"S. BATES, President."

The following anonymous summary, well written and evidently authentic, is taken from Macdonald's collection:

[History of the Wisconsin Phalanx, by a member.]

"In the winter of 1843—4 there was considerable excitement in the village of Southport, Wisconsin (now Kenosha City), on the subject of Association. The subject was taken up with much feeling and interest at the village lyceum and in various public meetings. Among the advocates of Association were a few persons who determined in the spring of 1844 to make a practical experiment. For that purpose a constitution was drawn up, and a voluntary Association formed, which styled itself 'The Wisconsin Phalanx.' As the movement began to ripen into action, the friends fell off, and the circle narrowed down from about seventy to twenty persons. This little band was composed mostly of men with small means, sturdy constitutions, below the middle age, and full of energy; men who had been poor, and had learned early to buffet with the antagonisms of civilization; not highly cultivated in the social and intellectual faculties, but more so in the moral and industrial.

"They raised about $ 1,000 in money, which they sent to the land-office at Green Bay, and entered a tract of land selected by their committee, in a congressional township in the north-west corner of Fond du Lac County, a township six miles square, without a single inhabitant, and with no settlement within twenty miles, except a few scattered families about Green Lake.

"With teams, stock, tents, and implements of husbandry and mechanism, they repaired to this spot in the latter part of May 1844, a distance of about one hundred and twenty-five miles from their homes, and commenced building and breaking up land, etc. They did not erect a log house, but split out of the tongh burr and white oak of the 'openings,' shingles, clapboards, floors, frames and all the materials of a house, and soon prepared a shelter. Their families were then moved on Late in the fall a saw-mill was built, and every thing prepared as well as could be for the winter. Their dwellings would have been unendurable at other times and under other circumstances; but at this time zeal, energy, excitement and hope kept them from complaining. Their land, which was subsequently increased to 1,800 acres, mostly at $1.25 per acre, consisted of 'openings,' prairie and timber, well watered, and with several small water-powers on the tract; a fertile soil, with as healthy a climate as could be found in the Western States.

"It was agreed to name the new town Ceresco, and a post-office was applied for under that name, and obtained. One of the members always held the office of post-master, until the administration of General Taylor, when the office was removed about three-quarters of a mile to a rival village. In the winter of 1844—5, the Association asked the Legislature to organize their town, which was readily done under the adopted name. A few settlers had by this time moved into the town (which, owing to the large proportion of prairie, was not rapidly settled), and in the spring they held their election. Every officer chosen was a member of the society, and as they were required to elect Justices and had no need of any, they chose the three oldest men. From that time until the dissolution of the society nearly every town-office of importance was filled by its members. They had also one of their members in both Constitutional Conventions of the State, and three in the State Senate for one term of two sessions. Subsequently one of their members was a candidate for Governor, receiving more votes in his town than both of the other candidates together; but only a small vote in the State, as he was the free-soil candidate.

"The Association drew up and prepared a charter or act of incorporation upon which they agreed, and applied to the Legislature for its passage; which was granted; and thus they became a body corporate and politic, known in the land as the 'Wisconsin Phalanx.' All the business was done in accordance with and under this charter, until the property was divided and the whole affair closed up. One clause in the charter prohibited the sale of the land. This was subsequently altered at the society's request, in an amendatory act in the session of 1849—50, for the purpose of allowing them to divide their property.

" In the spring of 1845, after their organization under the charter, they had considerable accession to their numbers, and might have had greater; but were very careful about admitting new members, and erred very much in making a property qualification. About this time (1845) a question of policy arose among the members, the decision of which is supposed by many good judges to have been the principal cause of the ultimate division and dissolution; it was, whether the dwellings should be built in unitary blocks adapted to a common boarding-house, or in isolated style, adapted to the separate family and single living. It was decided by a small majority to pursue the unitary plan, and this policy was persisted in until there was a division of property. Whether this was the cause of failure or not, it induced many of the best members to leave; and although it might have been the true policy under other circumstances and for other persons, in this case it was evidently wrong, for the members were not socially developed sufficiently to maintain such close relations. Notwithstanding this, they continued to increase slowly, rejecting many more applicants than they admitted; and often rejecting the better and admitting the worse, because the worse had the property qualifications. In this way they increased to the maximum of thirty-three families. They had no pecuniary difficulties, for they kept mostly out of debt.

"It was a great reading Community; often averaging as many as five or six regular newspapers to a family, and these constantly exchanging with each other. They were not religious, but mostly rather skeptical, except a few elderly orthodox persons. [This hardly agrees with the statement and protest on the 436th page.]

" They were very industrious, and had many discussions and warm arguments about work, manners, progress, etc. ; but still they continued to work and scold, and scold and work, with much energy, and to much effect. They raised one season ten thousand bushels of wheat, and much other grain ; had about seven hundred acres under cultivation ; but committed a great error in cultivating four hundred acres on the school lands adjoining their own, because it lay a little better for a large field. They had subsequently to remove their fences and leave that land, for they did not wish to buy it.

" Their charter elections were annual, and were often warmly contested, and turned mainly on the question of unitary or isolated households ; but they never went beyond words in their contentions.

" They were all temperance men and women : no ardent spirits were kept or sold for the first four years in the township, and never on the domain, while it was held as joint-stock.

" Their system of labor and pay was somewhat complicated, and never could be satisfactorily arranged. The farmers and mechanics were always jealous of each other, and could not be brought to feel near enough to work on and divide the profits at the end of the year ; but as they ever hoped to get over this difficulty, they said but very little about it. In their system of labor they formed groups for each kind of work ; each group, when consisting of three or more, choosing its own foreman, who kept the account of the time worked by each member, and reported weekly to a meeting of all the members, which regulated the average ; and then the Secretary copied it ; and at the end of the fiscal year each person drew, on his labor account, his proportion of the three-fourths of the increase and products which was allotted to labor, and on his stock shares, his proportion of the one-fourth that was divided to stock. The amount so divided was ascertained by an annual appraisal of all the property, thus ascertaining the rise or increase in value, as well as the product of labor. The dividend to capital was, however, usually considered too large and disproportionate.

" The books and accounts were accurately kept by the Secretary, and most of the individual transactions passed through this form, thus leaving all accounts in the hands of a disinterested person, open to inspection at all times, and bringing about an annual settlement which avoided many difficulties incident to civilization.

" The table of the Community, when kept as a public boarding-house, where the families and visitors or travelers were mostly seated, was set with plain but substantial food, much like the tables of farmers in newly settled agricultural States ; but it often incurred the ridicule of loafers and epicures, who travel much and fare better with strangers than at home.

" They had among their number a few men of leading intellect who always doubted the success of the experiment, and hence determined to accumulate property individually by any and every means called fair in competitive society. These would occasionally gain some important positions in the society, and representing it in part at home and abroad, caused much trouble. By some they were accounted the principal cause of the final failure.

"In the summer and fall of 1849 it became evident that a dissolution and division was inevitable, and plans for doing it within themselves, without recourse to courts of law, were finally got up, and they determined to have it done by their legal advisers as other business was done. At the annual election in December 1849, the officers were elected with a view to that particular business. They had already sold much of the personal property and cancelled much of the stock. The highest amount of stock ever issued was about $33,000, and this was reduced by the sale of personal property up to January 1850, to about $23,000; soon after which the charter was amended, allowing the sale of real estate and the discontinuance of annual settlement, schools, etc.

"In April 1850 they fixed on an appraisal of their lands in small lots (having some of them cut into village and farm lots), and commenced selling at public sale for stock, making the appraisal the minimum, and leaving any lands open to entry, after they had been offered publicly. During the summer of 1850 most of the lands were sold and most of the stock cancelled in this way, under an arrangement by which each stockholder should receive his proportional share of any surplus, or make up any deficiency. Most of the members bought either farming lands or village lots and became permanent inhabitants, thus continuing the society and its influences to a considerable extent. They divided about eight per cent. above par on the stock.

"Thus commenced, flourished and decayed this attempt at industrial Association. It never attempted to follow Fourier or any other teacher, but rather to strike out a path for itself. It failed because its leading minds became satisfied that under existing circumstances no important progress could be made, rather than from a want of faith in the ultimate practicability of Association.

"Many of the members regretted the dissolution, while others who had gained property and become established in business through the reputation of the Phalanx for credit and punctuality, seemed to care very little about it. Being absorbed in the world-wide spirit of speculation, and having their minds thus occupied, they forgot the necessity for a social change, which once appeared to them so important."

The writer of the foregoing was probably one of the leading members. In a paragraph preceding the account he says that the Wisconsin Phalanx had these three peculiarities, viz:

" 1. The same individual who was the principal originator and organizer of it, was also the one, who, throughout the experiment, had the entire confidence of the members and stockholders; and finally did nearly all the business in the closing up of its affairs.

" 2. At the division of its property, it paid a premium on its stock, instead of sustaining a loss.

" 3. Neither the Association nor any of its members ever had a lawsuit of any kind during its existence, or at its close.

" The truth is," he adds, " this attempt was pecuniarily successful; but socially, a failure."

Macdonald concludes with the following note: "Mr. Daniels, a gentleman who saw the whole progress of the Wisconsin Phalanx, says that the cause of its breaking up was speculation; the love of money and the want of love for Association. Their property becoming valuable, they sold it for the purpose of making money out of it."

This explanation of the mystery of the failure agrees with the hints at the conclusion of the previous account.

On the whole, the coroner's verdict in this case must be—'DIED, not by any of the common diseases of Associations, such as poverty, dissension, lack of wisdom, morality or religion, but by deliberate suicide, for reasons not fully disclosed.'

CHAPTER XXXVI.

THE NORTH AMERICAN PHALANX.

THIS was the test-experiment on which **Fourierism** practically staked its all in this country. Brisbane was busy in its beginnings; Greeley was Vice-President and stockholder. Its ambitious name and its location near New York City helped to set it apart as the model Phalanx. It was managed with great ability, and on the whole was more successful both in business and duration, than any other Fourier Association. It not only saw all the Phalanxes die around it, but it outlasted the *Harbinger* that blew the trumpet for them; and fought on, after the battle was given up. Indeed it outlived our friend Macdonald, the 'Old Mortality' of Socialism. Three times he visited it; and the record of his last visit, which was written in the year of his death, 1854, and was probably the last of his literary labors, closes with an acknowledgement of the continuance and prosperity of the North American. We shall have to give several chapters to this important experiment. We will begin with a semi-official expose of its foundations.

A History of the first nine years of the North American Phalanx, written
by its practical chief, Mr. Charles Sears, at the request of Macdonald;
dated December, 1852.

" Prior to the spring of 1843, Mr. Albert Brisbane had
been publishing, principally in the New York *Tribune*,
a series of articles on the subject of social science.
He had also published his larger work on Association,
which was followed by his pamphlet containing a summary of the doctrines of a new form of society, and the
outline of a project to found a practical Association, to
be called the North American Phalanx.

" There was nominally a central organization in the
city of New York, and affiliated societies were invited
to co-operate by subscribing the means of endowing the
proposed Phalanx, and furnishing the persons to engage
personally in the enterprise. It was proposed to raise
about four hundred thousand dollars, thus making the
attempt with adequate means to establish the conditions
of attractive industry.

" The essays and books above mentioned had a wide
circulation, and many were captivated with the glowing
pictures of a new life thus presented ; others were
attracted by the economies of the combined order which
were demonstrated ; still others were inspired by the
hopes of personal distinction in the brilliant career thus
opened to their ambition ; others again, were profoundly
impressed by Fourier's sublime annunciation of the
general destinies of globes and humanities ; that progressive development through careers, characterized all
movement and all forms ; that in all departments of
creation, the law of the series was the method observed
in distributing harmonies ; consequently, that human society and human activity, to be in harmony with the

universe of relations, can not be an exception to the great law of the series; consequently, that the existing order of civilization and the societies that preceded it are but phases in the growth of the race, and having subserved their more active uses, become bases of further development.

" Among those who became interested in the idea of social progress, were a few persons in Albany, New York, who from reading and interchange of views, were induced to unite in an organization for the purpose of deliberately and methodically investigating the doctrines of a new social order as announced by Fourier, deeming these doctrines worthy of the most profound and serious consideration.

" This body, after several preliminary meetings, formally adopted rules of organization on the 6th of April, 1843, and the declaration of their objects is in the following words: 'We, the undersigned, for the purpose of investigating Fourier's theory of social reform as expounded by Albert Brisbane, and if deemed expedient, of co-operating with like organizations elsewhere, do associate, with the ulterior view of organizing and founding an industrial and commercial Phalanx.'

"Proceeding in this direction, the body assumed the name of 'The Albany Branch of the North American Phalanx;' opened a correspondence with Messrs. Brisbane, Greeley, Godwin, Channing, Ripley and others; had lectures of criticism on existing institutions and in exposition of the doctrines of the proposed new order.

" During the summer practical measures were so matured, that a commission was appointed to explore the country, more particularly in the vicinity of New York and of Philadelphia, for a suitable domain upon which to commence the foundation of new social institutions. Mr. Brisbane was the delegate on the part of the New York friends, and Mr. Allen Worden on the part of the Albany Branch. A site was selected in Monmouth County, New Jersey, about forty miles south of New York; and on the 12th day of August, 1843, pursuant to public notice, a convention was held in the Albany Exchange, at which the North American Phalanx was organized by adopting a constitution, and subscribing to a covenant to invest in the capital stock.

"At this convention were delegates from New York, Catskill, Troy, Brook Farm Association, and the Albany Branch; and when the real work of paying money and elevating life to the effort of social organization was to be done, about a dozen subscribers were found equal to the work, ten of whom finally co-operated personally in the new life, with an aggregate subscription of eight thousand dollars. This by common consent was the absolute minimum of men and means; and, contrasted with the large expectations and claims originally stated, was indeed a great falling-off; but the few who had committed themselves with entire faith to the movement, went forward, determined to do what they could to make a worthy commencement, hoping that with their own families and such others as would from time to time be induced to co-operate, the germs of new institutions might fairly be planted.

"Accordingly in the month of September, 1843, a few families took possession of the domain, occupying to over-fullness the two farm-houses on the place, and commenced building a temporary house, forty feet by eighty, of two stories, for the accommodation of those who were to come the following spring.

"During the year 1844 the population numbered about ninety persons, including at one period nearly forty children under the age of sixteen years. Crops were planted, teams and implements purchased, the building of shops and mills was commenced, measures of business and organization were discussed, the construction of social doctrines debated, personal claims canvassed, and thus the business of life was going on at full tide; and now also commenced the real development of character.

"Hitherto there had been no settled science of society. Fourier, the man of profound insight, announced the law of progress and indicated the new forms that society would take. People accepted the new ideas gladly, and would as gladly institute new forms; but there was a lack of well-defined views on the precise work to be done. Besides, education tended strongly to confirm in most minds the force of existing institutions, and after attaining to middle age, and even before this period, the character usually becomes quite fixed; so that to break up habitudes, relinquish prejudices, sunder ties, and to adopt new modes of action, accept of modified results, and re-adjust themselves to new relations, was a difficult, and to the many, almost impossible work, as is proved by the fact that, of the thirty or forty similar attempts at associated life within the past ten years in this country, only the North American Phalanx now [1852] remains. Nor did this Association escape the inevitable consequences of bringing together a body of grown-up people with their families, many of whom came reluctantly, and whose characters were formed under other influences.

"Personal difficulties occurred as a matter of course,

but these were commonly overruled by a healthy sentiment of self-respect.   Parties also began to form, but
they were not fully developed until the first annual
settlement and distribution of profits was attempted.
Then, however, they took a variety of forms according
to the interest or ambition of the partisans ; though two
principal views characterized the more permanent and
clearly defined party divisions ; one party contending
for authority, enforced with stringent rules and final
appeal to the dictation of the chief officer; the other
party standing out for organization and distribution of
authority.   The former would centralize power and
make administration despotic, claiming that thus only
could order be maintained ; the latter claimed that to
do this, would be merely to repeat the institutions of
civilization ; that Association thus controlled would be
devoid of corporate life, would be dependent upon individuals, and quite artificial ; whereas what we wanted
was a wholly different order, viz., the enfranchisement
of the individual ; order through the natural method of
the series ; institutions that would be instinct with the
life that is organic, from the sum of the series, down to
the last subdivision of the group.   The strife to maintain these several views was long and vigorous ; and it
would scarcely be an exaggeration to say that our days
were spent in labor and our nights in legislation, for the
first five years of our associative life.   The question at
issue was vital.   It was whether the infant Association
should or should not have new institutions ; whether it
should be Civilizee or Phalansterian ; whether it should
be a mere joint-stock corporation such as had been
before, or whether the new form of industrial organization indicated by Fourier should be initiated.   In the

contest between the two principles of civilized joint-stock Association, and of the Phalansterian or Serial organization, the latter ultimately prevailed ; and in this triumph of the idea of the natural organic forms of society through the method of the series, we see distinctly the development of the germ of the Phalanx. For when we have a true principle evolved, however insignificant the development may be, the results, although limited by the smallness of the development, will nevertheless be right in kind. It is perhaps important, to the end that the results of our experience be rightly comprehended, to indicate the essential features of the order of society that is to succeed present disorder, and wherein it differs from other social forms.

"A fundamental feature is, that we deny the bald atheism that asserts human nature to be a melancholy failure and unworthy of respect or trust, and therefore to be treated as an alien and convict. On the contrary, we hold that, instead of chains, man requires freedom ; instead of checks, he requires development ; instead of artificial order through coercion, he requires the Divine harmony that comes through counterpoise. Hence society is bound by its own highest interests, by the obligation it owes to its every member, to make organic provision for the entire circle of human wants, for the entire range of human activity ; so that the individual shall be emancipated from the servitude of nature, from personal domination, from social tyrannies ; and that thus fully enfranchised and guaranteed by the whole force of society, into all freedoms and the endowment of all rights pertaining to manhood, he may fulfill his own destiny, in accordance with the laws written in his own organization.

"In the Phalanx, then, we have, in the sphere of production, the relation of employer and employed stricken out of the category of relations, not merely as in the simple joint-stock corporations, by substituting for the individual employer the still more despotic and irresistible corporate employer; but by every one becoming his own employer, doing that which he is best qualified by endowment to do, receiving for his labor precisely his share of the product, as nearly as it can be determined while there is no scientific unit of value.

"In the sphere of circulation or currency, we have a representative of all the wealth produced, so that every one shall have issued to him for all his production, the abstract or protean form of value, which is convertible into every other form of value; in commerce or exchanges, reducing this from a speculation as now, to a function; employing only the necessary force to make distributions; and exchanging products or values on the basis of cost.

"In the sphere of social relations, we have freedom to form ties according to affinities of character.

"In the sphere of education, we establish the natural method, not through the exaltation into professorships of this, that or other notable persons, but through a body of institutions reposing upon industry, and having organic vitality. Commencing with the nursery, we make, through the living corporation, through adequately endowed institutions that fail not, provision for the entire life of the child, from the cradle upward; initiating him step by step, not into nominal, ostensible education apart from his life, but into the real business of life, the actual production and distribution of wealth, the science of accounts and the administration of affairs; and providing that, through uses, the science that lies back of uses shall be acquired ; so theory and practice, the application of science to the pursuits of life shall, through daily use, become as familiar as the mother tongue ; and thus place our children at maturity in the ranks of manhood and womanhood, competent to all the duties and activities of life, that they may be qualified by endowment to perform.

" In the sphere of administration, we have a graduated hierarchy of orders, from the simple chief of a group, or supervisor of a single function, up to the unitary administration of the globe.

" In the sphere of religion, we have religious life as contrasted with the profession of a religious faith. The intellect requires to be satisfied as well as the affections, and is so with the scientific and therefore universal formula, that the religious element in man is the passion of unity; that is, that all the powers of the soul shall attain to true equilibrium, and act normally in accordance with Divine law, so that human life in all its powers and activities shall be in harmonious relations with nature, with itself, and with the supreme center of life.

" Of course we speak of the success of an idea, and only expect realization through gradual development. It is obvious also that such realization can be attained only through organization ; because, unaided, the individual makes but scanty conquests over nature, and but feeble opposition to social usurpations.

" The principle, then, of the Serial Organization being established, the whole future course of the Association, in respect to its merely industrial institutions, was plain, viz. : to develop and mature the serial form.

"Not that the old questions did not arise subsequently; on the contrary on the admission of new members from time to time, they did arise and have discussion anew; but the contest had been virtually decided. The Association had pronounced with such emphasis in favor of the organization of labor upon the basis of co-operative efforts, joint-stock property, and unity of interests, that those holding adverse views gradually withdrew; and the harmony of the Association was never afterward in serious jeopardy.

"During the later as well as earlier years of our associated life, the question of preference of modes of realization came under discussion in the Phalansterian school, one party advocating the measure of obtaining large means, and so fully endowing the Phalanx with all the external conditions of attractive industry, and then introducing gradually a body of select associates. The North American Phalanx, as represented in the conventions of the school, held to the view that new social institutions, new forms into which the life of a people shall flow, can not be determined by merely external conditions and the elaboration of a theory of life and organization, but are matters of growth.

"Our view is that the true Divine growth of the social, as of the individual man, is the progressive development of a germ; and while we would not in the slightest degree oppose a scientific organization upon a large scale, it is our preference to pursue a more progressive mode, to make a more immediately practical and controllable attempt.

"The call of to-day we understand to be for evidence, First: Of the possibility of harmony in Association; Second: That by associated effort, and the control of machinery, the laborer may command the means, not only of comfort and the necessaries of life, but also of education and refinement ; Third : that the nature of the relations we would establish are essentially those of religious justice.

"The possibility of establishing true social relations, increased production, and the embodiment of the religious sentiment, are, if we read the signs aright, the points upon which the question of Association now hinges in the public mind.

" Because, First : Man's capacity for these relations is doubted ; Because, Second : Production is an essential and permanent condition of life, and means of progress ; Because, Third : It is apprehended that the religious element is not sufficiently regarded and provided for in Association.

" Demonstrate that capacity, prove that men by their own efforts may command all the means of life, show in institutions the truly religious nature of the movement and the relations that are to obtain, and the public will be gained to the idea of Association.

" Another question still has been pressed upon us offensively by the advocates of existing institutions, as though their life were pure and their institutions perfect, while no terms of opprobrium could sufficiently characterize the depravity of the Socialists ; and this question is that of the marriage relation. Upon this question a form of society that is so notoriously rotten as existing civilization is, a society that has marriage and prostitution as complementary facts of its relations of the sexes, a society which establishes professorships of abortion, which methodizes infanticide, which outlaws woman, might at least assume the show of modesty, might treat

with common candor any and all who are seeking the
Divine law of marriage. Instead, therefore, of recognizing its right to defame us, we put that society upon
its defense, and say to it, Come out of your infidelities,
and your crimes, and your pretenses ; seek out the law
of righteousness, and deal justly with woman. Nevertheless this is a question in which we, in common with
others, have a profound interest ; it is a question which
has by no means escaped consideration among us, and
we perhaps owe it to ourselves to state our position.

"What the true law of relationship of the sexes is,
we as a body do not pretend to determine. Here, as
elsewhere, individual opinion is free; but there are certain conditions, as we think, clearly indicated, which are
necessary to the proper consideration of the question ;
and our view is that it is one that must be determned
mainly by woman herself. When she shall be fully
enfranchised, fully endowed with her rights, so that she
shall no longer be dependent on marriage for position,
no longer be regarded as a pensioner, but as a constituent of the State; in a single phrase, when society shall,
independently of other considerations than that of inherent right, assure to woman social position and
pecuniary independence, so that she can legislate on a
footing of equality, then she may announce the law
of the sexual relations. But this can only occur in
organized society; society in which there is a complete
circle of fraternal institutions that have public acceptance; can only occur when science enters the
domain of human society, and determines relations,
as it now does in astronomy or physic.

"We therefore say to civilization, You have no adequate solution of this problem that is convulsing you,

and in which every form of private and public protest against the actual condition is expressing itself. Besides this we claim what can not be claimed for any similar number of people in civilization, viz., that we have been here over nine years, with an average population of nearly one hundred persons of both sexes and all ages, and, judged by the existing standard of morals, we are above reproach on this question.

"Thus we have proceeded, disposing of our primary legislation, demonstrating to general acceptance the rectitude of our awards and distributions of profit, determining questions of social doctrine, perfecting methods of order, and developing our industry, with a fair measure of success. In this latter respect the following statistics will indicate partially the progress we have made.

"We commenced in 1843, as before mentioned, with a dozen subscribers, and an aggregate subscription of $8,000. On the 30th of November, 1844, upon our first settlement, our property amounted in round numbers to $28,000; of which we owed in capital stock and balances due members, say, $18,000. The remainder was debt incurred in purchasing the land, $9,000; implements, etc., $1,000; total, $10,000.

"Our population at this period, including members and applicants, was nearly as follows: Men, thirty-two; women, nineteen; children of both sexes under sixteen years, twenty-six; making an aggregate of seventy-seven. At one period thereafter our numbers were reduced to about sixty-five persons.

"On the 30th of November, 1852, our property was estimated at $80,000, held as follows: capital stock and balances of account due members, say, $62,800; permanent debt, $12,103; floating debt, $5,097; total, $80,000. Dividing this sum by 673, the number of acres, the entire cost of our property is $119 per acre.

"At this period our population of members and applicants is as follows: men, forty-eight; women, thirty-seven; adults, eighty-five; children under sixteen years, twenty-seven; making an aggregate of one hundred and twelve.

"Dividing the sum of property by this number, we have an average investment for each man, woman and child, of over $700, or for each family of five persons, say, $3,600. Dividing the sum of our permanent debt by the number of our population, the average to each person is, say, $107.

"For the purpose of comparing the pecuniary results of our industry to the individual, with like pursuits elsewhere, we make the following exhibition: In the year 1844 the average earnings of adults, besides their board, was three dollars and eighty cents a month, and the dividend for the use of capital was 4.7 per cent.

1845.	Earnings of labor was	. . .	$ 8.21 per month.
	of capital	. . . . . .	05.1 per cent
1846.	Earnings of labor	. . . . .	2.73 per month.
	of capital	. . . .	04.4 per cent.
1847.	Earnings of labor	. . . . .	12.02 per month.
	of capital	. . . .	05.6 per cent.
1848.	Earnings of labor	. . . . .	14 10 per month
	of capital	. . . .	05.7 per cent
1849.	Earnings of labor	. . . .	13.58 per month.
	of capital	. . . .	05.6 per cent.
1850.	Earnings of labor	. . . .	13.58 per month.
	of capital	. . . .	05.52 per cent.
1851.	Earnings of labor	. . . . .	14.59 per month.
	of capital	. . . .	04.84 per cent.

"It is to be noted that when we took possession of our domain, the land was in a reduced condition; and upon our improvements we have made no profit excepting subsequent increased revenue, they having been valued at cost. Also that our labors were mainly agricultural until within the last three years, when milling was successfully introduced. We have, it is true, carried on various mechanical branches for our own purposes, such as building, smith-work, tin-work, shoe-making, etc.; but for purposes of revenue, we have not to much extent succeeded in introducing mechanical branches of industry.

"Furthermore, we divide our profits upon the following general principles: For labors that are necessary, but repulsive or exhausting, we award the highest rates; for such as are useful, but less repugnant or taxing, a relatively smaller award is made; and for the more agreeable pursuits, a still smaller rate is allowed.

"Thus observing this general formula in our classification of labor, viz.: the necessary, the useful, and the agreeable; and also awarding to the individual, first, for his labor, secondly, for the talent displayed in the use of means, or in adaptation of means to ends, wise administration, etc., and thirdly, for the use of his capital; it will be perceived that we make our award upon a widely different basis from the current method. We have a theory of awards, a scientific reason for our classification of labor and our awards to individuals; and one of the consequences is that women earn more, relatively, among us than in existing society.

"In matters of education we have hitherto done little else than keep, as we might, the common district school, introducing, however, improved methods of instruction.

Other interests have pressed upon us; other questions clamored for solution. We were to determine whether or not we could associate in all the labors of life; and if yea, then whether we could sufficiently command the material means of life, until we should have established institutions that would supersede the necessity of strenuous personal effort. It will be understood that this work has been sufficiently arduous, and consequently that our children, being too feeble in point of numbers to assert their rights, have been pushed aside."

Here follows a labored disquisition on the possibilities of serial education, which we omit, as the substance of it can be found in the standard expositions of Fourierism.

"If now we are asked, what questions we have determined, what results we may fairly claim to have accomplished through our nine years of associated life and efforts at organization, we may answer in brief, that so far as the members of this body are concerned, we meet the universal demand of this day with institutions which guarantee the rights of labor and the products thereof, of education, and a home, and social culture. This is not a mere declaration of abstract rights that we claim to make, but we establish our members in the possession and enjoyment of these rights; and we venture to claim that, so far as the comforts of home, private rights and social privileges are concerned, our actual life is greatly in advance of that of any mixed population under the institutions of existing civilization, either in town or country. We claim, so far as with our small number we could do, to have organized labor through voluntary Association, upon the principle of unity of interests; so reconciling the hitherto hostile parties of laborer and capitalist; so settling the world-old, world-wide quarrel, growing out of antagonistic interests among men; that is, we have organized the production and distribution of wealth in agricultural and domestic labor, and in some branches of mechanics and manufactures, and thus have abolished the servile character of labor, and the servile relation of employer and employed. And it is precisely in the point where failure was most confidently predicted, viz., in domestic labor, that we have most fully succeeded, because mainly, as we suppose, in the larger numbers attached to this industry we had the conditions of carrying out more fully the serial method of organization.

"In distributing the profits of industry we have adopted a law of equitable proportion, so that when the facts are presented, we have initiated the measure of attaining to practical justice, or in the formula of Fourier, 'equitable distribution of profits.' We claim also that we guarantee the sale of the products of industry; that is, we secure the means of converting any and every form of product or fruit of labor at the cost thereof, into any other form also at cost. For all our labor is paid for in a domestic currency. In other words, when value is produced, a representative of that value is issued to the producer; and only so far as there is the production of value, is there any issue of the representative of value; so that property and currency are always equal, and thus we solve the problem of banking and currency; thus we have in practical operation, what Proudhon vainly attempted to introduce into France; what Kellogg proposed to introduce under governmental sanction in this country; what Warren proposes to accomplish by his labor notes and exchanges at cost.

"We might state other facts, but let this suffice for the present; and we will only say in conclusion, that when the organization of our educational series shall be completed, as we hope to see it, we shall thus have established as a body a measurably complete circle of fraternal institutions, in which social and private rights are guaranteed; we shall then fairly have closed the first cycle of our societary life and efforts, fairly have laid the germs of living institutions, of the corporations which have perpetual life, which gather all knowledges, which husband all experiences, and into the keeping of which we commit all material interests, and which only need a healthy development to change without injustice, to absorb without violence, the discords of existing society, and to unfold, as naturally as the chrysalis unfolds into a form of beauty, a new and higher order of human society.

"To carry on this work we need additional means to endow our agricultural, our educational, our milling and other interests, and to build additional tenements; and above all we need additional numbers of people who are willing to work for an idea; men and women who are competent to establish or conduct successfully some branch of profitable industry; who understand the social movement; who will come among us with worthy motives, and with settled purpose of fraternal co-operation; who can appreciate the labor, the conditions of life, the worth of the institutions we have and propose to have, in contrast with the chances of private gain accompanied by the prevailing disorder, the denial of right, and the ever-increasing oppressions of existing civilization.

"The views of members and applicants upon the

foregoing statement are expressed by the position of
their signatures affixed below :

Aye.

H. T. Stone,
Lucius Eaton,
Alcander Longley,
Herman Schette:,
W. A. French,
John Ash, Jr ,
John H. Steel,
Phebe T. Drew,
John Gray,
Robert J. Smith,
J. R. Vanderburgh,
James Renshaw,
J. G. Drew,
S. Martin,
Joseph T. French,
N. H. Stockwell,
C has. G. French,

Eugenia Thomson,
Leemon Stockwell,
R. N. Stockwell,
A. P. French,
Nathaniel H. Colson,
John French,
Mary E. F. Grey,
Althea Sears,
H. Bell Munday,
Caroline M. Hathaway,
Anna E. Hathaway,
Anne Guillauden,
L. Munday,
Chloe Sears,
James Renshaw, Jr.,
Emile Guillauden, Jr.,
Ellen M. Stockwell,

E. L. Holmes,
Gertrude Sears,
E. A. Angell,
J. Bucklin,
L. E. Bucklin,
Edwin D. Sayre,
O. S. Holmes,
John V. Sears,
P. French,
M. A. Martin,
L. French,
Z. King, Jr.,
D. H. King,
A. J. Lanotte,
W. K. Prentice,
Julia Bucklin,
—— Maynet.

Nay.

"Geo. Perry believes that difficulty arises from the selfishness, class-interest and personal ambition, of Class No. 1
and 2 ; also, last and not least, absence of uniformity of
attractions.

"J. R. Coleman endorses the above sentiments. James
Warren, do. H. N. Coleman, do.

"M. Hammond has very reluctantly concluded that the difficulty is in the Institution and not in the members."

CHAPTER XXXVII.

LIFE AT THE NORTH AMERICAN PHALANX.

THE following pictures from the files of the *Harbinger*, with the subsequent reports of Macdonald's three visits, give a tolerable view of life at the North American in its early and its latter days.

[Fourth of July (1845) at the Phalanx.]

"As soon as the moisture was off the grass, a group went down to the beautiful meadows to spread the hay; and the right good will, quickness, and thoroughness with which they completed their task, certainly illustrated the attractiveness of combined industry. Others meanwhile were gathering for dinner the vegetables, of which, by the consent of the whole neighborhood, they have a supply unsurpassed in early maturity and excellence; and still others were busy in the various branches of domestic labor.

"And now, the guests from New York and the country around having come in, and the hour for the meeting being at hand, the bell sounded, and men, women and children assembled in a walnut grove near the house, where a semicircle of seats had been arranged in the cool shade. Here addresses were given by William H. Channing and Horace Greeley, illustrating the position that Association is the truly consistent embodiment in practice of the professed principles of our nation.

"After some hour and a half thus spent, the company adjourned to the house, where a table had been spread the whole length of the hall, and partook of a most abundant and excellent dinner, in which the hospitable sisters of the Phalanx had most satisfactorily proved their faith by their works. Good cold water was the only beverage, thanks to the temperance of the members. A few toasts and short speeches seasoned the feast.

"And now once again, the afternoon being somewhat advanced, the demand for variety was gratified by a summons to the hay-field. Every rake and fork were in requisition; a merrier group never raked and pitched; never was a meadow more dexterously cleared; and it was not long before there was a demand that the right to labor should be honored by fresh work, which the chief of the group lamented he could not at the moment gratify. To close the festivities the young people formed in a dance, which was prolonged till midnight. And so ended this truly cheerful and friendly holiday.

[George Ripley's visit to the Phalanx.]

May, 14, 1846.

"Arriving about dinner time at the Mansion, we received a cordial welcome from our friends, and were soon seated at their hospitable table, and were made to feel at once that we were at home, and in the midst of those to whom we were bound by strong ties. How could it be otherwise? It was a meeting of those whose lives were devoted to one interest, who had chosen the lot of pioneers in a great social reform, and who had been content to endure sacrifices for the realization of ideas that were more sacred than life itself. Then, too, the similarity of pursuits, of the whole mode of life in our infant Associations, produces a similarity of feeling, of manners, and I could almost fancy, even of expression of countenance. I have often heard strangers remark upon the cheerfulness and elasticity of spirit which struck them on visiting our little Association at Brook Farm; and here I found the same thing so strongly displayed, that in conversing with our new friends, it seemed as if they were the same that I had left at home, or rather that I had been side by side with them for months or years, instead of meeting them to-day for the first time. I did not need any formal introduction to make me feel acquainted, and I flatter myself that there was as little reserve cherished on their part.

"After dinner we were kindly attended by our friend Mr. Sears over this beautiful, I may truly say, enchanting domain. I had often heard it spoken of in terms of high commendation; but I must confess, I was not prepared to find an estate combining so many picturesque attractions with such rare agricultural capabilities.

"Our friends here have no doubt been singularly fortunate in procuring so valuable a domain as the scene of their experiment, and I see nothing which, with industry and perseverance, can create a doubt of their triumphant success, and that at no very distant day.

"I was highly gratified with the appearance of the children, and the provision that is made for their education, physical as well as intellectual. I found them in a very neat school-room, under the intelligent care of

Mrs. B., who is devoting herself to this department with a noble zeal and the most pleasing results. It is seldom that young people in common society have such ample arrangements for their culture, or give evidence of such a healthy desire for improvement.

"This Association has not been free from difficulties. It has had to contend with the want of sufficient capital, and has experienced some embarrassment on that account. It has also suffered from the discouragement of some of its members—a result always to be expected in every new enterprise, and by no means formidable in the long run—and discontent has produced depression. Happily, the disaffected have retired from the premises, and with few, if any, exceptions, the present members are heartily devoted to the movement, with strong faith in the cause and in each other, and determined to deserve success, even if they do not gain it. Their prospects, however, are now bright, and with patient industry and internal harmony they must soon transform their magnificent domain into a most attractive home for the associative household. May God prosper them!"

[N. C. Neidhart's visit to the Phalanx.]

July 4, 1847.

"It is impossible for me to describe the deep impression which the life and genial countenances of our brethren have made upon us. Although not belonging to what are very unjustly called the higher classes, I discovered more true refinement, that which is based upon humanitary feeling, than is generally found among those of greater pretensions. There is a serene, earnest love about them all, indicating a determination on their part to abide the issue of the great experiment in which they are engaged.

"After a fatiguing walk over the domain, I found their simple but refreshing supper very inviting. Here we saw for the first time the women assembled, of whom we had only caught occasional glimpses before. They appeared to be a genial band, with happy, smiling countenances, full of health and spirits. Such deep and earnest eyes, it seemed to me, I had never seen before. Most of the younger girls had wreaths of evergreen and flowers wound around their hair, and some also around their persons in the form of scarfs, which became them admirably.

"After tea we resorted to the reading-room, where are to be found on files all the progressive and reformatory, as well as the best agricultural, papers of the Union, such as the *New York Tribune*, *Practical Christian*, *Young America*, *Harbinger*, etc. There is also the commencement of a small library.

"Only one thing was wanting to enliven the evening, and that was music. They possess, I believe, a guitar, flutes, and other instruments, but the time necessary for their cultivation seems to be wanting. The want of this so necessary accompaniment of universal harmony, was made up to us by some delightful hours which we spent in the parlor of Mrs. B., who showed us some of her beautiful drawings, and in whose intelligent society we spent the evening. This lady was formerly a member of the Clermont Phalanx, Ohio. I was sorry there was not time enough to receive from her an account of the causes of the disbandment of this society. She must certainly have been satisfied of the superiority of associated life, to encourage her to join immediately another.

"It was my good fortune (notwithstanding the large

number of visitors), to obtain a nice sleeping-room, from which I was sorry to see I had driven some obliging member of the Phalanx. The orderly simplicity of this room was quite pleasing. It enabled us to form some judgment of the order which pervaded the Community.

"Next morning we took an early breakfast, and accompanied by Mr. Wheeler, a member of the society, we wandered over the whole domain. On our way home we struck across Brisbane Hill, where they intend to erect the future Phalansterian house on a more improved and extensive plan.

"There is religious worship here every Sunday, in which all those who feel disposed may join The members of the society adhere to different religious persuasions, but do not seem to care much for the outward forms of religion.

"As far as I could learn, the health of the Phalanx has been generally very good. They have lost, however, several children by different diseases. During the prevalence of the small-pox in the Community, the superiority of the combined order over the isolated household was most clearly manifested. Quite lately they have constructed a bathing-house. The water is good, but must contain more or less iron, as the whole country is full of it."

Macdonald's first visit to the Phalanx.

October, 1851.

"It was dark when I arrived at the Phalanstery. Lights shone through the trees from the windows of several large buildings, the sight of which sent a cheering glow through me, and as I approached, I inwardly fancied that what I saw was part of an early dream. The glancing lights, the sounds of voices, and the notes of music, while all nature around was dark and still, had a strange effect, and I almost believed that this was a Community where people were really happy.

"I entered and inquired for Mr. Bucklin, whose name had been given me. At the end of a long hall I found a small reading-room, with four or five strange-looking beings sitting around a table reading newspapers. They all appeared eccentric, not alone because they were unshaven and unshorn, but from the peculiar look of their eyes and form of their faces. Mr. Bucklin, a kind man, came to me, glancing as if he anticipated something important. I explained my business, and he sat down beside me; but though I attempted conversation, he had very little to say. He inquired if I wished for supper, and on my assenting, he left me for a few minutes and then returned, and very soon after he led me out to another building. We passed through a passage and up a short flight of steps into a very handsome room, capable, I understood, of accommodating two hundred persons at dinner. It had a small gallery or balcony at one end of it, and six windows on either side. It was furnished with two rows of tables and chairs, each table large enough for ten or twelve persons to dine at. There were three bright lamps suspended from the ceiling. At one end of the room the chairs and tables had been removed, and several ladies and gentlemen were dancing cotillions to the music of a violin, played by an amateur in the gallery. At the other end of the room there was a doorway leading to the kitchen, and near this my supper was laid, very nice and tidy. Mr. Bucklin introduced me to Mr. Holmes, a gentleman who had lived in the Skaneateles and Trumbull experiments; and Mr. Holmes introduced me to Mr. Williston, who gave me some of the details of the early days of the North American Phalanx, during which he sometimes lived in high style, and sometimes was almost starved. He told of the tricks which the young members played upon the old members, many of whom had left.

"On looking at the dancers I perceived that several of the females were dressed in the new costume, which is no more than shortening the frock and wearing trowsers the same as men. There were three or four young women, and three or four children so dressed. I had not thought much of this dress before, but was now favorably impressed by it, when I contrasted it with the long dresses of some of the dancers. This style is decidedly superior, I think, for any kind of active employment. The dress seems exceedingly simple. The frocks were worn about the same length as the Highland *kilt*, ending a little above the knee; the trowsers were straight, and both were made of plain material. Afterward I saw some of the ladies in superior suits of this fashion, looking very elegant.

"Mr. Holmes shewed me to my bed, which was in the top of another building. It was a spacious garret with four cots in it, one in each corner. There were two windows, one of which appeared to be always open, and at that window a young man was sleeping, although the weather was very wet. The mattress I had was excellent, and I slept well; but the accommodations were rather rude, there being no chairs or pegs to hang the clothes upon. The young men threw their clothes upon the floor.   There was no carpet, but the floor seemed very clean.

"It rained hard all night, and the morning continued wet and unpleasant.   I rose about seven, and washed in a passage-way leading from the sleeping-rooms, where I found water well supplied; passed rows of small sleeping-rooms, and went out for a stroll.   The morning was too unpleasant for walking much, but I examined the houses, and found them to be large framed buildings, the largest of the two having been but recently built. It formed two sides of a square, and had a porch in front and on part of the back.   It appeared as if the portion of it which was complete was but a wing of a more extensive design, intended to be carried out at some future time.   The oldest building reminded me of one of the Rappite buildings in New Harmony, excepting that it was built of wood and theirs of brick. It formed a parallelogram, two stories high, with large garrets at the top.   A hall ran nearly the whole length of the building, and terminated in a small room which is used as a library, and to which is joined the office. Apartments were ranged on either side of the hall up stairs.   All the rooms appeared to be bed-rooms, and were in use.   The new building was more commodious. There were well furnished sitting-rooms on either side of the principal entrance.   The dining-hall, which I have before mentioned, was in the rear of this.   Up stairs the rooms were ranged in a similar manner to the old building, and appeared to be very comfortable. I was informed that they were soon to be heated by steam.   All these apartments were rented to the members at various prices, according to the relative superiority of each room.

" As the bell at the end of the building rang a second time for breakfast, I followed some of the members into the room, and on entering took my seat at the table nearest the door. I afterward learned that this was the vegetarian table, and also that it was customary for each person always to occupy the same seat at his meals. The tables were well supplied with excellent, wholesome food, and I think the majority of the members took tea and coffee and ate meat. Young men and women waited upon the tables, and seemed active and agreeable. An easy freedom and a harmonious feeling seemed to prevail.

" On leaving the room I was introduced to Mr. Sears, who, I ascertained, was what they called the ' leading mind.' He was rather tall, of a nervous temperament, the sensitive predominating, and was easy and affable. On my informing him of the object of my visit, he very kindly led me to his office and showed me several papers, which gave me every information I required. He introduced me to Mr. Renshaw, a gentleman who had been in the Ohio Phalanx. Mr. Renshaw was engaged in the blacksmith-shop; looked quite a philosopher, so far as form of head and length of beard and hair was concerned ; but he had a little too much of the sanguine in his temperament to be cool at all times. He very rapidly asked me the object of my book : what good would it do ? what was it for ? and seemed disposed to knock down some imaginary wrong, before he had any clear idea of what it was. I explained, and together with Mr. Sears, had a short controversy with him, which had a softening tendency, though it did not lead to perfect agreement. Mr. Sears contended that Community experiments failed because the accounts were not clearly and faithfully kept ; but Mr. Renshaw maintained that they all failed for want of means, and that the public impression that the members always disagreed was quite erroneous. At dinner I found a much larger crowd of persons in the room than at breakfast. I was introduced to several members, and among them to Mr. French, a gentleman who had once been a Universalist preacher. He was very kind, and gave me some information relative to the Jefferson County Industrial Association.

"I also made the acquaintance of Mr. John Gray, a gentleman who had lived five years among the Shakers, and who was still a Shaker in appearance. Mr. Gray is an Englishman, as would readily be perceived by his peculiar speech ; but with his English he had gotten a little mixture of the 'down east,' where he had lately been living. Mr. Gray was very fluent of speech, and what he said to me would almost fill a volume. He spoke chiefly of his Shaker experience, and of the time he had spent among the Socialists of England. He said it was his intention to visit other Communities in the United States, and gain all the experience he could among them, and then return to England and make it known. He was a dyer by trade (on which account he was much valued by the Shakers), and was very useful in taking care of swine. He spoke forcibly of the evils of celibacy among the Shakers, and of their strict regulations. He preferred living in the North American Phalanx, feeling more freedom, and knowing that he could go away when he pleased without difficulty. He thought the wages too low. Reckoning, for instance, that he earned about 90 cts. per day for ten hours labor, he got in cash every two weeks three-fourths of it, the remaining fourth going to the Phalanx as capital. Out of these wages he had to pay $ 1.50 per week for board, and $ 12 a year rent, besides extras; but he had a very snug little room, and lived well. He thought single men and women could do better there than married ones; but either could do better, so far as making money was the object, in the outer world. He decidedly preferred the single family and isolated cottage arrangement. I made allowances for Mr. Gray's opinions, when I remembered that he had been living five years among the Shakers, and but four months at the North American, whose regulations about capital and interest he was not very clear upon.

"I had a conversation with a lady who had lived two years at Hopedale. She was intelligent, but very sanguine; well-spoken and agreeable, but had too much enthusiasm. She described to me the early days of Hopedale and its present condition. She did not like it, but preferred the North American and its more unitary arrangements. She thought that the single-cottage system was wrong, and that woman would never attain her true position in such circumstances. She had a great opinion of woman's abilities and capacities for improvement; was sorry that the Phalanx had such a bombastic name; had once been very sanguine, but was now chastened down; believed that the North American could not be called an experiment on Fourier's plan; the necessary elements were not there, and never had been, and no experiment had ever been attempted with such material as Fourier proposed; until that is done, we can not say the system is false, etc.

"After supper I had conversation with several persons on Mr. Warren's plan of 'Equitable Commerce.'

Most of them were well disposed toward his views of 'individuality,' but not toward his 'cost principle,' many believing the difficulties of estimating the cost of many things not to be overcome; the details in carrying out the system would be too trifling and fine-drawn. Conversation turned upon the Sabbath. Some thought it would be good to have periodical meetings for reading or lecturing, and others thought it best to have nothing periodical, but leave every thing and every body to act in a natural manner, such as eating when you are hungry, drinking when you are thirsty, and resting when you are tired; let the child play when it is so inclined, and teach it when it demands to be taught. There were all kinds of opinions among them regarding society and its progress. My Shaker friend thought that society was progressing 'first-rate' by means of Odd-Fellowship, Freemasonry, benevolent associations, railroads, steamboats, and especially all kinds of large manufactories, without such little attempts as these of the North American to regenerate mankind.

"I might speculate on this strange mixture of minds, but prefer that the reader should take the facts and philosophize for himself. Here were persons who, for many years, had tried many schemes of social reorganization in various parts of the country, brought together not from a personal knowledge and attraction for each other, but through a common love of the social principles, which like a pleasant dream attracted them to this, the last surviving of that extensive series of experiments which commenced in this country about the year 1843.

"I retired to my cot about ten o'clock, and passed a restless night. The weather was warm and wet, and continued so in the morning. Rose at five o'clock and took breakfast with Dr. Lazarus and the stage-driver, and at a quarter to six we left the Phalanx in their neat little stage.

"During the journey to Keyport the Doctor seemed to be full of Association, and made frequent allusions to that state in which all things would be right, and man would hold his true position; thought it wrong to cut down trees, to clear land, to raise corn, to fatten pigs to eat, when, if the forest was left alone, we could live on the native deer, which would be much better food for man; he would have fruit-trees remain where they are found naturally; and he would have many other things done which the world would deem crazy nonsense."

Macdonald's second visit to the Phalanx.

"I visited the North American Phalanx again in July, 1852. The visit was an interesting one to me; but I will only refer to the changes which have taken place since my last visit.

"They have altered their eating and drinking arrangements, and adopted the eating-house system. At the table there is a bill of fare, and each individual calls for what he wants; on obtaining it the waiter gives him a check, with the price of the article marked thereon. After the meal is over, the waiters go round and enter the sum marked upon the check which each person has received, in a book belonging to that person; the total is added up at the end of each month and the payments are made. Each person finds his own sugar, which is kept upon the table. Coffee is half-a-cent per cup, including milk; bread one cent per plate; butter, I think, half-a-cent; meat two cents; pie two cents; and other things in like proportion. On Mr. Holmes's book, the cost of living ran thus: breakfast from one and a-half cents to three and a-half cents; dinner four and a-half cents to nine cents; supper four and a-half cents to eight cents. In addition to this, as all persons use the room alike, each pays the same rent, which is thirty-six and a-half cents per week; each person also pays a certain portion for the waiting labor, and for lighting the room. The young ladies and gentlemen who waited on table, as well as the Phalanx Doctor (a gentleman of talent and politeness), who from attraction performed the same duty, got six and a-quarter cents per hour for their labor.

" The wages of various occupations, agricultural, mechanical and professional, vary from six cents to ten cents per hour; the latter sum is the maximum. The wages are paid to each individual in full every month, and the profits are divided at the end of the year. Persons wishing to become members are invited to become visitors for thirty days. At the end of that time it is sometimes necessary for them to continue another thirty days; then they may be admitted as probationers for one year, and if they are liked by the members at the end of that time, it is decided whether they shall become full members or not.

" They had commenced brick-making, intending to build a mill; thought of building at Keyport or Red Bank. Some anticipated a loan from Horace Greeley Their stock was good; some said it was at par; one said, at seventy-five per cent. premium. (?) The profits were invested in things which they thought would bring them the largest interest; they had shares in two steamboats running to New York from Keyport and Red Bank.

"Their crops looked well, superior to any in the vicinity. There were large fields of corn and potatoes and a fine one of tomatoes. The first bushel of the latter article had just been sent to the New York market, and was worth eight dollars. There was a field of good melons, quite a picture to look upon. Since my last visit, there had been an addition made to the large building. A man had built the addition at a cost of $800, and had put $200 into the Phalanx, making $1,000 worth of stock. He lived in the house as his own. There is a neat cottage near the large building, which I suppose is also Association property, put in by the gentleman who built it and uses it—a Mr. Manning, I believe.

"The wages were all increased a little since my last visit, and there seemed to be more satisfaction prevailing, especially with the eating-house plan, which I understood had effected a saving of about two-thirds in the expenditure; this was especially the case in the article of sugar.

"The stage group was abolished; and the stage sold. It called there, however, regularly with the mails and passengers as before.

"I gleaned the following: The Phalanx property could support one thousand people, yet they can not get them, and they have not accommodations for such a number. Some doubt the advantage of taking more members until they are richer. All say they are doing well; yet some admit that individually they could do better, or that an individual with that property could have done better than they have done. They hire about sixteen

Dutch laborers, and say they are better treated than they would be elsewhere. These board in a room beneath the Phalanx dining-room, and lodge in various out-places around. They had an addition of six Frenchmen to their numbers, said to be exiles ; these persons were industrious and well liked.

"In a conversation with one of the discontented members, who had been there five years, he said that after an existence of nine years, there were fewer members than at the commencement ; there was something wrong in the system they were practicing; and if that was Association, then Association was wrong ; thinks there are some persons who try to crush and oust those who differ from them in opinion, or who wish to change the system so as to increase their number.

"There was more than enough work for all to do, mechanics especially. Carpenters were in demand. They had to hire the latter at $ 1.50 per day. They don't get any to join them. Some thought the wages too low ; yet the cost of living was not much over $ 2. per week, including washing and all else but clothing and luxuries.

"My acquaintance, John Gray, had been away from the Phalanx for some months, but had returned, having found that he could not live in 'old society' again ; sooner than that, he would return to the Shakers. He spoke much more favorably of the North American than before, and was particularly pleased with the eating arrangement ; he wanted to see the individual system carried out still further among them ; for in proportion as they adopted that, they were made free and happy ; but in proportion as they progressed toward Communism, the result was the reverse. After alluding to their many little difficulties, he pointed out so many advantages, that they seemed to counter-balance all the evils spoken of by himself and others. Criticism, he said, was the most potent regulator and governor.

"The charges were increased at the Phalanx. For five meals and very inferior sleeping accommodations twice, I paid $ 1.75. The Phalanx had paid five per cent. dividend on stock, for the past year."

Macdonald's third visit to the Phalanx.

"In the fall of 1853 I made another pilgrimage to the North American. On my journey from Red Bank I had for my fellow-passengers, the well-known Albert Brisbane and a young man named Davidson. The ride was diversified by interesting debates upon Spiritualism and Association.

"At the Phalanx I was pleased with the appearance of things during this visit. I saw the same faces, and felt assured they were 'sticking to it.' I also fell in with some strangers who had lately been attracted there. I was informed by one or two of the members that the articles which had been published about the Phalanx in the New York *Herald*, had done them good. It made the place known, and caused many strangers to visit them; among whom were some capitalists who offered to lend their aid ; a Dr. Parmelee was named as one of these. The articles also did good in criticising their peculiarities, letting them know what the 'world' thought of them, and shaking them up, like wind upon a stagnant pond.

"Mr. Sears informed me that they had had a freshet in August, which destroyed a large quantity of their forage ; and the dams were broken down, causing a loss of two or three hundred dollars. Their peach-orchard had failed, causing a deficiency of nearly two-thirds the usual amount of peaches. He was of the opinion that in five years they would be able to show something more tangible to the world. He thought that in about that time the experiment would have completed a marked phase in its history, and become more worthy of notice.

"In a conversation with Mr. French I learned that he had been away from the Phalanx for three weeks, seeing his friends in the country; but it made him happy to return; he felt he could not live elsewhere. He said their grand object was to provide a fitting education for their children. They had been neglected, though often thought of; and ere long something important would be done for them, if things turned out as he hoped. Last year, for the first time since their commencement, they declared a dividend to labor; this year they anticipated more, but the accidents would probably reduce it. Their total debts were $ 18,000, but the value of the place was $ 55,000. They bought the land at $ 20 per acre, and it had increased in value, not so much by their improvements as by the rise of land all through that country. They were not troubled about their debts; it was an advantage to them to let them remain; they could pay them at any time if necessary."

CHAPTER XXXVIII.

END OF THE NORTH AMERICAN PHALANX.

THE *Harbinger* and Macdonald both fail us in our search for the history of the last days of the North American; and having asked in vain for an authentic account of its failure from one at least of its leaders, we must content ourselves with such scraps of information on this interesting catastrophe, as we have picked up here and there in various publications. And first we will bring to view one or two facts which preceded the failure, and apparently led to it.

In the spring of 1853—the tenth year of the Phalanx—there was a split and secession, resulting in the formation of another Association, called the Raritan Bay Union, at Perth Amboy, New Jersey. A correspondent of the New York *Herald*, who visited this new Union in June, 1853, speaks of its founders and foundations as follows:

"The subscriptions already amount to over forty thousand dollars. Among the names of the stock-holders I notice that of Mrs. Tyndale, formerly an extensive crockery dealer in Chestnut street, Philadelphia, who carried on the business in her own name until she accumulated a handsome fortune, and then relin-

quished it to her son and son-in-law; also Marcus
Spring, commission merchant of New York; Rev.
William Henry Channing of Rochester, and Clement O.
Read, late superintendent of the large wash-house in
Mott street, New York.

"The President of the corporation, George B. Arnold
Esq., was last year President of the North American
Phalanx. Many years ago he was a minister at large in
the city of New York. He afterward removed to Illinois,
where he established an extensive nursery, working with
his own hands at the business, which he carried on successfully. He is an original thinker, a practical man, of
clear, strong common sense.

"The founders of the Union believe that many
branches of business may be carried on most advantageously here, and that the best class of mechanics will
soon find their interest and happiness promoted by joining them. Extensive shops will be erected, and either
carried on directly by the corporation, or leased, with
sufficient steam-power, to companies of its own members. The different kinds of business will be kept
separate, and every tub left to stand upon its own
bottom. They aim at combination, not confusion.
Every man will have pay for what he does, and no man
is to be paid for doing nothing. Whether they will drag
the drones out, if they find any, and kill them as the bees
do in autumn, or whether their ferryman will be directed
to take them out in his boat and tip them into the bay,
or what will be done with them, I can not say. But the
creed of this new Community seems to be, that 'Labor
is praise.' In religious matters the utmost freedom
exists, and every man is left to follow the dictates of his
own conscience."

Macdonald briefly mentions this Raritan Bay Association, and characterizes it as "a joint-stock concern, that undertook to hold an intermediate position between the North American and ordinary society;" meaning, we suppose, that it was less communistic than the Phalanx. He furnishes also a copy of its constitution, the preamble of which declares that its object is to establish "various branches of agriculture and mechanics, whereby industry, education and social life may, in principle and practice, be arranged in conformity to the Christian religion, and where all ties, conjugal, parental, filial, fraternal and communal, which are sanctioned by the will of God, the laws of nature, and the highest experience of mankind, may be purified and perfected; and where the advantages of co-operation may be secured, and the evils of competition avoided, by such methods of joint-stock Association as shall commend themselves to enlightened conscience and common sense."

The board of officers whose names are attached to this constitution were,

President, George B. Arnold; *Directors*, Clement O. Read, Marcus Spring, George B. Arnold, Joseph L. Pennock, Sarah Tyndale; *Treasurer*, Clement O. Read; *Secretary*, Angelina G. Weld.

It is evident that this offshoot drew away a portion of the members and stockholders of the North American. It amounted to little as an Association, and disappeared with the rest of its kindred; but its secession certainly weakened the parent Phalanx.

During the summer after this secession, the North American appears to have had an acrimonious controversy about religion with somebody, inside or outside, the nature of which we can only guess from the following mysterious hints in a long article written by Mr. Sears in the fall of 1853, on behalf of the Association, and published in the New York *Tribune* under the caption, "*Religion in the North American Phalanx.*" Mr. Sears said:

"I am incited to these remarks by the recent imposition of a missionary effort among us, and by a letter respecting it, indicating the failure of a cherished scheme, in a spirit which shows that the old sanctions only are wanting, to kindle the old fires. And, lest our silence be further misconstrued, and we subjected to further discourtesy, I am induced to say a few words in defense.

"Neither our quiet nor our good character have quite sufficed to protect us from the customary officiousness of busy sectaries, who professed not to understand how a people could associate, how a commonwealth could exist, without adopting some sectarian profession of religious faith, some partisan form of religious observance.

"In vain we urged that our institutions were religious; that here, before their eyes, was made real and practical in daily life and established as a real societary feature, that fraternity which the church in every form has held as its ideal; that here the Christian rule of life is made possible in the only way that it can be made possible, viz., through social guarantees which confirm the just claims of every member. In vain we showed that in the matter of private faith we did not propose to interfere, but in this respect held the same relation of a body to its constituent members, that the State of New

Jersey or any other commonwealth does to its citizens; that tolerance was our only proper course, and must continue to be; that the professors of any name could organize a society and have a fellowship of the same religious communion, if they chose; but that our effort was to seek out the divine mathematics of societary relations, and to determine a formula that would be of universal application; and that to allow our organization to be taken possession of as an agency for pushing private constructions of doctrine, would be an impossible descent for us; that any who choose could make such profession and have such observances as they liked, and by arrangement have equal use of our public rooms. Still from time to time various parties have urged their private views upon us, and whenever they wished, have had, by arrangement, the use of room and such audience as they could attract. But never until the past summer has there been such a persistent effort to press upon us private observance as to excite much attention; and for the first time in our history there arose, through a reprehensible effort, a public discussion of religious dogmas; and, to our regret and annoyance, the usual sectarian uncharitableness was exhibited and has since been expressed to us."

A further glimpse at the difficulty alluded to, is afforded by the following paragraph, which appeared in print about the same time, written by Eleazer Parmlee, a partizan of the other side:

"I received the inclosed letter from Marcus Spring, who requested me to co-operate with himself and others (at the two Phalanxes) in sustaining a preacher; as he insists 'that the religious and moral elements in man

should be cultivated for the true success of Association.'
I shall write to Mr. Spring that it is not my opinion that
religious cultivation or teaching will be allowed, certainly
at one of the Associations; and I would advise all persons who have any respect or regard for the religion of
the Bible, and who do not wish to have their feelings
outraged by a total want of common courtesy, to keep
entirely away, at least from the North American."

It seems probable that this controversy, whatever it
may have been, was complicated with the secession
movement in the spring before. We notice that Marcus
Spring, who was originally a prominent stockholder in
the North American, and who went over, as we have
seen, to the rival Phalanx at Perth Amboy, was mixed
up with this controversy, and apparently instigated the
"missionary imposition" of which Mr. Sears complains.
It may be reasonably conjectured that this theological
quarrel led to the ultimate withdrawal of stock which
brought the Association to its end.

In September 1853, after the secession and after the
quarrel about religion, the following gloomy picture of
the Phalanx was sent abroad in the columns of the New
York *Tribune*, the old champion of Socialism in general
and of the North American in particular. Whether its
representations were true or not, it must have had a
very depressing effect on the Association, and doubtless
helped to realize its own forebodings:

[Correspondence of the New York *Tribune*.]

"I remained nine days at the North American
Phalanx. They appear to be on a safe material basis.
Good wages are paid the laborers, and both sexes are
on an equality in every respect; the younger females

wear bloomers ; are beautiful and apparently refined ; but both sexes grow up in ignorance, and seem to have but little desire for mental progression. Their mode of life, however, is a decided improvement on the old one : the land appears to be well cultivated and very productive ; the majority of the men, and some of the women, are hard workers ; the wages of labor and profits on capital are constantly increasing and likely to increase ; probably in a few years more the stock will be as good an investment as any other stock, and the wages of labor much better than elsewhere. The standard of agricultural and mechanical labor is now nine cents per hour ; kitchen-work, waiting, etc., about the same. Their arrangements for economizing domestic labor seem very efficient ; but they have no sewing-machine and no store that amounts to any thing. If a hat of any kind is wanted, they have to go to Red Bank for it. They appear to make no effort to redeem their stock, which is now mostly in the hands of non-residents. The few who do save any thing, I understand, usually prefer something that 'pays' better. Most of them are decent sort of people, have few bad qualities and not many good ones, but they are evidently not working for an idea. They make no effort to extend their principles, and do not build, as a general thing, unless a person wanting to join builds for himself. Under such circumstances the progress of the movement must be necessarily slow, if even it progress at all. Latterly the number of members and probationers has decreased. They find it necessary to employ hired laborers to develop the resources of the land.

" So far as regards the material aspect, however, they get along tolerably well. But I regard the mechanism merely as a means for general progress—a basis for a superstructure of unlimited mental and spiritual development. They seem to regard it as the end. This absence of facilities for education and mental improvement is astonishing, in a Community enjoying so many of the advantages of co-operation. Those engaged in nurseries should have some acquaintance with physiology and hygiene; but such things are scarcely dreamed of as yet among any of the members, except two or three : or if so, they keep very quiet about it. A considerable portion of their hard earnings ends in smoke and spittoons, or some other form of mere animal gratification, to which they are in a measure compelled to resort, in the absence of any rational mode of applying their small amount of leisure. Their reading-room is supplied by two *New York Tribunes*, a *Nauvoo Tribune*, and two or three worthless local papers. The library consists of between three and four hundred volumes, not many of them progressive or the reverse. I believe there is a sort of a school, but should think they don't teach much there worth knowing, if results are to be the criterion. Cigar smoking is bad enough in men, but particularly objectionable in twelve-year olds. A number of papers are taken by individuals, but those that most need them don't have much chance at them ; besides, it is the end of associate life to economise by co-operation in this as in other matters. Some of them make miserable apologies for neglect of these matters, on the score of want of leisure, means, etc., but all amounts to nothing.

"The Phalanx people, having deferred improving the higher faculties of themselves and children until their lower wants are supplied, which can never be, are heavily in debt ; and so far as any effect on the outer world is concerned, the North American Phalanx is a total failure. No movement based on a mere gratification of the animal appetites can succeed in extending itself. There must be intellectual and spiritual life and progress ; matter can not move itself."

A year later the Phalanx suffered a heavy loss by fire, which was reported in the *Tribune*, September 13, 1854, as follows :

Destruction of the Mills of the North American Phalanx.

" About six and a-half o'clock Sunday morning, a fire broke out in the extensive mills of the North American Phalanx, located in Monmouth County, New Jersey. The fire was first discovered near the center of the main edifice, and had at that time gained great headway. It is supposed to have originated in the eastern portion of the building, and a strong easterly wind prevailing at the time, the flames were carried toward the center and western part of the edifice. This was a wooden building about one hundred feet square, three stories high, with a thirty horse-power steam-engine in the basement, and two run of burr-stones and superior machinery for the manufacture of flour, meal, hominy and samp, on the floors above. Adjoining the mill on the north was the general business office, containing the account books of the Association, the most valuable of which were saved by Mr. Sears at the risk of his life. Adjoining the office was the saw-mill, blacksmith-shop, tin-shop, etc., with valuable machinery, driven by the engine, all of which was destroyed. About two thousand bushels of wheat and corn were stored in the mill directly over the engine, which, in falling, covered it so as to preserve the machinery from the fire. There was a large quantity

of hominy and flour and feed destroyed with the mill.
The carpenters' shop, a little south of the grain mill,
was saved by great exertion of all the members, men
and women. All else in that vicinity is a smouldering
mass. Nothing was insured but the stock, valued at
$3,000, for two-thirds that amount. The loss is from
$7,000 to $10,000."

Alcander Longley, at present the editor of a Communist paper, was a member of the North American,
and should be good authority on its history. He
connects this fire very closely with the breaking-up of
the Phalanx. In a criticism of one of Brisbane's late
socialistic schemes, he says :

"A little reminiscence just here. We were a member
of the North American Phalanx. A fire burned our
mills and shops one unlucky night. We had plenty of
land left and plenty else to do. But we called the
'money bags' [stockholders] together for more stock to
rebuild with. Instead of subscribing more, they dissolved the concern, because it didn't pay enough
dividend! And the honest resident working members
were scattered and driven from the home they had
labored so hard and long for years to make. Would
Mr. Brisbane repeat such a farce ?"

Yet it appears that the crippled Phalanx lingered
another year ; for we find the following in the editorial
correspondence of *Life Illustrated* for August 1855 :

Last Picture of the North American.

"After supper (the hour set apart for which is from
five to six o'clock) the lawn, gravel walks and little lake
in front of the Phalanstery, present an animated and
charming scene. We look out upon it from our window.

Nearly the whole population of the place is out of doors. Happy papas and mammas draw their baby wagons, with their precious freight of smiling innocence, along the wide walks ; groups of little girls and boys frolic in the clover under the big walnut-trees by the side of the pond ; some older children and young ladies are out on the water in their light canoes, which they row with the dexterity of sailors ; men and women are standing here and there in groups engaged in conversation, while others are reclining on the soft grass ; and several young ladies in their picturesque working and walking cos-tume—a short dress or tunic coming to the knees, and loose pantaloons—are strolling down the road toward the shaded avenue which leads to the highway.

"There seems to be a large measure of quiet happi-ness here ; but the place is now by no means a gay one. If we observe closely we see a shadow of anxiety on most countenances. The future is no longer assured. Henceforth it must be 'each for himself,' in isolation and antagonism. Some of these people have been clamorous for a dissolution of the Association, which they assert has, so far as they are concerned at least, proved a failure ; but some of them, we have fancied, now look forward with more fear than hope to the day which shall sunder the last material ties which bind them to their associates in this movement."

The following from the *Social Revolutionist*, January, 1856, was written apparently in the last moments of the Phalanx.

[Alfred Cridge's Diagnosis in Articulo Mortis.]

"The North American Phalanx has decided to dis-solve. When I visited it two years since it seemed to be managed by practical men, and was in many respects thriving. The domain was well cultivated, labor well paid, and the domestic department well organized. With the ·exception of the single men's apartments being overcrowded, comfort reigned supreme. The following were some of the defects:

" 1. The capital was nearly all owned by non-residents, who invested it, however, without expectation of profit, as the stock was always below par, yielding at that time but 4 1-2 per cent. of interest, which was a higher rate than that formerly allowed. Probably the majority of the Community were hard workers, many of them to the extent of neglecting mental culture. I was informed that they generally lived from hand to mouth, saving nothing, though living was cheap, rent not high, and the par rate of wages ninety cents for ten hours, but varying from sixty cents to $ 1.20, according to skill, efficiency, unpleasantness, etc. Nearly all those who did save, invested in more profitable stock, leaving absentees to keep up an Association in which they had no particular interest. As the generality of those on the ground gave no tangible indications of any particular interest in the movement, it is no matter of surprise that, notwithstanding the zeal of a few disinterested philanthropists engaged in it, the institution failed to meet the sanguine expectations of its projectors.

" 2. They neglected the intellectual and æsthetic element. Some residents there attributed the failure of the Brook Farm Association to an undue predominance of these, and so ran into the opposite error. A well-known engraver in Philadelphia wished to reside at the Phalanx and practice his profession ; but no ; he must work on the farm ; if allowed to join, he would not be permitted to follow his attractions. So he did not come.

" 3. The immediate causes of the dissolution of both Associations were disastrous fires, and no way attributable to the principles on which they were based.

" 4. The formation of Victor Considerant's colony in Texas probably hastened the dissolution of the Phalanx, as many of the members preferred establishing themselves in a more genial latitude, to working hard one year or two for nothing, which they must have done, to regain the loss of $20,000 by fire, to say nothing of the indirect loss occasioned by the want of the buildings.

"Thus endeth the North American Phalanx! *Requiescat in pace!* Where is the Phœnix Association that is to arise from its ashes?

"P. S. Since the above was written, the domain of the North American Phalanx has been sold."

N. C. Meeker, who wrote those enthusiastic letters from the Trumbull Phalanx (now one of the editors of the *Tribune*), is the author of the following picturesque account of the North American, which we will call its

Post Mortem and Requiem, by an old Fourierist.

[From the New York *Tribune* of November 3, 1866.]

"Once in about every generation, attention is called to our social system. Many evils seem to grow from it. A class of men peculiarly organized, unite to condemn the whole structure. If public affairs are tranquil, they attempt to found a new system. So repeatedly and for so many ages has this been done, that it must be said that the effort arises from an aspiration. The object is not destructive, but beneficent. Twenty-five years ago an attempt was made in most of the Northern States. There are signs that another is about to be made. To those who are interested, a history of life in a Phalanx will be instructive. It is singular that none of the many thousand Fourierists have related their experience. (!) Recently I visited the old grounds of the North American Phalanx. Additional information is brought from a similar institution [the Trumbull] in a Western State. Light will be thrown on the problem; it will not solve it.

"Four miles from Red Bank, Monmouth County, New Jersey, six hundred acres of land were selected about twenty years ago, for a Phalanx on the plan of Fourier. The founders lived in New York, Albany and other places. The location was fortunate, the soil naturally good, the scenery pleasing and the air healthful. It would have been better to have been near a shipping-port. The road from Red Bank was heavy sand.

"First, a large building was erected for families; afterward, at a short distance, a spacious mansion was built, three stories high, with a front of one hundred and fifty feet, and a wing of one hundred and fifty feet. It is still standing in good repair, and is about to be used for a school. The rooms are of large size and well finished, the main hall spacious, airy, light and elegant. Grape-vines were trained by the side of the building, flowers were cultivated, and the adjoining ground was planted with shade-trees. Two orchards of every variety of choice fruit (one of forty acres) were planted, and small fruits and all kinds of vegetables were raised on a large scale. The Society were the first to grow okra or gumbo for the New York market, and those still living there continue its cultivation and control supplies. A durable stream ran near by; on its banks were pleasant walks, which are unchanged, shaded by chestnut and walnut trees. On this stream they built a first-class grist-mill. Not only did it do good work, but they established the manufacture of hominy and other products which gave them a valued reputation, and the profits of this mill nearly earned their bread.

"It was necessary to make the soil highly productive, and many German and other laborers were employed. The number of members was about one hundred, and visitors were constant. Of all the Associations, this was the best, and on it were fixed the hopes of the reformers. The chief pursuit was agriculture. Education was considered important, and they had good teachers and schools. Many young persons owed to the Phalanx an education which secured them honorable and profitable situations.

"The society was select, and it was highly enjoyed. To this day do members, and particularly women, look back to that period as the happiest in their lives. Young people have few proper wishes which were not gratified They seemed enclosed within walls which beat back the storms of life. They were surrounded by whatever was useful, innocent and beautiful. Neighborhood quarrels were unknown, nor was there trouble among children. There were a few white-eyed women who liked to repeat stories, but they soon sunk to their true value.

"After they had lived this life fourteen years,* their mill burned down. Mr. Greeley offered to lend them

---

* To be exact, this should be eleven years instead of fourteen. The Phalanx commenced operations in September, 1843, and the fire occurred in September, 1854. The whole duration of the experiment was only a little over twelve years, as the domain was sold, according to Alfred Cridge, in the winter of 1855—6.

$ 12,000 to rebuild it. They were divided on the subject of location. Some wanted to build at Red Bank, to save hauling. They could not agree. But there was another subject on which they did agree. Some suggested that they had better not build at all! that they had better dissolve! The question was put, and to every one's surprise, decided that they would dissolve. Accordingly the property was sold, and it brought sixty-six cents on a dollar. In a manner the sale was forced. Previously the stockholders had been receiving yearly dividends, and they lost little.

" While the young had been so happy, and while the women, with some exceptions, enjoyed society, with scarcely a cause for disquiet, fathers had been considering the future prospects of those they loved. The pay for their work was out of the profits, and on a joint-stock principle. Work was credited in hours, and on striking a dividend, one hour had produced a certain sum. A foreman, a skillful man, had an additional reward. It was five cents a day. One of the chief foremen told me that after working all day with the Germans, and working hard, so that there would be no delay he had to arrange what each was to do in the morning. Often he would be awakened by falling rain. He would long be sleepless in re-arranging his plans. A skillful teacher got an additional five cents. All this was in accordance with democratic principles. I was told that the average wages did not exceed twenty cents a day. You see capital drew a certain share which labor had to pay. But this was of no consequence, providing the institution was perpetual. There they could live and die. Some, however, ran in debt each year. With large families and small wages, they could not hold their own.   These men had long been uneasy.

"There was a public table where all meals were eaten. At first there was a lack of conveniences, and there was much hard work.   Mothers sent their children to school, and became cooks and chamber-maids.   The most energetic lady took charge of the washing group.   This meant she had to work hardest.   Some of the best women, though filled with enthusiasm for the cause, broke down with hard work.   Afterward there were proper conveniences; but they did not prevent the purchase of hair-dye.   The idea that woman in Association was to be relieved of many cares, was not realized.

"On some occasions, perhaps for reasons known at the time, there was a scarcity of victuals.   One morning all they had to eat was buckwheat cakes and water.   I think they must have had salt.   In another Phalanx, one breakfast was mush.   Every member felt ashamed.

"The combined order had been strongly recommended for its economies.   All articles were to be purchased at wholesale; food would be cheaper; and cooking when done for many by a few, would cost little.   In practice there were developments not looked for.   The men were not at all alike.   Some so contrived their work as not to be distant at meal-time.   They always heard the first ringing of the bell.   In the preparation of food, naturally, there will be small quantities which are choice. In families these are thought much of, and are dealt out by a mother's good hands.   They come last.   But here, in the New Jerusalem, those who were ready to eat, seized upon such the first thing.   If they could get enough of it, they would eat nothing else.

"You know that in all kinds of business there must

be men to see that nothing is neglected. On a farm teams must be fed and watered, cattle driven up or out, and bars or gates closed. They who did these things were likely to come to their meals late. They were sweaty and dirty, their feet dragged heavy. First they must wash. On sitting down they had to rest a little. Naturally they would look around. At such times one's wife watches him. At a glance she can see a cloud pass across his face. He need not speak to tell her his thoughts. She can read him better than a Bible in large type. In one Phalanx where I was acquainted, the public table was thrown up in disgust, like a pack of unlucky cards.

"But our North Americans were determined. To give to all as good food as the early birds were getting, it was necessary to provide large quantities. When this was done, living became very expensive and the economies of Association disappeared.

"They had to take another step. They established an eating-house on what is called the European plan. The plainest and the choicest food was provided. Whatever one might desire he could have. His meal might cost him ten cents or five dollars. When he finished eating he received a counter or ticket, and went to the office and settled. He handed over his ticket, and the amount printed on it was charged to him. For instance, a man has the following family: first, wifey, and then, George, Emily, Mary, Ralph and Rosa. They sit at a table by themselves, unless wifey is in the kitchen, with a red face, baking buckwheat cakes with all her might. They select their breakfast—a bill of fare is printed every day—and they have ham and eggs, fifteen cents; sausage, ten cents; cakes, fifteen cents; fish, ten cents ; and a cup of coffee and six glasses of water, five cents ; total, fifty-five cents, which is charged, and they go about their business. If wifey had been to work, she would eat afterward, and though she too would have to pay, she was credited with cake-baking. One should be so charitable as to suppose that she earned enough to pay for the meal that she ate sitting sideways. To keep these accounts, a book-keeper was required all day. One would think this a curious way ; but it was the only one by which they could choke off the birds of prey. One would think, too, that Rosa, Mary and Co., might have helped get breakfast ; but the plan was to get rid of drudgery.

"Again, there was another class. They were sociable and amiable men. Everybody liked to hear them talk, and chiefly they secured admission for these qualities. Unfortunately they did not bring much with them. All through life they had been unlucky. There was what was called the Council of Industry, which discussed and decided all plans and varieties of work. With them originated every new enterprise. If a man wanted an order for goods at a store, they granted or refused it. Some of these amiable men would be elected members ; it was easy for them to get office, and they greatly directed in all industrial operations. At the same time those really practical would attempt to counteract these men ; but they could not talk well, though they tried hard. I have never seen men desire more to be eloquent than they ; their most powerful appeals were when they blushed with silent indignation. But there was one thing they could do well, and that was to grumble while at work. They could make an impression then. Fancy the result.

"Lastly: the rooms where families lived adjoined each other, or were divided by long halls. Young men do not always go to bed early. Perhaps they would be out late sparking, and they returned to their rooms before morning. A man was apt to call to mind the words of the country mouse lamenting that he had left his hollow tree. Sometimes one had a few words to say to his wife when he was not in good humor on account of bad digestion. When some one overheard him, they would think of her delicate blooming face, and her ear-rings and finger-rings, and wonder, but keep silent; while others thought that they had a good thing to tell of. But let no one be troubled. These two will cling to each other, and nothing but death can separate them. He will bear these things a long time, winking with both eyes; but at last he thinks that they should have a little more room, and she heartily agrees.

"Fourteen years make a long period. At last they learned that it was easy enough to get lazy men, but practical and thorough business men were scarce. Five cents a day extra was not sufficient to secure them. A promising, ambitious young man growing up among them, did not see great inducements. He heard of the world; men made money there. His curiosity was great. One can see that the Association was likely to be childless.

"Learning these things which Fourier had not set down, their mill took fire. Still they were out of debt. They were doing well. The soil had been brought to a high state of cultivation. Of the fifteen or twenty Associations through the country, their situation and advantages were decidedly superior. I inquired of the old members remaining on the ground, and who bought the property and are doing well, the reason for their failure. They admit there was no good reason to prevent their going on, except the disposition. But Fourier did not recommend starting with less than eighteen hundred. When I asked them what would have been the result if they had had this number, they said they would have broken up in less than two years. Generally men are not prepared. Association is for the future.

" I found one still sanguine. He believes there are now men enough afloat, successfully to establish an Association. They should quietly commence in a town. There should be means for doing work cheaply by machinery. A few hands can wash and iron for several hundred in the same manner as it is done in our public institutions. Baking, cooking and sewing can be done in the same way. There is no disputing the fact that these means did not exist twenty years ago. Gradually family after family could be brought together. In time a whole town would be captured.

"The plausible and the easy again arise in this age. Let no one mistake a mirage for a real image. Disaster will attend any attempt at social reform, if the marriage relation is even suspected to be rendered less happy. The family is a rock against which all objects not only will dash in vain, but they will fall shivered at its base.

"N. C. M."

But even marriage and family, rocks though they are, have to yield to earthquakes: and Fourierism, in which Meeker delighted, was one of the upheavals that have unsettled them. They will have to be reconstructed.

The latest visitor to the remains of the North American whose observations have fallen under our notice, is Mr. E. H. Hamilton, a leading member of the Oneida

Community. His letter in the *Circular* of April 13, 1868, will be a fitting conclusion to this account; as well for the new peep it gives us into the causes of failure, as for its appropriate reflections.

Why the North American Phalanx failed.

"*New York, March* 31, 1868.

"Business called me a short time ago to visit the domain once occupied by the North American Phalanx. The gentleman whom I wished to see, resided in a part of the old mansion, once warm and lively with the daily activities and bright anticipations of enthusiastic Associationists. The closed windows and silent halls told of failure and disappointment. When individuals or a Community push out of the common channel, and with great self-sacrifice seek after a better life, their failure is as disheartening as their success would have been cheering. Why did they fail?

"The following story from an old member and eye-witness whom I chanced to meet in the neighboring village, impressed me, and was so suggestive that I entered it in my note-book. After inquiring about the Oneida Community, he told his tale almost word for word, as follows:

C.—My interest in Association turns entirely on its relations to industry. In our attempt, a number of persons came together possessed of small means and limited ideas. After such a company has struggled on a few years as we did, resolutely contending with difficulties, a vista will open, light will break in upon them, and they will see a pathway opening. So it was with us. We prospered in finances. Our main business grew better; but the mill with which it was connected grew poorer, till the need of a new building was fairly before us. One of our members offered to advance the money to erect a new mill. A stream was surveyed, a site selected. One of our neighbors whose land we wanted to flow, held off for a bonus. This provoked us and we dropped the project for the time. At this juncture it occurred to some of us to put up a steam-mill at Red Bank. This was the vista that opened to us. Here we would be in water-communication with New York city. Some $2,000 a year would be saved in teaming. This steam-mill would furnish power for other industries. Our mechanics would follow, and the mansion at Red Bank become the center of the Association, and finally the center of the town. Our secretary was absent during this discussion. I was fearful he would not approve of the project, and told some of our members so. On his return we laid the plan before him, and he said no. This killed the Phalanx. A number of us were dissatisfied with this decision, and thirty left in a body to start another movement, which broke the back of the Association. The secretary was one of our most enthusiastic members and a man of good judgment ; but he let his fears govern him in this matter. I believe he sees his mistake now. The organization lingered along two years, when the old mill took fire and burned down ; and it became necessary to close up affairs.

E. H. H.—Would it not have been better if your company of thirty had been patient, and gone on quietly till the others were converted to your views ? If truth were on your side, it would in time have prevailed over their objections.

C.—I would not give a cent for a person's conversion. When a truth is submitted to a body of persons, a few only will accept it. The great body can not, because their minds are unprepared.

E. H. H.—How did your company succeed in their new movement?

C.—We failed because we made a mistake. The great mistake Associationists every where made, all through these movements, was to locate in obscure places which were unsuitable for becoming business centers. Fourier's system is based on a township. An Association to be successful must embrace a township.

E. H. H.—Well, suppose you get together a number sufficient to form a township, and become satisfactorily organized, will there not still remain this liability to be broken up by diversity of judgments arising, as in the instance you have just related to me?

C.—No; let the movement be organized aright and it might break up every day and not fail.

"Here ended the conversation. The story interested me especially, because it taught so clearly that the success of Communism depends upon something else besides money-making. When Hepworth Dixon visited this country and inquired about the Oneida Community, Horace Greeley told him he would 'find the O. C. a trade success.' Now according to C.'s story the North American Phalanx entered the stage of 'trade success,' and then failed because it lacked the *faculty of agreement*. It is patent to every person of good sense, that 'a house divided against itself can not stand.' Divisions in a household, in an army, in a nation, are disastrous, and unless healed, are finally fatal. The great lesson that the Oneida Community has been learning, is, that agreement is possible. In cases where diversity of judgment has arisen, we have always secured unanimity by being patient with each other, waiting, and submitting all minds to the Spirit of Truth. We have experienced this result over and over again, until it has become a settled conviction through the Community, that when a project is brought forward for discussion, the best thing will be done, and we shall all be of one mind about it. How many times questions have arisen that would have destroyed us like the North American Phalanx, were it not for this ability to come to an agreement! Prosperity puts this power of harmony to a greater test than adversity. When we built our new house, how many were the different minds about material, location, plan! How were our feelings wrought up! Party-spirit ran high. There was the stone party, the brick party, and the concrete-wall party. Yet by patience, forbearing one with another and submitting one to another, the final result satisfied every one. Unity is the essential thing. Secure that, and financial success and all other good things will follow."

CHAPTER XXXIX.

CONVERSION OF BROOK FARM TO FOURIERISM.

AT the beginning of our history of the Fourier epoch, we gave an account of the origin of the Brook Farm Association in 1841, and traced its career till the latter part of 1843. So far we found it to be an original American experiment, not affiliated to Fourier, but to Dr. Channing; and we classed it with the Hopedale, Northampton and Skaneateles Communities, as one of the preparations for Fourierism. Now, at the close of our history, we must return to Brook Farm and follow it through its transformation into a Fourierist Phalanx, and its career as a public teacher and propagandist.

In the final number of the *Dial*, dated April 1844, Miss E. P. Peabody published an article on Fourierism, which commences as follows :

"In the last week of December, 1843, and first week of January, 1844, a convention was held in Boston, which may be considered as the first publication of Fourierism in this region.

"The works of Fourier do not seem to have reached us, and this want of text has been ill supplied by various conjectures respecting them; some of which are more remarkable for the morbid imagination they display than for their sagacity. For ourselves we confess to some remembrances of vague horror connected with this name, as if it were some enormous parasitic plant, sucking the life principles of society, while it spread apparently an equal shade, inviting man to repose under its beautiful but poison-dropping branches. We still have a certain question about Fourierism, considered as a catholicon for evil; but our absurd horrors were dissipated, and a feeling of genuine respect for the friends of the movement ensured, as we heard the exposition of the doctrine of Association, by Mr. Channing and others. That name [Channing] already consecrated to humanity, seemed to us to have worthily fallen, with the mantle of the philanthropic spirit, upon this eloquent expounder of Socialism; in whose voice and countenance, as well as in his pleadings for humanity, the spirit of his great kinsman still seemed to speak. We can not sufficiently lament that there was no reporter of the speech of Mr. Channing."

At the close of this article Miss Peabody says:

"We understand that Brook Farm has become a Fourierist establishment. We rejoice in this, because such persons as form that Association, will give it a fair experiment. We wish it Godspeed. May it become a University, where the young American shall learn his duties, and become worthy of this broad land of his inheritance."

William H. Channing, in the *Present*, January 15, 1844, gives an account of this same Boston convention, from which we extract as follows:

"This convention marked an era in the history of

New England. It was the commencement of a public movement upon the subject of social reform, which will flow on, wider, deeper, stronger, until it has proved in deeds the practicability of societies organized, from their central principle of faith to the minutest detail of industry and pleasure, according to the order of love. This movement has been long gathering. A hundred rills and rivers of humanity have fed it.

"The number of attendants and their interest increased to the end, as was manifested by the continuance of the meetings from Wednesday, December 27th, when the convention had expected to adjourn, through Thursday and Friday. The convention was organized by the choice of William Bassett, of Lynn, as President; of Adin Ballou, of Hopedale, G. W. Benson, of Northampton, George Ripley, of Brook Farm, and James N. Buffum, of Lynn, as Vice-Presidents; and of Eliza J. Kenney, of Salem, and Charles A. Dana, of Brook Farm, as Secretaries. The Associations of Northampton, Hopedale and Brook Farm, were each well represented.

"It was instructive to observe that practical and scientific men constantly confirmed, and often apparently without being aware of it, the doctrines of social science as announced by Fourier. Indeed, in proportion to the degree of one's intimacy with this profound student of harmony, does respect increase for his admirable intellectual power, his foresight, sagacity, completeness. And for one, I am desirous to state, that the chief reason which prevents my most public confession of confidence in him as the one teacher now most needed, is, that honor for such a patient and conscientious investigator demands, of all who would justify his views, a simplicity of affection, an extent and accuracy of knowledge, an intensity of thought, to which very few can now lay claim. Quite far am I from saying, that as now enlightened, I adopt all his opinions; on the contrary, there are some I reject; but it is a pleasure to express gratitude to Charles Fourier, for having opened a whole new world of study, hope and action. It does seem to me, that he has given us the clue out of our scientific labyrinth, and revealed the means of living the law of love."

The *Phalanx* of February 5, 1844, refers to the revolution going on at Brook Farm, as follows:

" The Brook Farm Association, near Boston, is now in process of transformation and extension from its former condition of an educational establishment mainly, to a regularly organized Association, embracing the various departments of industry, art and science. At the head of this movement, are George Ripley, Minot Pratt and Charles A. Dana. We can not speak in too high terms of these men and their enterprise. They are gentlemen of high standing in the community, and unite in an eminent degree, talent, scientific attainments and refinement, with great practical energy and experience. This Association has a fine spiritual basis in those already connected with it, and we hope that it will be able to rally to its aid the industrial skill and capital necessary to organize an Association, in which productive labor, art, science, and the social and the religious affections, will be so wisely and beautifully blended and combined, that they will lend reciprocal strength, support, elevation and refinement to each other, and secure abundance, give health to the body, development and expansion to the mind, and exaltation to the soul.   We are convinced that there are abundant means and material in New England now ready to form a fine Association ; they have only to be sought out and brought together."

From these hints it is evident that the Brook Farmers were fully converted to Fourierism in the winter of 1843—4, and that William H. Channing led the way in this conversion.   He had been publishing the *Present* since September 1843, side by side with the *Phalanx* (which commenced in October of that year); and though he, like the rest of the Massachusetts Socialists, began with some shyness of Fourierism, he had gradually fallen into the Brisbane and Greeley movement, till at last the *Present* was hardly distinguishable in its general drift from the *Phalanx*. Accordingly in April, 1844, just at the time when the *Dial* ended its career, as we have seen, with a confession of quasi-conversion to Fourierism, the *Present* also concluded its labors with a twenty-five-page exposition of Fourier's system, and the *Phalanx* assumed its subscription list.

The connection of the Channings with Fourierism, then, stands thus: Dr. Channing, the first medium of the Unitarian afflatus, was the father (by suggestion) of the Brook Farm Association, which was originally called the West Roxbury Community.   William H. Channing, the second medium according to Miss Peabody, converted this Community to Fourierism and changed it into a Phalanx.   The *Dial*, which Emerson says was also a suggestion of Dr. Channing, and the *Present*, which was edited by William H.

Channing, ended their careers in the same month, both hailing the advent of Fourierism, and the *Phalanx* and *Harbinger* became their successors.

The *Dial* and *Present*, in thus surrendering their Roxbury daughter as a bride to Fourierism, did not neglect to give her with their dying breath some good counsel and warning. We will grace our pages with a specimen from each. Miss Peabody in the *Dial* moralizes thus:

"The social passions, set free to act, do not carry within them their own rule, nor the pledge of conferring happiness. They can only get this from the free action upon them of the intellectual passions which constitute human reason.

"But these functions of reason, do they carry within themselves the pledge of their own continued health and harmonious action?

"Here Fourierism stops short, and, in so doing, proves itself to be, not a life, a soul, but only a body. It may be a magnificent body for humanity to dwell in for a season; and one for which it may be wise to quit old diseased carcases, which now go by the proud name of civilization. But if its friends pretend for it any higher character than that of a body, thus turning men from seeking for principles of life essentially above organization, it will prove but another, perhaps a greater curse.

"The question is, whether the Phalanx acknowledges its own limitations of nature, in being an organization, or opens up any avenue into the source of life that shall keep it sweet, enabling it to assimilate to itself contrary elements, and consume its own waste; so that, phœnix-like, it may renew itself forever in greater and finer forms.

"This question, the Fourierists in the convention, from whom alone we have learned any thing of Fourierism, did not seem to have considered. But this is a vital point.

"The life of the world is now the Christian life. For eighteen centuries, art, literature, philosophy, poetry, have followed the fortunes of the Christian idea. Ancient history is the history of the apotheosis of nature, or natural religion; modern history is the history of an idea, or revealed religion. In vain will any thing try to be, which is not supported thereby. Fourier does homage to Christianity with many words. But this may be cant, though it thinks itself sincere. Besides, there are many things which go by the name of Christianity, that are not it.

"Let the Fourierists see to it, that there be freedom in their Phalanxes for churches, unsupported by their material organization, and lending them no support on their material side. Independently existing, within them but not of them, feeding on ideas, forgetting that which is behind petrified into performance, and pressing on to the stature of the perfect man, they will finally spread themselves in spirit over the whole body.

"In fine, it is our belief, that unless the Fourierist bodies are made alive by Christ, 'their constitution will not march;' and the galvanic force of reäction, by which they move for a season, will not preserve them from corruption. As the corruption of the best is the worst, the warmer the friends of Fourierism are, the more awake should they be to this danger, and the more energetic to avert it."

Charles Lane in the *Present* discoursed still more profoundly, as follows :

" Some questions, of a nice importance, may be considered by the Phalanx before they set out, or at least
on the journey, for they will have weighty, nay, decisive
influences on the final result. One of these, perhaps
the one most deserving attention, nay, perhaps that
upon which all others hinge, is the adjustment of those
human affections, out of which the present family
arrangements spring. In a country like the United
States of North America, where food is very cheap, and
all the needs of life lie close to the industrious hand, it
is very rare to find a family of old parents with their
sons and daughters married and residing under the same
roof. The universal bond is so weak, or the individual
bond is so strong, that one married pair is deemed a
sufficient swarm of human bees to hive off and form a
new colony. How, then, can it be hoped that there is
universal affection sufficient to unite many such families
in one body for the common good ? If, with the natural
affections to aid the attempt to meliorate the hardships
and difficulties in natural life, it is rare, nay, almost impossible, to unite three families in one bond of fellowship, how shall a greater number be brought together ?
If, in cases where the individual characters are known,
can be relied on, are trusted with each other's affections,
property and person, such union can not be formed, how
shall it be constructed among strangers, or doubtful, or
untried characters ? The pressing necessities in isolated
families, the great advantages in even the smallest
union, are obvious to all, not least to the country families in this land ; yet they unite not, but out of every
pair of affectionate hearts they construct a new roof-

tree, a new hearth-stone, at which they worship as at their exclusive altar.

"Is there some secret leaven in this conjugal mixture, which declares all other union to be out of the possible affinities? Is this mixture of male and female so very potent, as to hinder universal or even general union? Surely it can not happen, in all those numerous instances wherein re-unions of families would obviously work so advantageously for all parties, that there are qualities of mind so foreign and opposed, that no one could beneficially be consummated. Or is it certain, that in these natural affections and their consequences in living offspring, there is an element so subversive of general Association that the two can not co-exist? The facts seem to maintain such a hypothesis. History has not yet furnished one instance of combined individual and universal life. Prophecy holds not very strong or clear language on the point. Plato scarcely fancied the possible union of the two affections; the religious Associations of past or present times have not attempted it; and Fourier, the most sanguine of all futurists, does not deliver very succinct or decisive oracles on the subject.

"Can we make any approximation to axiomatical truth for ourselves? May we not say that it is no more possible for the human affections to flow at once in two opposite directions, than it is for a stream of water to do so? A divided heart is an impossibility. We must either serve the universal (God), or the individual (Mammon). Both we can not serve. Now, marriage, as at present constituted, is most decidedly an individual, and not a universal act. It is an individual act, too, of a depreciated and selfish kind.

The spouse is an expansion and enlargement of one's self, and the children participate of the same nature. The all-absorbent influence of this union is too obvious to be dwelt upon. It is used to justify every glaring and cruel act of selfish acquisition. It is made the ground-work of the institution of property, which is itself the foundation of so many evils. This institution of property and its numerous auxiliaries must be abrogated in associative life, or it will be little better than isolated life. But it can not, it will not be repealed, so long as marital unions are indulged in; for, up to this very hour, we are celebrating the act as the most sacred on earth, and what is called providing for the family, as the most onerous and holy duty.

"The lips of the purest living advocates of human improvement, Pestalozzi, J. P. Greaves and others, are scarcely silent from the most strenuous appeals to mothers, to develop in their offspring the germs of all truth, as the highest resource for the regeneration of our race; and we are now turning round upon them and declaring, that naught but a deeper development of mortal selfishness can result from such a course. At least such seems to be a consequence of the present argument. Yet, if it be true, we must face it. This is at least an inquiry which must be answered. It is certain, indeed, that if there be a source of truth in the human soul, deeper than all selfishness, it may be consciously opened by appeals which shall enforce their way beneath the human selfishness which is superincumbent on the divine origin. Then we may possibly be at work on that ground whereon universal Association can be based. But must not, therefore, individual (or dual) union cease? Here is our predicament. It haunts us at every turn;

as the poets represent the disturbed wanderings of a departed spirit. And reconciliation of the two is not yet so clearly revealed to the faithful soul, as the headlong indulgence is practiced by the selfish. It is an axiom that new results can only be arrived at by action on new principles, or in new modes. The old principle and mode of isolated families has not led to happy results. This is a fact admitted on all hands. Let us then try what the consociate, or universal family will produce. But, then, let us not seduce ourselves by vain hopes. Let us not fail to see, that to this end the individual selfishness, or, if so they must be called, the holy gratifications of human nature, must be sacrificed and subdued. As has been affirmed above, the two can not be maintained together. We must either cling to heaven, or abide on earth; we must adhere to the divine, or indulge in the human attractions. We must either be wedded to God or to our fellow humanity. To speak in academical language, the conjunction in this case is the disjunctive 'or,' not the copulative 'and.' Both these marriages, that is, of the soul with God, and of soul with soul, can not exist together. It remains, therefore, for us, for the youthful spirit of the present, for the faithfully intelligent and determinedly true, to say which of the two marriages they will entertain."

In consummation of their union with Fourierism, the Brook Farmers formed and published a new constitution, confessing in its preamble their conversion, and offering themselves to Socialists at large as a nucleus for a model Phalanx. They say:

"The Association at Brook Farm has now been in existence upwards of two years. Originating in the

thought and experience of a few individuals, it has hitherto worn, for the most part, the character of a private
experiment, and has avoided rather than sought the
notice of the public. It has, until the present time,
seemed fittest to those engaged in this enterprise to
publish no statements of their purposes or methods, to
make no promises or declarations, but quietly and sincerely to realize as far as might be possible, the great
ideas which gave the central impulse to their movement.
It has been thought that a steady endeavor to embody
these ideas more and more perfectly in life, would give
the best answer, both to the hopes of the friendly and
the cavils of the skeptical, and furnish in its results the
surest grounds for any larger efforts.

"Meanwhile every step has strengthened the faith
with which we set out ; our belief in a divine order of
human society, has in our own minds become an absolute certainty ; and considering the present state of
humanity and of social science, we do not hesitate to
affirm that the world is much nearer the attainment of
such a condition than is generally supposed. The deep
interest in the doctrine of Association which now fills
the minds of intelligent persons every where, indicates
plainly that the time has passed when even initiative
movements ought to be prosecuted in silence, and makes
it imperative on all who have either a theoretical or practical knowledge of the subject, to give their share to the
stock of public information.

"Accordingly we have taken occasion at several public
meetings recently held in Boston, to state some of the
results of our studies and experience, and we desire here
to say emphatically, that while on the one hand we yield
an unqualified assent to that doctrine of universal unity

which Fourier teaches, so on the other, our whole observation has shown us the truth of the practical arrangements which he deduces therefrom. The law of groups and series is, as we are convinced, the law of human nature, and when men are in true social relations their industrial organization will necessarily assume those forms.

"But beside the demand for information respecting the principles of Association, there is a deeper call for action in the matter. We wish, therefore, to bring Brook Farm before the public, as a location offering at least as great advantages for a thorough experiment as can be found in the vicinity of Boston. It is situated in West Roxbury, three miles from the depot of the Dedham Branch Railroad, and about eight miles from Boston, and combines a convenient nearness to the city, with a degree of retirement and freedom from unfavorable influences, unusual even in the country. The place is one of great natural beauty, and indeed the whole landscape is so rich and various as to attract the notice even of casual visitors. The farm now owned by the Association contains two hundred and eight acres, of as good quality as any land in the neighborhood of Boston, and can be enlarged by the purchase of land adjoining, to any necessary extent. The property now in the hands of the Association is worth nearly or quite thirty thousand dollars, of which about twenty-two thousand dollars is invested either in the stock of the company, or in permanent loans at six per cent., which can remain as long as the Association may wish.

"The fact that so large an amount of capital is already invested and at our service, as the basis of more extensive operations, furnishes a reason why

Brook Farm should be chosen as the scene of that practical trial of Association which the public feeling calls for in this immediate vicinity, instead of forming an entirely new organization for that purpose. The completeness of our educational department is also not to be overlooked. This has hitherto received our greatest care, and in forming it we have been particularly successful. In any new Association it must be many years before so many accomplished and skillful teachers in the various branches of intellectual culture could be enlisted. Another strong reason is to be found in the degree of order our organization has already attained, by the help of which a large Association might be formed without the losses and inconveniences which would otherwise necessarily occur. The experience of nearly three years in all the misfortunes and mistakes incident to an undertaking so new and so little understood, carried on throughout by persons not entirely fitted for the duties they have been compelled to perform, has, we think, prepared us to assist in the safe conduct of an extensive and complete Association.

"Such an institution, as will be plain to all, can not by any sure means be brought at once and full-grown into existence. It must, at least in the present state of society, begin with a comparatively small number of select and devoted persons, and increase by natural and gradual aggregations. With a view to an ultimate expansion into a perfect Phalanx, we desire to organize immediately the three primary departments of labor, agriculture, domestic industry and the mechanic arts. For this purpose additional capital will be needed, etc.

GEORGE RIPLEY, MINOT PRATT, CHARLES A. DANA.

"*Brook Farm, January* 18, 1844."

Here follows the usual appeal for co-operation and investments. In October following a second edition of this constitution was issued, in the preamble of which the officers say:

"The friends of the cause will be gratified to learn, that the appeal in behalf of Brook Farm, contained in the introductory statement of our constitution, has been generously answered, and that the situation of the Association is highly encouraging. In the half-year that has elapsed, our numbers have been increased by the addition of many skillful and enthusiastic laborers in various departments, and our capital has been enlarged by the subscription of about ten thousand dollars. Our organization has acquired a more systematic form, though with our comparatively small numbers we can only approximate to truly scientific arrangements. Still with the unavoidable deficiencies of our groups and series, their action is remarkable, and fully justifies our anticipations of great results from applying the principles of universal order to industry.

"We have made considerable agricultural improvements; we have erected a work-shop sixty feet by twenty-eight for mechanics of several trades, some of which are already in operation; and we are now engaged in building a section one hundred and seventy-five feet by forty, of a Phalanstery or unitary dwelling. Our first object is to collect those who, from their character and convictions, are qualified to aid in the experiment we are engaged in, and to furnish them with convenient and comfortable habitations, at the smallest possible outlay. For this purpose the most careful economy is used, though we are yet able to attain many of the peculiar advantages of the Associated household. Still for transitional society, and for comparatively temporary use, a social edifice can not be made free from the defects of civilized architecture. When our Phalanx has become sufficiently large, and has in some measure accomplished its great purposes, the serial organization of labor and unitary education, we shall have it in our power to build a Phalanstery with the magnificence and permanence proper to such a structure."

Whereupon the appeal for help is repeated. Finally, in May 1845 this new constitution was published in the *Phalanx*, with a new preamble. In the previous editions the society had been styled the "Brook Farm Association for Education and Industry;" but in this issue, Article 1 Section 1 declares that "the name of this Association shall be The Brook Farm Phalanx." We quote a few paragraphs from the preamble :

"At the last session of the legislature of Massachusetts, our Association was incorporated under the name which it now assumes, with the right to hold real estate to the amount of one hundred thousand dollars. This confers upon us all the usual powers and privileges of chartered companies.

" Nothing is now necessary to the greatest possible measure of success, but capital to furnish sufficient means to enable us to develop every department to advantage. This capital we can now apply profitably and without danger of loss. We are well aware that there must be risk in investing money in an infant Association, as well as in any other untried business ; but with the labors of nearly four years we have arrived at a point where this risk hardly exists.

"By that increasing number whose most ardent desire is to see the experiment of Association fairly tried, we are confident that the appeal we now make will not be received without the most generous response in their power. As far as their means and their utmost exertions can go, they will not suffer so favorable an opportunity for the realization of their fondest hopes to pass unimproved. Nor do we call upon Americans alone, but upon all persons of whatever nation, to whom the doctrines of universal unity have revealed the destiny of man. Especially to those noble men who in Europe have so long and so faithfully labored for the diffusion and propagation of these doctrines, we address what to them will be an occasion of the highest joy, an appeal for fraternal co-operation in behalf of their realization. We announce to them the dawning of that day for which they have so hopefully and so bravely waited, the up-springing of those seeds that they and their compeers have sown. To them it will seem no exaggeration to say that we, their younger brethren, invite their assistance in a movement which, however humble it may superficially appear, is the grandest both in its essential character and its consequences, that can now be proposed to man; a movement whose purpose is the elevation of humanity to its integral rights, and whose results will be the establishment of happiness and peace among the nations of the earth.

"By order of the Central Council,

"GEORGE RIPLEY, *President.*

"*West Roxbury, May 20, 1845.*"

CHAPTER XL.

BROOK FARM PROPAGATING FOURIERISM.

Brook Farm having attained the dignity of incorporation and assumed the title of Phalanx, was ready to undertake the enterprise of propagating Fourierism. Accordingly, in the same number of the *Phalanx* that published the appeal recited at the close of our last chapter, appeared the prospectus of a new paper to be called the *Harbinger*, with the following editorial notice:

" Our subscribers will see by the prospectus that the name of the *Phalanx* is to be changed for that of the *Harbinger*, and that the paper is to be printed in future by the Brook Farm Phalanx."

From this time the main function of Brook Farm was propagandism. It published the *Harbinger* weekly, with a zeal and ability of which our readers have seen plenty of specimens. It also instituted a missionary society and a lecturing system, of which we will now give some account.

New York had hitherto been the head-quarters of Fourierism. Brisbane, Greeley and Godwin, the primary men of the cause, lived and published there; the *Phalanx* was issued there ; the National Conventions had

been held there ; and there was the seat of the Executive Committee that made several abortive attempts to
institute a confederation of Associations and a national
organization of Socialists. But after the conversion of
Brook Farm, the center of operations was removed from
New York to Massachusetts. As the *Harbinger* succeeded to the subscription-list and propagandism of the
Phalanx, so a new National Union of Socialists, having
its head-quarters nominally at Boston, but really at
Brook Farm, took the place of the old New York Conventions. Of this organization, William H. Channing
was the chief-engineer ; and his zeal and eloquence in
that capacity for a short time, well entitled him to the
honors of the chief Apostle of Fourierism. In fact he
succeeded to the post of Brisbane. This will be seen in
the following selections from the *Harbinger:*

[From William H. Channing's Appeal to Associationists.]

"BRETHREN :

"Your prompt and earnest co-operation is requested in
fulfilling the design of a society organized May 27, 1846,
at Boston, Massachusetts, by a general convention of
the friends of Association. This design may be learned
from the following extracts from its constitution :

"'I. The name of this society shall be the American
Union of Associationists.

"'II. Its purpose shall be the establishment of an order of society based on a system of joint-stock property;
co-operative labor; association of families ; equitable
distribution of profits ; mutual guarantees ; honors according to usefulness ; integral education ; unity of
interests : which system we believe to be in accord with
the laws of divine providence and the destiny of man.

" ' 111. Its method of operation shall be the appointment of agents, the sending out of lecturers, the issuing
of publications, and the formation of a series of affiili-
ated societies which shall be auxiliary to the parent
society ; in holding meetings, collecting funds, and in
every way diffusing the principles of Association : and
preparing for their practical application, etc.'

"We have a solemn and glorious work before us :
1, To indoctrinate the whole people of the United States
with the principles of associative unity ; 2, To prepare
for the time when the nation, like one man, shall re-
organize its townships upon the basis of perfect justice.

"A nobler opportunity was certainly never opened to
men, than that which here and now welcomes Associationists. To us has been given the very word which
this people needs as a guide in its onward destiny.
This is a Christian Nation ; and Association shows how
human societies may be so organized in devout obedience to the will of God, as to become true brotherhoods,
where the command of universal love may be fulfilled
indeed. Thus it meets the present wants of Christians ;
who, sick of sectarian feuds and theological controver-
sies, shocked at the inconsistencies which disgrace the
religious world, at the selfishness, ostentation, and caste
which pervade even our worshiping assemblies, at the
indifference of man to the claims of his fellow-man
throughout our communities in country and city, at
the tolerance of monstrous inhumanities by professed
ministers and disciples of him whose life was love, are
longing for churches which may be really houses of
God, glorified with an indwelling spirit of holiness, and
filled to overflowing with heavenly charity.

"Brethren ! Can men engaged in so holy and hu-

mane a cause as this, which fulfills the good and destroys
the evil in existing society throughout our age and
nation, which teaches unlimited trust in Divine love, and
commands perfect obedience to the laws of Divine order
among all people, which heralds the near advent of the
reign of heaven on earth—be timid, indifferent, sluggish? Abiding shame will rest upon us, if we put not
forth our highest energies in fulfillment of the present
command of Providence. Let us be up and doing with
all our might.

"The measures which you are now requested at once
and energetically to carry out, are the three following:
1, Organize affiliated societies to act in concert with the
American Union of Associationists; 2, Circulate the
Harbinger and other papers devoted to Association;
3, Collect funds for the purpose of defraying the expenses of lectures and tracts. It is proposed in the
autumn and winter to send out lecturers, in bands and
singly, as widely as possible.

"Our white flag is given to the breeze. Our three-
fold motto,

"Unity of man with man in true society,

"Unity of man with God in true religion,

"Unity of man with nature in creative art and
industry,

"Is blazoned on its folds. Let hearts, strong in the
might of faith and hope and charity, rally to bear it on
in triumph. We are sure to conquer. God will work
with us; humanity will welcome our word of glad
tidings. The future is ours. On! in the name of the
Lord.   WILLIAM HENRY CHANNING,

"*Cor. Sec. of the Am. Un. of Associationists.*

"*Brook Farm, June 6, 1846.*"

In connection with this appeal, an editorial announced

The Mission of Charles A. Dana.

" The operations of the 'American Union,' will be commenced without delay. Mr. Dana will shortly make a tour through the State of New York as its agent. He will lecture in the principal towns, and take every means to diffuse a knowledge of the principles of Association. Our friends are requested to use their best exertions to prepare for his labors, and give efficiency to them."

A meeting of the American Union of Associationists is reported in the *Harbinger* of June 27, at which all the speakers except Mr. Brisbane, were Brook Farmers. The session continued two days, and William H. Channing made the closing and electric speeches for both days. The editor says :

" Mr. Channing closed the first day in a speech of the loftiest and purest eloquence, in which he declared the great problem and movement of this day to be that of realizing a unitary church ; showed how utterly unchristian is every thing now calling itself a church, and how impossible the solution of this problem, so long as industry tends only to isolate those who would be Christians, and to make them selfish ; and ended with announcing the life-long pledge into which the believers in associative unity in this country have entered, that they will not rest nor turn back until the mind of this whole nation is made to see and own the truth which there is in their doctrines. The effect upon all present was electric, and the resolution to adjourn to the next evening, was a resolution to commence then in earnest a great work."

After mentioning many good things said and done on the second day, the editor says :

" It was understood that the whole would be brought to a head and the main and practical business of the meeting set forth by Mr. Channing. His appeal, alike to friends and to opposers of the cause, will dwell like a remembered inspiration in all our minds. It spoke directly to the deepest religious sentiment in every one, and awakened in each a consciousness of a new energy. All the poetic wealth and imagery of the speaker's mind seemed melted over into the speech, as if he would pour out all his life to carry conviction into the hearts of others. He seemed an illustration of a splendid figure which he used, to show the present crisis in this cause. ' It was,' said he, 'nobly, powerfully begun in this country ; but, there has been a pause in our movement. When Benvenuto Cellini was casting his great statue, wearied and exhausted he fell asleep. He was roused by the cries of the workmen ; Master, come quick, the fires have gone down, and the metal has caked in the running ! He hesitated not a moment, but rushed into the palace, seized all the gold and silver vessels, money, ornaments, which he could find, and poured them into the furnace ; and whatever he could lay hands on that was combustible, he took to renew the fire. We must begin anew, said he. And the flames roared, and the metal began to run, and the Jupiter came out in complete majesty. Just so our greater work has caked in the running. We have been luke-warm ; we have slept. But shall not we throw in all our gold and silver, and throw in ourselves too, since our work is to produce not a mere statue, but a harmonious life of man made perfect in the image of God ? Who ever had such motive for

action ? The Crusaders, on their knees and upon the
hilts of their swords, which formed a cross, daily dedi-
cated their lives and their all to the pious resolution of
re-conquering the sepulcher in which the dead Lord was
laid. But ours is the calling, not to conquer the sepulcher of the dead Lord, but to conquer the world, and
bring it in subjection to truth, love and beauty, that
the living Christ may at length return and enter upon
his Kingdom of Heaven on the earth.'

"We by no means intend this as a report of Mr.
Channing's speech. To reproduce it at all would be
impossible. We only tell such few things as we easily
remember. He closed with requesting all who had
signed the constitution, or who were ready to co-operate
with the American Union, to remain at a business
meeting.

"The hour was late and the business was made short.
The plans of the executive committee were stated and
approved. These were, 1, to send out lecturers; a
beginning having been already made in the appointment
of Mr. Charles A. Dana as an agent of the society, to
proceed this summer upon a lecturing tour through
New York, Western Pennsylvania and Ohio; 2, to support the *Harbinger;* and 3, to publish tracts."

This report is followed by another stirring appeal
from the Secretary, of which the following is the
substance:

"Action!—Fellow Associationists, Brethren, Sisters,
each and all! You are hereby once again earnestly
entreated, in the name of our cause of universal unity,
at once to co-operate energetically in carrying out the
proposed plans of the American Union :

" 1. Form societies. 2. Circulate the *Harbinger*. 3. Raise funds. We wish to find one hundred persons in the United States, who will subscribe $ 100 a year for three years, in permanently establishing the work of propagation ; or two hundred persons who will subscribe $ 50. Do you know any persons in your neighborhood who will for one year, three years, five years, contribute for this end ? Be instant, friends, in season and out of season, in raising a permanent fund, and an immediate fund. This whole nation must hear our gospel of glad tidings. Will you not aid?

" WILLIAM H. CHANNING.

" *Cor. Sec. of the Am. Un. of Associationists.*

How far Mr. Dana fulfilled the missionary programme assigned to him, we have not been able to discover. But we find that the two most conspicuous lecturers sent abroad by the American Union were Messrs John Allen and John Orvis. These gentlemen made two or three tours through the northern part of New England ; and in the fall of 1847 they were lecturing or trying to lecture in Utica, Syracuse, Rochester, and other parts of the state of New York, as we mentioned in our account of the Skaneateles and Sodus Bay Associations. But the harvest of Fourierism was past, and they complained sorely of the neglect they met with, in consequence of the bad odor of the defunct Associations. This is the last we hear of them. The American Union continued to advertise itself in the *Harbinger* till that paper disappeared in February 1849 ; but its doings after 1846 seem to have been limited to anniversary meetings.

CHAPTER XLI.

BROOK FARM PROPAGATING SWEDENBORGIANISM.

OUR history of the career of Brook Farm in its final function of public teacher and propagandist, would not be complete without some account of its agency in the great Swedenborgian revival of modern times.

In a series of articles published in the Oneida *Circular* a year or two ago, under the title of *Swedenborgiana*, the author of this history said :

"The foremost and brightest of the Associations that rose in the Fourier excitement, was that at Brook Farm. The leaders were men whose names are now high in literature and politics. Ripley, Dana, Channing, Dwight and Hawthorne, are specimens of the list. Most of them were from the Unitarian school, whose head-quarters are at Boston and Cambridge. The movement really issued as much from transcendental Unitarianism as from Fourierism. It was religious, literary and artistic, as well as social. It had a press, and at one time undertook propagandism by missionaries and lectures. Its periodical, the *Harbinger*, was ably conducted, and very charming to all enthusiasts of progress. Our Putney school, which had not then reached Communism, was among the admirers of this periodical, and undoubtedly took an impulse from its teachings. The

Brook Farm Association, as the leader and speaker of the hundred others that rose with it, certainly contributed most largely to the effect of the general movement begun by Brisbane and Greeley. But the remarkable fact, for the sake of which I am calling special attention to it, is, that in its didactic function, it brought upon the public mind, not only a new socialism but a new religion, and that religion was *Swedenborgianism.*

"The proof of this can be found by any one who has access to the files of the *Harbinger.* I could give many pages of extracts in point. The simple truth is that Brook Farm and the *Harbinger* meant to propagate Fourierism, but succeeded only in propagating Swedenborgianism. The Associations that arose with them and under their influence, passed away within a few years, without exception; but the surge of Swedenborgianism which they started, swept on among their constituents, and, under the form of Spiritualism, is sweeping on to this day.

"Swedenborgianism went deeper into the hearts of the people than the Socialism that introduced it, because it was a *religion.* The Bible and revivals had made men hungry for something more than social reconstruction. Swedenborg's offer of a new heaven as well as a new earth, met the demand magnificently. He suited all sorts. The scientific were charmed, because he was primarily a son of science, and seemed to reduce the universe to scientific order. The mystics were charmed, because he led them boldly into all the mysteries of intuition and invisible worlds. The Unitarians liked him, because, while he declared Christ to be Jehovah himself, he displaced the orthodox ideas of Sonship and tri-personality, and evidently meant only that Christ was an illusive representation of the Father. Even the infidels liked him, because he discarded about half the Bible, including all Paul's writings, as 'not belonging to the Word,' and made the rest a mere 'nose of wax' by means of his doctrine of the 'internal sense.' His vast imaginations and magnificent promises chimed in exactly with the spirit of the accompanying Socialisms. Fourierism was too bald a materialism to suit the higher classes of its disciples, without a religion corresponding. Swedenborgianism was a godsend to the enthusiasts of Brook Farm ; and they made it the complement of Fourierism.

"Swedenborg's writings had long been circulating feebly in this country, and he had sporadic disciples and even churches in our cities, before the new era of Socialism. But any thing like a general interest in his writings had never been known, till about the period when Brook Farm and the *Harbinger* were in the ascendant. Here began a movement of the public mind toward Swedenborg, as palpable and portentous as that of Millerism or the old revivals.

"But Young America could not receive an old and foreign philosophy like Swedenborg's, without reacting upon it and adapting it to its new surroundings. The old afflatus must have a new medium. In 1845 the movement which commenced at Brook Farm was in full tide. In 1847 the great American Swedenborg, Andrew Jackson Davis, appeared, and Professor Bush gave him the right hand of fellowship, and introduced him into office as the medium and representative of the 'illustrious Swede,' while the *Harbinger* rejoiced over them both.

"Here I might show by chapter and verse from

Davis's and Bush's writings, exactly how the conjunction between them took place; how Davis met Swedenborg's ghost in a graveyard near Poughkeepsie in 1844, and from him received a commission to help the 'inefficient' efforts of Christ to regulate mankind; how he had another interview with the same ghost in 1846, and was directed by him to open correspondence with Bush; how Bush took him under his patronage, watched and studied him for months, and finally published his conclusion that Davis was a true medium of Swedenborg, providentially raised up to confirm his divine mission and teachings; and finally, how Bush and Davis quarreled within a year, and mutually repudiated each other's doctrines; but I must leave details and hurry on to the end.

"After 1847 Swedenborgianism proper subsided, and 'Modern Spiritualism' took its place. But the character of the two systems, as well as the history of their relations to each other, proves them to be identical in essence. Spiritualism is Swedenborgianism Americanized. Andrew Jackson Davis began as a medium of Swedenborg, receiving from him his commission and inspiration, and became an independent seer and revelator, only because, as a son, he outgrew his father. The omniscient philosophies which the two have issued are identical in their main ideas about intuition, love and wisdom, familiarity of the living with the dead, classification of ghostly spheres, astronomical theology, etc. Andrew Jackson Davis is more flippant and superficial than Swedenborg, and less respectful toward the Bible and the past, and in these respects he suits his customers."

We understand that some of the Brook Farmers think

this view of the Swedenborgian influence of Brook Farm and the *Harbinger* is exaggerated. It will be appropriate therefore now to set forth some of the facts and teachings which led to this view.

The first notable statement of the essential dualism between Swedenborg and Fourier that we find in the writings of the Socialists, is in the last chapter of Parke Godwin's "*Popular View*," published in the beginning of 1844, a standard work on Fourierism, second in time and importance only to Brisbane's "*Concise Exposition.*" Godwin says :

"Thus far we have given Fourier's doctrine of Universal Analogy ; but it is important to observe that he was not the first man of modern times who communicated this view. Emanuel Swedenborg, between whose revelations in the sphere of spiritual knowledge, and Fourier's discoveries in the sphere of science, there has been remarked the most exact and wonderful coïncidence, preceded him in the annunciation of the doctrine in many of its aspects, in what is termed the doctrine of correspondence. These two great minds, the greatest beyond all comparison in our later days, were the instruments of Providence in bringing to light the mysteries of His Word and Works, as they are comprehended and followed in the higher states of existence. It is no exaggeration, we think, to say, that they are the two commissioned by the Great Leader of the Christian Israel, to spy out the promised land of peace and blessedness.

"But in the discovery and statement of the doctrine of Analogy, these authorities have not proceded according to precisely the same methods. Fourier has arrived at it by strictly scientific synthesis, and Swedenborg by the study of the Scriptures aided by Divine illumination. What is the aspect in which Fourier views it we have shown ; we shall next attempt to elucidate the peculiar development of Swedenborg."

From this Mr. Godwin goes on to show at length the parallelism between the teachings of these "incomparable masters." It will be seen that he intimates that thinkers and writers before him had taken the same view. One of these, doubtless, was Hugh Doherty, an English Fourierist, whose writings frequently occur in the *Phalanx* and *Harbinger*. A very long article from him, maintaining the identity of Fourierism and Swedenborgianism, appeared in the *Phalanx* of September 7, 1844. The article itself is dated London, January 30, 1844. Among other things Mr. Doherty says :

" I am a believer in the truths of the New Church, and have read nearly all the writings of Swedenborg, and I have no hesitation in saying that without Fourier's explanation of the laws of order in Scriptural interpretation, I should probably have doubted the truth of Swedenborg's illumination, from want of a ground to understand the nature of spiritual sight in contradistinction from natural sight ; or if I had been able to conceive the opening of the spiritual sight, and credit Swedenborg's doctrines and affirmations, I should probably have understood them only in the same degree as most of the members of the New Church whom I have met in England, and that would seem to me, in my present state, a partial calamity of cecity. I say this in all humility and sincerity of conscience, with a view to future reference to Swedenborg himself in the spiritual world, and as a means of inducing the members of the New Church generally not to. be content with a superficial or limited knowledge of their own doctrines."

In another passage Mr. Doherty claims to have been "a student of Fourier fourteen years, and of Swedenborg two years."

In consequence partly of the new appreciation of Swedenborg that was rising among the Fourierists, a movement commenced in England in 1845 for republishing the scientific works of "the illustrious Swede." An Association for that purpose was formed, and several of Swedenborg's bulkiest works were printed under the auspices of Wilkinson, Clissold and others. This Wilkinson was also a considerable contributor to the *Phalanx* and *Harbinger*, as the reader will see by recurring to a list in our chapter on the Personnel of Fourierism.

Following this movement, came the famous lecture of Ralph Waldo Emerson on " *Swedenborg, the Mystic,*" claiming for him a lofty position as a scientific discoverer. That lecture was first published in this country in a volume entitled, "*Representative Men,*" in 1849; but according to Mr. White (the biographer of Swedenborg), it was delivered in England several times in 1847 ; and we judge from an expression which we italicize in the following extract from it, that it was written and perhaps delivered in this country in 1845 or 1846, i. e. very soon after the republication movement in England:

"The scientific works [of Swedenborg] have *just now* been translated into English, in an excellent edition. Swedenborg printed these scientific books in the ten years from 1734 to 1744, and they remained from that time neglected ; and now, after their century is complete, he has at last found a pupil in Mr. Wilkinson, in London, a philosophic critic, with a coequal vigor of understanding and imagination comparable only to Lord Bacon's, who has produced his master's buried books to the day, and transferred them, with every advantage, from their forgotten Latin into English, to go round the world in our commercial and conquering tongue. This startling reäppearance of Swedenborg, after a hundred years, in his pupil, is not the least remarkable fact in his history. Aided, it is said, by the munificence of Mr. Clissold, and also by his literary skill, this piece of poetic justice is done. The admirable preliminary discourses with which Mr. Wilkinson has enriched these volumes, throw all the cotemporary philosophy of England into shade."

Emerson, it is true, was not a Brook Farmer; but he was the spiritual fertilizer of all the Transcendentalists, including the Brook Farmers. It is true also that in his lecture he severely criticised Swedenborg; but this was his vocation: to judge and disparage all religious teachers, especially seers and thaumaturgists. On the whole he gave Swedenborg a lift, just as he helped the reputation of all "ethnic Scriptures." His criticism of Swedenborg amounts to about this: "He was a very great thinker and discoverer; but his visions and theological teachings are humbugs; still they are as good as any other, and rather better."

William H. Channing, another fertilizer of Brook Farm, was busy at the same time with Emerson, in the work of calling attention to Swedenborg. His conversions to Fourierism and Swedenborgianism seem to have proceeded together. The last three numbers of the *Present* are loaded with articles extolling Swedenborg, and the editor only complains of them that they "by no means do justice to the great Swedish philosopher and seer." The very last article in the volume is an item headed, "Fourier and Swedenborg," in which Mr. Channing says:

"I have great pleasure in announcing another work upon Fourier and his system, from the pen of C. J. Hempel. This book is a very curious and interesting one, from the attempt of the author to show the identity or at least the extraordinary resemblance between the views of Fourier and Swedenborg. How far Mr. Hempel has been successful I cannot pretend to judge. But this may be safely said, no one can examine with any care the writings of these two wonderful students of Providence, man and the universe, without having most sublime visions of divine order opened upon him. Their doctrine of Correspondence and Universal Unity accords with all the profoundest thought of the age."

Such were the influences under which Brook Farm assumed its final task of propagandism. Let us now see how far the coupling of Fourier and Swedenborg was kept up in the *Harbinger*.

The motto of the paper, displayed under its title from first to last, was selected from the writings of the Swedish seer. In the editors' inaugural address they say:

"In the words of the illustrious Swedenborg, which we have selected for the motto of the *Harbinger*, "All things, at the present day, stand provided and prepared, and await the light. The ship is in the harbor; the sails are swelling; the east wind blows; let us weigh anchor, and put forth to sea."

In a glancing run through the five semi-annual volumes of the *Harbinger* we find between thirty and forty articles on Swedenborg and Swedenborgian subjects, chiefly editorial reviews of books, pamphlets, etc., with a considerable amount of correspondence from Wilkinson, Doherty and other Swedenborgian Fourierists in England. The burden of all these articles is the same, viz., the unity of Swedenborgianism and Fourierism. On the one hand the Fourierists insist that Swedenborg revealed the religion that Fourier anticipated; and on the other the Swedenborgians insist that Fourier discovered the divine arrangement of society that Swedenborg foreshadowed. The reviews referred to were written chiefly by John S. Dwight and Charles A. Dana.* We will give a few specimens of their utterances :

[From Editorials by John S. Dwight.]

* * * "In religion we have Swedenborg; in social economy Fourier ; in music Beethoven.

* * * "Swedenborg we reverence for the greatness and profundity of his thought. We study him continually for the light he sheds on so many problems of human destiny, and more especially for the remarkable correspondence, as of inner with outer, which his revelations present with the discoveries of Fourier concerning social organization, or the outward forms of life. The one is the great poet and high-priest, the other the great

---

* Henry James also wrote many articles for the *Harbinger* in the interest of Swedenborg. His subsequent career as a promulgator of the Swedenborgian philosophy, in which he has even scaled the heights of the *North American Review*, is well known ; but perhaps it is not so well known that he commenced that career in the *Harbinger*. He has continued faithful to both Swedenborg and Fourier, to the present time.

economist, as it were, of the harmonic order, which all things are preparing.

* * * "Call not our praises of Swedenborg 'hollow;' if he offered us ten times as much which we could not assent to, it would not detract in the least from our reverence for the man, or our great indebtedness to his profoundly spiritual insight.

* * * "Deeper foundations for science have not been touched by any sounding-line as yet, than these same philosophical principles of Swedenborg. Fourier has not gone deeper; but he has shed more light on these deep foundations, taken their measurement with a more bold precision, and reared a no insignificant portion of the everlasting superstructure. But in their ground they are both one. Taken together they are the highest expression of the tendency of human thought to universal unity.

[From Editorials by Charles A. Dana.]

* * * "We recommend the writings of Swedenborg to our readers of all denominations, as we should recommend those of any other providential teacher. We believe that his mission is of the highest importance to the human family, and shall take every fit occasion to call the attention of the public to it.

* * * "No man of unsophisticated mind can read Swedenborg without feeling his life elevated into a higher plane, and his intellect excited into new and more reverent action on some of the sublimest questions which the human mind can approach. Whatever may be thought of the doctrines of Swedenborg or of his visions, the spirit which breathes from his works is pure and heavenly.

* * * "We do not hesitate to say that the publication and study of Swedenborg's scientific writings must produce a new era in human knowledge, and thus in society.

* * * " Though Swedenborg and Fourier differ in the character of their minds, and the immediate end of their studies, the method they adopted was fundamentally the same; their success is thus due, not to the vastness of their genius alone, but in a measure also to the instruments they employed. The logic of Fourier is imperfectly stated in his doctrine of the Series, of Universal Analogy, and of Attractions proportional to Destinies; that of Swedenborg in the incomplete and often very obscure and difficult expositions which appear here and there in his works, of the doctrine of Forms; of Order and Degrees; of Series and Society; of Influx; of Correspondence and Representation; and of Modification. This logic appears to have existed complete in the minds of neither of these great men; but even so much of it as they have communicated, puts into the hands of the student the most invaluable assistance, and attracts him to a path of thought in which the successful explorers will receive immortal honors from a grateful race.

* * * " The chief characteristic of this epoch is, its tendency, everywhere apparent, to unity in universality; and the men in whom this tendency is most fully expressed are Swedenborg, Fourier and Goethe. In these three eminent persons is summed up the great movement toward unity in universality, in religion, science and art, which comprise the whole domain of human activity. In speaking of Swedenborg as the teacher of this century in religion, some of the most obvious con-

siderations are his northern origin, his peculiar education, etc.

* * * "We say without hesitation, that, excepting the writings of Fourier, no scientific publications of the last fifty years are to be compared with [the Wilkinson edition of Swedenborg] in importance. To the student of philosophy, to the savan, and to the votary of social science, they are alike invaluable, almost indispensable. Whether we are inquiring for truth in the abstract, or looking beyond the aimlessness and contradictions of modern experimentalism in search of the guiding light of universal principles, or giving our constant thought to the laws of Divine Social Order, and the re-integration of the Collective Man, we can not spare the aid of this loving and beloved sage. His was a grand genius, nobly disciplined. In him, a devotion to truth almost awful, was tempered by an equal love of humanity and a supreme reverence for God. To his mind, the order of the universe and the play of its powers were never the objects of idle curiosity or of cold speculation. He entered into the retreats of nature and the occult abode of the soul, as the minister of humanity, and not as a curious explorer eager to add to his own store of wonders or to exercise his faculties in those difficult regions. No man had ever such sincerity, such absolute freedom from intellectual selfishness as he."

The reader, we trust, will take our word for it, that there is a very large amount of this sort of teaching in the volumes of the *Harbinger*. Even Mr. Ripley himself wielded a vigorous cudgel on behalf of Swedenborg against certain orthodox critics, and held the usual language of his socialistic brethren about the "sublime visions of the illustrious Swedish seer," his " bold poetic revelations," his "profound, living, electric principles," the "piercing truth of his productions," etc. Vide *Harbinger*, Vol. 3, p. 317.

On these and such evidences we came to the conclusion that the Brook Farmers, while they disclaimed for Fourierism all sectarian connections, did actually couple it with Swedenborgianism in their propagative labors; and as Fourierism soon failed and passed away, it turned out that their lasting work was the promulgation of Swedenborgianism ; which certainly has had a great run in this country ever since. It would not perhaps be fair to call Fourierism, as taught by the *Harbinger* writers, the stalking-horse of Swedenborgianism ; but it is not too much to say that their Fourierism, if it had lived, would have had Swedenborgianism for its state-religion. This view agrees with the fact that the only sectarian Association, avowed and tolerated in the Fourier epoch, was the Swedenborgian Phalanx at Leraysville.

The entire historical sequence which seems to be established by the facts now before us, may be stated thus : Unitarianism produced Transcendentalism ; Transcendentalism produced Brook Farm ; Brook Farm married and propagated Fourierism ; Fourierism had Swedenborgianism for its religion ; and Swedenborgianism led the way to Modern Spiritualism.

CHAPTER XLII.

THE END OF BROOK FARM.

It only remains to tell what we know of the causes that brought the Brook Farm Phalanx to its end.

Within a year from the time when it assumed the task of propagating Fourierism, i. e. on the 3d of March, 1846, a disastrous fire prostrated the energies and hopes of the Association. We copy from the *Harbinger* (March 14) the entire article reporting it:

"FIRE AT BROOK FARM.—Our readers have no doubt been informed before this, of the severe calamity with which the Brook Farm Association has been visited, by the destruction of the large unitary edifice which it has been for some time erecting on its domain. Just as our last paper was going through the press, on Tuesday evening the 3d inst., the alarm of fire was given at about a quarter before nine, and it was found to proceed from the 'Phalanstery;' in a few minutes the flames were bursting through the doors and windows of the second story; the fire spread with almost incredible rapidity throughout the building; and in about an hour and a-half the whole edifice was burned to the ground. The members of the Association were on the spot in a few moments, and made some attempts to save a quantity of lumber that was in the basement story; but so rapid was the progress of the fire, that this was found to be impossible, and they succeeded only in rescuing a couple of tool-chests that had been in use by the carpenters.

"The neighboring dwelling-house called the 'Eyry,' was in imminent danger while the fire was at its height, and nothing but the stillness of the night, and the vigilance and activity of those who were stationed on its roof, preserved it from destruction. The vigorous efforts of our nearest neighbors, Mr. T. J. Orange, and Messrs. Thomas and George Palmer, were of great service in protecting this building, as a part of our force were engaged in another direction, watching the work-shop, barn, and principal dwelling-house.

"In a short time our neighbors from the village of West Roxbury, a mile and a-half distant, arrived in great numbers with their engine, which together with the engines from Jamaica Plain, Newton, and Brookline, rendered valuable assistance in subduing the flaming ruins, although it was impossible to check the progress of the fire, until the building was completely destroyed. We are under the deepest obligations to the fire companies which came, some of them five or six miles, through deep snow on cross roads, and did every thing in the power of skill or energy, to preserve our other buildings from ruin. Many of the engines from Boston came four or five miles from the city, but finding the fire going down, returned without reaching the spot. The engines from Dedham, we understand, made an unsuccessful attempt to come to our aid, but were obliged to turn back on account of the condition of the roads. No efforts, however, would have probably been successful in arresting the progress of the flames. The building was divided into nearly a hundred rooms in the upper stories, most of which had been lathed for several months, without plaster, and being almost as dry as tinder, the fire flashed through them with terrific rapidity.

"There had been no work performed on this building during the winter months, and arrangements had just been made to complete four out of the fourteen distinct suites of apartments into which it was divided, by the first of May. It was hoped that the remainder would be finished during the summer, and that by the first of October, the edifice would be prepared for the reception of a hundred and fifty persons, with ample accommodations for families, and spacious and convenient public halls and saloons. A portion of the second story had been set apart for a church or chapel, which was to be finished, in a style of simplicity and elegance, by private subscription, and in which it was expected that religious services would be performed by our friend William H. Channing, whose presence with us, until obliged to retire on account of ill health, has been a source of unmingled satisfaction and benefit.

On the Saturday previous to the fire, a stove was put in the basement story for the accommodation of the carpenters, who were to work on the inside; a fire was kindled in it on Tuesday morning which burned till four o'clock in the afternoon; at half past eight in the evening, the building was visited by the night-watch, who found every thing apparently safe; and at a quarter before nine, a faint light was discovered in the second story, which was supposed at first to have proceeded from the lamp, but, on entering to ascertain the fact, the smoke at once showed that the interior was on fire. The alarm was immediately given, but almost before the people had time to assemble, the whole edifice was wrapped in flames. From a defect in the construction of the chimney, a spark from the stove-pipe had probbly communicated with the surrounding wood-work; and from the combustible nature of the materials, the flames spread with a celerity that made every effort to arrest their violence without effect.

" This edifice was commenced in the summer of 1844, and has been in progress from that time until November last, when the work was suspended for the winter, and resumed, as before stated, on the day in which it was consumed. It was built of wood, one hundred and seventy-five feet long, three stories high, with attics divided into pleasant and convenient rooms for single persons. The second and third stories were divided into fourteen houses independent of each other, with a parlor and three sleeping-rooms in each, connected by piazzas which ran the whole length of the building on both stories. The basement contained a large and commodious kitchen, a dining-hall capable of seating from three to four hundred persons, two public saloons, and a spacious hall or lecture-room. Although by no means a model for the Phalanstery or unitary edifice of a Phalanx, it was well adapted for our purposes at present, situated on a delightful eminence, which commanded a most extensive and picturesque view, and affording accommodations and conveniences in the combined order, which in many respects would gratify even a fastidious taste. The actual expenditure upon the building, including the labor performed by the Association, amounted to about $7,000; and $3,000 more, it was estimated, would be sufficient for its completion. As it was not yet in use by the Association, and until the day of its destruction, not exposed to fire, no insurance had been effected. It was built by investments in our loan-stock, and the loss falls upon the holders of partnership-stock and the members of the Association.

"It is some alleviation of the great calamity which we have sustained, that it came upon us at this time rather than at a later period. The house was not endeared to us by any grateful recollections; the tender and hallowed associations of home had not yet begun to cluster around it; and although we looked upon it with joy and hope, as destined to occupy an important sphere in the social movement to which it was consecrated, its destruction does not rend asunder those sacred ties which bind us to the dwellings that have thus far been the scene of our toils and of our satisfactions. We could not part with either of the houses in which we have lived at Brook Farm, without a sadness like that which we should feel at the departure of a bosom friend. The destruction of our edifice makes no essential change in our pursuits. It leaves no family destitute of a home; it disturbs no domestic arrangements; it puts us to no immediate inconvenience. The morning after the disaster, if a stranger had not seen the smoking pile of ruins, he would not have suspected that any thing extraordinary had taken place. Our schools were attended as usual; our industry in full operation; and not a look or expression of despondency could have been perceived. The calamity is felt to be great; we do not attempt to conceal from ourselves its consequences; but it has been met with a calmness and high trust, which gives us a new proof of the power of associated life to quicken the best elements of character, and to prepare men for every emergency.

"We shall be pardoned for entering into these almost

personal details, for we know that the numerous friends of Association in every part of our land, will feel our misfortune as if it were a private grief of their own. We have received nothing but expressions of the most generous sympathy from every quarter, even from those who might be supposed to take the least interest in our purposes ; and we are sure that our friends in the cause of social unity will share with us the affliction that has visited a branch of their own fraternity.

"We have no wish to keep out of sight the magnitude of our loss. In our present infant state, it is a severe trial of our strength. We can not now calculate its ultimate effect. It may prove more than we are able to bear ; or like other previous calamities, it may serve to bind us more closely to each other, and to the holy cause to which we are devoted. We await the result with calm hope, sustained by our faith in the universal Providence, whose social laws we have endeavored to ascertain and embody in our daily lives.

"It may not be improper to state, as we are speaking of our own affairs more fully than we have felt at liberty to do before in the columns of our paper, that, whatever be our trials of an external character, we have every reason to rejoice in the internal condition of our Association. For the last few months it has more nearly than ever approached the idea of a true social order. The greatest harmony prevails among us ; not a discordant note is heard ; a spirit of friendship, of brotherly kindness, of charity, dwells with us and blesses us ; our social resources have been greatly multiplied ; and our devotion to the cause which has brought us together, receives new strength every day. Whatever may be in reserve for us, we have an infinite satisfaction in the true relations which have united us, and the assurance that our enterprise has sprung from a desire to obey the Divine law. We feel assured that no outward disappointment or calamity can chill our zeal for the realization of a Divine order of society, or abate our effort in the sphere which may be pointed out by our best judgment as most favorable to the cause which we have at heart."

In the next number of the *Harbinger* (March 21), an editorial addressed to the friends of Brook Farm, indicated some depression and uncertainty. The following are extracts from it :

" We do not altogether agree with our friends, in the importance which they attach to the special movement at Brook Farm ; we have never professed to be able to represent the idea of Association with the scanty resources at our command ; nor would the discontinuance of our establishment or of any of the partial attempts which are now in progress, in the slightest degree weaken our faith in the associative system, or our conviction that it will sooner or later be adopted as the only form of society suited to the nature of man and in accordance with the Divine will. We have never attempted any thing more than to prepare the way for Association, by demonstrating some of the leading ideas on which the theory is founded ; in this we have had the most gratifying success ; but we have always regarded ourselves only as the humble pioneers in the work, which would be carried on by others to its magnificent consummation, and have been content to wait and toil for the development of the cause and the completion of our hope.

"Still we have established a center of influence here for the associative movement, which we shall spare no effort to sustain. We are fully aware of the importance of this ; and nothing but the most inexorable necessity, will withdraw the congenial spirits that are gathered in social union here, from the work which has always called forth their most earnest devotedness and enthusiasm. Since our disaster occurred, there has not been an expression or symptom of despondency among our number ; all are resolute and calm ; determined to stand by each other and by the cause ; ready to encounter still greater sacrifices than have as yet been demanded of them ; and desirous only to adopt the course which may be presented by the clearest dictates of duty. The loss which we have sustained occasions us no immediate inconvenience, does not interfere with any of our present operations ; although it is a total destruction of resources on which we had confidently relied, and must inevitably derange our plans for the enlargement of the Association and the extension of our industry. We have a firm and cheerful hope, however, of being able to do much for the illustration of the cause with the materials that remain. They are far too valuable to be dispersed, or applied to any other object ; and with favorable circumstances will be able to accomplish much for the realization of social unity."

This fire was a disaster from which Brook Farm never recovered. The organization lingered, and the *Harbinger* continued to be published there, till October 1847 ; but the hope of becoming a model Phalanx died out long before that time. The *Harbinger* is very reticent in relation to the details of the dissolution. We can only give the reader the following scraps hinting at the end :

[From the New York *Tribune* (August, 1847), in answer to an allegation in the New York *Observer* that "the Brook Farm Association, which was near Boston, had wound up its affairs some time since."]

"The Brook Farm Association not only was, but is near Boston, and the *Harbinger* is still published from its press. But, having been started without capital, experience or industrial capacity, without reference to or knowledge of Fourier's or any other systematic plan of Association, on a most unfavorable locality, bought at a high price, and constantly under mortgage, this Association is about to dissolve, when the paper will be removed to this city, with the master-spirits of Brook Farm as editors. The *Observer* will have ample opportunity to judge how far experience has modified their convictions or impaired their energies."

[From a report of a Boston Convention of Associationists, in the *Harbinger*, October 23, 1847.]

"The breaking up of the life at Brook Farm was frequently alluded to, especially by Mr. Ripley, who, on the eve of entering a new sphere of labor for the same great cause, appeared in all his indomitable strength and cheerfulness, triumphant amid outward failure. The owls and bats and other birds of ill omen which utter their oracles in leading political and sectarian religious journals, and which are busily croaking and screeching of the downfall of Association, had they been present at this meeting, could their weak eyes have borne so much light, would never again have coupled failure with the thought of such men, nor entertained a feeling other than of envy of experience like theirs."

The next number of the *Harbinger* (October 30, 1847) announced that that paper would in future be published in New York under the editorial charge of

Parke Godwin, assisted by George Ripley and Charles A. Dana in New York, and William H. Channing and John S. Dwight in Boston. This of course implied the dispersion of the Brook Farmers, and the dissolution of the Association; and this is all we know about it.

The years 1846 and 1847 were fatal to most of the Fourier experiments. Horace Greeley, under date of July 1847, wrote to the *People's Journal* the following account of what may be called,

Fourierism reduced to a Forlorn Hope.

"As to the Associationists (by their adversaries termed 'Fourierites'), with whom I am proud to be numbered, their beginnings are yet too recent to justify me in asking for their history any considerable space in your columns. Briefly, however, the first that was heard in this country of Fourier and his views (beyond a little circle of perhaps a hundred persons in two or three of our large cities, who had picked up some notion of them in France or from French writings), was in 1840, when Albert Brisbane published his first synopsis of Fourier's theory of industrial and household Association. Since then, the subject has been considerably discussed, and several attempts of some sort have been made to actualize Fourier's ideas, generally by men destitute alike of capacity, public confidence, energy and means. In only one instance that I have heard of was the land paid for on which the enterprise commenced; not one of these vaunted 'Fourier Associations' ever had the means of erecting a proper dwelling for so many as three hundred people, even if the land had been given them. Of course, the time for paying the first installment on the mortgage covering their land has generally witnessed the dissipation of their sanguine dreams. Yet there are at least three of these embryo Associations still in existence; and, as each of these is in its third or fourth year, they may be supposed to give some promise of vitality. They are the North American Phalanx, near Leedsville, New Jersey; the Trumbull Phalanx, near Braceville, Ohio; and the Wisconsin Phalanx, Ceresco, Wisconsin. Each of these has a considerable domain nearly or wholly paid for, is improving the soil, increasing its annual products, and establishing some branches of manufactures. Each, though far enough from being a perfect Association, is animated with the hope of becoming one, as rapidly as experience, time and means will allow."

Of the three Phalanxes thus mentioned as the rear-guard of Fourierism, one—the Trumbull—disappeared about four months afterward (very nearly at the time of the dispersion of Brook Farm), and another—the Wisconsin—lasted only a year longer, leaving the North American alone for the last four years of its existence.

Brook Farm in its function of propagandist (which is always expensive and exhausting at the best), must have been sadly depressed by the failures that crowded upon it in its last days; and it is not to be wondered that it died with its children and kindred.

If we might suggest a transcendental reason for the failure of Brook Farm, we should say that it had naturally a *delicate constitution*, that was liable to be shattered by disasters and sympathies; and the causes of this weakness must be sought for in the character of the afflatus that organized it. The transcendental afflatus, like that of Pentecost, had in it two elements, viz., Communism, and "the gift of tongues;" or in other words, the tendency to religious and social unity, represented by Channing and Ripley; and the tendency to literature, represented by Emerson and Margaret Fuller. But the proportion of these elements was different from that of Pentecost. *The tendency to utterance was the strongest.* Emerson prevailed over Channing even in Brook Farm; nay, in Channing himself, and in Ripley, Dana and all the rest of the Brook Farm leaders. In fact they went over from practical Communism to literary utterance when they assumed the propagandism of Fourierism; and utterance has been their vocation ever since. A similar phenomenon occurred in the history of the great literary trio of England, Coleridge, Wordsworth and Southey. Their original afflatus carried them to the verge of Communism; but "their gift of tongues" prevailed and spoiled them. And the tendency to literature, as represented by Emerson, is the farthest opposite of Communism, finding its *summum bonum* in individualism and incoherent instead of organic inspiration.

The end of Brook Farm was virtually the end of Fourierism. One or two Phalanxes lingered afterward, and the *Harbinger*, was continued a year or two in New York; but the enthusiasm of victory and hope was gone; and the Brook Farm leaders, as soon as a proper transition could be effected, passed into the service of the *Tribune*.

During the fatal year following the fire at Brook Farm, the famous controversy between Greeley and Raymond took place, which we have mentioned as Greeley's last battle in defense of retreating Fourierism. It commenced on the 20th of November, 1846, and ended on the 20th of May, 1847, each of the combatants delivering twelve well-shotted articles in their respective papers, the *Tribune* and the *Courier and Enquirer*, which were afterward published together in pamphlet-form by the Harpers. Parton, in his biography of Greeley, says at the beginning of his report of that discussion, " It *finished* Fourierism in the United States ;" and again at the close—" Thus ended Fourierism. Thenceforth the *Tribune* alluded to the subject occasionally, but only in reply to those who sought to make political or personal capital by reviving it."

CHAPTER XLIII.

THE SPIRITUALIST COMMUNITIES.

WE proposed at the beginning to trace the history of the Owen and Fourier movements, as comprising the substance of American Socialisms. After reaching the terminus of this course, it is still proper to avail ourselves of the station we have reached, to take a birdseye view of things beyond.

We must must not, however, wander from our subject. CO-OPERATION is the present theme of enthusiasm in the *Tribune,* and among many of the old representatives of Fourierism. But Co-operation is not Socialism. It is a very interesting subject, and doubtless will have its history ; but it does not belong to our programme. Its place is among the *preparations* of Socialism. It is not to be classed with Owenism, Fourierism and Shakerism ; but with Insurance, Saving's Banks and Protective Unions. It is not even the offspring of the theoretical Socialisms, but rather a product of general common sense and experiment among the working classes. It is the application of the principle of combination to the business of buying and distributing goods ; whereas Socialism proper is the application of that principle to domestic arrangements, and requires at the lowest, local gatherings and combinations of homes. If the old

Socialists have turned aside or gone back to Co-operation, it is because they have lost their original faith, and
like the Israelites that came out of Egypt, are wandering their forty years in the wilderness, instead of entering the promised land in three days, as they expected.

We do not believe that the American people have
lost sight of the great hope which Owen and Fourier
set before them, or will be contented with any thing
less than unity of interests carried into all the affairs of
life. Co-operation as one of the preparations for this
unity, is interesting them at the present time, in the
absence of any promising scheme of real Socialism.
But they are interested in it rather as a movement
among the oppressed operatives of Europe, where nothing higher can be attempted, than as a consummation
worthy of the progress that has commenced in Young
America.

Our present business as historians of American
Socialisms, is not with Co-operation, but with experiments in actual Association which have occurred since
the downfall of Fourierism.

The terminus we have reached is 1847, the year of
Brook Farm's decease. Since then " Modern Spiritualism" has been the great American excitement. And it
is interesting to observe that all the Socialisms that we
have surveyed, sent streams (if they did not altogether
debouch) into this gulf. It is well known that Robert
Owen in his last days was converted to Spiritualism, and
transferred all he could of his socialistic stock to that
interest. His successor, Robert Dale Owen, has not
carried forward the communistic schemes of his father,
but has been the busy patron of Spiritualism. Several
other indirect but important *anastomoses* of Owenism

with Spiritualism may be traced ; one, through Josiah Warren and his school of Individual Sovereignty at Modern Times, where Nichols and Andrews developed the germ of spiritualistic free-love ; another (curiously enough), through Elder Evans of New Lebanon, who was originally an Owen man, and now may be said to be a common center of Shakerism, Owenism and Spiritualism. In his auto-biographical articles in the *Atlantic Monthly* he maintained that Shakerism was the actual mother of Spiritualism, and had the first run of the " manifestations," that afterwards were called the " Rochester rappings." And lastly, Fourierism, by its marriage with Swedenborgianism at Brook Farm, and in many other ways, gave its strength to Spiritualism.

It is a point of history worth noting here, that Mr. Brisbane is mentioned in the introduction to Andrew Jackson Davis's Revelations, as one of the witnesses of the *seances* in which that work was uttered. C. W. Webber, a spiritualistic expert, in the introduction to his story of "Spiritual Vampirism," refers to this conjunction of Fourierism with Spiritualism, as follows :

" No man, who has kept himself informed of the psychological history and progress of his race, can by any means fail to recognize at once, in the pretended 'revelations' of Davis, the mere *disjecta membra* of the systems so extensively promulgated by Fourier and Swedenborg. Davis, during the whole period of his 'utterings,' was surrounded by groups, consisting of the disciples of Fourier and Swedenborg ; as, for instance, the leading Fourierite of America [Mr. Brisbane] was, for a time, a constant attendant upon those mysterious meetings, at which the myths of innocent Davis were formally announced from the condition of clairvoyance, and transcribed by his keeper, for the press ; while the chief exponent and minister of Swedenborgianism in New York [George Bush] was often seated side by side with him. Can it be possible that these men failed to comprehend, as thought after thought, principle after principle, was enunciated in their presence, which they had previously supposed to belong exclusively to their own schools, that the 'revelation' was merely a sympathetic reflex of their own derived systems? It was no accident; for, as often as Fourierism predominated in 'the evening lecture,' it was sure that the prime representative of Fourier was present; and when the peculiar views of Swedenborg prevailed, it was equally certain that he was forcibly represented in the conclave. Sometimes both schools were present; and on those identical occasions we have a composite system of metaphysics promulgated, which exhibited, most consistently, the doctrines of Swedenborg and Fourier, jumbled in liberal and extraordinary confusion."

As might be expected, Spiritualism has taken something from each of the Socialisms which have emptied into it. It is obvious enough that it has the omnivorous marvelousness of the Shakers, combined with the infidelity of the Owenites. But probably the world knows little of the tendency to socialistic speculation and experiment which it has inherited from all three of its confluents. It has had very little success in its local attempts at Association; and this has been owing chiefly to the superior tenacity of its devotion to the great antagonist of Association, Individual Sovereignty, which devotion also it inherited specially from Owen through Warren, and generally from both the Owen and Fourier schools. In consequence of its never having been able to produce more than very short-lived abortions of Communities, its Socialisms have not attracted much attention; but it has been continually speculating and scheming about Association, and its attempts on all sorts of plans ranging between Owenism and Fourierism, with inspiration superadded, have been almost numberless.

One of the first of these spiritualistic attempts, and probably a favorable specimen of the whole, was the Mountain Cove Community. Having applied in vain for information, to several persons who had the best opportunity to know about this Community, we must content ourselves with a very imperfect sketch, obtained chiefly from statements and references furnished by Macdonald, and from documents in the files of the Oneida *Circular*.

All the witnesses we have found, testify that this Community was set on foot by the rapping spirits in a large circle of Spiritualists at Auburn, New York, sometime between the years 1851 and 1853. It appears to have had active constituents at Oneida, Verona, and other places in Oneida and Madison Counties. Several of the leading "New York Perfectionists" in those places were conspicuous in the preliminary proceedings, and some of them actually joined the emigration to Virginia. The first reference to the movement that we have found, is in a letter from Mr. H. N. Leet, published in the *Circular*, November 16, 1851. He says:

"The 'rappings' have attracted my attention. I have scarcely known whether I should have to consider them as wholly of earth, or regard them as from Hades; or even be 'sucked in' with the other old Perfectionists.

The reports I hear from abroad are wonderful, and some of them well calculated to make men exclaim, ' This is the great power of God!' But what I see and hear partakes largely of the ridiculous, if not the contemptible. They have had frequent meetings at the houses of Messrs. Warren, Foot, Gould, Stone, Mrs. Hitchcock, etc.; and 'a chiel's amang them them taking notes;' but whether he will 'prent 'em' or or not, is uncertain. I have from time to time been writing out what facts have come under my observation, and do so yet.

"Yesterday in their meeting, I heard extracts of letters from Mr. Hitchcock written from Virginia; in which he states that they have found the garden of Eden, the identical spot where our first parents sinned, and on which no human foot has trod since Adam and Eve were driven out; that himself, Ira S. Hitchcock, was the first who has been permitted to set his foot upon it; and further, that in all the convulsions of nature, the upheavings and depressions, this spot has remained undisturbed as it originally appeared. This is the spot that is to form the center in the redemption now at hand; and parts adjacent are, by convulsions and a reverse process, to be restored to their primeval state. This is the substance of what I heard read. The revelation was said to have been spelled out to them by raps from Paul."

In a subsequent letter published in the *Circular* December 14, 1851, Mr. Leete sent us the spiritual document which summoned the saints to Mountain Cove, introducing it as follows:

"I send inclosed an authentic copy of a printed circular, said to have been received by Mr. Scott, the spiritual leader of the Virginia movement, in this manner, viz.: the words were seen in a vision, printed in space, one at a time, declared off by him, and written down by some one else."

Mountain Cove Circular.

"Go! Scarcely let time intervene. Escape the vales of death. Pass from beneath the cloud of magnetic human glory. Flee to the mountains whither I direct. Rest in their embrace, and in a place fashioned and appointed of old. There the dark cloud of magnetic death has never rested. For I, the Lord, have thus decreed, and in my purpose have I sworn, and it shall come to pass. Time waiteth for no man.

"For above the power of sin a storm is gathering that shall sweep away the refuge of lies. Come out of her, O, my people! for their sun shall be darkened, and their moon turned into blood, and their stars shall fall from their heaven. The Samson of strength feeleth for the pillars of the temple. Her foundation already moveth. Her ruin stayeth for the rescue of my people.

"The city of refuge is builded as a hiding place and a shelter; as the shadow of a great rock in a weary land; as an asylum for the afflicted; a safety for those fleeing from the power of sin which pursueth to destroy. In that mountain my people shall rest secure. Above it the cloud of glory descendeth. Thence it encompasseth the saints. There angels shall ascend and descend. There the soul shall feast and be satisfied. There is the bread and the water of life. 'And in this mountain shall the Lord of hosts make unto all people a feast of fat things, a feast of wines on the lees, of fat things full of marrow, of wines on the lees well refined. And he will destroy in this mountain the face of the covering cast over all people, and the vail that is spread over all nations. He will swallow up death in victory ; and the Lord God will wipe away tears from off all faces ; and the rebuke of his people shall he take away from off all the earth; for the Lord hath spoken it.' And I will defend Zion, for she is my chosen. There shall the redeemed descend. There shall my people be made one. There shall the glory of the Lord appear, descending from the tabernacle of the Most High.

"The end is not yet.

" You are the chosen. Go, bear the reproaches of my people. Go without the camp. Lead in the conquest. Vanquish the foe. As ye have been bidden, meekly obey. Paradise hath no need of the things that ye love so dearly. For earthly apparel, if obedient, ye shall have garments of righteousness and salvation. For earthly treasures, ye shall gather grapage from your Maker's throne. For tears, ye shall have jewels, as dewdrops from heaven. For sighs, notes of celestial melody. For death, ye shall have life. For sorrow, ye shall have fulness of joy. Cease, then, your earthly struggle. All ye love or value, ye shall still possess. Earth is departing. The powers and imaginations of men are rolling together like a scroll. Escape the wreck ere it leaps into the abyss of woe. Forget not each other. Bear with each other. Love each other. Go forth as lambs to the slaughter. For lo, thy King cometh, and ere thou art slain he shall defend. Kiss the rod that smites thee, and bow chastened at thy Maker's throne."

Here occurs a long break in our information, extending from December 1851, to July 1853. How the Community was established and what progress it made in that interval, the reader must imagine for himself. Our leap is from the beginning to near the end. The *Spiritual Telegraph* of July 2, 1853, contained the following :

"MOUNTAIN COVE COMMUNITY.—We copy below an article from the *Journal of Progress*, published in New York. It is from the pen of Mr. Hyatt, who was for a time a member of the Community at Mountain Cove. Mr. Hyatt is a conscientious man, and is still a firm believer in a rational Spiritualism. We have never regarded the claims of Messrs. Scott and Harris with favor, though we have thought and still think, that the motives and life of the latter were always honorable and pure. There are other persons at the Mountain who are justly esteemed for their virtues ; but we most sincerely believe they are deluded by the absurd pretensions of Mr. Scott."

[From the *Journal of Progress*.]

"Most of our readers are undoubtedly aware that there is a company of Spiritualists now residing at Mountain Cove, Virginia, whose claims of spiritual intercourse are of a somewhat different nature from those usually put forth by believers in other parts of the country.

"This movement grew out of a large circle of Spiritualists at Auburn, New York, nearly two years since; but the pretensions on the part of the prime movers became of a far more imposing nature than they were in Auburn, soon after their location at Mountain Cove. It is claimed that they were directed to the place which they now occupy, by God, in fulfillment of certain prophecies in Isaiah, for the purpose of redeeming all who would co-operate with them and be dictated by

their counsel; and the place which they occupy is denominated 'the Holy Mountain, which was sanctified
and set apart for the redemption of his people.'

"The principal mediums, James L. Scott and Thomas
L. Harris, profess absolute Divine inspiration, and entire infallibility; that the infinite God communicates
with them directly, without intermediate agency; and
that by him they are preserved from the possibility of
error in any of their dictations which claim a spiritual
origin.

"By virtue of these assumptions, and claiming to be
the words of God, all the principles and rules of practice, whether of a spiritual or temporal nature, which
govern the believers in that place, are dictated by the
individuals above mentioned.   Among the communications thus received, which are usually in the form of
arbitrary decrees, are requirements which positively
forbid those who have once formed a belief in the
divinity of the movement, the privilege of criticising, or
in any degree reasoning upon, the orders and communications uttered; or in other words, the disciples are
forbidden the privilege of having any reason or conscience at all, except that which is prescribed to them
by this oracle.   The most unlimited demands of the
controlling intelligence must be acceded to by its followers, or they will be thrust without the pale of the
claimed Divine influence, and utter and irretrievable
ruin is announced as the penalty.

"In keeping with such pretensions, these 'Matthiases'
have claimed for God his own property; and hence men
are required to yield up their stewardships: that is, relinquish their temporal possessions to the Almighty.
And, in pursuance of this, there has been a large

quantity of land in that vicinity deeded without reserve by conscientious believers, to the human vicegerents of God above mentioned, with the understanding that such conveyance is virtually made to the Deity !

"As would inevitably be the case, this mode of operations has awakened in the minds of the more reasoning and reflective members, distrust and unbelief, which has caused some, with great pecuniary loss, to withdraw from the Community, and with others who remain, has ripened into disaffection and violent opposition ; and the present condition of the ' Holy Mountain' is anything but that of divine harmony. Discord, slander and vindictiveness is the order of proceedings, in which one or both of the professed inspired mediators take an active part ; and the prospect now is, that the claims of divine authority in the temporal matters of 'the Mountain,' will soon be tested, and the ruling power conceded to be absolute, or else completely dethroned."

After the above, came the following counter-statement in the *Spiritual Telegraph*, August 6, 1853 :

Cincinnati, July 14, 1853.

"MR. S. B. BRITTAN—Sir : A friend has handed me the *Telegraph* of July 2, and directed my attention to an article appearing in that number, headed 'Mountain Cove Community,' which, although purporting to be from the pen of one familiar with our circumstances at the Cove, differs widely from the facts in our case.

"Suffice it for the present to say, that Messrs. Scott and Harris, either jointly or individually, for themselves, or as the 'human vicegerents of God,' have and hold no deed (as the article quoted from the *Journal of Progress* represents) of lands at the Cove. Neither have they pecuniary supporters there. Nor are men residing there required or expected to deal with them upon terms aside from the ordinary rules of business transactions. They have no claims upon men there for temporal benefits. They exact no tithes, or even any degree of compensation for public services; and, although they have preached and lectured to the people there during their sojourn in that country, they have never received for such services a penny; and, except what they have received from a few liberal friends who reside in other portions of the country, they secure their temporal means by their own industry. Moreover, for land and dwellings occupied by them, they are obligated to pay rent or lease-money; and should they at any time obtain a deed, according to present written agreement, they are to pay the full value to those who are the owners of the soil and by virtue thereof still retain their stewardship.

"I have thus briefly stated facts; facts of which I should have an unbiassed knowledge, and of which I ought to be a competent judge. These facts I have ample means to authenticate, and together with a full and explicit statement of the nature of the lease, when due the public, if ever, I shall not hesitate to give. And from these the reader may determine the character of the entire expose, so liberally indorsed, as also other statements so freely trumpeted, relative to us at Mountain Cove.

"From some years of the most intimate intercourse with the Rev. T. L. Harris, surrounded by circumstances calculated to try men's souls, I am prepared to bear testimony to your statements relative to his goodness and purity; and will add, that were all men of like character, earth would enjoy a saving change, and that right speedily.

" Assured that your sense of right will secure for this brief statement, equal notoriety with the charges pre-ferred against us—hence a place in the columns of the *Telegraph*;   I am, &c,   J. L. SCOTT."

This counter-statement has the air of special pleading, and all the information that we have obtained by com-munication with various ex-members of the Mountain Cove Community, goes to confirm the substance of the preceding charges. The following extracts from a letter in reply to some of our questions, is a specimen :

" There were indications in the acts of one or more individuals at Mountain Cove, that plainly showed their desire to get control of the possessions which other indi-viduals had saved as the fruits of their industry and economy. Those evil designs were frustrated by those who were the intended victims of the crafty, though not without some pecuniary sacrifice to the innocent.

From all this we infer that the Mountain Cove Com-munity came to its end in the latter part of 1853, by a quarrel about property ; which is all we know about it.

This was the most noted of the Spiritualist Com-munities. The rest are not noticed by Macdonald, and, so far as we know, hardly deserve mention.

CHAPTER XLIV.

THE BROCTON COMMUNITY.

WE are forbidden to class this Association with the Spiritualist Communities, by a positive disclaimer on the part of its founders : as the reader will see further on. Otherwise we should have said that the Brocton Community is the last of the series which commenced at Mountain Cove. Thomas L. Harris, the leader at Brocton, was also one of the two leaders at Mountain Cove, and as Swedenborgianism, his present faith, is certainly a species of Spiritualism, not altogether unrelated to the more popular kind which he held in the times of Mountain Cove, we can not be far wrong in counting the Brocton Community as one of the *sequelæ* of Fourierism, and in the true line of succession from Brook Farm.

After the bad failure of non-religious Socialism in the Owen experiments, and the worse failure of semi-religious Socialism in the Fourier experiments, a lesson seems to have been learned, and a tendency has come on, to lay the foundations of socialistic architecture in some kind of Spiritualism, equivalent to religion. This tendency commenced, as we have seen, among the Brook Farmers, who promulgated Swedenborgianism almost as zealously as they did Fourierism. The same tendency is seen in the history of the Owens, father and son. Thus, it is evident that the entire Spiritualistic platform has been pushed forward by a large part of its constituency, as a hopeful basis of future Socialisms. And the Brocton Community seems to be the final product and representative of this tendency to union between Spiritualism and Socialism.

As Mr Harris and Mr. Oliphant, the two conspicuous men at Brocton, are both Englishmen, we might almost class that Community with the exotics, which do not properly come into our history. But the close connection of Brocton with the Spiritualistic movement, and the general interest it has excited in this country, on the whole entitle it to a place in the records of American Socialisms. The following account is compiled from a brilliant report in the *New York Sun* of April 30, 1869, written by Oliver Dyer:

History and Description of the Brocton Community.

" Nine miles beyond Dunkirk, on the southerly shore of Lake Erie, in the village of Brocton, New York, is a Community which, in some respects, and especially as to the central idea around which the members gather, is probably without a parallel in the annals of mankind.

"The founder of this Community is the Rev. Thomas Lake Harris, an Englishman by birth, but whose parents came to this country when he was three years old. He was for several years a noted preacher of the Universalist denomination in New York. Subsequently he went to England, where he had a noticeable career as a preacher of strange doctrines. Between five and six years ago he returned to this country, and settled in

Amenia, Duchess County, where he prospered as a banker and agriculturist, until in October, 1867, he (as he claims), in obedience to the direct leadings of God's spirit, took up his abode at his present residence in Chautauqua County, on the southerly shore of Lake Erie, and founded the Brocton Community.

"The tract of land owned and occupied by the Community, comprises a little over sixteen hundred acres, and is about two and a-half miles long, by one mile in breadth. One-half of this tract was purchased by Mr. Harris with his own money; the residue was purchased with the money of his associates. and at their request is held by him in trust for the Community. The main building on the premises (for there are several residences) is a low, two-story edifice straggling over much ground.

"A deep valley runs through the estate, and along the bed of the valley winds a copious creek, on the northerly bank of which, at a well-selected site, stands a saw-mill, [the inevitable !] which seems to have constant use for all its teeth.

" The land for the most part lies warm to the sun, and its quality and position are such that it does not require under-draining, which is a great advantage. It is bountifully supplied with wood and water and is variegated in surface and in soil.

"About eighty acres are in grapes, of several varieties, among which are the Concord, Isabella, Salem, Iona, Rogers's Hybrid and others. They expect much from their grapes. The intention is to strive for quality rather than quantity, and to run principally to table fruit of an excellence which will command the highest prices.

"It is the intention of the Community to go extensively into the dairy business, and considerable progress has already been made in that direction. Other industrial matters are also being driven ahead with skill and vigor; but a large portion of the estate has yet to be brought under cultivation, and there is a deal of hard work to be done to make the 1,600 acres presentable, and to secure comfortable homes for the workers.

"There are about sixty adult members of the Community, besides a number of children. Among the rest are five orthodox clergymen; several representatives from Japan; several American ladies of high social position and exquisite culture, etc.

"But the members who attract the most attention, at least of the newspaper world, are Lady Oliphant and her son, Lawrence Oliphant, who are understood to be exiles from high places in the aristocracy of England.

All these work together on terms of entire equality, and all are very harmonious in religion, notwithstanding their previous diversity of position and faith.

"This is a very religious Community. Swedenborg furnishes the original doctrinal and philosophical basis of its faith, to which Mr. Harris, as he conceives, has been led by Providence to add other and vital matters, which were unknown until they were revealed through him. They reverence the Scriptures as the very word of God.

"The fundamental religious belief of the Community may be summed up in the dogma, that there is one God and only one, and that he is the Lord Jesus Christ. The religion of the Community is intensely practical, and may be stated as, faith in Christ, and a life in accordance with his commandments.

"And here comes in the question, What is a life in accordance with Christ's commandments ? Mr. Harris and his fellow believers hold that when a man is 'born of the Spirit,' he is inevitably drawn into communal relations with his brethren, in accordance with the declaration that 'the disciples were of one heart and one mind, and had all things in common.'

"This doctrine of Communism has been held by myriads, and repeated attempts have been made, but made in vain, to embody it in actual life. It is natural, therefore, to distrust any new attempt in the same direction. Mr. Harris is aware of this general distrust, and of the reasons for it ; but he claims that he has something which places his attempt beyond the vicissitudes of chance, and bases it upon immutable certainty ; that hitherto there has been no palpable criterion whereby the existence of God could be tested, no tangible test whereby the indication of his will could be determined ; but that such criterion and test have now been vouchsafed, and that on such criterion and test to him communicated, his Community is founded.

"The pivot on which this movement turns, the foundation on which it rests, the grand secret of the whole matter, is known in the Community as 'open respiration,' also as 'divine respiration ;' and the starting point of the theory is, that God created man in his own image and likeness, and breathed into him the breath of life. That the breathing into man of the breath of life was the sensible point of contact between the divine and human, between God and man. That man in his holy state was, so to speak, directly connected with God, by means of what might be likened to a spiritual respiratory umbilical chord, which ran from God to man's inmost or celestial nature, and constantly suffused him with airs from heaven, whereby his spiritual respiration or life was supported, and his entire nature, physical as well as spiritual, kept in a state of godlike purity and innocence, without, however, any infringement of man's freedom.

"That after the fall of man this spiritual respiratory connection between God and man was severed, and the spiritual intercourse between the Creator and the creature brought to an end, and hence spiritual death. That the great point is to have this respiratory connection with God restored. That Mr. Harris and those who are co-operating with him have had it restored, and are in the constant enjoyment thereof. That it is by this divine respiration, and by no other means, that a human being can get irrefragable, tangible, satisfactory evidence that God is God, and that man has or can have conjunction with God. This divine respiration retains all that is of the natural respiration as its base and fulcrum, and builds upon and employs it for its service.

"In the new respiration, God gives an atmosphere that is as sensitive to moral quality as the physical respiration is to natural quality; and this higher breath, whose essence is virtue, builds up the bodies of the virtuous, wars against disease, expels the virus of hereditary maladies, renews health from its foundations, and stands in the body as a sentinel against every plague. When this spiritual respiration descends and takes possession of the frame, there is thenceforth a guiding power, a positive inspiration, which selects the recipient's calling, which trains him for it, which leads him to favorable localities, and which co-ordinates affairs on a large scale. It will deal with groups as with individuals;

it will re-distribute mankind ; it will re-organize the village, the town, the workshop, the manufactory, the agricultural district, the pastoral region, gathering human atoms from their degradation, and crystallizing them in resplendent unities.

"This primary doctrine has for its accompaniment a special theory of love and marriage, which is this: In heaven the basis of social order is marital order, and so it must be in this world. There, all the senses are completed and included in the sense of chastity ; that sense of chastity is there the body for the soul of conjugal desire ; there, the corporeal element of passion is excluded from the nuptial senses : there, the utterly pure alone are permitted to enter into the divine state involved in nuptial union; and so it must be here below. The 'sense of chastity' is the touchstone of conjugal fitness, and is bestowed in this wise:

"When the Divine breaths have so pervaded the nervous structures that the higher attributes of sensation begin to waken from their immemorial torpor, and to react against disease, a sixth sense is as evident as hearing is to the ear, or sight to vision. It is distributed through the entire frame. So exquisitely does it pervade the hands that the slightest touch declares who are chaste and who are unchaste. And this sixth sense is the sense of chastity. It comes from God, who is the infinite chastity.

"Within this sense of chastity nuptial love has its dwelling-place. So utterly hostile is it by nature to what the world understands by desire and passion, that the waftings of an atmosphere bearing these elements in its bosom affect it with loathing. This sense of chastity literally clothes every nerve. A living, sensitive garment, without spot or seam, it invests the frame of the universal sensations, and gives instant warning of the approach of impurity even in thought.

"In true nuptial love, which is born of love to God, the nuptial pair, from the inmost oneness of the divine being, are embosomed each in each, as loveliness in loveliness, innocence in innocence, blessedness in blessedness. In possessing each other they possess the Lord, who prepares the two to become one heart, one mind, one soul, one love, one wisdom, one felicity. There are ladies and gentlemen in the Community who claim to have attained this sense of chastity to such a degree that they instantly detect the presence of an impure person.

"It may surprise the reader to hear that what is called 'Spiritualism' finds no favor in this Community. All phases of the spirit-rapping business are abhorred.

"A cardinal principle of government, as to their own affairs in the Community, is unity of conviction. The Council of Direction consists of nineteen members; and if any one of them fails to perceive the propriety of a course or plan agreed upon by the other eighteen, it is accepted as an indication of Providence that the time for carrying out the course or plan has not yet come; and they patiently wait until the entire Council becomes 'of one heart and one mind' as to the matter proposed.

"They do not hunger for proselytes, nor seek public recognition. They know that the spirit is the great matter; and that an enterprise, as well as a human being, or a tree, must grow from the internal, vital principle, and not from external agglomerations. Whosoever, therefore, applies for admission to their circle is subject to crucial spiritual tests and a revealing probation. Unconditional surrender to God's will, absolute chastity not only in act but in spirit, complete self-abnegation, a full acceptance of Christ as the only and true God, are fundamental conditions even to a probationship.

"Painting, sculpture, music and all the accomplishments are to have fitting development. There is no Quakerism or Puritanism in them. Man (including woman) is to be developed liberally, thoroughly, grandly, but all in the name of the Lord, and with an eye single to God's glory. Science, art, literature, languages, mechanics, philosophy, whatever will help to give back to man his lost mastership of the universe, is to be subordinated for that purpose.

" Their domestic affairs, including cooking and washing, are carried on much as in the outside world. They live in many mansions, and have no unitary household. But they are alive to all the teachings of science and sociology on these topics, and intend to make machinery and organization do as much of the drudgery of the Community as possible.

" They have no peculiar costume or customs. They eat, drink, dress, converse and worship God just like cultivated Christians elsewhere. They have no regular preaching at present, nor literary entertainments, but all these are to come in due season. They intend, as their numbers increase, and as the organization solidifies, to inaugurate whatever institutions may be necessary to promote their intellectual and spiritual welfare, and also to establish such industries and manufactures on the domain, as sound, economical discretion, vivified and guided by the new respiration, shall dictate.

"By means of the new respiration they think that, in the lapse of time, mankind will become regenerate, and society be reconstructed, and physical disease banished from the earth, and a millennial reign inaugurated under the domination of Divine order. They especially expect great things in the East; that the doctrine of the Lord, as set forth by Swedenborg and Mr. Harris, and re-inforced by the new respiration, will by and by sweep over Asia, where the people are already beginning to be tossed on the waves of spiritual unrest, and are longing for a higher religious development."

After this luminous introduction, Mr. Dana, the editor of the *Sun*, followed with the article ensuing:

"WILL IT SUCCEED?

"The account which we published yesterday, from the accomplished pen of Mr. Oliver Dyer, of the new Community in Chautauqua County, which Mr. Harris, Mr. Oliphant and their associates are engaged in founding, will, we think, excite attention everywhere. Considered as a religious movement alone, the enterprise merits a candid and even sympathetic attention. Its fundamental ideas are such as must promote thought and inquiry wherever they are promulgated. That they are all true, as a matter of theological doctrine, we certainly are not prepared to affirm; but that they challenge a respectful interest in the minds of all sincere inquirers after spiritual truth, can not be disputed. But it is not as a new form of Christianity, with new dogmas and new pretensions, that we have to deal with the system proclaimed at Brocton. What especially engages our observation is the social aspect of the undertaking. Is it founded upon notions that promise any considerable advance upon the present form of society ? Does it contain within itself the elements of success ?

" As respects the first question, we are free to answer that the scheme of the Brocton philosophers is too little developed, too immature in their own minds, to allow of any dogmatic judgment respecting it. The religious phase of the Community, and the enthusiasm which belongs to it, have not yet crystallized in relations of industry, art, education and external life, sufficiently to show the precise end at which it will aim. Indeed it would seem that its founders have avoided rather than cultivated those speculations on the organization of society to which most social innovators give the first place in their thoughts. Starting from man's highest spiritual nature alone, they prefer to leave every practical problem to be solved as it rises, not by scientific theory or business shrewdness, but by the help of that supernatural inspiration which forms a vital point in their theology. But on the other hand, they are pledged to democratic equality, to perfect respect for the dignity of labor, and to brotherly justice in the distribution alike of the advantages of life and the earnings of the common toil. We may conclude, then, that despite the Communism which seems to lie at the foundation of their design, with its annihilation of individual property, and its tendency to annihilate individual character also, all persons who can adopt the religion of this Community will find a happier life within its precincts than they can look for elsewhere. But that it will initiate a new stage in the world's social progress, or exercise any perceptible influence upon the general condition of mankind, is not to be expected.

" As to the probability of its lasting, that seems to us

to be strong. Communities based upon peculiar religious views, have generally succeeded. The Shakers and the Oneida Community are conspicuous illustrations of this fact ; while the failure of the various attempts made by the disciples of Fourier, Owen and others, who have not had the support of religious fanaticism, proves that without this great force the most brilliant social theories are of little avail. Have the Brocton people enough of it to carry them safely through ? Or is their religion of too transcendental a character to form a sure and tenacious cement for their social structure ? These questions only time can positively answer ; but we incline to the belief that they are likely to live and prosper, to become numerous and wealthy, and to play a much more influential part in the world than either of the bodies of religious Socialists that have preceded them."

The reader will perhaps expect us to say something from our stand-point, in answer to Mr. Dana's question, "Will it succeed?" and as the name of the Oneida Community is called in connection with the Shakers and the Broctonians, it seems proper that we should do what we can to help on a fair comparison of these competing Socialisms.

In the first place, many of the cardinal principles reported in Mr. Dyer's account, command our highest respect and sympathy. Religion as the basis, inspiration as the guide, Providence as the insurer, reverence for the Bible, Communism of property, unanimity in action, abstinence from proselytism, self-improvement instead of preaching and publicity, liberality of culture in science, art, literature, language, mechanics, philosophy, and whatever will help to give back man his lost mastership of the universe, these and many other of the fundamentals at Brocton we recognize as old acquaintances and very dear friends. With this acknowledgment premised, we will be free to point out some things which we regard as unpromising weaknesses in the constitution of the new Socialism.

The Brocton Community is evidently very religious, and so far may be regarded as strong in the first element of success. Its religion, however, is Swedenborgianism, revised and adapted to the age, but not essentially changed; and we have seen that the experiments in Socialism which Swedenborgians have heretofore made, have not been successful. The Yellow Spring Community in Owen's time, and the Leraysville Phalanx in the Fourier epoch, were avowedly Swedenborgian Associations; but they failed as speedily and utterly as their contemporaries. Notwithstanding the claim of a wonderful affinity between Swedenborgianism and Fourierism which the *Harbinger* used to make, it seems probable that the afflatus of pure Swedenborgianism is not favorable to Communism or to close Association of any kind. Swedenborg in his personal character was not a Socialist or an organizer in any way, but a very solitary speculator; and the heavens he set before the world were only sublimated embodiments of the ordinary principle of private property, in wives and in every thing else.

When we say that the Brocton Community is Swedenborgian, we do not forget that Mr. Harris professes to have made important additions to the Teutonic revelations. But we see that the fundamental doctrines reported by Mr. Dyer are essentially the same as those we have found in Swedenborg's works. Even the pivotal discovery of "internal respiration" is not original with Mr. Harris. Swedenborg had it in theory and in personal experience. He ascribes the purity of the Adamic church to this condition, and its degeneracy and destruction, to the loss of it. Thus he says:

"It was shown me, that [at the time of the degeneracy of the Adamites] the internal respiration, which proceeded from the navel toward the interior region of the breast, retired toward the region of the back and toward the abdomen, thus outward and downward. Immediately before the flood scarce any internal respiration existed. At last it was annihilated in the breast, and its subjects were choked or suffocated. In those who survived, external respiration was opened. With the cessation of internal respiration, immediate intercourse with angels and the instant and instinctive perception of truth and falsehood, were lost."

And Mr. White, the latest biographer of Swedenborg, says of him:

"The possession by him of the power of easy transition of sense and consciousness from the lower to the upper world, arose, it would appear, from some peculiarities in his physical organization. The suspension of respiration under deep thought, common to all men, was preternaturally developed in him; and in his diary he makes a variety of observations on his case; as for instance he says:

"'My respiration has been so formed by the Lord, as to enable me to breathe inwardly for a long time without the aid of the external air, my respiration being directed within, and my outward senses, as well as actions, still continuing in their vigor, which is only possible with persons who have been so formed by the Lord. I have also been instructed that my breathing was so directed, without my being aware of it, in order to enable me to be with spirits, and to speak with them.'

" Again, he tells us that there are many species of respirations inducing divers introductions to the spirits and angels with whom the lungs conspire ; and goes on to say, that he was at first habituated to insensible breathing in his infancy, when at morning and evening prayers, and occasionally afterward when exploring the concordance between the heart, lungs and brain, and particularly when writing his physiological works ; that for a number of years, beginning with his childhood, he was introduced to internal respiration mainly by intense speculations in which breathing stops, for otherwise intense thought is impossible. When heaven was open to him, and he spoke with spirits, sometimes for nearly an hour he scarcely breathed at all. The same phenomena occurred when he was going to sleep, and he thinks that his preparation went forward during repose. So various was his breathing, so obedient did it become, that he thereby obtained the range of the higher world, and access to all its spheres."

Thus it would seem that what Mr. Harris is attempting at Brocton is, to realize on a large scale the experience of Swedenborg, and reproduce the Adamic church. This "open respiration," however, must be an oracular influx not essentially different from that which guides the Shakers, the Ebenezers, and all the religious Communities. We have called it afflatus. It does not appear to be strong enough in the Brocton Community to dissolve old-fashioned familism ; which we consider a bad sign, as our readers know. There is an inevitable competition between the family-spirit and the Community-spirit, which all the "internal respiration" that we have enjoyed, has never been able to harmonize in any other way than by thoroughly subordinating family interests, and making the Community the prime organization. And it is quite certain that this has been the experience of the Shakers and all the other successful Communities. Indeed this is the very revolution that is involved in real Christianity. The private family has been and is the unit of society in naturalism, i. e. in the pre-Christian, pagan state. But the Church, which is equivalent to the Association, or Community, or Phalanx, is clearly the unit of society in the Christian scheme.

The Brocton philosophy of love and marriage is manifestly Swedenborgian. In some passages it seems like actual Shakerism, but the prevailing sense is that of intensified conjugality, *a la* Swedenborg. Here again the Swedenborgian afflatus will be very unfavorable to success. Swedenborg wrote in the same vein as Mr. Harris talks, about chastity; but withal he kept mistresses at several times in his life; and he recommends mistress-keeping to those who "can not contain." Moreover he gives married men thirty-four reasons, many of them very trivial, for keeping concubines. Above all, his theory of marriage in heaven, involving the sentimentalism of predestined mating (which doubtless is retained entire in the Brocton philosophy), not only leads directly to contempt of ordinary marriage, as being an artificial system of blunders, but necessarily authorizes the "right of search" to find the true mate. The practical result of this theory is seen in the system of "free love," or experimenting for "affinities," which has prevailed among Spiritualists. It will require a very high power of "internal respiration" to steer the Brocton Community through these dangers, resulting from its affiliation with the Swedenborgian principality. Close Association is a worse place than ordinary society for working out the delicate problems of the negative theory of chastity.

The Broctonians are reported as reverencing the Bible, but this can only mean that they reverence it in Swedenborg's fashion. He rejected about half of it (including all of Paul's writings) as uninspired ; and worshiped the rest as full of divinity, stuffed in every letter and dot with double and triple significance, of which significance he alone had the key.

Probably Mr. Harris's principal deviation from the Swedenborgian theology, is the introduction of his original faith of Universalism. Swedenborg lived and wrote before modern benevolence was developed so far as to require the elimination of future punishment ; and with all his laxity on other points, he was more orthodox and uncompromising in regard to the eternity of hell-torments, and even as to their sulphuric nature, than any writer the world has ever seen before or since. Hence the Spiritualists, who generally belong to the Universalist school, either have to quarrel with Swedenborg openly, as Andrew Jackson Davis did, or modify his system on this point, as T. L. Harris has done.

We were surprised, as Mr. Dyer supposes his readers might be, to learn that the Brocton Communists abhor "all phases of the rapping business ; " for we remember that Mr. Harris was counted among Spiritualists in old times, and we see that he is still in pursuit of the

Adamic status and other attainments that were the objective points of the Mountain Cove Community.

As to externals, the Brocton Community, we fear, has got the land-mania, which ruined so many of the Owen and Fourier Associations. Sixteen hundred acres must be a dreary investment for a young and small Community. If our experience is worth any thing, and if we might offer our advice, we should say, Sell two-thirds of that domain and put the proceeds into a machine-shop. Agriculture, after all, is not a primary business. Machinery goes before it; always did and always will more and more. Plows and harrows, rakes and hoes, were the dynamics even of ancient farming; and the men that invented and made them were greater than farmers. The Oneida Community made its fortune by first sinking forty thousand dollars in training a set of young men as machinists. The business thus started has proved to be literally a high school in comparison with farming or almost any other business, not excepting that of academies and colleges. With that school always growing in strength and enthusiasm, we can make the tools for all other businesses, and the whole range of modern enterprise is open to us.

If the Brocton leaders have plenty of money at interest, we see no reason why they may not live pleasantly and do well in some form of loose co-operation. But with the weaknesses we have noticed, we doubt whether their "internal respiration" will harmonize them in close Association, or enable them to get their living by amateur farming.

CHAPTER XLV.

THE SHAKERS.

We should hardly do justice to the Shakers if we should leave them undistinguished among the obscure exotics. Their influence on American Socialisms has been so great as to set them entirely apart from the other antique religious Communities. Macdonald makes more of them than of any other single Community, devoting nearly a hundred pages to their history and peculiarities. Most of his material relating to them, however, may be found in their own current publications ; and need not be reproduced here. But there is one document in his collection giving an "inside view" of their social and religious life, which we are inclined to publish for special reasons. It is, in the first place, a picture of their daily routine, as faithful as could be expected from one who appears to have been neither a friend nor an enemy to them ; and its representations in this respect are verified substantially by various Shaker publications. But it is specially interesting to us as a disclosure of the historical secret which connects Shakerism with "modern Spiritualism." Elder Evans, the conspicuous man of the Shakers, in his late autobiography alludes to this secret in the following terms :

"In 1837 to 1844, there was an influx from the spirit world, confirming the faith of many disciples, who had lived among believers for years, and extending through-out all the eighteen [Shaker] societies, making media by the dozen, whose various exercises, not to be suppressed even in their public meetings, rendered it imperatively necessary to close them all to the world during a period of seven years, in consequence of the then unprepared state of the world, to which the whole of the manifesta-tions, and the meetings too, would have been as unadul-terated foolishness, or as inexplicable mysteries.

"The spirits then declared, again and again, that, when they had done their work among the inhabitants of Zion, they would do a work in the world, of such magnitude, that not a place nor a hamlet upon earth should remain unvisited by them.

"After their mission among us was finished, we supposed that the manifestations would immediately begin in the outside world ; but we were much disap-pointed ; for we had to wait four years before the work began, as it finally did, at Rochester, New York. But the rapidity of its course throughout the nations of the earth (as also the social standing and intellectual importance of the converts), has far exceeded the predictions."   —*Atlantic Monthly*, May, 1869.

The narrative we are about to present relates to the period of closed doors here mentioned, and to some of the "manifestations" which had to be withdrawn from public view, lest they should be regarded as "unadulter-ated foolishness." It is perhaps the only testimony the world has in regard to the events which, according to Evans, were the real beginnings of modern Spiritualism.

Macdonald does not give the name of the writer, but says that he was an "intimate and esteemed friend, who went among the Shakers partly to escape worldly troubles, and partly through curiosity; and that his story is evidently clear-headed and sincere."

Four Months Among the Shakers.

"Circumstances that need not be rehearsed, induced me to visit the Shaker Society at Watervliet, in the winter of 1842—3. Soon after my arrival, I was conducted to the Elder whose business it was to deal with inquirers. He was a good-looking old man, with a fine open countenance, and a well-formed head, as I could see from its being bald. I found him very intelligent, and soon made known to him my business, which was to learn something about the Shakers and their conditions of receiving members. On my observing that I had seen favorable accounts of their society in the writings of Mr. Owen, Miss Martineau, and other travelers in the United States, he replied, that 'those who wished to know the Shakers, must live with them;' and this remark proved to be true. He propounded to me at considerable length their faith, 'the daily cross' they were obliged to take up against the devil and the flesh, and the supreme virtue of a life of celibacy. When he had concluded I asked if those who wished to join the society were expected to acknowledge a belief in all the articles of their faith? To which he replied, 'that they were not, for many persons came there to join them, who had never heard their gospel preached; but they were always received, and an opportunity given them of ac-

cepting or rejecting it.' He then informed me of the
conditions under which they received candidates : ' All
new comers have one week's trial, to see how they like ;
and after that, if they wish to continue they must take up
the daily cross, and commence the work of regeneration
and salvation, following in the footsteps of Jesus Christ
and Mother Ann.' My first cross, he informed me,
would be to confess all the wicked acts I had ever committed. I asked him if he gave absolution like a Catholic priest. He replied, ' that God forgave sins and not
they ; but it was necessary in beginning the work of
salvation, to unburden the mind of all its past sins.' I
thought this confession (demanded of strangers) was a
piece of good policy on their part ; for it enabled the
Elder who received the confession, to form a tolerable
opinion of the individual to be admitted. I agreed
however before confession to make a week's trial of the
place, and was accordingly invited to supper ; after
which I was shown to the sleeping room specially set
apart for new members. I was not left here more than
an hour when a small bell rang, and one of the brothers
entered the room and invited me to go to the family
meeting ; where I saw for the first time their mode of
worshiping God in the dance. I thought it was an
exciting exercise, and I should have been more pleased
if they had had instrumental, instead of vocal music.

"At first my meals were brought to me in my room,
but after a few days I was invited to commence the
work of regeneration and prepare for confession, that I
might associate with the rest of the brothers. On
making known my readiness to confess, I was taken to
the private confession-room, and there recounted a brief
history of my past life. This appeared rather to please

the Elder, and he observed that I 'had not been very wicked.' I replied, 'No, I had not abounded in acts of crime and debauchery.' But the old man, to make sure I was not deceiving him, tried to frighten me, by telling me of individuals who had not made a full confession of their wickedness, and who could find no peace or pleasure until they came back and revealed all. He assured me moreover that no wicked person could continue there long without being found out. I was curious to know how such persons would be detected; so he took me to the window and pointed out the places where 'Mother Ann' had stationed four angels to watch over her children; and 'these angels,' he said, 'always communicated any wickedness done there, or the presence of any wicked person among them.' 'But,' he continued, 'you can not understand these things; neither can you believe them, for you have not yet got faith enough.' I replied: 'I can not see the angels!' 'No,' said he, 'I can not see them with the eye of sense; but I can see them with the eye of faith. You must labor for faith: and when any thing troubles you that you can not understand or believe, come to me, and do not express doubts to any of the brethren.' The Elder then put on my eyes a pair of spiritual golden spectacles, to make me see spiritual things. I instinctively put up my hands to feel them, which made the old gentleman half laugh, and he said, 'Oh, you can not feel them; they will not incommode you, but will help you to see spiritual things.'

"After this I was permitted to eat with the family and invited to attend their love-meetings. I was informed that I had perfect liberty to leave the village whenever I chose to do so; but that I was to receive no pay for my services if I were to leave; I should be provided for, the same as if I were one of the oldest members, with food, clothing and lodgings, according to their rules.

DAILY ROUTINE.

"The hours of rising were five o'clock in the summer, and half-past five in the winter. The family all rose at the toll of the bell, and in less than ten minutes vacated the bed-rooms. The sisters then distributed themselves throughout the rooms, and made up all the beds, putting every thing in the most perfect order before breakfast. The brothers proceeded to their various employments, and made a commencement for the day. The cows were milked, and the horses were fed. At seven o'clock the bell rang for breakfast, but it was ten minutes after when we went to the tables. The brothers and sisters assembled each by themselves, in rooms appointed for the purpose; and at the sound of a small bell the doors of these rooms opened, and a procession of the family was formed in the hall, each individual being in his or her proper place, as they would be at table. The brothers came first, followed by the sisters, and the whole marched in solemn silence to the dining-room. The brothers and sisters took separate tables, on opposite sides of the room. All stood up until each one had arrived at his or her proper place, and then at a signal from the Elder at the head of the table, they all knelt down for about two minutes, and at another signal they all arose and commenced eating their breakfast. Each individual helped himself; which was easily done, as the tables were so arranged that between every four persons there was a supply of every article intended for the meal. At the conclusion they all arose and marched away from the tables in the same manner as they marched to them; and during the time of marching, eating, and re-marching, not one word was spoken, but the most perfect silence was preserved.

"After breakfast all proceeded immediately to their respective employments, and continued industriously occupied until ten minutes to twelve o'clock, when the bell announced dinner. Farmers then left the field and mechanics their shops, all washed their hands, and formed procession again, and marched to dinner in the same way as to breakfast. Immediately after dinner they went to work again, (having no hour for resting), and continued steady at it until the bell announced supper. At supper the same routine was gone through as at the other meals, and all except the farmers went to work again. The farmers were supposed to be doing what were called 'chores,' which appeared to mean any little odd jobs in and about the stables and barns. At eight o'clock all work was ended for the day, and the family went to what they called a 'union meeting.' This meeting generally continued one hour, and then, at about nine o'clock, all retired to bed."

UNION MEETINGS.

"The two Elders and the two Eldresses held their meetings in the Elders' room. The three Deacons and the three Deaconesses met in one of their rooms. The rest of the family, in groups of from six to eight brothers and sisters, met in other rooms. At these meetings it was customary for the seats to be arranged in two rows about four feet apart. The sisters sat in one row, and the brothers in the other, facing each other. The meetings were rather dull, as the members had nothing to converse about save the family affairs; for those who troubled themselves about the things of the world, were not considered good Shakers. It was expected that in coming there we should leave the 'world' behind us. The principal subject of conversation was eating and drinking. One brother sometimes eulogized a sister whom he thought to be the best cook, and who could make the best 'Johnny-cake.' At one meeting that I attended, there was a lively conversation about what we had for dinner; and by this means, it might be said, we enjoyed our dinner twice over.

"I have thus given the routine for one day; and each week-day throughout the year was the same. The only variation was in the evening. Besides these union meetings, every alternate evening was devoted to dancing. Sundays also had a routine of their own, which I will not detail.

"During the time I was with the Shakers, I never heard one of them read the Bible or pray in public. Each one was permitted to pray or let it alone as he pleased, and I believe there was very little praying among them. Believing as they did that all 'worldly things' should be left in the 'world' behind them, they did not even read the ordinary literature of the day. Newspapers were only for the use of the Elders and Deacons. The routine I have described was continually going on; and it was their boast that they were then the same in their habits and manners as they were sixty years before. The furniture of the dwellings was of the same old-fashioned kind that the early Dutch settlers used; and every thing about them and their dwellings, I was taught, was originally designed in heaven, and the designs transmitted to them by angels. The plan of their buildings, the style of their furniture, the pattern of their coats and pants, and the cut of their hair, is all regulated according to communications received from heaven by Mother Ann. I was gravely told by the first Elder, that the inhabitants of the other world were Shakers, and that they lived in Community the same as we did, but that they were more perfect.

THE DANCING MEETINGS.

" At half-past seven P. M. on the dancing days, all the members retired to their separate rooms, where they sat in solemn silence, just gazing at the stove, until the silver tones of a small tea-bell gave the signal for them to assemble in the large hall. Thither they proceeded in perfect order and solemn silence. Each had on thin dancing-shoes; and on entering the door of the hall they walked on tip-toe, and took up their positions as follows: the brothers formed a rank on the right, and the sisters on the left, facing each other, about five feet apart. After all were in their proper places the chief Elder stepped into the center of the space, and gave an exhortation for about five minutes, concluding with an invitation to them all to 'go forth, old men, young men and maidens, and worship God with all their might in the dance.' Accordingly they 'went forth,' the men stripping off their coats and remaining in their shirt-sleeves. First they formed a procession and marched around the room at double-quick time, while four brothers and four sisters stood in the center singing for them. After marching in this manner until they got a little warm, they commenced dancing, and continued it until they were all pretty well tired. During the dance the sisters kept on one side, and the brothers on the other, and not a a word was spoken by any of them. After they appeared to have had enough of this exercise, the Elder gave the signal to stop, when immediately each one took his or her place in an oblong circle formed around the room, and all waited to see if any one had received a 'gift,' that is, an inspiration to do something odd. Then two of the sisters would commence whirling round like a top, with their eyes shut; and continued this motion for about fifteen minutes; when they suddenly stopped and resumed their places, as steady as if they had never stirred. During the 'whirl' the members stood round like statues, looking on in solemn silence.

A MESSAGE FROM MOTHER ANN.

"On some occasions when a sister had stopped her whirling, she would say, 'I have a communication to make;' when the head Eldress would step to her side and receive the communication, and then make known the nature of it to the company. The first message I heard was as follows: 'Mother Ann has sent two angels to inform us that a tribe of Indians has been round here two days, and want the brothers and sisters to take them in. They are outside the building there, looking in at the windows.' I shall never forget how I looked round at the windows, expecting to see the yellow faces, when this announcement was made; but I believe some of the old folks who eyed me, bit their lips and smiled. It caused no alarm to the rest, but the first Elder exhorted the brothers 'to take in the poor spirits and assist them to get salvation.' He afterward repeated more of what the angels had said, viz., 'that the Indians were a savage tribe who had all died before Columbus discovered

America, and had been wandering about ever since. Mother Ann wanted them to be received into the meeting to-morrow night.' After this we dispersed to our separate bed-rooms, with the hope of having a future entertainment from the Indians.

INDIAN ORGIES.

" The next dancing night we again assembled in the same manner as before, and went through the marching and dancing as usual; after which the hall doors were opened, and the Elder invited the Indians to come in. The doors were soon shut again, and one of the sisters (the same who received the original communication) informed us that she saw Indians all around and among the brothers and sisters. The Elder then urged upon the members the duty of 'taking them in.' Whereupon eight or nine sisters became possessed of the spirits of Indian squaws, and about six of the brethren became Indians. Then ensued a regular pow-wow, with whooping and yelling and strange antics, such as would require a Dickens a describe. The sisters and brothers squatted down on the floor together, Indian fashion, and the Elders and Eldresses endeavored to keep them asunder, telling the men they must be separated from the squaws, and otherwise instructing them in the rules of Shakerism. Some of the Indians then wanted some 'succotash,' which was soon brought them from the kitchen in two wooden dishes, and placed on the floor; when they commenced eating it with their fingers. These performances continued till about ten o'clock; then the chief Elder requested the Indians to go away, telling them they would find some one waiting to conduct them to the Shakers in the heavenly world. At this announcement the possessed men and women became themselves again, and all retired to rest.

"The above was the first exhibition of the kind that I witnessed, but it was a very trifling affair to what I afterward saw. To enable you to understand these scenes, I must give you as near as I can, the ideas the Shakers have of the other world. As I gathered from conversations with the Elder, and from his teaching and preaching at the meetings, it is as follows : Heaven is a Shaker Community on a very large scale. Every thing in it is spiritual. Jesus Christ is the head Elder, and Mother Ann the head Eldress. The buildings are large and splendid, being all of white marble. There are large orchards with all kinds of fruit. There are also very large gardens laid out in splendid style, with beautiful rivers flowing through them ; but all is spiritual. Outside of this heaven the spirits of the departed wander about on the surface of the earth (which is the Shaker hell), till they are converted to Shakerism. Spirits are sent out from the aforesaid heaven on missionary tours, to preach to the wandering ones until they profess the faith, and then they are admitted into the heavenly Community.

SPIRITUAL PRESENTS.

"At one of the meetings, after a due amount of marching and dancing, by which all the members had got pretty well excited, two or three sisters commenced whirling, which they continued to do for some time, and then stopped suddenly and revealed to us that Mother Ann was present at the meeting, and that she had brought a dozen baskets of spiritual fruit for her children ; upon which the Elder invited all to go forth to the baskets in the center of the floor, and help themselves. Accordingly they all stepped forth and went through the various motions of taking fruit and eating it. You will wonder if I helped myself to the fruit, like the rest. No; I had not faith enough to see the baskets or the fruit; and you may think, perhaps, that I laughed at the scene; but in truth, I was so affected by the general gravity and the solemn faces I saw around me, that it was impossible for me to laugh.

"Other things as well as fruit were sometimes sent as presents, such as spiritual golden spectacles. These heavenly ornaments came in the same way as the fruit, and just as much could be seen of them. The first presents of this kind that were received during my residence there, came as follows: A sister whirled for some time; then stopped and informed the Eldress as usual that Mother Ann had sent a messenger with presents for some of her most faithful children. She then went through the action of handing the articles to the Eldress, at the same time mentioning what they were, and for whom. As near as I can remember, there was a pair of golden spectacles, a large eye-glass with a chain, and a casket of love for the Elder to distribute. The Eldress went through the act of putting the spectacles and chain upon the individuals they were intended for: and the Elder in like manner opened the casket and threw out the love by handsful, while all the members stretched out their hands to receive, and then pressed them to their bosoms. All this appeared to me very childish, and I could not help so expressing myself to the Elder, at the first opportunity that offered. He replied, 'that this was what he labored for, viz., to be a simple Shaker; that the proud and worldly, the so-called great men of this

world, must become as simple as they, as simple as little children, before they can enter the Kingdom of
Heaven.   They must suffer themselves to be called fools
for the Kingdom of Heaven's sake.   These were the
crosses they had to bear.'

"The Elder would sometimes kindly invite me to his
room and ask me what I thought of the meeting last
night.   This was generally after those meetings at
which there had been some great revelation from heaven,
or some pow-wow with the spirits.   I could only reply
that I was much astonished, and that these things were
altogether new to me.   He would then tell me that I
would see greater things than these.   But I replied that
it required more faith to believe them than I possessed.
Then he would exhort me to 'labor for faith, and I would
get it.   He did not expect young believers to get faith
all at once; although some got it faster than others.'

SPIRITUAL MUSIC AND BATHING.

"On the second Sunday I spent with the Shakers,
there was a curious exhibition, which I saw only once.
After dinner all the members assembled in the hall and
sang two songs; when the Elder informed them that it
was a 'gift for them to march in procession, with their
golden instruments playing as they marched, to the holy
fountain, and wash away all the stains that they had
contracted by sinful thoughts or feelings; for Mother
was pleased to see her children pure and holy.'   I looked
around for the musical instruments, but as they were
spiritual I could not see them.   The procession marched
two and two, into the yard and round the square, and
came to a halt in the center.   During the march each
one made a sound with the mouth, to please him or her-

self, and at the same time went through the motions of playing on some particular instrument, such as the Clarionet, French-horn, Trombone, Bass-drum, etc. ; and such a noise was made, that I felt as if I had got among a band of lunatics. It appeared to me much more of a burlesque overture than any I ever heard performed by Christy's Minstrels. The yard was covered with grass, and a stick marked the center of the fountain. Another song was sung, and the Elder pointed to the spiritual fountain, at the same time observing, 'it could only be seen by those who had sufficient faith.' Most of the brethren then commenced going through the motions of washing the face and hands ; but finally some of them tumbled themselves in all over; that is, they rolled on the grass, and went through many comical and fantastic capers. My room-mate, Mr. B., informed me that he had seen several such exhibitions during the time he had been living there.

A SHAKER FUNERAL.

"One of the sisters of a neighboring family died, and our family were notified to attend the funeral. On arriving at the place, we were shown into a room, and at a signal from a small bell, we were formed into a procession and marched to the large dancing-hall, at the entrance to which the corpse was laid out in a coffin, so as to be seen by all as they passed in. The company then formed in two grand divisions, the brothers on one side, and the sisters on the other, one division facing the other. The service commenced by singing ; after which the funeral sermon was preached by the Elder. He set forth in as forcible a manner as he seemed capable of, the uncertainty of life, the character of the deceased sister, what a true and faithful child of Mother's she was, and how many excellent qualities she possessed. The head Eldress also gave her testimony of praise to the deceased, alluding to her patience and resignation while sick, and her desire to die and go to Mother. After a little more singing one of the sisters announced that the spirit of the deceased was present, and that she desired to return her thanks to the various sisters who waited upon her while she was sick; and named the different individuals who had been kindest to her. She had seen Mother Ann in heaven, and had been introduced to the brothers and sisters, and she gave a flattering account of the happiness enjoyed in the other world. Another sister joined in and corroborated these statements, and gave about the same version of the message. After another song the coffin was closed, put into a sleigh, and conveyed to the grave, and buried without further ceremony.

A DAY OF SWEEPING AND SCRUBBING.

"An order was received from Mother Ann that a day should be set apart for purification. I had no information of this great solemnity until the previous evening, when the Elder announced that to-morrow would be observed as a day for general purification. 'The brothers must clean their respective work-shops, by sweeping the walls, and removing every cobweb from the corners and under their work-benches, and wash the floors clean by scrubbing them with sand. By doing this they would remove all the devils and wicked spirits that might be lodging in the different buildings; for where cobwebs and dust were permitted to accumulate, there the evil spirits hide themselves. Mother had sent a message that there were evil spirits lodging about ; and she wished them to be removed ; and also that those members who had committed any wickedness, should confess it, and thus make both outside and inside clean.'

"At early dawn next morning, the work commenced, and clean work was made in every building and room, from the grand hall down to the cow-house. At ten o'clock eight of the brothers, with the Elders at their head, commenced their journey of inspection through every field, garden, house, work-shop and pig-pen, chanting the following rhyme as they passed along :

' Awake from your slumbers, for the Lord of Hosts is going through the land !
He will sweep, He will clean his Holy Sanctuary !
Search ye your lamps ! read and understand !
For the Lord of Hosts holds the lamp in his hand ! '

A REVIVAL IN HADES.

"During my whole stay with the Shakers a revival was going on among the spirits in the invisible world. Information of it was first received by one of the families in Ohio, through a heavenly messenger. The news of the revival soon spread from Ohio to the families in New York and New England. It was caused as follows : George Washington and most of the Revolutionary fathers had, by some means, got converted, and were sent out on a mission to preach the gospel to the spirits who were wandering in darkness. Many of the wild Indian tribes were sent by them to the different Shaker Communities, to receive instruction in the gospel. One of the tribes came to Watervliet and was 'taken in,' as I have described.

"At one of the Sunday meetings, when the several families were met for worship, one of the brothers

declared himself possessed of the spirit of George
Washington; and made a speech informing us that
Napoleon and all his Generals were present at our meeting, together with many of his own officers, who fought
with him in the Revolution. These, as well as many
more distinguished personages, were all Shakers in the
other world, and had been sent to give information
relative to the revival now going on. In a few minutes
each of the persons present at the meeting, fell to representing some one of the great personages alluded to.

"This revival commenced when I first went there;
and during the four months I remained, much of the
members' time was spent in such performances. It
appeared to me, that whenever any of the brethren or
sisters wanted to have some fun, they got possessed of
spirits, and would go to cutting up capers; all of which
were tolerated even during the hours of labor, because
whatever they chose to do, was attributed to the spirits.
When they became affected they were conveyed to the
Elder's room; and sometimes he would have six or
seven of them at once. The sisters who gave vent to
their frolicsome feelings, were of course attended to by
the Eldress. I might occupy great space if I were to
go into the details of these spiritual performances; but
there was so much similarity in them, that I must ask
the reader to let the above suffice."

We have omitted many paragraphs of this narrative,
relating to matters generally known through Shaker
publications and others, and many personal details; our
principal object being to give a view of some of the
Shaker manifestations which seem to have been the
first stage of Modern Spiritualism.

The reader will notice that the date of these manifestations—the winter of 1842—3—coïncides with the focal period of the Fourier excitement (which, as we have seen, lapsed into Swedenborgianism, as that did into Spiritualism); also that, on the larger scale, the seven years of manifestations and closed doors designated by Evans, from 1837 to 1844, coïncide with the epoch of Transcendentalism. In the times of the *Dial* there was a noticeable liking for Shakerism among the Transcendentalists; and some of their leaders have lately shown signs of preferring Shakerism to Fourierism. We mention these coïncidences only as affording glimpses of connections and mysterious affinities, that we do not pretend to understand. Only we see that both forms of Socialism favored by the Transcendentalists—Shakerism and Fourierism—have contributed their whole volume to swell the flood of Spiritualism.

CHAPTER XLVI.

THE ONEIDA COMMUNITY.

LAST of all, we must venture a sketch of the Association in the bosom of which, this history has been written and printed.

The Oneida Community belongs to the class of religious Socialisms, and, so far as we know, is the only religious Community of American origin. Its founder and most of its members are descendants of New England Puritans, and were in early life converts and laborers in the Revivals of the Congregational and Presbyterian churches. As Unitarianism ripened into Transcendentalism at Boston, and Transcendentalism produced Brook Farm, so Orthodoxy ripened into Perfectionism at New Haven, and Perfectionism produced the Oneida Community.

The story of the founder and foundations of the Oneida Community, told in the fewest possible words, is this :

John Humphrey Noyes was born at Brattleboro, Vermont, in 1811. The great Finney Revival found him at twenty years of age, a college graduate, studying law, and sent him to study divinity, first at Andover and afterward at New Haven. Much study of the Bible, under the instructions of Moses Stuart, Edward Robinson and Nathaniel Taylor, and under the continued and increasing influence of the Revival afflatus, soon landed him in a new experience and new views of the way of salvation, which took the name of Perfectionism. This was in February, 1834. The next twelve years he spent in studying and teaching salvation from sin; chiefly at Putney, the residence of his father and family. Gradually a little school of believers gathered around him. His first permanent associates were his mother, two sisters, and a brother. Then came the wives of himself and his brother, and the husbands of his two sisters. Then came George Cragin and his family from New York, and from time to time other families and individuals from various places. They built a chapel, and devoted much of their time to study, and much of their means to printing. So far, however, they were not in form or theory Socialists, but only Revivalists. In fact, during the whole period of the Fourier excitement, though they read the *Harbinger* and the *Present* and watched the movement with great interest, they kept their position as simple believers in Christianity, and steadfastly criticised Fourierism. Nevertheless during these same years they were gradually and almost unconsciously evolving their own social theory, and preparing for the trial of it. Though they rejected Fourierism, they drank copiously of the spirit of the *Harbinger* and of the Socialists; and have always acknowledged that they received a great impulse from Brook Farm. Thus the Oneida Community really issued from a conjunction between the Revivalism of Orthodoxy and the Socialism of Unitarianism. In 1846, after the fire at Brook Farm, and when Fourierism was manifestly passing away, the little church at Putney began cautiously to experiment in Communism. In the fall of 1847, when Brook Farm was breaking up, the Putney Community was also breaking up, but in the agonies, not of death, but of birth. Putney conservatism expelled it, and a Perfectionist Community, just begun at Oneida under the influence of the Putney school, received it.

The story of the Community since it thus assumed its present name and form, has been told in various Annual Reports, Hand-books, and even in the newspapers and Encyclopædias, till it is in some sense public property. In the place of repeating it here, we will endeavor to give definite information on three points that are likely to be most interesting to the intelligent reader; viz: 1, the religious theory of the Community; 2, its social theory; and 3, its material results.

As the early experiences of the Community were of two kinds, religious and social, so each of these experiences produced a book. The religious book, called *The Berean*, was printed at Putney in 1847, and consisted mainly of articles published in the periodicals of the Putney school during the previous twelve years. The socialistic book, called *Bible Communism*, was published in 1848, a few months after the settlement at Oneida, and was the frankest possible disclosure of the theory of entire Communism, for which the Community was then under persecution. Both of these books have long been out of print. Our best way to give a faithful representation of the religious and social theories of the Community in the shortest form, will be, to rehearse the contents of these books.

Religious Theory.

has an invisible organization that is as substantial as his body.

XI. Animal Magnetism: showing that the phenomena of Mesmerism are as incredible as the Bible miracles.

XII. The Divine Nature: showing that God is dual, and that man, as male and female, is made in the image of God.

XIII. Creation: an act of God's faith.

XIV. The Origin of Evil: showing that Christ's theory was that evil comes from the Devil as good comes from God.

XV. The Parable of the Sower: illustrating the preceding doctrine.

XVI. Parentage of Sin and Holiness: illustrating the same doctrine.

XVII. The Cause and the Cure: showing that all diseases of body and soul are traceable to diabolical influence ; and that all rational medication and salvation must overcome this cause.

XVIII. The Atonement: showing that Christ, in the sacrifice of himself, destroyed the power of the Devil.

XIX. The Cross of Christ: Continuation of the preceding.

XX. Bread of Life: showing that the eucharist symbolizes actual participation in that flesh and blood of Christ " which came down from heaven."

XXI. The New Covenant: showing that a dispensation of grace commenced at the manifestation of Christ, entirely different from the preceding Jewish dispensation.

XXII. Salvation from Sin: showing that this was the special promise and gift of the new dispensation.

XXIII. Perfectionism: defining the term as referring to God's righteousness, and not self-righteousness.

XXIV. "He that Committeth Sin is of the Devil:"
showing that this means what it says.

XXV. Paul not Carnal: showing that he was an
actual example of salvation from sin.

XXVI. A Hint to Temperance Men: showing that
the common interpretation of the seventh chapter of
Romans, which refers the confession "When I would
do good evil is present with me," etc., to Christian
experience, exactly suits the drunkard, and is the
greatest obstacle to all reform.

XXVII. Paul's Views of Law: showing that while
he was a champion of the law as a standard of
righteousness, he had no faith in its power to secure its
own fulfillment, but believed in the grace of Christ as
the end of the law, saving men from sin, which the law
could not do.

XXVIII. Anti-Legality not Antinomianism: showing that the effectual government of God rules by grace
and truth, and in displacing the law, fulfils the law.

XXIX. Two Kinds of Antinomianism: showing that
the worst kind is that which cleaves to the law of
commandments, and neglects the law of the Spirit of
life.

XXX. The Second Birth: showing that this attainment includes salvation from sin, and was never experienced till the manifestation of Christ.

XXXI. The Two-Fold Nature of the Second Birth:
showing that the "water and spirit" which are the
elements of it, are not material water and air, but truth
and grace, or intellectual and spiritual influences.

XXXII. Two Classes of Believers: showing that

there were in the Primitive Church two distinct grades of experience: one that of the carnal believers, called *nepioi;* the other that of the regenerate, called *teleioi.*

XXXIII. The Spiritual Man : showing that a stable mind, a loving heart and an unquenchable desire of progress, are the characteristics of the *teleioi.*

XXXIV. Spiritual Puberty: illustrating regeneration by the change of life which takes place at natural puberty.

XXXV. The Power of Christ's Resurrection: showing that regeneration, i. e. salvation from sin, comes by faith in the resurrection of Christ, communicating to the believer the same power that raised Christ from the dead.

XXXVI. An Outline of all Experience: describing four grades, viz., 1, the natural state ; 2, the legal state ; 3, the spiritual state ; 4, the glorified state.

XXXVII. The Way into the Holiest: showing that the life given by Christ has opened new access to God.

XXXVIII. Christian Faith: showing how it differs from Jewish faith ; and how it is to be experienced.

XXXIX. Settlement with the Past: showing the Judaistic character of the experiences of popular modern saints, and appealing from them to the standards and examples of the Primitive Church.

XL. The Second Coming of Christ: showing that Christ predicted, and that the Primitive Church expected, this event to take place within one generation from his first coming ; that all the signs of its approach which Christ foretold, actually came to pass before the close of the apostolic age ; consequently that simple faith is compelled to affirm that he did come at the time appointed, and the mistake about the matter has not been in his predictions or the expectations of his disciples, but in the imaginations of the world as to the physical and public nature of the event.

XLI. A Criticism of Stuart's Commentary on Romans 13 : 11, and 2 Thessalonians 2 : 1—8 : showing that the premature excitement of the Thessalonians, instead of disproving the theory that the Second Advent was near at that time, confirms it.

XLII. "The Man of Sin:" showing that the diabolical power designated by this title, was already at work when the epistle to the Thessalonians was written ; that Paul himself was withstanding it ; and that on his departure it was fully manifested.

XLIII. A Criticism of Robinson's Commentary on the 24th and 25 chapters of Matthew: showing that the Second Coming is the theme of discourse from the 29th verse of the 24th chapter to the 31st of the 25th ; and that then the prophecy passes to the subsequent reign of Christ and the general judgment.

XLIV. A Criticism of the Rev. Messrs. Bush and Barnes's allegation that the Apostles were mistaken in their expectations of the Second Coming within their own lifetime.

XLV. Date of the Apocalypse: showing that it was written before the destruction of Jerusalem.

XLVI. Scope of the Apocalypse: showing that it relates to the same course of events as those predicted in the 24th and 25th of Matthew.

XLVII. The Dispensation of the Fullness of Times: showing that, as the Second Advent with the first resurrection and judgment took place at the end of the times of the Jews, so there is to be a second resurrection and final judgment at the end of the "times of the Gentiles," or in the "dispensation of the fullness of times."

XLVIII. The Millennium: showing that the period designated by this term is past.

XLIX. The Two Witnesses. L. The First Resurrection.

LI. A Criticism of Bush's Theory of the Resurrection.

LII. The Keys of Death and Hell. LIII. Objections Answered. The two last chapters are a continuation of the controversy with Bush.

LIV. Criticism of Ballou's Theory of the Resurrection.

LV. Connection of Regeneration with the Resurrection: showing that regeneration or salvation from sin is the incipient stage of the resurrection.

LVI. The Second Advent to the Soul: showing that there was an intermediate coming of Christ in the Holy Spirit, between his first personal coming and his second.

LVII. The Throne of David: showing that Christ became king of heaven and earth *de jure* and *de facto* at the end of the Jewish dispensation.

LVIII. The Birthright of Israel: showing that the Jews are, by God's perpetual covenant, the royal nation.

LIX. The Sabbath. LX. Baptism. LXI. Marriage.

LXII. Apostolical Succession: a criticism of the Oxford tracts.

LXIII. Puritan Puseyism. LXIV. Unity of the kingdom of God. LXV. Peace Principles.

LXVI. The Primary Reform: showing that salvation from sin is the foundation needed by all other reforms.

LXVII. Leadings of the Spirit: showing that true

inspiration does not make a man a fanatic or a puppet.

LXVIII. The Doctrine of Disunity: aimed against a theory that prevailed among Perfectionists, similar to Warren's Individual Sovereignty.

LXIX. Fiery Darts Quenched: showing that the failings and apostasies of Perfectionists are no argument against the doctrine of salvation from sin.

LXX. The Love of Life: showing that the anxiety about the body that is encouraged by doctors and hygienists, is the central lust of the flesh.

LXXI. Abolition of Death: to come in this world, as the last result of Christ's victory over sin and the Devil.

LXXII. Condensation of Life: showing that the unity for which Christ prayed in John 17: 21—23, is to be the element of the good time coming, reconstructing all things and abolishing Death.

LXXIII. Principalities and Powers: referring all our experience to the invisible hosts that are contending over us.

LXXIV. Our Relations to the Primitive Church: showing that the original organization instituted by Christ and the apostles, is accessible to us, and that our main business as reformers is, to open communication with that heavenly body.

Social Theory.

[Leading propositions of *Bible Communism* slightly condensed.]

CHAPTER I.—*Showing what is properly to be anticipated concerning the coming of the Kingdom of Heaven and its institutions on earth.*

PROPOSITION 1.—The Bible predicts the coming of the Kingdom of Heaven on earth. Dan. 2: 44. Isa. 25: 6–9.

2.—The administration of the will of God in his kingdom on earth, will be the same as the administration of his will in heaven. Matt. 6: 10. Eph. 1: 10.

3.—In heaven God reigns over body, soul, and estate, without interference from human governments. Dan. 2: 44. 1 Cor. 15: 24, 25. Isa. 26: 13, 14, and 33: 22.

4.—The institutions of the Kingdom of Heaven are of such a nature, that the general disclosure of them in the apostolic age would have been inconsistent with the continuance of the institutions of the world through the times of the Gentiles. They were not, therefore, brought out in detail on the surface of the Bible, but were disclosed verbally by Paul and others, to the interior part of the church. 1 Cor. 2: 6. 2 Cor. 12: 4. John 16: 12, 13. Heb. 9: 5.

CHAPTER II.—*Showing that Marriage is not an institution of the Kingdom of Heaven, and must give place to Communism.*

PROPOSITION 5.—In the Kingdom of Heaven, the institution of marriage, which assigns the exclusive possession of one woman to one man, does not exist. Matt. 22: 23—30.

6.—In the Kingdom of Heaven the intimate union of life and interest, which in the world is limited to pairs, extends through the whole body of believers; i. e. complex marriage takes the place of simple. John 17: 21. Christ prayed that all believers might be one, even as he and the Father are one. His unity with the Father is defined in the words, "All mine are thine, and all thine are mine." Ver. 10. This perfect community of interests, then, will be the condition of all, when his prayer is answered. The universal unity of the members of Christ, is described in the same terms that are used to describe marriage unity. Compare 1 Cor. 12 : 12—27, with Gen. 2: 24. See also 1 Cor. 6: 15—17, and Eph. 5 : 30—32.

7.—The effects of the effusion of the Holy Spirit on the day of Pentecost, present a practical commentary on Christ's prayer for the unity of believers, and a sample of the tendency of heavenly influences, which fully confirm the foregoing proposition. "All that believed were together and had all things common ; and sold their possessions and goods, and parted them to all, as every man had need." " The multitude of them that believed were of one heart and of one soul ; neither said any of them that aught of the things which he possessed was his own ; but they had all things common." Acts 2: 44, 45, and 4 : 32. Here is unity like that of the Father and the Son : " All mine thine, and all thine mine."

8.—Admitting that the Community principle of the day of Pentecost, in its actual operation at that time, extended only to material goods, yet we affirm that there is no intrinsic difference between property in persons and property in things ; and that the same spirit which abolished exclusiveness in regard to money, would abolish, if circumstances allowed full scope to it, exclusiveness in regard to women and children. Paul expressly places property in women and property in goods in the same category, and speaks of them together, as ready to be abolished by the advent of the Kingdom of Heaven. "The time," says he, "is short ; it remaineth that they that have wives be as though they had none ; and they that buy as though they possessed not ; for the fashion of this world passeth away." 1 Cor. 7: 29–31.

9.—The abolishment of appropriation is involved in

the very nature of a true relation to Christ in the gospel. This we prove thus: The possessive feeling which expresses itself by the possessive pronoun *mine*, is the same in essence when it relates to persons, as when it relates to money or any other property. Amativeness and acquisitiveness are only different channels of one stream. They converge as we trace them to their source. Grammar will help us to ascertain their common center; for the possessive pronoun *mine*, is derived from the personal pronoun *I*; and so the possessive feeling, whether amative or acquisitive, flows from the personal feeling, that is, it is a branch of egotism. Now egotism is abolished by the gospel relation to Christ. The grand mystery of the gospel is vital union with Christ; the merging of self in his life; the extinguishment of the pronoun *I* at the spiritual center. Thus Paul says, "I live, yet not I, but Christ liveth in me." The grand distinction between the Christian and the unbeliever, between heaven and the world, is, that in one reigns the We-spirit, and in the other the I-spirit. From *I* comes *mine*, and from the I-spirit comes exclusive appropriation of money, women, etc. From *we* comes *ours*, and from the We-spirit comes universal community of interests.

10.—The abolishment of exclusiveness is involved in the love-relation required between all believers by the express injunction of Christ and the apostles, and by the whole tenor of the New Testament. "The new commandment is, that we love one another," and that, not by pairs, as in the world, but *en masse*. We are required to love one another fervently. The fashion of the world forbids a man and woman who are otherwise appropriated, to love one another fervently. But if they obey Christ they must do this ; and whoever would allow them to do this, and yet would forbid them (on any other ground than that of present expediency), to express their unity, would " strain at a gnat and swallow a camel ;" for unity of hearts is as much more important than any external expression of it, as a camel is larger than a gnat.

11.—The abolishment of social restrictions is involved in the anti-legality of the gospel. It is incompatible with the state of perfected freedom toward which Paul's gospel of " grace without law" leads, that man should be allowed and required to love in all directions, and yet be forbidden to express love except in one direction. In fact Paul says, with direct reference to sexual inter-course—" All things are lawful for me, but all things are not expedient; all things are lawful for me, but I will not be brought under the power of any ;" (1 Cor. 6: 12 ;) thus placing the restrictions which were necessary in the transition period on the basis, not of law, but of ex-pediency and the demands of spiritual freedom, and leaving it fairly to be inferred that in the final state, when hostile surroundings and powers of bondage cease, all restrictions also will cease.

12.—The abolishment of the marriage sytem is in-volved in Paul's doctrine of the end of ordinances. Marriage is one of the " ordinances of the worldly sanc-tuary." This is proved by the fact that it has no place in the resurrection. Paul expressly limits it to life in the flesh. Rom. 7: 2, 3. The assumption, therefore, that believers are dead to the world by the death of Christ (which authorized the abolishment of Jewish ordinances), legitimately makes an end of marriage. Col. 2: 20.

13.—The law of marriage is the same in kind with the Jewish law concerning meats and drinks and holy days, of which Paul said that they were "contrary to us, and were taken out of the way, being nailed to the cross." Col. 2: 14. The plea in favor of the worldly social system, that it is not arbitrary, but founded in nature, will not bear investigation. All experience testifies (the theory of the novels to the contrary notwithstanding), that sexual love is not naturally restricted to pairs. Second marriages are contrary to the one-love theory, and yet are often the happiest marriages. Men and women find universally (however the fact may be concealed), that their susceptibility to love is not burnt out by one honey-moon, or satisfied by one lover. On the contrary, the secret history of the human heart will bear out the assertion that it is capable of loving any number of times and any number of persons, and that the more it loves the more it can love. This is the law of nature, thrust out of sight and condemned by common consent, and yet secretly known to all.

14.—The law of marriage "worketh wrath." 1. It provokes to secret adultery, actual or of the heart. 2. It ties together unmatched natures. 3. It sunders matched natures. 4. It gives to sexual appetite only a scanty and monotonous allowance, and so produces the natural vices of poverty, contraction of taste and stinginess or jealousy. 5. It makes no provision for the sexual appetite at the very time when that appetite is the strongest. By the custom of the world, marriage, in the average of cases, takes place at about the age of twenty-four; whereas puberty commences at the age of fourteen. For ten years, therefore, and that in the very flush of life, the sexual appetite is starved. This law of society bears hardest on females, because they have less opportunity of choosing their time of marriage than men. This discrepancy between the marriage system and nature, is one of the principal sources of the peculiar diseases of women, of prostitution, masturbation, and licentiousness in general.

CHAPTER III.—*Showing that death is to be abolished, and that, to this end, there must be a restoration of true relations between the Sexes.*

PROPOSITION 15.—The Kingdom of Heaven is destined to abolish death in this world. Rom. 8 : 19—25. 1. Cor. 15 : 24—26. Isa. 25 : 8.

16.—The abolition of death is to be the last triumph of the Kingdom of Heaven ; and the subjection of all other powers to Christ must go before it. 1 Cor. 15 : 24—26. Isa. 33 : 22—24.

17.—The restoration of true relations between the sexes is a matter second in importance only to the reconciliation of man to God. The distinction of male and female is that which makes man the image of God, i. e. the image of the Father and the Son. Gen. 1 : 27. The relation of male and female was the first social relation. Gen. 2 : 22. It is therefore the root of all other social relations. The derangement of this relation was the first result of the original breach with God. Gen. 3 : 7 ; comp. 2 : 25. Adam and Eve were, at the beginning, in open, fearless, spiritual fellowship, first with God, and secondly, with each other. Their transgression produced two corresponding alienations, viz., first, an alienation from God, indicated by their fear of meeting him and their hiding themselves among the trees of the garden ; and secondly, an alienation from each other, indicated by their shame at their nakedness and their hiding themselves from each other by clothing. These were the two great manifestations of original sin—the only manifestations presented to notice in the record of the apostacy. The first thing then to be done, in an attempt to redeem man and reörganize society, is to bring about reconciliation with God; and the second thing is to bring about a true union of the sexes. In other words, religion is the first subject of interest, and sexual morality the second, in the great enterprise of establishing the Kingdom of Heaven on earth.

18.—We may criticise the system of the Fourierists, thus : The chain of evils which holds humanity in ruin, has four links, viz., 1st, a breach with God; (Gen. 3: 8;) 2d, a disruption of the sexes, involving a special curse on woman ; (Gen. 3: 16;) 3d, the curse of oppressive labor, bearing specially on man ; (Gen. 3: 17—19;) 4th, the reign of disease and death. (Gen. 3: 22—24.) These are all inextricably complicated with each other. The true scheme of redemption begins with reconciliation with God, proceeds first to a restoration of true relations between the sexes, then to a reform of the industrial system, and ends with victory over death. Fourierism has no eye to the final victory over death, defers attention to the religious question and the sexual question till some centuries hence, and confines itself to the rectifying of the industrial system. In other words, Fourierism neither begins at the beginning nor looks to the end of the chain, but fastens its whole interest on the third link, neglecting two that precede it, and ignoring that which follows it. The sin-system, the marriage-system, the work-system, and the death-system, are all one, and must be abolished together. Holiness, free-love, association in labor, and immortality, constitute the chain of redemption, and must come together in their true order.

19.—From what precedes, it is evident that any attempt to revolutionize sexual morality before settlement with God, is out of order. Holiness must go before free love. Bible Communists are not responsible for the proceedings of those who meddle with the sexual question, before they have laid the foundation of true faith and union with God.

20.—Dividing the sexual relation into two branches, the amative and propagative, the amative or love-relation is first in importance, as it is in the order of nature. God made woman because "he saw it was not good for man to be alone;" (Gen. 2 : 18); i. e., for social, not primarily for propagative, purposes. Eve was called Adam's "help-meet." In the whole of the specific account of the creation of woman, she is regarded as his companion, and her maternal office is not brought into view. Gen. 2: 18—25. Amativeness was necessarily the first social affection developed in the garden of Eden. The second commandment of the eternal law of love, "Thou shalt love thy neighbor as thyself," had amativeness for its first channel; for Eve was at first Adam's only neighbor. Propagation and the affections connected with it, did not commence their operation during the period of innocence. After the fall God said to the woman, "I will greatly multiply thy sorrow and thy conception;" from which it is to be inferred that in the original state, conception would have been comparatively infrequent.

21.—The amative part of the sexual relation, separate from the propagative, is eminently favorable to life. It is not a source of life (as some would make it), but it is the first and best distributive of life. Adam and Eve, in their original state, derived their life from God. Gen. 2 : 7. As God is a dual being, the Father and the Son, and man was made in his image, a dual life passed from God to man. Adam was the channel specially of the life of the Father, and Eve of the life of the Son. Amativeness was the natural agency of the distribution and mutual action of these two forms of life. In this primitive position of the sexes (which is their normal position in Christ), each reflects upon the other the love of God ; each excites and develops the divine action in the other.

22.—The propagative part of the sexual relation is in its nature the expensive department. 1. While amativeness keeps the capital stock of life circulating between two, propagation introduces a third partner. 2. The propagative act is a drain on the life of man, and when habitual, produces disease. 3. The infirmities and vital expenses of woman during the long period of pregnancy, waste her constitution. 4. The awful agonies of child-birth heavily tax the life of woman. 5. The cares of the nursing period bear heavily on woman. 6. The cares of both parents, through the period of the childhood of their offspring, are many and burdensome. 7. The labor of man is greatly increased by the necessity of providing for children. A portion of these expenses would undoubtedly have been curtailed, if human nature had remained in its original integrity, and will be, when it is restored. But it is still self-evident that the birth of children, viewed either as a vital or a mechanical operation, is in its nature expensive ; and the fact that multiplied conception was imposed as a curse, indicates that it was so regarded by the Creator.

CHAPTER IV.—*Showing how the Sexual Function is to be redeemed, and true relations between the sexes restored.*

PROPOSITION 23.—The amative and propagative functions are distinct from each other, and may be separated practically. They are confounded in the world, both in the theories of physiologists and in universal practice. The amative function is regarded merely as a bait to the propagative, and is merged in it. But if amativeness is, as we have seen, the first and noblest of the social affections, and if the propagative part of the sexual relation was originally secondary, and became paramount by the subversion of order in the fall, we are bound to raise the amative office of the sexual organs into a distinct and paramount function. [Here follows a full exposition of the doctrine of self-control or Male Continence, which is an essential part of the Oneida theory, but may properly be omitted in this history.]

CHAPTER V.—*Showing that Shame, instead of being one of the prime virtues, is a part of original Sin and belongs to the Apostasy.*

PROPOSITION 24.—Sexual shame was the consequence of the fall, and is factitious and irrational. Gen. 2: 25 ; compare 3: 7. Adam and Eve, while innocent, had no shame ; little children have none ; other animals have none.

CHAPTER VI.—*Showing the bearings of the preceding views on Socialism, Political Economy, Manners and Customs, etc.*

PROPOSITION 25.—The foregoing principles concerning the sexual relation, open the way for Association. 1. They furnish motives. They apply to larger partnerships the same attractions that draw and bind together pairs in the worldly partnership of marriage. A Community home in which each is married to all, and where love is honored and cultivated, will be as much more attractive than an ordinary home, as the Community out-numbers a pair. 2. These principles remove the principal obstructions in the way of Association. There is plenty of tendency to crossing love and adultery, even in the system of isolated households. Association increases this tendency. Amalgamation of interests, frequency of interview, and companionship in labor, inevitably give activity and intensity to the social attractions in which amativeness is the strongest element. The tendency to extra-matrimonial love will be proportioned to the condensation of interests produced by any given form of Association; that is, if the ordinary principles of exclusiveness are preserved, Association will be a worse school of temptation to unlawful love than the world is, in proportion to its social advantages. Love, in the exclusive form, has jealousy for its complement; and jealousy brings on strife and division. Association, therefore, if it retains one-love exclusiveness, contains the seeds of dissolution; and those seeds will be hastened to their harvest by the warmth of associate life. An Association of States with customhouse lines around each, is sure to be quarrelsome. The further States in that situation are apart, and the more their interests are isolated, the better. The only way to prevent smuggling and strife in a confederation of contiguous States, is to abolish custom-house lines from the interior, and declare free-trade and free transit, collecting revenues and fostering home products by one custom-house line around the whole. This is the policy of the heavenly system—' that they *all* [not two and two] may be one.'

26.—In vital society, strength will be increased and the necessity of labor diminished, till work will become sport, as it would have been in the original Eden state. Gen. 2 : 15 ; compare 3 : 17—19. Here we come to the field of the Fourierists—the third link of the chain of evil. And here we shall doubtless ultimately avail ourselves of many of the economical and industrial discoveries of Fourier. But as the fundamental principle of our system differs entirely from that of Fourier, (our foundation being his superstructure, and *vice versa*,) and as every system necessarily has its own complement of external arrangements, conformed to its own genius, we will pursue our investigations for the present independently, and with special reference to our peculiar principles.—Labor is sport or drudgery according to the proportion between strength and the work to be done. Work that overtasks a child, is easy to a man. The amount of work remaining the same, if man's strength were doubled, the result would be the same as if the amount of work were diminished one-half. To make labor sport, therefore, we must seek, first, increase of strength, and secondly, diminution of work : or, (as in the former problem relating to the curse on woman), first, enlargement of income, and secondly, diminution of expenses. Vital society secures both of these objects. It increases strength, by placing the individual in a vital organization, which is in communication with the source of life, and which distributes and circulates life with the highest activity; and at the same time, by its compound economies, it reduces the work to be done to a minimum.

27.—In vital society labor will become attractive. Loving companionship in labor, and especially the mingling of the sexes, makes labor attractive. The present divison of labor between the sexes separates them entirely. The woman keeps house, and the man labors abroad. Instead of this, in vital society men and women will mingle in both of their peculiar departments of work. It will be economically as well as spiritually profitable, to marry them in-doors and out, by day as well as by night. When the partition between the sexes is taken away, and man ceases to make woman a propagative drudge, when love takes the place of shame, and fashion follows nature in dress and business, men and women will be able to mingle in all their employments, as boys and girls mingle in their sports ; and then labor will be attractive.

28.—We can now see our way to victory over death. Reconciliation with God opens the way for the reconciliation of the sexes. Reconciliation of the sexes emancipates woman, and opens the way for vital society. Vital society increases strength, diminishes work, and makes labor attractive, thus removing the antecedents of death. First we abolish sin ; then shame ; then the curse on woman of exhausting child-bearing ; then the curse on man of exhausting labor ; and so we arrive regularly at the tree of life.

CHAPTER VII.—*A concluding Caveat, that ought to be noted by every Reader of the foregoing Argument.*

PROPOSITION 29.—The will of God is done in heaven, and of course will be done in his kingdom on earth, not merely by general obedience to constitutional principles, but by specific obedience to the administration of his Spirit. The constitution of a nation is one thing, and the living administration of government is another. Ordinary theology directs attention chiefly, and almost exclusively, to the constitutional principles of God's government; and the same may be said of Fourierism, and all schemes of reform based on the development of "natural laws." But as loyal subjects of God, we must give and call attention to his actual administration; i. e., to his will directly manifested by his Spirit and the agents of his Spirit, viz., his officers and representatives. We must look to God, not only for a Constitution, but for Presidential outlook and counsel; for a cabinet and corps of officers; for national aims and plans; for direction, not only in regard to principles to be carried out, but in regard to time and circumstance in carrying them out. In other words, the men who are called to usher in the Kingdom of God, will be guided, not merely by theoretical truth, but by the Spirit of God and specific manifestations of his will and policy, as were Abraham, Moses, David, Jesus Christ, Paul, &c. This will be called a fanatical principle, because it requires *bona fide* communication with the heavens, and displaces the sanctified maxim that the "age of miracles and inspiration is past." But it is clearly a Bible principle; and we must place it on high, above all others, as the palladium of conservatism in the introduction of the new social order.

Two expressions occur in the foregoing summaries which need some explanation; viz., in the first, the word *Spiritualist*; and in the second, the term *Free Love*. Without explanation, the modern reader might suppose these expressions to be used in the sense commonly attached to them at the present time. But if he will consider that the articles in *The Berean* were first published long before the birth of Modern Spiritualism, and that *Bible Communism* was published long before the birth of Free Love among Spiritualists, he will see that these expressions do not mean in the above documents, what they mean in popular usage, and do not in any way connect the Oneida Community with Modern Spiritualists, or with their system of Free Love. The simple truth is, that the Putney school invented the term *Spiritualist* to designate all believers in immediate communication with the spiritual world, referring at the time specially to Perfectionists and Revivalists, and marking the distinction between them and the legalists of the churches; and they invented the term *Free Love* to designate the social state of the Kingdom of Heaven as defined in *Bible Communism*. Afterward these terms were appropriated and specialized by the followers of Andrew Jackson Davis and Thomas L. Nichols. The Oneida Communists have for many years printed and re-printed in their various publications the following protest, which may fitly close this account of their religious and social theories:

FREE LOVE.

[From the *Hand-Book* of the Oneida Community.]

"This terrible combination of two very good ideas—freedom and love—was first used by the writers of the Oneida Community about twenty-one years ago, and probably originated with them. It was however soon taken up by a very different class of speculators scattered about the country, and has come to be the name of a form of socialism with which we have but little affinity. Still it is sometimes applied to our Communities; and as we are certainly responsible for starting it into circulation, it seems to be our duty to tell what meaning we attach to it, and in what sense we are willing to accept it as a designation of our social system.

"The obvious and essential difference between marriage and licentious connections may be stated thus:

"Marriage is permanent union. Licentiousness deals in temporary flirtations.

"In marriage, Communism of property goes with Communism of persons. In licentiousness, love is paid for as hired labor.

"Marriage makes a man responsible for the consequnces of his acts of love to a woman. In licentiousness, a man imposes on a woman the heavy burdens of maternity, ruining perhaps her reputation and her health, and then goes his way without responsibility.

"Marriage provides for the maintenance and education of children. Licentiousness ignores children as nuisances, and leaves them to chance.

"Now in respect to every one of these points of difference between marriage and licentiousness, *we stand with marriage.* Free Love with us does *not* mean freedom to love to-day and leave to-morrow; nor freedom to take a woman's person and keep our property to ourselves; nor freedom to freight a woman with our offspring and send her down stream without care or help; nor freedom to beget children and leave them to the street and the poor-house. Our Communities are *families*, as distinctly bounded and separated from promiscuous society as ordinary households. The tie that binds us together is as permanent and sacred, to say the least, as that of marriage, for it is our religion. We receive no members (except by deception or mistake), who do not give heart and hand to the family interest for life and forever. Community of property extends just as far as freedom of love. Every man's care and every dollar of the common property is pledged for the maintenance and protection of the women, and the education of the children of the Community. Bastardy, in any disastrous sense of the word, is simply impossible in such a social state. Whoever will take the trouble to follow our track from the beginning, will find no forsaken women or children by the way. In this respect we claim to be in advance of marriage and common civilization.

" We are not sure how far the class of socialists called ' Free Lovers' would claim for themselves any thing like the above defense from the charge of reckless and cruel freedom ; but our impression is that their position, scattered as they are, without organization or definite separation from surrounding society, makes it impossible for them to follow and care for the consequences of their freedom, and thus exposes them to the just charge of licentiousness. At all events their platform is entirely different from ours, and they must answer for themselves. *We* are not ' Free Lovers ' in any sense that makes love less binding or responsible than it is in marriage." *

---

* We observe that the account of the Oneida Community given in the Supplement to Chambers' Encyclopædia, begins thus : "*Perfectionists* or *Bible Communists;* popularly known as Free Lovers or preachers of Free Love." The whole article, covering several pages, is very careless in its geographical and other details, and not altogether reliable in its statements of the doctrines and morals of the Communists. As materials that get into Encyclopædias may be presumed to be crystallizing for final history, it is to be hoped that the Messrs. Chambers will at least get this article corrected by some intelligent American, for future editions.

Material Results.

The concrete results of·Communism at Oneida, have been made public from time to time in the *Circular,* the weekly paper of the Community. The "journal" columns of this sheet, in which are given the ups and downs of Community progress, with much of the gossip of its home life, would fill several volumes. Referring the inquisitive reader to these for details, we shall limit our present sketch to the main outlines :

The Oneida Community has two hundred and two members, and two affiliated societies, one of forty members at Wallingford, Connecticut, and one of thirty-five members at Willow Place, on a detached part of the Oneida domain. This domain consists of six hundred and sixty-four acres of choice land, and three excellent water-powers. The manufacturing interest here created is valued at over $200,000. The Wallingford domain consists of two hundred and twenty-eight acres, with a water-power, a printing-office and a silk-factory. The three Community families (in all two hundred and seventy-seven persons) are financially and socially a unit.

The main dwelling of the Community is a brick structure consisting of a center and two wings, the whole one hundred and eighty-seven feet in length, by seventy in breadth. It has towers at either end and irregular extensions reaching one hundred feet in the rear. This is the Community Home. It contains the chapel, library, reception-room, museum, principal drawing-rooms, and many private apartments. The other buildings of the group are the "old mansion," containing the kitchen and dining-room, the Tontine, which is a work-building, the fruit-house, the store, etc. The manufacturing buildings in connection with the water-powers are large, and mostly of brick.   The organic principle of Communism in industry and domestic life, is seen in the common roof, the common table, and the daily meetings of all the members.

The extent and variety of industrial operations at the Oneida Community may be seen in part by the follow-ing statistics from the report of last year, (1868.)

No. of steel traps manufactured during the year, 278,000.
"   " packages of preserved fruits,   104,458.
Amount of raw silk manufactured,   4,664 lbs.
Iron cast at the foundry,   227,000 do.
Lumber manufactured at saw-mill,   305,000 feet.
Product of milk from the dairy,   31,143 gallons.
"   "   hay on the domain,   300 tons.
"   "   potatoes,   800 bushels.
"   "   strawberries,   740 do.
"   "   apples,   1,450 do.
"   "   grapes,   9,631 lbs.

Stock on the farm, 93 cattle and 25 horses.   Amount of teaming done, valued at $6,260.

In addition to these, many branches of industry neces-sary for the convenience of the family are pursued, such as shoemaking, tailoring, dentistry, etc.   The cash busi-ness of the Community during the year, as represented by its receipts and disbursements, was about $575,000. Amount paid for hired labor $34,000.   Family expenses (exclusive of domestic labor by the members, teaching, and work in the printing office), $41,533.43.

The amount of labor performed by the Community members during the year, was found to be approxi-mately as follows :

	Number.	Amount of labor per day.
Able-bodied men . . .	80	7 hours
" women . .	84	6 " 40 min.
Invalid and aged men .	6	3 " 40 "
Boys	4	3 " 40 "
Invalid and aged women	9	1 " 20 "
Girls	2	1 " 20 "

This is exclusive of care of children, school-teaching, printing and editing the *Circular*, and much head-work in all departments.

Taking 304 days for the working year, we have, as a product of the above figures, a total of 35,568 days' work at ten hours each. Supposing this labor to be paid at the rate of $1.50 per day, the aggregate sum for the year would be $53,352.00. By comparing this with the amount of family expenses, $41,533.43, we find, at the given rate of wages, a surplus of profit amounting to $11,818.57, or 33 cents profit for each person per day. This represents the saving which ordinary unskilled labor would make by means of the mere economy of Association. Were it possible for a skillful mechanic to live in co-operation with others, so that his wife and elder children could spend some time at productive labor, and his family could secure the economies of combined households, their wages at present rates would be more than double the cost of living. Labor in the Community being principally of the higher class, is proportionately rewarded, and in fact earns much more than $1.50 per day.

The entire financial history of the Community in brief is the following : It commenced business at its present location in 1848, but did not adopt the practice of taking annual inventories till 1857. Of the period between these dates we can give but a general account. The Community in the course of that period had five or six branches with common interests, scattered in several States. The "Property Register," kept from the beginning, shows that the amount of property brought in by the members of all the Communities, up to January 1, 1857, was $107,706.45. The amount held at Oneida at that date, as stated in the first regular inventory, was only $41,740. The branch Communities at Putney, Wallingford and elsewhere, at the same time had property valued at $25,532.22. So that the total assets of the associated Communities were $67,272.22, or $40,434.23 less than the amount brought in by the members. In other words between the years 1848 and 1857, the associated Communities sunk (in round numbers) $40,000. Various causes may be assigned for this, such as inexperience, lack of established business, persecutions and extortions, the burning of the Community store, the sinking of the sloop Rebecca Ford in the Hudson River, the maintenance of an expensive printing family at Brooklyn, the publication of a free paper, etc.

In the course of several years previous to 1857, the Community abandoned the policy of working in scattered detachments, and concentrated its forces at Oneida and Wallingford. From the first of January 1857, when its capital was $41,740, to the present time, the progress of its money-matters is recorded in the following statistics, drawn from its annual inventories:

In 1857, net earnings,	$5,470.11	In 1862, net earnings.	$9,859.78
" 1858, " "	1,763.60	" 1863, " "	44,755.30
" 1859, " "	10,278.38	" 1864, " "	61,382.62
" 1860, " "	15,611.03	" 1865, " "	12,382.81
" 1861, " "	5,877.89	" 1866, " "	13,198.74

Total net earnings in ten years, $180,580.26; being a yearly average income of $18,058.02, above all expenses. The succeeding inventories show the following result:

Net earnings in 1867, $21,416.02.
Net earnings in 1868, $55,100.83.

being an average for the last two years of over $38,000 per annnm.

During the year 1869 the following steps forward have been taken: 1, an entire wing has been added to the brick Mansion House, for the use of the children; 2, apparatus for heating the whole by steam has been introduced; 3, a building has been erected for an Academy, and systematic home-education has commenced; 4, silk-weaving has been introduced at Willow Place; 5, the manufacture of silk-twist has been established at Wallingford; 6, the Communities at Oneida and Wallingford have been more thoroughly consolidated than heretofore; 7, this book on *American Socialisms* has been prepared at Oneida and printed at Wallingford.

CHAPTER XLVII.

REVIEW AND RESULTS.

LOOKING back now over the entire course of this history, we discover a remarkable similarity in the symptoms that manifested themselves in the transitory Communities, and almost entire unanimity in the witnesses who testify as to the causes of their failure. GENERAL DEPRAVITY, all say, is the villain of the whole story.

In the first place Macdonald himself, after "seeing stern reality," confesses that in his previous hopes of Socialism he "had imagined mankind better than they are."

Then Owen, accounting for the failure at New Harmony, says, "he wanted honesty, and he got dishonesty; he wanted temperance, and instead he was continually troubled with the intemperate; he wanted cleanliness, and he found dirt," and so on.

The Yellow Spring Community, though composed of "a very superior class," found in the short space of three months, that "self-love was a spirit that would not be exorcised. Individual happiness was the law of nature, and it could not be obliterated; and before a single year had passed, this law had scattered the members of that society which had come together so earnestly and under such favorable circumstances, back into the selfish world from which they came."

The trustees of the Nashoba Community, in abandoning Frances Wright's original plan of common property, acknowledge their conviction that such a system can not succeed "without the members composing it are superior beings. That which produces in the world only common-place jealousies and every-day squabbles, is sufficient to destroy a Community."

The spokesman of the Haverstraw Community at first attributes their failure to the "dishonesty of the managers;" but afterward settles down into the more general complaint that they lacked "men and women of skillful industry, sober and honest, with a knowledge of themselves and a disposition to command and be commanded," and intimates that "the sole occupation of the men and women they had, was parade and talk."

The historian of the Coxsackie Community says "they had many persons engaged in talking and law-making, who did not work at any useful employment. The consequences were, that after struggling on for between one and two years, the experiment came to an end. There were few good men to steer things right."

Warren found that the friction that spoiled his experiments was "the want of common honesty."

Ballou complained that "the timber he got together was not suitable for building a Community. The men and women that joined him were very enthusiastic and commenced with great zeal; their devotion to the cause seemed to be sincere; but they did not know themselves."

At the meetings that dissolved the Northampton Community, "some spoke of the want of that harmony and brotherly feeling, which were indispensable to success; others spoke of the unwillingness to make sacrifices on the part of some of the members; also of the lack of industry and the right appropriation of time."

Collins lived in a quarrel with a rival during nearly the whole life of his Community, and finally gave up the experiment from "a conviction that the theory of Communism could not be carried out in practice; that the attempt was premature, the time had not yet arrived, and the necessary conditions did not yet exist." His experience led him to the conclusion that "there is floating upon the surface of society, a body of restless, disappointed, jealous, indolent spirits, disgusted with our present social system, not because it enchains the masses to poverty, ignorance, vice, and endless servitude; but because they can not render it subservient to their private ends. Experience shows that this class stands ready to mount every new movement that promises ease, abundance, and individual freedom; and that when such an enterprise refuses to interpret license for freedom, and insists that every member shall make their strength, skill and talent, subservient to the movement, then the cry of tyranny and oppression is raised against those who advocate such industry and self-denial; then the enterprise must become a scapegoat, to bear the fickleness, indolence, selfishness, and envy of this class."

The testimony in regard to the Sylvania Association is, that "young men wasted the good things at the commencement of the experiment; and besides victuals, dry-goods supplied by the Association were unequally obtained. Idle and greedy people find their way into such attempts, and soon show forth their character by burdening others with too much labor, and, in times of scarcity, supplying themselves with more than their allowance of various necessaries, instead of taking less."

The failure of the One Mentian Community is attributed to "ignorance and disagreements," and that of the Social Reform Unity to "lack of wisdom and general preparation."

The Leraysville Phalanx went to pieces in a grumble about the management.

Of the Clarkson Association a writer in the *Phalanx* says that they were "ignorant of Fourier's principles, and without plan or purpose, save to fly from the ills they had already experienced in civilization. Thus they assembled together such elements of discord, as naturally in a short time led to their dissolution."

The Sodus Bay Socialists quarreled about religion, and when they broke up, some decamped in the night, with as much of the common property as they could lay hands on. Whereupon Macdonald sententiously remarks—"The fact that mankind do not like to have their faults and failings made public, will probably account for the difficulty in obtaining particulars of such experiments."

The Bloomfield Association went to wreck in a quarrel about land-titles.

Of the Jefferson County Association, Macdonald says, "After a few months, disagreements became general. Their means were totally inadequate ; they were too ignorant of the principles of Association ; were too much crowded together, and had too many idlers among them. There was bad management on the part of the officers, and some were suspected of dishonesty."

The Moorhouse Union appears to have been almost wholly a gathering of worthless adventurers.

Mr. Moore, in his *Post Mortem* on the Marlboro

Association, very delicately observes that "the failure of the experiment may be traced to the fact that the minds of its originators were not homogeneous."

Macdonald, after studying the Prairie Home Community, says, "From all I saw I judged that it was too loosely put together, and that the members had not entire confidence in each other."

The malcontent who gives an account of the Trumbull Phalanx says: "Some came with the idea that they could live in idleness at the expense of the purchasers of the estate, and these ideas they practically carried out; while others came with good hearts for the cause. There were one or two designing persons, who came with no other intent than to push themselves into situations in which they could impose upon their fellow members; and this, to a certain extent, they succeeded in doing." And again: "I think most persons came there for a mere shift. Their poverty and their quarreling about what they called religion (for there were many notions as to which was the right way to heaven), were great drawbacks to success."

There were rival leaders in the Ohio Phalanx, and their respective parties quarreled about constitutions till they got into a lawsuit which broke them up. The member who gave the account of this Association says: "The most important causes of failure were said to be the deficiency of wealth, wisdom and goodness."

The Clermont Phalanx had jealousies among its women that led to a lawsuit; and a difficulty with one of its leading members about land-titles.

The story of the Alphadelphia Phalanx is briefly told thus: "The disagreement with Mr. Tubbs about a mill-race at the commencement of the experiment, threw a damper on it, from which it never recovered. All lived in clover so long as a ton of sugar or any other such luxury lasted. The officers made bad bargains. Laborers became discouraged. In the winter some of the influential members went away temporarily, and thus left the real friends of the Association in the minority; and when they returned after two or three months absence, every thing was turned up-side-down. There was a manifest lack of good management and foresight. The old settlers accused the majority of this, and were themselves elected officers; but they managed no better, and finally broke up the concern."

The Wisconsin Phalanx kept its quarrels below lawsuit point, but the leading member who gives account of it, says that the habit of the members was to "scold and work, and work and scold;" and that "they had among their number a few men of leading intellect who always doubted the success of the experiment, and hence determined to accumulate property individually by any and every means called fair in competitive society. These would occasionally gain some important positions in the society, and representing it in part at home and abroad, caused much trouble. By some they were accounted the principal cause of the final failure."

Mr. Daniels, a gentleman who saw the whole progress of the Wisconsin Phalanx, says that "the cause of its breaking up was speculation, the love of money and the want of love for Association. Their property becoming valuable, they sold it for the purpose of making money out of it."

The North American was evidently shattered by secessions, resulting partly from religious dissensions and partly from differences about business.

Brook Farm alone is reported as harmonious to
the end.

It should be observed that the foregoing disclosures
of disintegrating infirmities were generally made reluctantly, and are necessarily very imperfect. Large
departments of dangerous passion are entirely ignored.
For instance, in all the memoirs of the Owen and
Fourier Associations, not a word is said on the
"Woman Question!" Among all the disagreements and
complaints, not a hint occurs of any jealousies and quarrels about love matters. In fact women are rarely
mentioned; and the terrible passions connected with distinction of sex, which the Shakers, Rappites, Oneidians,
and all the rest of the religious Communities have had
so much trouble with, and have taken so much pains to
provide for or against, are absolutely left out of sight.
Owen, it is true, named marriage as one of the trinity
of man's oppressors: and it is, generally understood that
Owenism and Fourierism both gave considerable latitude
to affinities and divorces; but this makes it all the more
strange that there was no trouble worth mentioning, in
any of these Communities, about crossing love-claims.
Can it be, we ask ourselves, that Owen had such conflicts
with whiskey-tippling, but never a fight with the love-
mania? that all through the Fourier experiments, men
and women, young men and maidens, by scores and hundreds were tumbled together into unitary homes, and
sometimes into log-cabins seventeen feet by twenty-five,
and yet no sexual jostlings of any account disturbed
the domestic circle? The only conclusion we can come
to is, that some of the most important experiences of
the transitory Communities have not been surrendered
to history.

Nevertheless the troubles that do come to the surface show, as we have said, that human depravity is the dread "Dweller of the Threshold," that lies in wait at every entrance to the mysteries of Socialism.

Shall we then turn back in despair, and give it up that Association on the large scale is impossible ? This seems to have been the reaction of all the leading Fourierists. Greeley sums up the wisdom he gained from his socialistic experience in the following invective:

"A serious obstacle to the success of any socialistic experiment must always be confronted. I allude to the kind of persons who are naturally attracted to it. Along with many noble and lofty souls, whose impulses are purely philanthropic, and who are willing to labor and suffer reproach for any cause that promises to benefit mankind, there throng scores of whom the world is quite worthy—the conceited, the crotchety, the selfish, the headstrong, the pugnacious, the unappreciated, the played-out, the idle, and the good-for-nothing generally ; who, finding themselves utterly out of place and at a discount in the world as it is, rashly conclude that they are exactly fitted for the world as it ought to be. These may have failed again and again, and been protested at every bank to which they have been presented ; yet they are sure to jump into any new movement as if they had been born expressly to superintend and direct it, though they are morally certain to ruin whatever they lay their hands on. Destitute of means, of practical ability, of prudence, tact and common sense, they have such a wealth of assurance and self-confidence, that they clutch the responsible positions which the capable and worthy modestly shrink from ; so responsibilities that would tax the ablest, are mistakenly devolved on the blindest and least fit. Many an experiment is thus wrecked, when, engineered by its best members, it might have succeeded."

Meeker gloomily concludes that "generally men are not prepared; Association is for the future."

And yet, to contradict these disheartening persuasions and forbid our settling into despair, we have a respectable series of successes that can not be ignored. Mr. Greeley recognizes them, though he hardly knows how to dispose of them. "The fact," he says, "stares us in the face that, while hundreds of banks and factories, and thousands of mercantile concerns managed by shrewd, strong men, have gone into bankruptcy and perished, Shaker Communities, established more than sixty years ago, upon a basis of little property and less worldly wisdom, are living and prosperous to-day. And their experience has been imitated by the German Communities at Economy, Zoar, the Society of Ebenezer, etc. Theory, however plausible, must respect the facts."

Let us look again at these exceptional Associations that have not succumbed to the disorganizing power of general depravity. Jacobi's record of their duration and fortunes is worth recapitulating. Assuming that they are all still in existence, their stories may be epitomized as follows:

Beizel's Community has lasted one hundred and fifty-six years; was at one time very rich; has money at interest yet; some of its grand old buildings are still standing.

The Shaker Community, as a whole, is ninety-five years old; consists of eighteen large societies; many of them very wealthy.

Rapp's Community is sixty-five years old, and very wealthy.

The Zoar Community is fifty-three years old, and wealthy.

The Snowberger Community is forty-nine years old and " well off."

The Ebenezer Community is twenty-three years old ; and said to be the largest and richest Community in the United States.

The Janson Community is twenty-three years old and wealthy.

The Oneida Community (frequently quoted as belonging to this class) is twenty-one years old, and prosperous.

The one feature which distinguishes these Communities from the transitory sort, is their religion ; which in every case is of the earnest kind which comes by recognized afflatus, and controls all external arrangements.

It seems then to be a fair induction from the facts before us that earnest religion does in some way modify human depravity so as to make continuous Association possible, and insure to it great material success. Or if it is doubted whether it does essentially change human nature, it certainly improves in some way the *conditions* of human nature in socialistic experiments. It is to be noted that Mr. Greeley and other experts in socialism claim that there *is* a class of "noble and lofty souls" who are prepared for close Association ; but their attempts have constantly been frustrated by the throng of crotchety and selfish interlopers that jump on to their movements. Now it may be that the tests of earnest religion are just what are needed to keep a discrimination between the "noble and lofty souls" and the scamps of whom the Socialists complain. On the whole it seems probable that earnest religion does favorably modify both human depravity and its conditions, preparing some for Association by making them better, and shutting off others that would defeat the attempts of the best. Earnest men of one religious faith are more likely to be respectful to organized authority and to one another, than men of no religion or men of many religions held in indifference and mutual counteraction. And this quality of respect, predisposing to peace and subordination, however base it may be in the estimation of "Individual Sovereigns," and however worthless it may be in ordinary circumstances, is certainly the indispensable element of success in close Association.

The logic of our facts may be summed up thus: The non-religious party has tried Association under the lead of Owen, and failed; the semi-religious party has tried it under the lead of Fourier, and failed; the thoroughly religious party has not yet tried it; but sporadic experiments have been made by various religious sects, and so far as they have gone, they have indicated by their success, that earnest religion may be relied upon to carry Association through to the attainment of all its hopes. The world then must wait for this final trial; and the hope of the triumph of Association can not rationally be given up, till this trial has been made.

The question for the future is, Will the Revivalists go forward into Socialism; or will the Socialists go forward into Revivalism? We do not expect any further advance, till one or the other of these things shall come to pass; and we do not expect overwhelming victory and peace till both shall come to pass.

The best outlook for Socialism is in the direction of

the local churches. These are scattered every where, and under a powerful afflatus might easily be converted into Communities. In that case Communism would have the advantage of previous religion, previous acquaintance, and previous rudimental organizations, all assisting in the tremendous transition from the old world of selfishness, to the new world of common interest. We believe that a church that is capable of a genuine revival, could modulate into daily meetings, criticism, and all the self-denials of Communism, far more easily than any gathering by general proclamation for the sole purpose of founding a Community.

If the churches can not be put into this work, we do not see how Socialism on a large scale is going to be propagated. Exceptional Associations may be formed here and there by careful selection and special good fortune ; but how general society is to be resolved into Communities, without some such transformation of existing organizations, we do not pretend to foresee. Our hope is that churches of all denominations will by and by be quickened by the Pentecostal Spirit, and begin to grow and change, and finally, by a process as natural as the transformation of the chrysalis, burst forth into Communism.

CHAPTER XLVIII.

DEDUCTIVE AND INDUCTIVE SOCIALISMS.

IT is well for a theory to be subjected to the test of adverse criticism. Particularly in matters of contemporaneous history the public are interested to hear all sides. We have presented in this book our estimate of the French and English schools of Socialism; but as the reader may deem a Communist's judgment of the Phalansterian school necessarily defective, we are happy to insert here a communication from Mr. Brisbane himself, presenting a partizan's defence of Fourier. It was received and printed in the *Circular*, just as the last chapters of our history of Fourierism were preparing.

" FOURIER AND THE ATTEMPTS TO REALIZE HIS THEORY.

" *To the Editor of the Circular:*

" Will you allow me space in your journal to say that no practical trial, and no approach to one, has as yet been made of Fourier's theory of Social Organization. A trial of a theory supposes that the practical test is made in conformity with its principles; otherwise there is no trial. Let generous minds who are working for the social redemption of their race, be just to those who have labored conscientiously for this great end. Let them be just to Fourier, who, in silence during a long life strove to solve the great problem of the organization of society on a scientific basis, neglecting every thing else—the pursuit of fortune, the avenue to which was more than once open to him—and position and reputation in society.

"Fourier says: There are certain *Laws of Organization* in nature, which are the source of order and harmony in creation. These laws human reason must discover and apply in the organization of society, if a true social order is to be established on the earth. The moral forces in man, called sentiments, faculties, passions, etc., are framed or fashioned, and their action determined, in accordance with these laws. They tend naturally to act in conformity with them, and would do so, if not thwarted. If the Social Organization, which is the external medium in which these forces operate, is based on those laws, it will, it is evident, be adapted to the forces—to the nature of man. This will secure their true, natural and harmonious development, and with it the solution of the fundamental problem of social order and harmony. In organizing society on its true basis, begin, says Fourier, with Industry, which is the primary and material branch of the Social Organization. By the natural organization of Industry the productive labors of mankind will be *dignified and rendered attractive;* wealth will be increased ten-fold, so that abundance will be secured to all, and with abundance, the means of education and refinement, and of social equality and unity. When refinement and intelligence are rendered general, the superstructure of society will be built under the favorable circumstances which such a work requires.

"Briefly stated, such is Fourier's view. In his works he describes in detail the plan of Industrial Organization. He explains the laws of organization in Nature (as he understands them), on which Industry is to be based.   He takes special pains to give minute directions in relation to the subject, and warns those who may undertake the work of organization, to avoid mistakes—some of which he points out—that may easily be made, and would vitiate the undertaking.

"The little Associations started in this country, of which you have given an account, had for their object the realization of Fourier's industrial system.   Now, instead of avoiding the mistakes which he warned his followers against making, not one of those Associations realized *a single one of the conditions* which he laid down. Not one of them had the tenth, nor the twentieth part of the means and resources—pecuniary and scientific— necessary to carry out the organization he proposed.   In a word, no trial, and no approach to a trial of Fourier's theory has been made.   I do not say that his theory is true, or would succeed, if fairly tried.   I simply affirm that *no trial* of it has been made ; so that it is unjust to speak of it, as if it had been tested.   With ample, that is, vast resources, and some years to prepare the domain, erect buildings, and make all necessary arrangements, so as to thoroughly prepare the field of operations before the members or operators entered, then with men of organizing capacity to test fairly the principles which he has laid down, a fair trial could be made.

"I repeat, let us be just to those who have labored patiently and conscientiously for the social elevation of humanity.   Fourier's was a great soul.   To a powerful intellect he added nobility and goodness of heart. Clear, exact, strict and scientific in thought, he was at the same time kind and philanthropic in feeling.   Impelled by noble motives, he devoted his intellect to the most important of works, to the discovery of the natural principles of social organization.   Such a man deserves to be treated with profound respect.   Infantile attempts to realize his ideas should not, in their failure, be charged upon him, covering him with the ridicule or folly attached to them.   Let him stand on his Theory. That is his intellectual pedestal.   Let those who undertake to judge him, study his Theory.   When they overthrow that they will overthrow him.

"I will close by stating my estimate of Fourier, which is the result of some reflection.

"Social Science is a creation of the nineteenth century.   It has been developed in a regular form in the present century, as was Astronomy, for example, in the sixteenth.   Men have arisen almost simultaneously in different countries, who have conceived the possibility of such a science, and set themselves to work at it. Fourier took the lead.   He began in 1798, and published his first work in 1806.   Krause, in Germany, began to write in 1808.   St. Simon, in France, in 1811. Owen, in England, at a later period still.   Comte, a disciple of St Simon, began in 1824, I think.   Fourier and Comte were the only minds that undertook to base Social Science on, and to deduce it from, universal laws, having their source in the infallible wisdom of the universe   Comte, after laying a broad foundation with the aid of all the known sciences ; after seeking to determine the theory of each special science, and to construct a *Science of the Sciences* by which to guide himself, abandons his scientific construction (reared in his first work—"Positive Philosophy"), when he comes to elaborate his plan of practical organization.   He deduces his plan of the Social Order of the future from the historical past, and especially from the Middle Age *regime*, guided in so doing by his own personal feelings and views. His Social system is consequently a compound of historical deduction and personal sentiment. It is, I think, without practical value. His scientific demonstration of the possibility and the necessity of Social Science is of *great value*, and will secure to him unbounded respect in the future. Fourier, at the outset of his labors, conceived the necessity of discovering the laws of order and harmony in the universe—Nature's plan and theory of organization—and of deducing `from them *the Science of Social Organization.* Leaving aside all secondary considerations, he set about this great work. The discovery of the laws of order and organization in creation was his great end. The deduction of a Social Order from them was an accessory work. He claims to have succeeded; and claims for his plan of social organization no value outside of its conformity to Nature's laws. "I give no theory of my own," he says in a hundred places; "I DEDUCE. If I have deduced erroneously, let others establish the true deduction."

"Social Science is a vast and complex science; it can not be discovered and constituted by the aid of empirical observation and reasoning: the *Inductive method* can not do its work here. The laws of order and organization in nature must be discovered, and from them the science must be deduced. In astronomy, in order to solve its higher and more abstruse problems, it is necessary to deduce from one of the great laws of Nature; namely, that of gravitation. It is more necessary still in the case of the involved problems of Social Science.

"Now the merit of Fourier consists in having seen

clearly this great truth; in having sought carefully to discover Nature's laws of organization; and in having deduced from them with the greatest patience and fidelity the organization of the Social System which he has elaborated. His organization of Industry and of Education are master-pieces of deductive thought.

"If Fourier has failed, if he has not discovered the laws of natural organization, or has not deduced rightly from them, he has opened the way and pointed out the true path; he has shown *what must be done*, and furnished invaluable examples of the mode in which deduction must take place in Social organization. He has shown how the human mind is to create a Social Science, and effect the Social Reconstruction to which this science is to lead. If he went astray, and could not follow the difficult path he indicated, he has at least clearly described the ways and modes of proceeding. Others can now easily follow in his footsteps.

"If we would compare the pioneers in Social Science to those in astronomy, I would say that Fourier is the Kepler of the new science. Possessing, like Kepler, a vast and bold genius, he has, by far-reaching intuition and close analytic thought, discovered some of the fundamental principles of Social Science, enough to place it on a scientific foundation, and to constitute it regularly, as did Kepler in astronomy. Auguste Comte appears to me to be the Tycho Brahe of Social Science: learned and patient, but not original, not a discoverer of new laws and principles. Other great minds will be required to complete the science. It will have its Galileo, its Newton, its Laplace, and even still more all-sided minds; for the science is far more complex and abstruse than that of astronomy; it is the crowning intellectual evolu--

tion, which human genius is to effect in its scientific career.   Very truly yours,   A. BRISBANE."

This endeavor by a leading Phalansterian to set us right in regard to the merits of Fourier, is generous to him, and doubtless well meant for us, but not altogether necessary. The foregoing history bears witness that we have not held Fourier responsible for the American experiments made in his name, and have not treated him with ridicule or disrespect on account of their failures. In our comments on the Sylvania Association we said :

"It is evident enough that this was not Fourierism. Indeed the Sylvanian who wrote the account of his Phalanx, frankly admits for himself and doubtless for his associates, that their doings had in them no semblance of Fourierism. But then the same may be said, without much modification, of all the experiments of the Fourier epoch. Fourier himself, would have utterly disowned every one of them. * * * Here then arises a distinction between Fourierism as a theory propounded by Fourier, and Fourierism as a practical movement administered in this country by Brisbane. * * * The value of Fourier's ideas is not determined, nor the hope of good from them foreclosed, merely by the disasters of these local experiments. And, to deal fairly all around, it must further be said, that it is not right to judge Brisbane by such experiments as that of the Sylvania Association. Let it be remembered that, with all his enthusiasm, he gave warning from time to time, in his publications, of the deficiencies and possible failures of these hybrid ventures ; and was cautious enough to keep himself and his money out of them."

We then proposed a distribution of criticism as

follows : " 1. Fourier, though not responsible for Brisbane's administration, *was* responsible for tantalizing the world with a magnificent theory, without providing the means of translating it into practice. 2. Brisbane, though not altogether responsible for the inadequate attempts of the poor Sylvanians and the rest of the rabble volunteers, must be blamed for spending all his energy in drumming and recruiting ; while, to insure success, he should have given at least half his time to drilling the soldiers and leading them in actual battle. 3. The rank and file as they were strictly volunteers, should have taken better care of themselves, and not been so ready to follow and even rush ahead of leaders, who were thus manifestly devoting themselves to theorizing and propagandism, without experience."

These citations show, and a full reading of the text at page 247 and afterward, will show still more clearly, that we have not been inconsiderate in our treatment of the socialistic leaders.

Mr. Brisbane concludes his letter with an analysis of Fourier's claims as a Philosopher. He does not affirm that Fourier's theory is right, but only that he has pointed out the right way to discover a right theory. This, if true, is certainly a valuable service. Fourier's way, according to Mr. Brisbane, was to work by deduction, instead of induction. He first discovered certain fundamental laws of the universe ; how he discovered them we are not told ; but probably by intuitive assumption, as nothing is said of induction or proof in connection with them ; then from these laws he deduced his social theory, without recurrence to observation or experiment. This, according to Brisbane and Fourier, is the way that all future discoverers in

Social Science must pursue. Is this the right way?

The leaders of modern science say that sound theories in Astronomy and in every thing else are discovered by induction, and that deduction follows after, to apply and extend the principles established by induction. Let us hear one of them:

[From the Introduction to Youmans' New Chemistry.]

"The master minds of our race, by a course of toilsome research through thousands of years, gradually established the principles of mechanical force and motion. Facts were raised into generalities, and these into still higher generalizations, until at length the genius of NEWTON seized the great principle of attraction, which controls all bodies on the earth and in the heavens. He explained the mechanism and motions of the universe by the grandest induction of the human mind.

"The mighty principle thus established, now became the first step of the deductive method. Leverrier, in the solitude of his study, reasoning downward from the universal law through planetary perturbation, proclaimed the existence, place and dimensions of a new and hitherto unknown planet in our solar system. He then called upon the astronomer to verify his deduction by the telescope. The observation was immediately made, the planet was discovered, and the immortal prediction of science was literally fulfilled. Thus induction discovers principles, while deduction applies them.

"It is not by skillful conjecture that knowledge grows, or it would have ripened thousands of years ago. It was not till men had learned to submit their cherished speculations to the merciless and consuming ordeal of verification, that the great truths of nature began to be revealed.   Kepler tells us that he made and rejected nineteen hypotheses of the motion of Mars before he established the true doctrine that it moves in an ellipse.

"The ancient philosophers, disdaining nature, retired into the ideal world of pure meditation, and holding that the mind is the measure of the universe, they believed they could reason out all truths from the depths of the soul. They would not experiment: consequently they lacked the first conditions of science, observation, experiment and induction.   Their mistake was perhaps natural, but it was an error that paralyzed the world. The first step of progress was impossible."

If Youmans points the right way, Fourier, instead of being the Kepler of Social Science, was evidently one of the "ancient philosophers."

We frankly avow that we are at issue with Mr. Brisbane on the main point that he makes for his master.   We do not believe that cogitation without experiment is the right way to a true social theory. With us induction is first; deduction second; and verification by facts or the logic of events, always and everywhere the supreme check on both.   For the sake of this principle we have been studying and bringing to light the lessons of American Socialisms.   If Fourier and Brisbane are on the right track, we are on the wrong.   Let science judge between us.

But Mr. Brisbane thinks that social science is exceptional in its nature, too "vast and complex" to get help from observation and experiment.   All science is vast and complex, reaching out into the unfathomable; but social science seems to us exceptional, if at all, as the field that lies nearest home and most open to observation and experiment.   It is not like astronomy, looking away into the inaccessible regions of the universe, but like navigation or war, commanding us at our peril to study it in the immediate presence of its facts.

Mr. Brisbane insists that Fourier's theory has not had a practical trial: and we have said the same thing before him. Yet we must now say that in another sense it has had its trial. It was brought before the world with all the advantages that the most brilliant school of modern genius could give it; and it did not win the confidence of scientific men or of capitalists, because they saw, what Mr. Brisbane now confesses for it, that it came from the closet, and not from the world of facts. This nineteenth century, which has had thrift and faith enough to lay the Atlantic cable, would have accepted and realized Fourierism, if it had been a genuine product of induction. So that the reason why it never reached the stage of practical trial was, that it failed on the previous question of its scientific legitimacy. Mr. Brisbane himself, as a capitalist, never had confidence enough in it to risk his fortune on it. And poor as the actual experiments were, *human nature* had a trial in them, which convinced all rational observers, that if the numbers and means had been as great as Fourier required, the failures would have been swifter and worse.

We insist that God's appointed way for man to seek the truth in all departments, and above all in Social Science, which is really the science of righteousness, is to combine and alternate thinking with experiment and practice, and constantly submit all theories, whether obtained by scientific investigation or by intuition and inspiration, to the consuming ordeal of practical verification. This is the law established by all the experience of modern science, and the law that every loyal disciple of inspiration will affirm and submit to. And according to this law, the Shakers and Rappites, whom Mr. Brisbane does not condescend to mention, are really the pioneers of modern Socialism, whose experiments deserve a great deal more study than all the speculations of the French schools. By way of offset to Mr. Brisbane's account of the development of sociology in the nineteenth century, we here repeat our historical theory.

The great facts of modern Socialism are these: From 1776, the era of our national Revolution, the Shakers have been established in this country; first at two places in New York; then at four places in Massachusetts; at two in New Hampshire: two in Maine; one in Connecticut; and finally at two in Kentucky, and two in Ohio. In all these places prosperous religious Communism has been modestly and yet loudly preaching to the nation and to the world. New England and New York and the Great West have had actual Phalanxes before their eyes for nearly a century. And in all this time what has been acted on our American stage, has had England, France and Germany for its audience. The example of the Shakers has demonstrated, not merely that successful Communism is subjectively possible, but that this nation is free enough to let it grow. Who can doubt that this demonstration was known and watched in Germany from the beginning; and that it helped the successive experiments and emigrations of the Rappites, the Zoarites and the Ebenezers? These experiments, we have seen, were echoes of Shakerism, growing fainter and fainter, as the time-distance increased. Then the Shaker movement with its echoes was sounding also in England, when Robert Owen undertook to convert the world to Communism, and it is evident enough that he was really a far-off follower of the Rappites. France also had heard of Shakerism, before St. Simon or Fourier began to meditate and write Socialism. These men were nearly contemporaneous with Owen, and all three evidently obeyed a common impulse. That impulse was the sequel and certainly in part the effect of Shakerism. Thus it is no more than bare justice to say, that we are indebted to the Shakers more than to any or all other social architects of modern times. Their success has been the 'specie basis' that has upheld all the paper theories, and counteracted the failures, of the French and English schools. It is very doubtful whether Owenism or Fourierism would have ever existed, or if they had, whether they would have ever moved the practical American nation, if the facts of Shakerism had not existed before them and gone along with them. But to do complete justice we must go a step further. While we say that the Rappites, the Zoarites, the Ebenezers, the Owenites, and even the Fourierists are all echoes of the Shakers, we must also say that the Shakers are the far-off echoes of the PRIMITIVE CHRISTIAN CHURCH.

What then has been Fourier's function? Surely his vast labors and their results have not been useless.

His main achievement has been destruction. He was a merciless critic and scolder of the old civilization. His magnificent imaginations of good things to come have also served the purpose, in the general development of sociology, of what rhetoricians call *excitation*. But his theory of positive construction is, in our opinion, as worthless as the theories of St. Simon and Compte. And so many socialist thinkers have been fuddled by it, that it is at this moment the greatest obstruction to the healthy progress of Social Science. Practically it says to the world—"The experiments of the Shakers and other religious Communities, though successful, are unscientific and worthless; the experiments of the Fourierists that failed so miserably, were illegitimate and prove nothing; inductions from these or any other facts are useless; the only thing that can be done to realize true Association, is to put together eighteen hundred human beings on a domain three miles square, with a palace and outfit to match. Then you will see the equilibrium of the passions and spontaneous order and industry, insuring infinite success." As these conditions are well known to be impossible, because nobody believes in the promised equilibrium and success, the upshot of this teaching is despair. But the nineteenth century is not sitting at the feet of despair; and it will clear Fourierism out of its way.

THE INDUCTIVE SCHOOL OF SOCIALISM, instead of thus shutting the gates of mercy on mankind, says to all: The enormous economies and advantages of combination, which you see in ten thousand joint-stock companies around you, and in the wealth of the Shakers and other successful Associations, and even the blessings of magnificent and permanent HOMES, which you do *not* see in those combinations, are prizes offered to AGREE-MENT. They require no special number. If two or three of you shall agree, you can take those prizes; for by agreement and consequent success, two or three will soon become many. They require no special amount of capital. If you are poor, by combination you can become rich. Agreement can make its own fortune, and need not wait to be endowed. The blessing of heaven is upon it, and it can work its way from the lowest poverty to all the wealth that Fourier taught his disciples to beg from capitalists.

Thus demanding equilibrium of the passions and harmony at the outset, instead of looking for them as the miraculous result of getting together vast assemblages, we throw to the winds the limitations and impossible conditions of Fourierism. And the harmony we ask for as condition precedent, is not chimerical, but already exists. All the facts we have, indicate that it comes by religion ; and the idea is evidently growing in the public mind that religion is the *only* bond of agreement sufficient for family Association. If any dislike this condition, we say : Seek agreement in some other way, till all doubt on this point shall be removed by abundant experiment. The lists are open. We promise nothing to non-religious attempts ; but we promise all things to agreement, let it come as it may. If Paganism or infidelity or nothingarianism can produce the required agreement, they will win the prize. But on the other hand if it shall turn out in this great Olympic of the nineteenth century, that Christianity alone has the harmonizing power necessary to successful Association, then Christianity will at last get its crown.

INDEX.

A CATALOGUE OF SELECTED DOVER BOOKS
IN ALL FIELDS OF INTEREST

A CATALOGUE OF SELECTED DOVER BOOKS
IN ALL FIELDS OF INTEREST

AMERICA'S OLD MASTERS, James T. Flexner. Four men emerged unexpectedly from provincial 18th century America to leadership in European art: Benjamin West, J. S. Copley, C. R. Peale, Gilbert Stuart. Brilliant coverage of lives and contributions. Revised, 1967 edition. 69 plates. 365pp. of text.
21806-6 Paperbound $2.75

FIRST FLOWERS OF OUR WILDERNESS: AMERICAN PAINTING, THE COLONIAL PERIOD, James T. Flexner. Painters, and regional painting traditions from earliest Colonial times up to the emergence of Copley, West and Peale Sr., Foster, Gustavus Hesselius, Feke, John Smibert and many anonymous painters in the primitive manner. Engaging presentation, with 162 illustrations. xxii + 368pp.
22180-6 Paperbound $3.50

THE LIGHT OF DISTANT SKIES: AMERICAN PAINTING, 1760-1835, James T. Flexner. The great generation of early American painters goes to Europe to learn and to teach: West, Copley, Gilbert Stuart and others. Allston, Trumbull, Morse; also contemporary American painters—primitives, derivatives, academics—who remained in America. 102 illustrations. xiii + 306pp.
22179-2 Paperbound $3.00

A HISTORY OF THE RISE AND PROGRESS OF THE ARTS OF DESIGN IN THE UNITED STATES, William Dunlap. Much the richest mine of information on early American painters, sculptors, architects, engravers, miniaturists, etc. The only source of information for scores of artists, the major primary source for many others. Unabridged reprint of rare original 1834 edition, with new introduction by James T. Flexner, and 394 new illustrations. Edited by Rita Weiss. 6⅝ x 9⅝.
21695-0, 21696-9, 21697-7 Three volumes, Paperbound $13.50

EPOCHS OF CHINESE AND JAPANESE ART, Ernest F. Fenollosa. From primitive Chinese art to the 20th century, thorough history, explanation of every important art period and form, including Japanese woodcuts; main stress on China and Japan, but Tibet, Korea also included. Still unexcelled for its detailed, rich coverage of cultural background, aesthetic elements, diffusion studies, particularly of the historical period. 2nd, 1913 edition. 242 illustrations. lii + 439pp. of text.
20364-6, 20365-4 Two volumes, Paperbound $5.00

THE GENTLE ART OF MAKING ENEMIES, James A. M. Whistler. Greatest wit of his day deflates Oscar Wilde, Ruskin, Swinburne; strikes back at inane critics, exhibitions, art journalism; aesthetics of impressionist revolution in most striking form. Highly readable classic by great painter. Reproduction of edition designed by Whistler. Introduction by Alfred Werner. xxxvi + 334pp.
21875-9 Paperbound $2.25

VISUAL ILLUSIONS: THEIR CAUSES, CHARACTERISTICS, AND APPLICATIONS, Matthew Luckiesh. Thorough description and discussion of optical illusion, geometric and perspective, particularly; size and shape distortions, illusions of color, of motion; natural illusions; use of illusion in art and magic, industry, etc. Most useful today with op art, also for classical art. Scores of effects illustrated. Introduction by William H. Ittleson. 100 illustrations. xxi + 252pp.

21530-X Paperbound $1.50

A HANDBOOK OF ANATOMY FOR ART STUDENTS, Arthur Thomson. Thorough, virtually exhaustive coverage of skeletal structure, musculature, etc. Full text, supplemented by anatomical diagrams and drawings and by photographs of undraped figures. Unique in its comparison of male and female forms, pointing out differences of contour, texture, form. 211 figures, 40 drawings, 86 photographs. xx + 459pp. 5⅜ x 8⅜.

21163-0 Paperbound $3.00

150 MASTERPIECES OF DRAWING, Selected by Anthony Toney. Full page reproductions of drawings from the early 16th to the end of the 18th century, all beautifully reproduced: Rembrandt, Michelangelo, Dürer, Fragonard, Urs, Graf, Wouwerman, many others. First-rate browsing book, model book for artists. xviii + 150pp. 8⅜ x 11¼.

21032-4 Paperbound $2.00

THE LATER WORK OF AUBREY BEARDSLEY, Aubrey Beardsley. Exotic, erotic, ironic masterpieces in full maturity: Comedy Ballet, Venus and Tannhauser, Pierrot, Lysistrata, Rape of the Lock, Savoy material, Ali Baba, Volpone, etc. This material revolutionized the art world, and is still powerful, fresh, brilliant. With *The Early Work,* all Beardsley's finest work. 174 plates, 2 in color. xiv + 176pp. 8⅛ x 11.

21817-1 Paperbound $3.00

DRAWINGS OF REMBRANDT, Rembrandt van Rijn. Complete reproduction of fabulously rare edition by Lippmann and Hofstede de Groot, completely reedited, updated, improved by Prof. Seymour Slive, Fogg Museum. Portraits, Biblical sketches, landscapes, Oriental types, nudes, episodes from classical mythology—All Rembrandt's fertile genius. Also selection of drawings by his pupils and followers. "Stunning volumes," *Saturday Review.* 550 illustrations. lxxviii + 552pp. 9⅛ x 12¼.

21485-0, 21486-9 Two volumes, Paperbound $6.50

THE DISASTERS OF WAR, Francisco Goya. One of the masterpieces of Western civilization—83 etchings that record Goya's shattering, bitter reaction to the Napoleonic war that swept through Spain after the insurrection of 1808 and to war in general. Reprint of the first edition, with three additional plates from Boston's Museum of Fine Arts. All plates facsimile size. Introduction by Philip Hofer, Fogg Museum. v + 97pp. 9⅜ x 8¼.

21872-4 Paperbound $1.75

GRAPHIC WORKS OF ODILON REDON. Largest collection of Redon's graphic works ever assembled: 172 lithographs, 28 etchings and engravings, 9 drawings. These include some of his most famous works. All the plates from *Odilon Redon: oeuvre graphique complet,* plus additional plates. New introduction and caption translations by Alfred Werner. 209 illustrations. xxvii + 209pp. 9⅛ x 12¼.

21966-8 Paperbound $4.00

DESIGN BY ACCIDENT; A BOOK OF "ACCIDENTAL EFFECTS" FOR ARTISTS AND DESIGNERS, James F. O'Brien. Create your own unique, striking, imaginative effects by "controlled accident" interaction of materials: paints and lacquers, oil and water based paints, splatter, crackling materials, shatter, similar items. Everything you do will be different; first book on this limitless art, so useful to both fine artist and commercial artist. Full instructions. 192 plates showing "accidents," 8 in color. viii + 215pp. 8⅜ x 11¼. 21942-9 Paperbound $3.50

THE BOOK OF SIGNS, Rudolf Koch. Famed German type designer draws 493 beautiful symbols: religious, mystical, alchemical, imperial, property marks, runes, etc. Remarkable fusion of traditional and modern. Good for suggestions of timelessness, smartness, modernity. Text. vi + 104pp. 6⅛ x 9¼.
20162-7 Paperbound $1.25

HISTORY OF INDIAN AND INDONESIAN ART, Ananda K. Coomaraswamy. An unabridged republication of one of the finest books by a great scholar in Eastern art. Rich in descriptive material, history, social backgrounds; Sunga reliefs, Rajput paintings, Gupta temples, Burmese frescoes, textiles, jewelry, sculpture, etc. 400 photos. viii + 423pp. 6⅜ x 9¾. 21436-2 Paperbound $3.50

PRIMITIVE ART, Franz Boas. America's foremost anthropologist surveys textiles, ceramics, woodcarving, basketry, metalwork, etc.; patterns, technology, creation of symbols, style origins. All areas of world, but very full on Northwest Coast Indians. More than 350 illustrations of baskets, boxes, totem poles, weapons, etc. 378 pp.
20025-6 Paperbound $2.50

THE GENTLEMAN AND CABINET MAKER'S DIRECTOR, Thomas Chippendale. Full reprint (third edition, 1762) of most influential furniture book of all time, by master cabinetmaker. 200 plates, illustrating chairs, sofas, mirrors, tables, cabinets, plus 24 photographs of surviving pieces. Biographical introduction by N. Bienenstock. vi + 249pp. 9⅞ x 12¾. 21601-2 Paperbound $3.50

AMERICAN ANTIQUE FURNITURE, Edgar G. Miller, Jr. The basic coverage of all American furniture before 1840. Individual chapters cover type of furniture—clocks, tables, sideboards, etc.—chronologically, with inexhaustible wealth of data. More than 2100 photographs, all identified, commented on. Essential to all early American collectors. Introduction by H. E. Keyes. vi + 1106pp. 7⅞ x 10¾.
21599-7, 21600-4 Two volumes, Paperbound $7.50

PENNSYLVANIA DUTCH AMERICAN FOLK ART, Henry J. Kauffman. 279 photos, 28 drawings of tulipware, Fraktur script, painted tinware, toys, flowered furniture, quilts, samplers, hex signs, house interiors, etc. Full descriptive text. Excellent for tourist, rewarding for designer, collector. Map. 146pp. 7⅞ x 10¾.
21205-X Paperbound $2.00

EARLY NEW ENGLAND GRAVESTONE RUBBINGS, Edmund V. Gillon, Jr. 43 photographs, 226 carefully reproduced rubbings show heavily symbolic, sometimes macabre early gravestones, up to early 19th century. Remarkable early American primitive art, occasionally strikingly beautiful; always powerful. Text. xxvi + 207pp. 8⅜ x 11¼. 21380-3 Paperbound $3.00

ALPHABETS AND ORNAMENTS, Ernst Lehner. Well-known pictorial source for decorative alphabets, script examples, cartouches, frames, decorative title pages, calligraphic initials, borders, similar material. 14th to 19th century, mostly European. Useful in almost any graphic arts designing, varied styles. 750 illustrations. 256pp. 7 x 10.
21905-4 Paperbound $3.50

PAINTING: A CREATIVE APPROACH, Norman Colquhoun. For the beginner simple guide provides an instructive approach to painting: major stumbling blocks for beginner; overcoming them, technical points; paints and pigments; oil painting; watercolor and other media and color. New section on "plastic" paints. Glossary. Formerly *Paint Your Own Pictures.* 221pp.
22000-1 Paperbound $1.75

THE ENJOYMENT AND USE OF COLOR, Walter Sargent. Explanation of the relations between colors themselves and between colors in nature and art, including hundreds of little-known facts about color values, intensities, effects of high and low illumination, complementary colors. Many practical hints for painters, references to great masters. 7 color plates, 29 illustrations. x + 274pp.
20944-X Paperbound $2.50

THE NOTEBOOKS OF LEONARDO DA VINCI, compiled and edited by Jean Paul Richter. 1566 extracts from original manuscripts reveal the full range of Leonardo's versatile genius: all his writings on painting, sculpture, architecture, anatomy, astronomy, geography, topography, physiology, mining, music, etc., in both Italian and English, with 186 plates of manuscript pages and more than 500 additional drawings. Includes studies for the Last Supper, the lost Sforza monument, and other works. Total of xlvii + 866pp. $7\frac{7}{8}$ x $10\frac{3}{4}$.
22572-0, 22573-9 Two volumes, Paperbound $10.00

MONTGOMERY WARD CATALOGUE OF 1895. Tea gowns, yards of flannel and pillow-case lace, stereoscopes, books of gospel hymns, the New Improved Singer Sewing Machine, side saddles, milk skimmers, straight-edged razors, high-button shoes, spittoons, and on and on . . . listing some 25,000 items, practically all illustrated. Essential to the shoppers of the 1890's, it is our truest record of the spirit of the period. Unaltered reprint of Issue No. 57, Spring and Summer 1895. Introduction by Boris Emmet. Innumerable illustrations. xiii + 624pp. $8\frac{1}{2}$ x $11\frac{5}{8}$.
22377-9 Paperbound $6.95

THE CRYSTAL PALACE EXHIBITION ILLUSTRATED CATALOGUE (LONDON, 1851). One of the wonders of the modern world—the Crystal Palace Exhibition in which all the nations of the civilized world exhibited their achievements in the arts and sciences—presented in an equally important illustrated catalogue. More than 1700 items pictured with accompanying text—ceramics, textiles, cast-iron work, carpets, pianos, sleds, razors, wall-papers, billiard tables, beehives, silverware and hundreds of other artifacts—represent the focal point of Victorian culture in the Western World. Probably the largest collection of Victorian decorative art ever assembled—indispensable for antiquarians and designers. Unabridged republication of the Art-Journal Catalogue of the Great Exhibition of 1851, with all terminal essays. New introduction by John Gloag, F.S.A. xxxiv + 426pp. 9 x 12.
22503-8 Paperbound $4.50

A HISTORY OF COSTUME, Carl Köhler. Definitive history, based on surviving pieces of clothing primarily, and paintings, statues, etc. secondarily. Highly readable text, supplemented by 594 illustrations of costumes of the ancient Mediterranean peoples, Greece and Rome, the Teutonic prehistoric period; costumes of the Middle Ages, Renaissance, Baroque, 18th and 19th centuries. Clear, measured patterns are provided for many clothing articles. Approach is practical throughout. Enlarged by Emma von Sichart. 464pp.   21030-8 Paperbound $3.00

ORIENTAL RUGS, ANTIQUE AND MODERN, Walter A. Hawley. A complete and authoritative treatise on the Oriental rug—where they are made, by whom and how, designs and symbols, characteristics in detail of the six major groups, how to distinguish them and how to buy them. Detailed technical data is provided on periods, weaves, warps, wefts, textures, sides, ends and knots, although no technical background is required for an understanding. 11 color plates, 80 halftones, 4 maps. vi + 320pp. 6⅛ x 9⅛.   22366-3 Paperbound $5.00

TEN BOOKS ON ARCHITECTURE, Vitruvius. By any standards the most important book on architecture ever written. Early Roman discussion of aesthetics of building, construction methods, orders, sites, and every other aspect of architecture has inspired, instructed architecture for about 2,000 years. Stands behind Palladio, Michelangelo, Bramante, Wren, countless others. Definitive Morris H. Morgan translation. 68 illustrations. xii + 331pp.   20645-9 Paperbound $2.50

THE FOUR BOOKS OF ARCHITECTURE, Andrea Palladio. Translated into every major Western European language in the two centuries following its publication in 1570, this has been one of the most influential books in the history of architecture. Complete reprint of the 1738 Isaac Ware edition. New introduction by Adolf Placzek, Columbia Univ. 216 plates. xxii + 110pp. of text. 9½ x 12¾.
21308-0 Clothbound $10.00

STICKS AND STONES: A STUDY OF AMERICAN ARCHITECTURE AND CIVILIZATION, Lewis Mumford. One of the great classics of American cultural history. American architecture from the medieval-inspired earliest forms to the early 20th century; evolution of structure and style, and reciprocal influences on environment. 21 photographic illustrations. 238pp.   20202-X Paperbound $2.00

THE AMERICAN BUILDER'S COMPANION, Asher Benjamin. The most widely used early 19th century architectural style and source book, for colonial up into Greek Revival periods. Extensive development of geometry of carpentering, construction of sashes, frames, doors, stairs; plans and elevations of domestic and other buildings. Hundreds of thousands of houses were built according to this book, now invaluable to historians, architects, restorers, etc. 1827 edition. 59 plates. 114pp. 7⅞ x 10¾.
22236-5 Paperbound $3.00

DUTCH HOUSES IN THE HUDSON VALLEY BEFORE 1776, Helen Wilkinson Reynolds. The standard survey of the Dutch colonial house and outbuildings, with constructional features, decoration, and local history associated with individual homesteads. Introduction by Franklin D. Roosevelt. Map. 150 illustrations. 469pp. 6⅝ x 9¼.   21469-9 Paperbound $3.50

THE ARCHITECTURE OF COUNTRY HOUSES, Andrew J. Downing. Together with Vaux's *Villas and Cottages* this is the basic book for Hudson River Gothic architecture of the middle Victorian period. Full, sound discussions of general aspects of housing, architecture, style, decoration, furnishing, together with scores of detailed house plans, illustrations of specific buildings, accompanied by full text. Perhaps the most influential single American architectural book. 1850 edition. Introduction by J. Stewart Johnson. 321 figures, 34 architectural designs. xvi + 560pp.

22003-6 Paperbound $3.50

LOST EXAMPLES OF COLONIAL ARCHITECTURE, John Mead Howells. Full-page photographs of buildings that have disappeared or been so altered as to be denatured, including many designed by major early American architects. 245 plates. xvii + 248pp. 7⅞ x 10¾.

21143-6 Paperbound $3.00

DOMESTIC ARCHITECTURE OF THE AMERICAN COLONIES AND OF THE EARLY REPUBLIC, Fiske Kimball. Foremost architect and restorer of Williamsburg and Monticello covers nearly 200 homes between 1620-1825. Architectural details, construction, style features, special fixtures, floor plans, etc. Generally considered finest work in its area. 219 illustrations of houses, doorways, windows, capital mantels. xx + 314pp. 7⅞ x 10¾.

21743-4 Paperbound $3.50

EARLY AMERICAN ROOMS: 1650-1858, edited by Russell Hawes Kettell. Tour of 12 rooms, each representative of a different era in American history and each furnished, decorated, designed and occupied in the style of the era. 72 plans and elevations, 8-page color section, etc., show fabrics, wall papers, arrangements, etc. Full descriptive text. xvii + 200pp. of text. 8⅜ x 11¼.

21633-0 Paperbound $4.00

THE FITZWILLIAM VIRGINAL BOOK, edited by J. Fuller Maitland and W. B. Squire. Full modern printing of famous early 17th-century ms. volume of 300 works by Morley, Byrd, Bull, Gibbons, etc. For piano or other modern keyboard instrument; easy to read format. xxxvi + 938pp. 8⅜ x 11.

21068-5, 21069-3 Two volumes, Paperbound $8.00

HARPSICHORD MUSIC, Johann Sebastian Bach. Bach Gesellschaft edition. A rich selection of Bach's masterpieces for the harpsichord: the six English Suites, six French Suites, the six Partitas (Clavierübung part I), the Goldberg Variations (Clavierübung part IV), the fifteen Two-Part Inventions and the fifteen Three-Part Sinfonias. Clearly reproduced on large sheets with ample margins; eminently playable. vi + 312pp. 8⅛ x 11.

22360-4 Paperbound $5.00

THE MUSIC OF BACH: AN INTRODUCTION, Charles Sanford Terry. A fine, nontechnical introduction to Bach's music, both instrumental and vocal. Covers organ music, chamber music, passion music, other types. Analyzes themes, developments, innovations. x + 114pp.

21075-8 Paperbound $1.25

BEETHOVEN AND HIS NINE SYMPHONIES, Sir George Grove. Noted British musicologist provides best history, analysis, commentary on symphonies. Very thorough, rigorously accurate; necessary to both advanced student and amateur music lover. 436 musical passages. vii + 407 pp.

20334-4 Paperbound $2.25

JOHANN SEBASTIAN BACH, Philipp Spitta. One of the great classics of musicology, this definitive analysis of Bach's music (and life) has never been surpassed. Lucid, nontechnical analyses of hundreds of pieces (30 pages devoted to St. Matthew Passion, 26 to B Minor Mass). Also includes major analysis of 18th-century music. 450 musical examples. 40-page musical supplement. Total of xx + 1799pp.

(EUK) 22278-0, 22279-9 Two volumes, Clothbound $15.00

MOZART AND HIS PIANO CONCERTOS, Cuthbert Girdlestone. The only full-length study of an important area of Mozart's creativity. Provides detailed analyses of all 23 concertos, traces inspirational sources. 417 musical examples. Second edition. 509pp.
(USO) 21271-8 Paperbound $3.50

THE PERFECT WAGNERITE: A COMMENTARY ON THE NIBLUNG'S RING, George Bernard Shaw. Brilliant and still relevant criticism in remarkable essays on Wagner's Ring cycle, Shaw's ideas on political and social ideology behind the plots, role of Leitmotifs, vocal requisites, etc. Prefaces. xxi + 136pp.

21707-8 Paperbound $1.50

DON GIOVANNI, W. A. Mozart. Complete libretto, modern English translation; biographies of composer and librettist; accounts of early performances and critical reaction. Lavishly illustrated. All the material you need to understand and appreciate this great work. Dover Opera Guide and Libretto Series; translated and introduced by Ellen Bleiler. 92 illustrations. 209pp.

21134-7 Paperbound $1.50

HIGH FIDELITY SYSTEMS: A LAYMAN'S GUIDE, Roy F. Allison. All the basic information you need for setting up your own audio system: high fidelity and stereo record players, tape records, F.M. Connections, adjusting tone arm, cartridge, checking needle alignment, positioning speakers, phasing speakers, adjusting hums, trouble-shooting, maintenance, and similar topics. Enlarged 1965 edition. More than 50 charts, diagrams, photos. iv + 91pp.   21514-8 Paperbound $1.25

REPRODUCTION OF SOUND, Edgar Villchur. Thorough coverage for laymen of high fidelity systems, reproducing systems in general, needles, amplifiers, preamps, loudspeakers, feedback, explaining physical background. "A rare talent for making technicalities vividly comprehensible," R. Darrell, *High Fidelity*. 69 figures. iv + 92pp.
21515-6 Paperbound $1.00

HEAR ME TALKIN' TO YA: THE STORY OF JAZZ AS TOLD BY THE MEN WHO MADE IT, Nat Shapiro and Nat Hentoff. Louis Armstrong, Fats Waller, Jo Jones, Clarence Williams, Billy Holiday, Duke Ellington, Jelly Roll Morton and dozens of other jazz greats tell how it was in Chicago's South Side, New Orleans, depression Harlem and the modern West Coast as jazz was born and grew. xvi + 429pp.

21726-4 Paperbound $2.00

FABLES OF AESOP, translated by Sir Roger L'Estrange. A reproduction of the very rare 1931 Paris edition; a selection of the most interesting fables, together with 50 imaginative drawings by Alexander Calder. v + 128pp. 6½x9¼.

21780-9 Paperbound $1.25

AGAINST THE GRAIN (A REBOURS), Joris K. Huysmans. Filled with weird images, evidences of a bizarre imagination, exotic experiments with hallucinatory drugs, rich tastes and smells and the diversions of its sybarite hero Duc Jean des Esseintes, this classic novel pushed 19th-century literary decadence to its limits. Full unabridged edition. Do not confuse this with abridged editions generally sold. Introduction by Havelock Ellis. xlix + 206pp. 22190-3 Paperbound $2.00

VARIORUM SHAKESPEARE: HAMLET. Edited by Horace H. Furness; a landmark of American scholarship. Exhaustive footnotes and appendices treat all doubtful words and phrases, as well as suggested critical emendations throughout the play's history. First volume contains editor's own text, collated with all Quartos and Folios. Second volume contains full first Quarto, translations of Shakespeare's sources (Belleforest, and Saxo Grammaticus), Der Bestrafte Brudermord, and many essays on critical and historical points of interest by major authorities of past and present. Includes details of staging and costuming over the years. By far the best edition available for serious students of Shakespeare. Total of xx + 905pp. 21004-9, 21005-7, 2 volumes, Paperbound $5.25

A LIFE OF WILLIAM SHAKESPEARE, Sir Sidney Lee. This is the standard life of Shakespeare, summarizing everything known about Shakespeare and his plays. Incredibly rich in material, broad in coverage, clear and judicious, it has served thousands as the best introduction to Shakespeare. 1931 edition. 9 plates. xxix + 792pp. (USO) 21967-4 Paperbound $3.75

MASTERS OF THE DRAMA, John Gassner. Most comprehensive history of the drama in print, covering every tradition from Greeks to modern Europe and America, including India, Far East, etc. Covers more than 800 dramatists, 2000 plays, with biographical material, plot summaries, theatre history, criticism, etc. "Best of its kind in English," *New Republic.* 77 illustrations. xxii + 890pp.
20100-7 Clothbound $7.50

THE EVOLUTION OF THE ENGLISH LANGUAGE, George McKnight. The growth of English, from the 14th century to the present. Unusual, non-technical account presents basic information in very interesting form: sound shifts, change in grammar and syntax, vocabulary growth, similar topics. Abundantly illustrated with quotations. Formerly *Modern English in the Making.* xii + 590pp.
21932-1 Paperbound $3.50

AN ETYMOLOGICAL DICTIONARY OF MODERN ENGLISH, Ernest Weekley. Fullest, richest work of its sort, by foremost British lexicographer. Detailed word histories, including many colloquial and archaic words; extensive quotations. Do not confuse this with the Concise Etymological Dictionary, which is much abridged. Total of xxvii + 830pp. $6\frac{1}{2}$ x $9\frac{1}{4}$.
21873-2, 21874-0 Two volumes, Paperbound $5.50

FLATLAND: A ROMANCE OF MANY DIMENSIONS, E. A. Abbott. Classic of science-fiction explores ramifications of life in a two-dimensional world, and what happens when a three-dimensional being intrudes. Amusing reading, but also useful as introduction to thought about hyperspace. Introduction by Banesh Hoffmann. 16 illustrations. xx + 103pp. 20001-9 Paperbound $1.00

POEMS OF ANNE BRADSTREET, edited with an introduction by Robert Hutchinson. A new selection of poems by America's first poet and perhaps the first significant woman poet in the English language. 48 poems display her development in works of considerable variety—love poems, domestic poems, religious meditations, formal elegies, "quaternions," etc. Notes, bibliography. viii + 222pp.

22160-1 Paperbound $2.00

THREE GOTHIC NOVELS: THE CASTLE OF OTRANTO BY HORACE WALPOLE; VATHEK BY WILLIAM BECKFORD; THE VAMPYRE BY JOHN POLIDORI, WITH FRAGMENT OF A NOVEL BY LORD BYRON, edited by E. F. Bleiler. The first Gothic novel, by Walpole; the finest Oriental tale in English, by Beckford; powerful Romantic supernatural story in versions by Polidori and Byron. All extremely important in history of literature; all still exciting, packed with supernatural thrills, ghosts, haunted castles, magic, etc. xl + 291pp.

21232-7 Paperbound $2.00

THE BEST TALES OF HOFFMANN, E. T. A. Hoffmann. 10 of Hoffmann's most important stories, in modern re-editings of standard translations: Nutcracker and the King of Mice, Signor Formica, Automata, The Sandman, Rath Krespel, The Golden Flowerpot, Master Martin the Cooper, The Mines of Falun, The King's Betrothed, A New Year's Eve Adventure. 7 illustrations by Hoffmann. Edited by E. F. Bleiler. xxxix + 419pp.   21793-0 Paperbound $2.25

GHOST AND HORROR STORIES OF AMBROSE BIERCE, Ambrose Bierce. 23 strikingly modern stories of the horrors latent in the human mind: The Eyes of the Panther, The Damned Thing, An Occurrence at Owl Creek Bridge, An Inhabitant of Carcosa, etc., plus the dream-essay, Visions of the Night. Edited by E. F. Bleiler. xxii + 199pp.   20767-6 Paperbound $1.50

BEST GHOST STORIES OF J. S. LEFANU, J. Sheridan LeFanu. Finest stories by Victorian master often considered greatest supernatural writer of all. Carmilla, Green Tea, The Haunted Baronet, The Familiar, and 12 others. Most never before available in the U. S. A. Edited by E. F. Bleiler. 8 illustrations from Victorian publications. xvii + 467pp.   20415-4 Paperbound $2.50

THE TIME STREAM, THE GREATEST ADVENTURE, AND THE PURPLE SAPPHIRE— THREE SCIENCE FICTION NOVELS, John Taine (Eric Temple Bell). Great American mathematician was also foremost science fiction novelist of the 1920's. *The Time Stream,* one of all-time classics, uses concepts of circular time; *The Greatest Adventure,* incredibly ancient biological experiments from Antarctica threaten to escape; *The Purple Sapphire,* superscience, lost races in Central Tibet, survivors of the Great Race. 4 illustrations by Frank R. Paul. v + 532pp.

21180-0 Paperbound $2.50

SEVEN SCIENCE FICTION NOVELS, H. G. Wells. The standard collection of the great novels. Complete, unabridged. *First Men in the Moon, Island of Dr. Moreau, War of the Worlds, Food of the Gods, Invisible Man, Time Machine, In the Days of the Comet.* Not only science fiction fans, but every educated person owes it to himself to read these novels. 1015pp.   20264-X Clothbound $5.00

LAST AND FIRST MEN AND STAR MAKER, TWO SCIENCE FICTION NOVELS, Olaf Stapledon. Greatest future histories in science fiction. In the first, human intelligence is the "hero," through strange paths of evolution, interplanetary invasions, incredible technologies, near extinctions and reemergences. Star Maker describes the quest of a band of star rovers for intelligence itself, through time and space: weird inhuman civilizations, crustacean minds, symbiotic worlds, etc. Complete, unabridged. v + 438pp. 21962-3 Paperbound $2.00

THREE PROPHETIC NOVELS, H. G. WELLS. Stages of a consistently planned future for mankind. *When the Sleeper Wakes,* and *A Story of the Days to Come,* anticipate *Brave New World* and *1984,* in the 21st Century; *The Time Machine,* only complete version in print, shows farther future and the end of mankind. All show Wells's greatest gifts as storyteller and novelist. Edited by E. F. Bleiler. x + 335pp. (USO) 20605-X Paperbound $2.00

THE DEVIL'S DICTIONARY, Ambrose Bierce. America's own Oscar Wilde—Ambrose Bierce—offers his barbed iconoclastic wisdom in over 1,000 definitions hailed by H. L. Mencken as "some of the most gorgeous witticisms in the English language." 145pp. 20487-1 Paperbound $1.25

MAX AND MORITZ, Wilhelm Busch. Great children's classic, father of comic strip, of two bad boys, Max and Moritz. Also Ker and Plunk (Plisch und Plumm), Cat and Mouse, Deceitful Henry, Ice-Peter, The Boy and the Pipe, and five other pieces. Original German, with English translation. Edited by H. Arthur Klein; translations by various hands and H. Arthur Klein. vi + 216pp.
20181-3 Paperbound $1.50

PIGS IS PIGS AND OTHER FAVORITES, Ellis Parker Butler. The title story is one of the best humor short stories, as Mike Flannery obfuscates biology and English. Also included, That Pup of Murchison's, The Great American Pie Company, and Perkins of Portland. 14 illustrations. v + 109pp. 21532-6 Paperbound $1.00

THE PETERKIN PAPERS, Lucretia P. Hale. It takes genius to be as stupidly mad as the Peterkins, as they decide to become wise, celebrate the "Fourth," keep a cow, and otherwise strain the resources of the Lady from Philadelphia. Basic book of American humor. 153 illustrations. 219pp. 20794-3 Paperbound $1.25

PERRAULT'S FAIRY TALES, translated by A. E. Johnson and S. R. Littlewood, with 34 full-page illustrations by Gustave Doré. All the original Perrault stories—Cinderella, Sleeping Beauty, Bluebeard, Little Red Riding Hood, Puss in Boots, Tom Thumb, etc.—with their witty verse morals and the magnificent illustrations of Doré. One of the five or six great books of European fairy tales. viii + 117pp. 8⅛ x 11. 22311-6 Paperbound $2.00

OLD HUNGARIAN FAIRY TALES, Baroness Orczy. Favorites translated and adapted by author of the *Scarlet Pimpernel.* Eight fairy tales include "The Suitors of Princess Fire-Fly," "The Twin Hunchbacks," "Mr. Cuttlefish's Love Story," and "The Enchanted Cat." This little volume of magic and adventure will captivate children as it has for generations. 90 drawings by Montagu Barstow. 96pp.
(USO) 22293-4 Paperbound $1.95

THE RED FAIRY BOOK, Andrew Lang. Lang's color fairy books have long been children's favorites. This volume includes Rapunzel, Jack and the Bean-stalk and 35 other stories, familiar and unfamiliar. 4 plates, 93 illustrations x + 367pp.
21673-X Paperbound $1.95

THE BLUE FAIRY BOOK, Andrew Lang. Lang's tales come from all countries and all times. Here are 37 tales from Grimm, the Arabian Nights, Greek Mythology, and other fascinating sources. 8 plates, 130 illustrations. xi + 390pp.
21437-0 Paperbound $1.95

HOUSEHOLD STORIES BY THE BROTHERS GRIMM. Classic English-language edition of the well-known tales — Rumpelstiltskin, Snow White, Hansel and Gretel, The Twelve Brothers, Faithful John, Rapunzel, Tom Thumb (52 stories in all). Translated into simple, straightforward English by Lucy Crane. Ornamented with headpieces, vignettes, elaborate decorative initials and a dozen full-page illustrations by Walter Crane. x + 269pp.
21080-4 Paperbound $2.00

THE MERRY ADVENTURES OF ROBIN HOOD, Howard Pyle. The finest modern versions of the traditional ballads and tales about the great English outlaw. Howard Pyle's complete prose version, with every word, every illustration of the first edition. Do not confuse this facsimile of the original (1883) with modern editions that change text or illustrations. 23 plates plus many page decorations. xxii + 296pp.
22043-5 Paperbound $2.00

THE STORY OF KING ARTHUR AND HIS KNIGHTS, Howard Pyle. The finest children's version of the life of King Arthur; brilliantly retold by Pyle, with 48 of his most imaginative illustrations. xviii + 313pp. 6⅛ x 9¼.
21445-1 Paperbound $2.00

THE WONDERFUL WIZARD OF OZ, L. Frank Baum. America's finest children's book in facsimile of first edition with all Denslow illustrations in full color. The edition a child should have. Introduction by Martin Gardner. 23 color plates, scores of drawings. iv + 267pp.
20691-2 Paperbound $1.95

THE MARVELOUS LAND OF OZ, L. Frank Baum. The second Oz book, every bit as imaginative as the Wizard. The hero is a boy named Tip, but the Scarecrow and the Tin Woodman are back, as is the Oz magic. 16 color plates, 120 drawings by John R. Neill. 287pp.
20692-0 Paperbound $1.75

THE MAGICAL MONARCH OF MO, L. Frank Baum. Remarkable adventures in a land even stranger than Oz. The best of Baum's books not in the Oz series. 15 color plates and dozens of drawings by Frank Verbeck. xviii + 237pp.
21892-9 Paperbound $2.00

THE BAD CHILD'S BOOK OF BEASTS, MORE BEASTS FOR WORSE CHILDREN, A MORAL ALPHABET, Hilaire Belloc. Three complete humor classics in one volume. Be kind to the frog, and do not call him names . . . and 28 other whimsical animals. Familiar favorites and some not so well known. Illustrated by Basil Blackwell.
156pp. (USO) 20749-8 Paperbound $1.25

EAST O' THE SUN AND WEST O' THE MOON, George W. Dasent. Considered the best of all translations of these Norwegian folk tales, this collection has been enjoyed by generations of children (and folklorists too). Includes True and Untrue, Why the Sea is Salt, East O' the Sun and West O' the Moon, Why the Bear is Stumpy-Tailed, Boots and the Troll, The Cock and the Hen, Rich Peter the Pedlar, and 52 more. The only edition with all 59 tales. 77 illustrations by Erik Werenskiold and Theodor Kittelsen. xv + 418pp. 22521-6 Paperbound $3.00

GOOPS AND HOW TO BE THEM, Gelett Burgess. Classic of tongue-in-cheek humor, masquerading as etiquette book. 87 verses, twice as many cartoons, show mischievous Goops as they demonstrate to children virtues of table manners, neatness, courtesy, etc. Favorite for generations. viii + 88pp. 6½ x 9¼.
22233-0 Paperbound $1.25

ALICE'S ADVENTURES UNDER GROUND, Lewis Carroll. The first version, quite different from the final *Alice in Wonderland,* printed out by Carroll himself with his own illustrations. Complete facsimile of the "million dollar" manuscript Carroll gave to Alice Liddell in 1864. Introduction by Martin Gardner. viii + 96pp. Title and dedication pages in color. 21482-6 Paperbound $1.25

THE BROWNIES, THEIR BOOK, Palmer Cox. Small as mice, cunning as foxes, exuberant and full of mischief, the Brownies go to the zoo, toy shop, seashore, circus, etc., in 24 verse adventures and 266 illustrations. Long a favorite, since their first appearance in St. Nicholas Magazine. xi + 144pp. 6⅝ x 9¼.
21265-3 Paperbound $1.75

SONGS OF CHILDHOOD, Walter De La Mare. Published (under the pseudonym Walter Ramal) when De La Mare was only 29, this charming collection has long been a favorite children's book. A facsimile of the first edition in paper, the 47 poems capture the simplicity of the nursery rhyme and the ballad, including such lyrics as I Met Eve, Tartary, The Silver Penny. vii + 106pp. 21972-0 Paperbound $1.25

THE COMPLETE NONSENSE OF EDWARD LEAR, Edward Lear. The finest 19th-century humorist-cartoonist in full: all nonsense limericks, zany alphabets, Owl and Pussycat, songs, nonsense botany, and more than 500 illustrations by Lear himself. Edited by Holbrook Jackson. xxix + 287pp. (USO) 20167-8 Paperbound $1.75

BILLY WHISKERS: THE AUTOBIOGRAPHY OF A GOAT, Frances Trego Montgomery. A favorite of children since the early 20th century, here are the escapades of that rambunctious, irresistible and mischievous goat—Billy Whiskers. Much in the spirit of *Peck's Bad Boy,* this is a book that children never tire of reading or hearing. All the original familiar illustrations by W. H. Fry are included: 6 color plates, 18 black and white drawings. 159pp. 22345-0 Paperbound $2.00

MOTHER GOOSE MELODIES. Faithful republication of the fabulously rare Munroe and Francis "copyright 1833" Boston edition—the most important Mother Goose collection, usually referred to as the "original." Familiar rhymes plus many rare ones, with wonderful old woodcut illustrations. Edited by E. F. Bleiler. 128pp. 4½ x 6⅜. 22577-1 Paperbound $1.25

TWO LITTLE SAVAGES; BEING THE ADVENTURES OF TWO BOYS WHO LIVED AS INDIANS AND WHAT THEY LEARNED, Ernest Thompson Seton. Great classic of nature and boyhood provides a vast range of woodlore in most palatable form, a genuinely entertaining story. Two farm boys build a teepee in woods and live in it for a month, working out Indian solutions to living problems, star lore, birds and animals, plants, etc. 293 illustrations. vii + 286pp.

20985-7 Paperbound $2.50

PETER PIPER'S PRACTICAL PRINCIPLES OF PLAIN & PERFECT PRONUNCIATION. Alliterative jingles and tongue-twisters of surprising charm, that made their first appearance in America about 1830. Republished in full with the spirited woodcut illustrations from this earliest American edition. 32pp. 4½ x 6⅜.

22560-7 Paperbound $1.00

SCIENCE EXPERIMENTS AND AMUSEMENTS FOR CHILDREN, Charles Vivian. 73 easy experiments, requiring only materials found at home or easily available, such as candles, coins, steel wool, etc.; illustrate basic phenomena like vacuum, simple chemical reaction, etc. All safe. Modern, well-planned. Formerly *Science Games for Children.* 102 photos, numerous drawings. 96pp. 6⅛ x 9¼.

21856-2 Paperbound $1.25

AN INTRODUCTION TO CHESS MOVES AND TACTICS SIMPLY EXPLAINED, Leonard Barden. Informal intermediate introduction, quite strong in explaining reasons for moves. Covers basic material, tactics, important openings, traps, positional play in middle game, end game. Attempts to isolate patterns and recurrent configurations. Formerly *Chess.* 58 figures. 102pp. (USO) 21210-6 Paperbound $1.25

LASKER'S MANUAL OF CHESS, Dr. Emanuel Lasker. Lasker was not only one of the five great World Champions, he was also one of the ablest expositors, theorists, and analysts. In many ways, his Manual, permeated with his philosophy of battle, filled with keen insights, is one of the greatest works ever written on chess. Filled with analyzed games by the great players. A single-volume library that will profit almost any chess player, beginner or master. 308 diagrams. xli x 349pp.

20640-8 Paperbound $2.50

THE MASTER BOOK OF MATHEMATICAL RECREATIONS, Fred Schuh. In opinion of many the finest work ever prepared on mathematical puzzles, stunts, recreations; exhaustively thorough explanations of mathematics involved, analysis of effects, citation of puzzles and games. Mathematics involved is elementary. Translated by F. Göbel. 194 figures. xxiv + 430pp. 22134-2 Paperbound $3.00

MATHEMATICS, MAGIC AND MYSTERY, Martin Gardner. Puzzle editor for Scientific American explains mathematics behind various mystifying tricks: card tricks, stage "mind reading," coin and match tricks, counting out games, geometric dissections, etc. Probability sets, theory of numbers clearly explained. Also provides more than 400 tricks, guaranteed to work, that you can do. 135 illustrations. xii + 176pp.

20338-2 Paperbound $1.50

MATHEMATICAL PUZZLES FOR BEGINNERS AND ENTHUSIASTS, Geoffrey Mott-Smith. 189 puzzles from easy to difficult—involving arithmetic, logic, algebra, properties of digits, probability, etc.—for enjoyment and mental stimulus. Explanation of mathematical principles behind the puzzles. 135 illustrations. viii + 248pp.
20198-8 Paperbound $1.25

PAPER FOLDING FOR BEGINNERS, William D. Murray and Francis J. Rigney. Easiest book on the market, clearest instructions on making interesting, beautiful origami. Sail boats, cups, roosters, frogs that move legs, bonbon boxes, standing birds, etc. 40 projects; more than 275 diagrams and photographs. 94pp.
20713-7 Paperbound $1.00

TRICKS AND GAMES ON THE POOL TABLE, Fred Herrmann. 79 tricks and games—some solitaires, some for two or more players, some competitive games—to entertain you between formal games. Mystifying shots and throws, unusual caroms, tricks involving such props as cork, coins, a hat, etc. Formerly *Fun on the Pool Table*. 77 figures. 95pp.
21814-7 Paperbound $1.00

HAND SHADOWS TO BE THROWN UPON THE WALL: A SERIES OF NOVEL AND AMUSING FIGURES FORMED BY THE HAND, Henry Bursill. Delightful picturebook from great-grandfather's day shows how to make 18 different hand shadows: a bird that flies, duck that quacks, dog that wags his tail, camel, goose, deer, boy, turtle, etc. Only book of its sort. vi + 33pp. 6½ x 9¼. 21779-5 Paperbound $1.00

WHITTLING AND WOODCARVING, E. J. Tangerman. 18th printing of best book on market. "If you can cut a potato you can carve" toys and puzzles, chains, chessmen, caricatures, masks, frames, woodcut blocks, surface patterns, much more. Information on tools, woods, techniques. Also goes into serious wood sculpture from Middle Ages to present, East and West. 464 photos, figures. x + 293pp.
20965-2 Paperbound $2.00

HISTORY OF PHILOSOPHY, Julián Marias. Possibly the clearest, most easily followed, best planned, most useful one-volume history of philosophy on the market; neither skimpy nor overfull. Full details on system of every major philosopher and dozens of less important thinkers from pre-Socratics up to Existentialism and later. Strong on many European figures usually omitted. Has gone through dozens of editions in Europe. 1966 edition, translated by Stanley Appelbaum and Clarence Strowbridge. xviii + 505pp.
21739-6 Paperbound $2.75

YOGA: A SCIENTIFIC EVALUATION, Kovoor T. Behanan. Scientific but non-technical study of physiological results of yoga exercises; done under auspices of Yale U. Relations to Indian thought, to psychoanalysis, etc. 16 photos. xxiii + 270pp.
20505-3 Paperbound $2.50

Prices subject to change without notice.
Available at your book dealer or write for free catalogue to Dept. GI, Dover Publications, Inc., 180 Varick St., N. Y., N. Y. 10014. Dover publishes more than 150 books each year on science, elementary and advanced mathematics, biology, music, art, literary history, social sciences and other areas.